Intercultural Communication

An Ecological Approach

Amardo Rodriguez

Syracuse University

Devika Chawla

Ohio University

Kendall Hunt
publishing company

Book Team

Chairman and Chief Executive Officer   Mark C. Falb
President and Chief Operating Officer   Chad M. Chandlee
Vice President, Higher Education   David L. Tart
Director of Publishing Partnerships   Paul B. Carty
Editorial Manager   Georgia Botsford
Senior Editor   Angela Willenbring
Vice President, Operations   Timothy J. Beitzel
Assistant Vice President, Production Services   Christine E. O'Brien
Senior Production Editor   Carrie Maro
Permissions Editor   Renae Horstman
Cover Designer   Suzanne Millius

Cover image © Getty Images

Kendall Hunt
publishing company
www.kendallhunt.com
Send all inquiries to:
4050 Westmark Drive
Dubuque, IA 52004-1840

Printed in the United States of America
10 9 8 7 6 5 4 3 2 1

Brief Contents

Contents

About the Authors

Amardo Rodriguez (Ph.D., Howard University) is a Laura J. and L. Douglas Meredith Professor in the Department of Communication and Rhetorical Studies at Syracuse University. His research and teaching interests explore the potentiality of emergent conceptions of communication that foreground moral, existential, and spiritual assumptions about the human condition to redefine and enlarge contemporary understandings of democracy, diversity, and community. Publications include articles in *International and Intercultural Communication Annual, Journal of Intercultural Communication, Journal of Intergroup Relations, Journal of Religion and Society, Southern Communication Journal,* and elsewhere. His books include *On Matters of Liberation (I): The Case Against Hierarchy; Diversity as Liberation (II): Introducing a New Understanding of Diversity; Essays on Communication and Spirituality: Contributions to a New Discourse on Communication; Communication, Space, and Design: The Integral Relation Between Communication and Design; Diversity: Mestizos, Latinos and the Promise of Possibilities;* and *Embodying The Postcolonial Life.*

Devika Chawla (Ph.D., Purdue University) is Associate Professor in the School of Communication Studies at Ohio University. Her intellectual interests include performative and narrative approaches to identity and communication. She teaches graduate and undergraduate courses in ethnography and performance, critical ethnography, cross-cultural communication, post-colonial studies, family communication, and interpersonal communication. Publications include articles in *Qualitative Inquiry, Cultural Studies ↔ Critical Methodologies, International and Intercultural Communication Annual, Review of Communication, Women & Language, Teaching in Higher Education, Radical Pedagogy, Storytelling, Self, Society: An Interdisciplinary Journal of Storytelling Studies,* and contributed book chapters and essays in various edited volumes.

Introduction

Studying intercultural communication in the United States before September 11, 2001, is fundamentally different to studying intercultural communication after that date. Now any study of intercultural communication must begin with asking, What is the possibility of communication between people of fundamentally different religious persuasions and orientations? What can intercultural communication achieve between such people? Could intercultural communication have saved us from September 11? Could intercultural communication save us from the next September 11? In other words, what is the promise of intercultural communication in a post–September 11 world? Can intercultural communication bring peace and prosperity between different people, or is aggression and violent conflict inevitable? After September 11, many persons have increasingly claimed the latter. In this way, September 11 has in many ways elevated our distrust and suspicion of those persons who seem most different to us.

For instance, writing in the face of September 11, Morgan Norval (2002) claimed that "to a great extent, the war on terrorism is a clash of civilizations, as Islam is fundamentally anti-Western; thus, the prospects for success are limited. Unless we recognize that we are engaged in the revival of the centuries old clash between Islam and the Christian West and act accordingly" (p. 22).

Poll after poll in the United States show most respondents expressing unfavorable views of Islam and believing that Muslims are disproportionately prone to violence. A national poll by Cornell University found that about 27% of respondents believe "that all Muslim Americans should be required to register their location with the federal government, and 26% [believe] that mosques should be closely monitored by U.S. law enforcement agencies." In addition, "29% agreed that undercover law enforcement agents should infiltrate Muslim civic and volunteer organizations, in order to keep tabs on their activities and fund raising." Also, about 22% believe that the federal government should profile citizens as potential threats based on the fact that they are Muslim or have Middle Eastern heritage. In all, "about 44% said they believe that some curtailment of civil liberties is necessary for Muslim Americans." A *Washington Post–ABC News* poll found that a majority of Americans believe that Muslims are disproportionately prone to violence. This poll also found that nearly half of Americans have a negative view of Islam, and one in four Americans admits to harboring prejudice toward Muslims, the same proportion that expressed some personal bias against Arabs. These poll numbers are consistent with those found in Europe. In a Pew poll, most Europeans doubt that Muslims coming into their countries want to adopt their national customs and way of life. Substantial majorities in Germany (76%), Great Britain (64%), Spain (67%), and Russia (69%) believe that Muslims in their country want to remain distinct from the larger society. Interestingly, "only 30% of German Muslims believe that Muslims coming into that country today want to assimilate—most say they want to be separate and most Germans agree."

Writing in the face of September 11, Samuel Huntington, who until recently was Chairman of the Harvard Academy for International and Area Studies and the Albert J. Weatherhead III, University Professor at Harvard University, warns of the United States disintegrating and collapsing as a result of our increasing diversity from non-European nations. In *Who We Are: The Challenges to America's National Identity,* Huntington (2004) focuses on the threats that multiculturalism, bilingualism, cosmopolitanism, and globalism pose to the United States. He believes that the United States must vanquish these movements to preserve its ideological, cultural, and social stability. We must protect the "American Creed." According to Huntington, the "American Creed," as initially formulated by Thomas Jefferson and elaborated by many others, "is widely viewed" as the defining element of American identity. "The Creed, however, was the product of the distinct Anglo-Protestant culture of the founding settlers of America in the seventeenth and eighteenth centuries" (p. xv). Huntington claims that key elements of that culture include "the English language; Christianity; religious commitment; English concepts of the rule of law, responsibility of rulers, and the rights of individuals; and the dissenting Protestant values of individualism, the work ethic, and the belief that humans have the ability and duty to try to create a heaven on earth" (pp. xv–xvi). Huntington believes that in the face of September 11, "Americans should recommit themselves to the Anglo-Protestant culture, traditions, and values that for three and half centuries have been embraced by Americans of all races, ethnicities, and religions and that have been the source of their liberty, unity, power, prosperity, and moral leadership as a force for good in the world" (p. xvii).

Huntington claims that Latino immigration poses the greatest threat to the territorial, cultural, and political integrity of the United States. He calls for immediate and severe actions to neutralize this threat. He believes that Latino immigration constitutes the greatest challenge to our "existing cultural, political, legal, commercial, and educational systems," and "to the historical, cultural, and linguistic identity" of the United States. Thus Huntington professes to be "deeply concerned about the unity and strength of my country based on liberty, equality, law, and individual rights" (2004, p. xvi-xvii).

But population trends in United States are conspiring against Huntington. According to census figures, racial and ethnic minorities now account for 43% of Americans under age 20. Among people of all ages, minorities make up at least 40% of the population in more than one in six of the nation's 3,141 counties.

Moreover, one in four American counties has passed or is approaching the tipping point where Black, Hispanic, and Asian children constitute a majority of the under-20 population. According to the Pew Research Center, "If current trends continue, the population of the United States will rise to 438 million in 2050, from 296 million in 2005, and 82% of the increase will be due to immigrants arriving from 2005 to 2050 and their U.S.-born descendants (2008)." The latest population changes by race, ethnicity, and age, as of July 1, 2007, suggest that minorities—now about a third of the population—might soon constitute a majority of all Americans. In fact, according to new government projections, white people will no longer make up a majority of Americans by 2042. That is 8 years sooner than previous estimates, made in 2004. According to William Frey, a demographer at the Brookings Institution, "The white population is older and very much centered around the aging baby boomers who are well past their high fertility years. The future of America is epitomized by the young people today. They are basically the melting pot we are going to see in the future." The Pew Research Center also projects that nearly one in five Americans (19%) will be an immigrant in 2050, compared with one in eight (12%) in 2005. By 2025, the immigrant, or foreign-born, share of the population will surpass the peak during the last great wave of immigration a century ago.

- The Latino population, already the nation's largest minority group, will triple in size and will account for most of the nation's population growth from 2005 through 2050. Hispanics will make up 29% of the U.S. population in 2050, compared with 14% in 2005.
- Births in the United States will play a growing role in Hispanic and Asian population growth; as a result, a smaller proportion of both groups will be foreign born in 2050 than is the case now.
- The non-Hispanic white population will increase more slowly than other racial and ethnic groups.

As *The New York Times* observed, "The latest figures confirm the sweep of America's growing diversity." In *Day of Reckoning,* Patrick Buchanan (2007) echoes Samuel Huntington's many fears and warnings about what these changing demographics mean for the future of the United States. The primary thesis of Buchanan's book is that the United States is "decomposing" and is on a path to "national suicide." Buchanan is obsessed with the numbers and writes openly about the United States facing a "Third World invasion." Citing figures from the U.S. Census Bureau, Buchanan wrote, "Hispanics, 1% of the U.S. population in 1950, are now 14.4%. Since 2000, their numbers have soared 25% to 45 million. The U.S. Asian population grew by 24% since 2000, as the number of white kids of school age fell 4%. Half the children five and younger today are minority children" (p. 8). Also, "by 2050 the number of African Americans and Hispanics will have almost doubled from today's 85 million, to 160 million. The future seems more ominous than it did in the hopeful days of civil rights. For these burgeoning scores of millions will not long accept second-class accommodations in the affluent society, where they are the emerging majority. The long hot summers of yesterday may be returning" (p. 10).

Buchanan is also concerned about the apparent unwillingness of immigrants to learn English and various U.S. institutions allowing this to happen. "In Chicago's schools, children are taught in two hundred languages. Five million of the 9 million people in Los Angeles County speak a language other than English in their homes" (p. 9). As with Huntington, Buchanan believes that this kind of language diversity will ultimately bring chaos and disunity to the United States. Thus Buchanan wants English to be declared the official language of the United States. He believes that language commonality rather than language diversity is necessary for the creation of any great society. In fact, according to Buchanan, "no great republic or empire . . . ever arose because it embraced democracy, diversity, and equality" (2007, p. 174). So what is the United States to do, besides making English the country's official language? Buchanan wants the United States to immediately and drastically curb the number of immigrants legally admitted every year, build a great wall on the border with Mexico, and deny amnesty to the 12 to 20 million illegal immigrants already in the United States.

Huntington and Buchanan are by no means the only persons who are publicly contending that changing population trends threaten the stability and prosperity of the United States. Indeed, every new wave of immigrants to the United States has been met with dire warnings about chaos, disunity, and disease. For instance, the Chinese Exclusion Act of 1882 was the first significant restriction on free immigration in U.S. history. The Act excluded Chinese "skilled and unskilled laborers and Chinese employed in mining" from entering the country for 10 years under penalty of imprisonment and deportation. The Act also affected Chinese who were already in the United States. It made Chinese immigrants permanent aliens by excluding them from U.S. citizenship. The Act was renewed for 10 years by the 1892 Geary Act and again with no termination date in 1902. The Act's 1902 extension also required "each Chinese resident to register and obtain a certificate of residence. Without a certificate, he or she faced deportation." Republican Senator George Frisbie Hoar of Massachusetts described the Act as "nothing less than the legalization of racial discrimination." However, at the turn of the 20th century, unprecedented levels of immigration from Southern and Eastern Europe to the United States aroused widespread public support for restrictive immigration laws, and Congress passed many laws curbing immigration from Europe, including the 1917 Immigration Act, which excluded all "aliens over sixteen years of age, physically capable of reading, [but] who cannot read the English language, or some other language or dialect, including Hebrew or Yiddish." During congressional debate over the 1924 Immigration Act, Senator Ellison DuRant Smith of South Carolina made the following case before the U.S. Senate in support of the legislation that eventually passed with only six dissenting votes:

> I think that we have sufficient stock in America now for us to shut the door, Americanize what we have, and save the resources of America for the natural increase of our population. We all know that one of the most prolific causes of war is the desire for increased land ownership for the overflow of a congested population. We are increasing at such a rate that in the natural course of things in a comparatively few years the landed resources, the natural resources of the country, shall be taken up by the natural increase of our population. It seems to me the part of wisdom now that we have throughout the length and breadth of continental America a population which is beginning to encroach upon the reserve and virgin resources of the country to keep it in trust for the multiplying population of the country . . .
>
> It is of greater concern to us to maintain the institutions of America, to maintain the principles upon which this Government is founded, than to develop and exploit the underdeveloped resources of the country. There are some things that are dearer to us, fraught with more benefit to us, than the immediate development of the undeveloped resources of the country. I believe that our particular ideas, social, moral, religious, and political, have demonstrated, by virtue of the progress we have made and the character of people that we are, that we have the highest ideals of any member of the human family or any nation. We have demonstrated the fact that the human family, certainty the predominant breed in America, can govern themselves by a direct government of the people. If this Government shall fail, it shall fail by virtue of the terrible law of inherited tendency. Those who come from the nations which from time immemorial have been under the dictation of a master fall more easily by the law of inheritance and the inertia of habit into a condition of political servitude than the descendants of those who cleared the forests, conquered the savage, stood at arms and won their liberty from their mother country, England.
>
> I think we now have sufficient population in our country for us to shut the door and to breed up a pure, unadulterated American citizenship . . . Thank God we have in America perhaps the largest percentage of any country in the world of the pure, unadulterated Anglo-Saxon stock; certainly the greatest of any nation in the Nordic breed. It is for the preservation of that splendid stock that has characterized us that I would make this not an asylum for the oppressed of all countries, but a country to assimilate and perfect that splendid type of manhood that has made America the foremost Nation in her progress and in her power, and yet the youngest of all the nations. I myself believe that the preservation of her institutions depends upon us now taking counsel with our condition and our experience during the last World War.
>
> Without offense, but with regard to the salvation of our own, let us shut the door and assimilate what we have, and let us breed pure American citizens and develop our own American resources.

But what would be the United States without immigration? Consider the following: Albert Einstein (born in Germany, Einstein moved to the United States in

1933), Ieoh Ming Pei (one of United States' most famous architects, Pei was born in Canton in China in 1917 and came to the United States at the age of 18 to study architecture), Madeleine Albright (Secretary of State in the Clinton administration, Madeleine Albright was born in Czechoslovakia in 1937 and moved with her family to the United States in 1948), Subranhmanyan Chandrasekhar (1983 Nobel Laureate for Physics, Subranhmanyan Chandrasekhar was born in Lahore, India, in 1910), Ang Lee (this New York-based, Taiwan-born independent producer, director, and screenwriter won Best Director in the 2005 Academy Awards for *Brokeback Mountain*), Irving Berlin (composer), Jerry Yang (cofounder of Yahoo!), Sergey Brin (cofounder of Google), Alexander Graham Bell (famous inventor), Andrew Carnegie (this steel tycoon was born in Scotland and immigrated to the United States at the age of 13; he donated millions of dollars to thousands of libraries and educational institutions), Charlie Chaplin (famous actor, director, writer, and composer is considered one of the leading talents in film history), Thomas Mann (Mann was born in Germany and won the Nobel Prize for Literature in 1929, is considered one of the most acclaimed novelists of the 20th century, and became a U.S. citizen in 1944), Colin Powell (Secretary of State in President George W. Bush administration, is a child of immigrants from the Caribbean), Tiger Woods (whose mother is from Asia), and of course, President Barack Obama (whose father is from Kenya).

But our suspicion of immigration persists. There is no need for any of us to deny that dealing with persons who seem most different to us comes with much anxiety. These are natural human responses. In many ways, diversity is about the unknown. It is about things that seem to exceed our realm of understanding. In this regard, diversity requires a willingness to find new ways of perceiving and understanding each other, which involves a willingness to alter and even abandon our current ways of viewing the world. Without a willingness to do such renovation, those who seem most different to us will remain beyond our realm of understanding, and thereby forever subject to our prejudice and ignorance. In a word, diversity is about communication. It is about finding new ways to understand each other, especially when such understanding seems impossible. What distinguishes our position in this book from that of Huntington, Buchanan, and others is the belief that communication is always laden with possibility, including the possibility of harmony between different peoples. We share Mary Catherine Bateson's (1994) view that a "certain amount of friction is inevitable whenever peoples with different customs and assumptions meet." However, what "is miraculous is how often it is possible to work together to sustain joint performances in spite of disparate codes, evoking different belief systems to affirm that possibility. As migration and travel increase, we are going to have to become more self-conscious and articulate about differences, and to find acceptable ways of talking about insights gained through such friction-producing situations, gathering up the harvest of learning along the way" (p. 23).

POSITIONING OUR PERSPECTIVE

Our goal is to produce an intercultural communication book that deals openly and honestly with the many frustrations and tribulations that come with dealing with peoples who seem to be of fundamentally different traditions, predispositions, and persuasions. However, rather than merely present the issues that seem to make for these frustrations and tribulations for discussion, this book introduces a new framework that can potentially help us lessen these frustrations and tribulations by presenting a new way of understanding the origins of these issues. This framework operates both descriptively and prescriptively. It gives us a way of explaining and understanding our conflicts and tensions with different peoples, as well as a way of navigating and resolving these conflicts and tensions. As such, what most distinguishes this intercultural communication book from others is the premise that the differences that seem to put us at each other's throats can be negotiated, navigated, and even resolved. For us, the study of intercultural communication is about how the world can potentially unfold. As Asante, Miike, and Yin (2008) noted, "As globalization and localization intensify in every corner of the world . . . the field [intercultural communication] is increasingly confronted by more fundamental issues of identity, community, and humanity. In effect, intercultural communication is the only way to mitigate identity politics, social disintegration, religious conflicts, and ecological vulnerability in the global village. Human survival and flourishing depends on our ability to communicate successfully across differences" (p. 1). We agree completely with this sentiment. We also believe that these challenges require us to redefine intercultural communication so as to better understand the forces and motives that make for these challenges. We advocate for an expansive definition of intercultural communication, as communication is always cultural—that is, all communication involves peoples with different ethnicities, nationalities, geographies, spiritualities, sexualities, rationalities, sensibilities, modalities, and histories. ***Communication is always intercultural.*** We are always managing and negotiating differences in communication. The *success* of communication depends on how constructively we manage and negotiate our differences. We therefore believe that our intercultural problems are fundamentally communication problems rather than problems of differences.

DEFINITIONS OF INTERCULTURAL COMMUNICATION

How we define something shapes how we acquire knowledge of something and where we look for knowledge of that something. Just as well, how we define something influences what we define as knowledge about that something. Also, how we define something influences how we experience and relate to something. Finally, how we define something reflects what we believe, assume, and value.

Simply put, definitions matter. We found the following definitions of intercultural and cross-cultural communication in our review of various intercultural communication literatures and discourses:

- Intercultural communication generally involves face-to-face communication between people from different national cultures.
- Intercultural communication can be defined as the interpersonal interaction between members of different groups, which differ from each other in respect to the knowledge shared by their members and in respect to their linguistic forms of symbolic behavior.
- Intercultural communication occurs when large and important cultural differences create dissimilar interpretations and expectations about how to communicate competently.
- Intercultural communication occurs whenever a minimum of two persons from different cultures or microcultures come together and exchange verbal and nonverbal symbols.

All these definitions generally assume that intercultural communication occurs between peoples of different cultures—that is, between peoples of different beliefs, values, norms, fears, and so forth. We are also assuming that these different groups of peoples are stable and reflect distinct practices and behaviors that allow us to distinguish one group from another. We therefore use language like Western culture, Caribbean culture, Latino culture, Native American culture, African-American culture, Asian, culture, and so forth. We tend to believe that possessing knowledge of these different cultures is vital for good communication between peoples of different cultures. We also tend to believe that our lack of knowledge of each other's culture is what is fundamentally responsible for our communication problems with persons of other cultures.

Thus, many intercultural communication readings and courses spend a tremendous amount of time introducing us to the many ways that cultures are supposedly different. We eventually come to learn that whereas some cultures are high context (emphasis on nonverbal communication), others are low context (focus on verbal communication), and whereas some cultures are feminine, others are masculine, and whereas some cultures are collectivist, others are individualist, and whereas some cultures are patriarchal, others are matriarchal, and whereas some cultures are monochromic, others are polychromic, and whereas some cultures are active, others are passive, and whereas some cultures as vertical, others are horizontal, and whereas some cultures are universalist, others are particularist, and whereas some cultures are instrumental, others are expressive, and whereas some cultures are associative, others are abstractive, and so forth. We are encouraged to use this knowledge of how cultures are different to navigate, bridge, and manage our relations with persons of other cultures.

Most intercultural readings tend to begin on the assumption that cultures make for differences, such as peoples sharing different beliefs, values, fears, norms, expectations, truths, and ultimately, different behaviors. For example, Klopf and McCroskey (2007) contend that "unless we know the rules of other cultures practices, we will discover it is almost impossible to tell how members of other cultures will behave in similar situations" (p. 22). Many readings also focus a lot how cultures are learned and acquired. Also, communication is commonly cast as a tool that allows us to navigate and bridge our different cultures. The goal of most of these readings is to make us communicatively proficient by knowing how cultures are different and how best to use various communication skills and techniques to navigate and bridge such differences. For example, McDaniel, Samovar, and Porter (2006) claim that "the international community is riven with sectarian violence arising from ideological, cultural, and racial differences" (p. 15). Neuliep (2000) echoes Arthur Schlesinger's warning that "history tells an ugly story of what happens when people of diverse cultural, ethnic, religious, or linguistic background converge in one place" (p. 2). Finally, many intercultural communication readings claim that changing global demographics, economics, and pragmatics make being interculturally proficient vital in the current world. For instance, Rogers and Steinfatt (1999) noted, "If individuals could attain a higher degree of intercultural competence, they would presumably become better citizens, students, teachers, businesspeople, and so forth. Society would be more peaceful, more productive, and generally a more attractive place to live" (p. 222). Moreover, "individuals would be better able to understand others who are unlike themselves. Through such improved understanding, a great of conflict could be avoided; the world would be a better place" (p. 222). In short, most intercultural communication readings and discourses focus on how best different peoples can manage to bridge each other's cultural differences.

Language receives significant attention in most intercultural communication literatures and discourses. Yet these discussions also perpetuate assumptions that limit diversity and, in so doing, keep us bound to a set of fears and beliefs that maintain our suspicion and distrust of those who seem most different to us. A popular assumption is that a common language is vital for communication between peoples of different cultures. For instance, Samovar, Porter, and McDaniel (2007) wrote that "language diversity presents a problem in the United States" (p. 182). Although Samovar and company "do not endorse" legislative "proposals to make English the official language of the United States," they do believe "that knowledge of English and the ability to communicate in English are essential in American society" (pp. 182–183). However, the position that "language diversity presents a problem in the United States" still perpetuates the assumption—and the attending fear, anxiety, and paranoia—that diversity needs to be carefully managed and controlled to avoid social chaos. This position is in no way fundamentally different from that of proponents of English-only legislation and other ballot measures to limit linguistic diversity. It merely constitutes a gentler and milder version—one that seems progressive and even supportive of diversity, yet still perpetuates the belief that without all of us in the United States speaking English, chaos and disunity will result. This belief can be seen in a recent post by B. R. Myers (2008), a contributing editor for *Atlantic Monthly*, "The many immigrants who now refuse to learn more than a little transactional English are in effect saying that an economic community is all they want to be part of. The obvious irony is that a nation without one unifying language will end up poorer in economic terms as well."

Yet history makes no case that language diversity threatens stability and social evolution. In fact, the world's most horrendous crimes have occurred in places, such as Germany, Yugoslavia, Rwanda, Iraq, Turkey, and Somalia, where there was language homogeneity. But what of the widening gap between rich and poor, or our reckless and selfish plundering of the planet's natural resources? How did these come to present no problem to intercultural relations in the United States and are thereby absent in most intercultural communication readings? The goal of most intercultural communication readings is to make us communicatively proficient. But such proficiency in no way pushes us to reckon with the larger forces in our society that make for a widening gap between rich and poor and thereby our increasing anxiety of immigrants who are supposedly taking away jobs and being a drain on precious resources. Neither does the goal of communication proficiency push us to reckon with the fallout of our reckless plundering of the world's natural resources on the quality of life of different peoples, such as those native peoples in Alaska, whose homes are disappearing into the ocean as the ice caps melt. Just as well, neither does this proficiency push us to reckon with how our dependency on foreign oil make many persons in the Middle East have a deep hostility to the United States. Our point is that many forces impede understanding. No understanding evolves from a vacuum. There is always a historical context—a history that shapes our perception of the other person, a history that influences what each person is ready and willing to understand, a history that guides how each side encounters the other side. Understanding each other is about understanding the history that makes us different.

Language is by no means the most important component in communication. Language only achieves this status when one begins with the assumption that communication is fundamentally a linguistic and symbolic phenomenon. Yet a linguistic and symbolic-based definition pervades many intercultural communication readings and discourses. For instance, Neuliep (2000) asserts, "Intercultural communication occurs whenever a minimum of two persons from different cultures or microcultures come together and exchange verbal and nonverbal symbols" (p. 18). Likewise, Klopf and McCroskey (2007) hold that "communication is the process by which persons share information, meanings, and feelings through the exchange of verbal and nonverbal messages" (p. 34). For Samovar et al. (2007), "communication is the process through which symbols are transmitted for the purpose of elic-iting a response" (p. 12). Indeed, most intercultural communication readings forward definitions of communication that assume no profound relationship between communication and the human condition, or even between communication and the condition of the world. Communication is cast as purely a device to share our thoughts and emotions, and communication competency is presumably about mastery of various skills and techniques that allow us to convey our thoughts and emotions with precision and restraint. But this popular orientation to communication masks the implications of different communication practices on the human condition (Rodriguez, 2006; Thayer, 1987). To recognize the profound relationship between communication and the human condition is to recognize that communication is fundamentally moral—our communication practices and environs shape and define our humanity and the humanity of others, and the condition of our humanity affects our perception of the world, and as well as the condition of the world.

Our point is that the definitions of communication that are found in most intercultural communication readings lack the breath and depth to help us flourish in a world that is increasingly showcasing diversity more as a verb and less as a noun. In a world where our spaces and distances are collapsing and the boundaries between the local and the global disappearing, increasing numbers of persons are unwilling to yield to simplistic categories of difference (Conquergood, 2002). In our view, such a world requires a definition of communication that defines communication as a mode of being and becoming rather than a means of relaying and sharing of messages between separate bodies (Rodriguez, 2006). In this emergent definition, *communication is about being vulnerable to the humanity of others*. This emergent definition of communication promotes modes of being that lessen the threat of our differences by pushing us to understand and embody the world from new and different positions. It defines communication proficiency in terms of our capacity for empathy and compassion. To look at communication in terms of vulnerability is to recognize that language diversity poses no threat to progress and our social prosperity. What ultimately undermines social evolution is our lack of empathy and compassion for those who seem most different to us. However, although Martin and Nakayama (2007) have a generous discussion of forgiveness, and Gudykunst and Kim (2003) present an interesting discussion of community, most intercultural communication readings make no mention of compassion. Then again, love, mercy, compassion, selflessness, tenderness, and forgiveness, all notions that pertain to vulnerability and are necessary for the flourishing of diversity, remain on the periphery of communication theory, inquiry, and pedagogy.

POSITIONING OUR ARGUMENT

Various intercultural communication literatures and discourses present many reasons why the study of intercultural communication is important. The most prominent position is the *Global Argument.* Many persons point to the fact that the world is increasingly global, multicultural, and plural, and as a result, different peoples must peacefully coexist for social, political, and economic purposes. We have to be interculturally proficient to deal successfully with employees, contractors, and customers from diverse backgrounds, persuasions, and religions. Endless examples are dramatically given by intercultural communication consultants to show the negative consequences and costs that come from being interculturally incompetent and insensitive. This is the standard pitch that most intercultural communication consultants make to organizations and corporations. This is also how the argument typically appears in intercultural communication manuals:

> The businesses that succeed in the future are the businesses that can tap the limitless bounties of the global economy. However, to do so you need people with the right skills, experience, knowledge and understanding. Having employees that have attained a certain level of intercultural competence through training and on-the-ground experience provides access the aforementioned bounties. Employees that are flexible in manner and open in mind can approach the challenges of working in foreign environments much more easily.

DOCTORS MISS CULTURAL NEEDS, STUDY SAYS
Kevin Sack

As researchers ponder growing evidence that blacks have worse outcomes than whites in the treatment of chronic disease, they often theorize that members of minorities suffer disproportionately from poor access to quality care. Now a new study of diabetes patients has found stark racial disparities even among patients treated by the same doctors.

The lead author of the study said in an interview that he attributed the differences less to overt racism than to a systemic failure to tailor treatments to patients' cultural norms. The problem, said the author, Dr. Thomas D. Sequist, an assistant professor of health care policy at Harvard Medical School, may be that physicians do not discriminate in the way they counsel patients.

"It isn't that providers are doing different things for different patients," Dr. Sequist said. "It's that we're doing the same thing for every patient and not accounting for individual needs. Our one-size-fits-all approach may leave minority patients with needs that aren't being met."

For instance, he said, counseling black or Latino patients with diabetes to lower their carbohydrate intake by cutting rice from their diets may not be a realistic strategy if rice is a family staple.

"We may be listing fruits and vegetables that are part of one person's culture but not another," Dr. Sequist said. "We're not really giving them information they can use."

In the study, which was published Monday in The Archives of Internal Medicine, Dr. Sequist and his colleagues examined electronic medical records of 6,814 patients with diabetes. All were treated from 2005 to 2007 by at least one of 90 primary care physicians with Harvard Vanguard Medical Associates, which has 14 walk-in health clinics in eastern Massachusetts. Each doctor treated at least five white patients and five black ones.

The researchers looked at three standard measures of effective diabetes control: blood pressure, LDL cholesterol levels and hemoglobin A1C, which reflects blood sugar. Though similar proportions of black and white patients took each test, fewer black patients adequately controlled their levels on all three measures. The glucose test found, for example, that 71 percent of white patients and 63 percent of black ones were adequately controlling their blood sugar levels.

Socioeconomic factors like income or insurance status explained 13 percent to 38 percent of the racial differences, the authors calculated. But they found much larger racial disparities—from 66 percent to 75 percent—in patients who were treated by the same doctor. Adjusting for clinical differences among patients did not change the findings.

"Racial differences in outcomes were not related to black patients differentially receiving care from physicians who provide a lower quality of care, but rather that black patients experienced less ideal or even adequate outcomes than white patients within the same physician panel," the study concluded.

To attack such disparities, the authors recommended that doctors and other members of the health care system learn more about minority communities and that patients receive better education about diabetes and how and why it must be controlled.

"Our data suggest that the problem of racial disparities is not characterized by only a few physicians providing markedly unequal care," the authors wrote, "but that such differences in care are spread across the entire system, requiring the implementation of systemwide solutions."

There is also the ***Empirical Argument.*** This argument is premised on the fact that culturally heterogeneous groups and teams are more innovative and creative than culturally homogenous groups and teams. In a global economy that first and foremost rewards innovation, the success of organizations and corporations will depend on the ability of teams and groups to be consistently innovative and creative. As such, organizations and corporations will only recruit and retain persons who can thrive in culturally heterogeneous environments. This is how the Empirical Argument typically appears in intercultural communication manuals:

> Intercultural communication training enhances people's skills and therefore future employment opportunities. Having cross-cultural awareness gives people a competitive edge over others, especially when applying for positions in international companies with a large multicultural staff base.

There is also the ***International Argument.*** This argument is based on the notion that the problems that increasingly face all peoples are increasingly international in nature and, as a result, will require international solutions. These problems include global warming, access to clean water, hunger, poverty, proliferation of weapons of mass destruction, pandemics, collapse of nation states, and access to renewable energy resources. Resolving these problems will require working intensely with different peoples. We will also have to build alliances and form coalitions that serve the best interest of all. That moment in history when one nation can unilaterally impose its will on the world is over.

This book highlights the ***Moral Argument.*** An increasingly global, plural, and multicultural world allows us to enlarge our humanity and create new kinds of identity by giving us access to all manner of social, cultural, and relational resources that come from all corners of the world. To be interculturally competent is be open to all these resources. It is also about being open to new ways of being that exceed time and space. That is, being open to modes of being that exceed the bounds of geography and history. To be interculturally competent is also about recognizing our humanity in each other and, as a result, recognizing our obligation to each other, even when that recognition is most difficult to come by, as when a person is of a different religious persuasion.

Our position is that this emerging global, multicultural, and plural world is presenting us with new challenges and resources that can allow us to enter a new realm of being human that reflects a larger and richer version of what it means to be human. It allows us to build what Young Yun Kim (2003) nicely refers to as an intercultural personhood—"a way of life in which an individual develops an identity and a definition of self that integrates, rather than separates, humanity" (p. 436). Kim believes that in "becoming intercultural . . . we can rise above the hidden grips of our childhood culture and discover that there are many ways to be good, true, and beautiful. In this process, we attain a wider circle of identification, approaching the limits of many cultures and, ultimately, humanity itself. This process is not unlike climbing a mountain. As we reach the mountaintop, we see that all paths below lead to the same summit and that each path offers unique scenery. Likewise the process of becoming intercultural leads to an awareness of ourselves as being part of a larger, more inclusive whole and gives us a greater empathetic capacity" (Kim, 2003, p. 446). In this way, this emerging multicultural world is presenting us with a set of new possibilities and opportunities to be human.

We are excited about the prospects this emerging world offers. We have no dread about our ability to deal with the challenges this world presents. We accept disruption as a natural rhythm of the world. After all, how would life have texture and substance without disruption? How would possibility come into the world without disruption? Indeed, geologists now claim that the geological forces—the shifting and moving of the earth's tectonic plates—behind great earthquakes, volcanoes, and tsunamis are "advantageous for life on earth—especially human life." As William Broad points out in an article titled "Deadly and Yet Necessary, Quakes Renew the Planet," "The advantages began billions of years ago, when this crustal recycling made the oceans and atmosphere and formed the continents. Today, it builds mountains, enriches soils, regulates the planet's temperature, concentrates gold and other rare metals and maintains the sea's chemical balance" (2005). Jelle Zeilinga de Boer, a geologist at Wesleyan University and author of many books on earthquakes and volcanoes, points to how tsunamis distribute rich sediments from river systems across coastal plains, making the soil richer. "It brings fertile soils into the lowlands. In time, a more fertile jungle will develop." In fact, Dr. Frank Press, author of *Understanding Earth* and a past president of the National Academy of Sciences, claims, "On balance, it's possible that life on earth would not have originated without plate tectonics, or the atmosphere, or the oceans." We believe our social worlds are also prone to seismic and volcanic kinds of disruptions, and that these disruptions can be potentially positive for us. Changes in the conditions and environs that sustain our social and relational worlds can push us to develop new modes of being and understanding that can make for new and better social worlds. Thus these changes can be life affirming.

Our spaces and distances are no doubt collapsing and imploding. In many ways, our unfolding world seems to be inviting us to enter a new realm of being human by enlarging our obligation to each other. Successfully managing and resolving our tensions and conflicts with different peoples will require of us the ability to exercise the most compassion, the most forgiveness, and even the most mercy. Nothing less will get us beyond this moment in history. Yet the exercising of this compassion, forgiveness, and mercy is also what is most integral in making us human. It is also what will eventually save us from the conflicts that now seem on the brink of engulfing us. So, for us, a global, plural, and multicultural world must be engaged openly, honestly, and compassionately. We must engage each other, deliberate with each other, mediate with each other. Without doing any of this, or being committed to doing any of this, there is no possibility of us entering into a new realm of being human. We will remain at the mercy of our worse anxieties, insecurities, and paranoia and thereby forever be afraid and paralyzed by all that is new and different.

LOOKING FORWARD

The following sections of this book revisit and unpack all the issues and positions found in this overview. We employ a case study rich approach, which means that case studies surround and are woven into nearly every discussion. We aspire to show how theory deepens our understanding of reality and can also revise our perception and understanding of reality. We have chosen contemporary case studies from the United States, as well as from around the world. We have also chosen case studies that many even consider impossible to resolve. We hope to show how these cases conflicts can be managed and even resolved. But there is an important distinction between a resolution and a solution. A resolution is a process. It is about cultivating understanding between the different sides and encouraging both sides to experience the world from the position of the other side. Thus a resolution is about working toward a beginning, such as finding new ways to understand and enrich our understanding of each other, regardless of our differences.

CHAPTER 1

Intercultural Communication: Problems, Challenges, and Issues

KEY TERMS

Cognitive Stability

Uncertainty Reduction Theory

Intercultural Communication Cookbook Approach

INTRODUCTION

History seems to show rather plainly that all peoples struggle with getting along with other peoples of different orientations and persuasions. Many claim that this reality simply reflects the fact that this activity is *unnatural* to the human experience and, as a result, should never be fully encouraged. It will always bring a manner of problems. We should presumably keep to our kind. Marry our kind. Pray with our kind. Live with our kind. Go to school with our kind. In fact, most of us already tend to favor our kind. Commonality gives us *cognitive stability.* It lessens the anxiety that comes with dealing with the unknown. Commonality also is about safety. It allows us to distinguish friend from foe, and psychologists claim that this is necessary for us to do. In short, either embracing or celebrating, diversity is difficult for us to do. It is demanding, challenging, and even threatening. Most of us harbor all kinds of prejudices, biases, and fears of different groups. For instance, in the 2008 national election

1

in the United States, polls consistently found that ethnicity was a deciding factor for many white voters. Various ballot measures also found sexual orientation and religious persuasion to be deciding factors. Moreover, many now point, as Bill Bishop (2008) does in *The Big Sort: Why the Clustering of Like-Minded America Is Tearing Us Apart*, to an emerging body of research that shows no positive relation between diversity and education. "Education is presumed to nurture an appreciation of diversity: The more schooling, the greater the respect for works of literature and art, different cultures, and various types of music. Certainly, well-educated Americans see themselves as worldly, nuanced, and comfortable with difference. Education also should make us curious—ever eager to hear—different political points of view. But it doesn't. The more educated Americans become—and the richer—the less likely they are to discuss politics with those who have different points of view" (p. 286). These are examples of our reality of diversity. Diversity is difficult for us to do.

Our study of various intercultural communication literatures and discourses finds an unwillingness to deal openly with all problems, challenges, and issues that disrupt the promotion of intercultural communication. We found a consistent focus on promoting good news about diversity and outlining the many promises and rewards that will come to those who are interculturally proficient. Often, intercultural communication education is cast as an investment with measurable outcomes. In the end, the reality of intercultural communication is often much different from what is found in many intercultural communication readings. We wish to end this schism. This schism does a disservice to intercultural communication by undermining the openness that is necessary to understand each other. It also impedes the development of intercultural communication frameworks and perspectives that are reliable, credible, and believable. In fact, this schism most hurts intercultural communication discourses by reinforcing the false belief that achieving diversity is unnatural and thereby in no way leads to elegant processes and outcomes.

We have no fear of diversity. This is ultimately the goal of this book—to release us of this fear. Yes, achieving diversity is difficult. It can be challenging, frustrating, and even excruciating. But achieving diversity is necessary for moral rather than merely practical reasons. It allows us to expand our humanity, to look at the world and each other in new ways. It even allows us to look at ourselves in new ways. Achieving diversity enriches our social worlds. Still, working through this life-affirming process can be difficult. But there is no need to be afraid of the challenges that surround intercultural communication. The following sections of this chapter present many of the difficult problems, challenges, and issues that surround intercultural communication, but yet tend to be absent in too many intercultural communication readings.

THE PROBLEM WITH DIVERSITY

Our worldviews reflect the ways we perceive, experience, and make sense of ourselves, each other, and the world. In this way, our worldviews reflect our beliefs, values, assumptions, truths, expectations, and fears. The dominant worldview in the Western world divides the world between the forces of homogeneity, order, life, unity, progress, and meaning and the forces of diversity, death, disunity, anarchy, and ambiguity. It also pits these sets of forces against each other. We therefore perceive, experience, and make sense of the world through this lens. We trust homogeneity. We are comfortable with homogeneity. Diversity, on the other hand, makes us anxious. We are suspicious of diversity. We would prefer that diversity to be monitored, controlled, and limited. In the end, our worldview favors homogeneity, as seen in the popular sentiment about the need for all U.S. citizens to speak Standard English and submit to "the American Creed." This sentiment reflects the fear that without a common language, diversity, chaos, and anarchy will presumably result. Regardless of how tolerant many of us consider ourselves, our suspicion of diversity is always present. Still, every sticker tells us that our differences make us stronger. We are told again and again to celebrate diversity and embrace our differences.

But what happens when reality seems to confirm our deep suspicions of diversity? In a massive new study, based on interviews of nearly 30,000 people across the United States, Robert Putnam of Harvard University found that the greater the diversity in a community, the less people volunteer, give to charity, work on community projects, and vote. In the most diverse communities, neighbors trust one another about half as much as they do in the most homogenous settings. The study also found that virtually all measures of social involvement are lower in more diverse settings. According to Scott Page, a University of Michigan political scientist, "The extent of the effect is shocking." Many opponents of immigration have already begun to use Putnam's study as proof of the harm large-scale immigration causes to the nation's social integrity.

Edward Glaeser, an economist at Harvard University, claims that Putnam's study is "an important addition to a growing body of evidence on the challenges created by diversity." In a recent study, Glaeser and colleague Alberto Alesina argued that roughly half the difference in social welfare spending between the United States and Europe can be attributed to the greater ethnic diversity of the U.S. population. Economists Matthew Kahn of UCLA and Dora Costa of MIT also link diversity with lower levels of participation in voluntary organizations and lower levels of school funding, census response rates, and trust in others.

Management and organization literatures also show problems with diversity. Various management diversity literatures discuss diversity in terms of functionality and utility. That is, diversity affords superior decision making, promotes creativity, expands access to new markets and resources, enables better relations with customers, and so forth. We look at diversity as a means to an end. In a review of diversity management literatures, Diane Grimes (2002) found that the reasons given for the need to manage diversity included "(a) the need to adapt to changing workplace demographics; (b) the desire to increase business effectiveness (for example, to decrease conflict, increase productivity, keep the business out of court, and/or to respond to changing markets and customer bases); and (c) a concern for justice (including a desire to decrease discrimination, increase alternative perspectives, recognize bias, and increase cultural awareness)" (p. 388).

Other research also shows that group diversity (a) increases the determination and will of collectives, (b) mobilizes in the community the resources to solve complex and fuzzy problems, (c) gives collectives the ability to reach out to the broader society and to explore novel opportunities, (d) promotes entrepreneurialism within collectives, (e) lessens conflict between groups, (f) increases innovation and creativity within groups, and (g) enhances the ability of groups to find reasonable solutions for complex problems (Bandura & Wood, 1989; Burt, 1992; Goldenberg & Mazursky, 2002; Granovetter, 1974; Lowndes & Skelcher, 1998; Surowiecki, 2004).

Diversity training programs and initiatives focus on harnessing the rewards of diversity. Presumably, diversity is a commodity that comes with the addition of peoples of different races, gender, ethnicity, and so forth. Organizations can supposedly become diverse through the process of addition, specifically the addition and accommodation of different kinds of people. Recognizing the many rewards that diversity brings, organizations are committed to adding all kinds of differences. Persons of historically marginalized and disenfranchised groups are vigorously pursued, always strongly encouraged to apply for different offerings and job openings. However, management diversity literature also shows that diversity continues to present many problems. Various literatures commonly refer to diversity as a double-edge sword. On one hand, research consistently correlates diversity with creativity and superior decision making (Watson, Kumar, & Michaelson, 1993), and on the other, diversity is associated with higher turnover rates, less job satisfaction levels, higher levels of deviancy, higher levels of absenteeism, and less-integrated collectives (Wagner, Pfeffer, & O'Reilly, 1984).

In a review of organizational diversity literatures, Milliken and Martins (1996) observed, "One of the most striking and most important findings of research on diversity is that groups that are diverse have lower levels of member satisfaction and higher rates of turnover than more homogenous groups." (p. 420). Milliken and Martins (1996) speculated about whether organizations can continue to afford the trade-off between the benefits and costs of diversity. "If so, are there ways in which organizations can perform a balancing act between the costs and benefits of diversity?" (p. 421).

We are by no means of the view that diversity is a problem, as various literatures seem to suggest. Our point is that diversity is evidently still a problem for many persons, even after being saturated with messages about how diversity is good for us. To deny this reality is simply dishonest. As for Putnam's findings about how diversity fragments a community, these findings merely point to the growing pains that come with a society that is only now beginning to deal with a rich amount of diversity. We will hopefully soon develop the communication practices that are vital to properly process this diversity. Diversity problems are really problems of empathy and compassion, or the lack thereof. There will always be tension between human beings.

But such tensions are in no way the cause of destructive strife between different human beings. What causes such conflict is our failure to develop the communication temperament to engage, manage, and resolve these tensions. In this way, Putnam's findings are merely revealing that our own empathy and compassion are deficient. Yet to look at such findings from the standpoint of diversity reinforces the view that the problem is solely with those who seem most different to us. But, of course, nothing could be further from the truth. Regardless of how homogenous a society is, or how homogeneous a society pretends to be, no society can flourish without empathy and compassion. Without communication, only aggression will result.

THE PROBLEM WITH COMMUNICATION

One of the most popular frameworks in intercultural communication is *uncertainty reduction theory.* This theory claims that communication is a process of reducing uncertainty. It also claims that through this process of reducing uncertainty, understanding, meaning, and clarity appear. In this way, uncertainty reduction theory associates uncertainty with confusion. So communication is presumably a process that moves from uncertainty to clarity. As such, communication problems are fundamentally seen as uncertainty problems—our failure to successfully remove uncertainty. In uncertainty reduction theory, communication is a distilling and refining process. It is about removing the noise that impedes clarity of thought, clarity of purpose, and ultimately, clarity of expression.

The threat of noise, uncertainty, and confusion supposedly resides in our lack of knowledge of other cultures. Thus most intercultural readings and discourses focus on introducing us to the customs, norms, traditions, beliefs, behaviors, and other practices that distinguish cultures. We are to know which cultures are high context or low context, linear or nonlinear, masculine or feminine, hierarchical or circular, associative or abstractive, and so forth. This is commonly (and often disparagingly) referred to as the *intercultural communication cookbook approach.* But this practice cultivates stereotyping by promoting the notion that persons of certain cultures share a common set of beliefs, values, behaviors, attitudes, expectations, ambitions, and predispositions. Yes, many cultures and peoples do have high degrees of commonality, but there is always diversity, tension, and conflict even among the most homogenous peoples. Also, in an increasingly multicultural, plural, and global world, maintaining commonality is increasingly difficult, as our spaces and distances are collapsing through travel, technology, and migration. In short, the problem with employing an uncertainty reduction approach in intercultural communication is that noise and confusion cannot be removed from the human experience. To do so is humanly impossible.

Uncertainty permeates everything. It pervades language. We will always have different meanings for language. This is why every religious text allow for so many different religions and denominations. Many religions even differ as to whether Jesus Christ is God, or the Son of God. In fact, all religious texts allow for uncertainty. Uncertainty also permeates life. Who can know for certain what will happen next Monday, or next Friday? Uncertainty also permeates the human condition. We have no way of knowing for certain how we will respond to new experiences, new environs. We also have no way of knowing how new experiences will shape us. Our experiences shape our understanding of ourselves. We become what our experiences allow us to become. There is simply no way for us to fully process the world's mystery. Yet no human being can escape this mystery, which means that even our best understandings of the world will reflect mystery, and our questions will always exceed our answers. Thus, a person who believes in God must accept the uncertainty that comes with, "Who made God, and who made the entity that made God?" Just as well, a person who believes in evolution must accept the uncertainty that comes with, "What activity set evolution in motion, and what activity set that activity in motion?" No human being can bring certainty to these questions.

Thus uncertainty reduction theory is by no means the most constructive framework by which to approach intercultural communication in an increasingly multicultural world. In fact, this theory, by pushing to do something that is simply impossible, actually undermines intercultural communication by putting us in conflict with the natural order of the world. Communication is impossible without uncertainty. ***Uncertainty catalyzes communication.*** Without uncertainty, there would be no need to understand anything, to ask anything, to probe anything. Through uncertainty communication unfolds. Yet the fact that communication can never conquer uncertainty means that uncertainty is the lifeblood of communication. Through uncertainty the world seems to be inviting us to create our own meanings and understandings of the world. It is also reminding us that even our *best* understandings and meanings will be bound by uncertainty. Thus every meaning and understanding can allow for a different interpretation. By making communication possible, uncertainty makes diversity possible. This, again, is why communication is always about managing and negotiating our differences. Communication and diversity share a common womb. Neither can flourish without the other. When communication thrives, diversity flourishes. But both can only flourish when uncertainty flourishes. Thus, trying to limit uncertainty only succeeds in limiting communication and diversity. However, without communication, there is simply no way for us to lessen the threat of our differences, much less understand each other. In an increasingly global, plural, and multicultural world, this can never be constructive. So rather than trying to end uncertainty, our goal should be to develop a communication competency and resiliency that allows to be in harmony—rather than in conflict—with uncertainty. Without this capacity, we will continue to believe that our intercultural problems are fundamentally about our differences rather than our communication practices.

THE PROBLEM WITH BOXES

Nearly every application form and census survey asks us to check off boxes that identify our race, ethnicity, gender, religion, and sexual orientation. The purpose of these boxes is to categorize and organize human experience. We assume that these boxes capture important differences between human beings that need to be noted and navigated. But increasing numbers of persons are refusing to check off these boxes. These boxes increasingly make no sense for many of us. Our identity is too racially, ethnically, sexually, and religiously complex to fit neatly into these boxes. Thus, what becomes of intercultural communication in a world without boxes? What becomes of the intercultural cookbook approach that is so dependent on boxes? What would diversity mean in a world without boxes? What differences would be navigated in intercultural communication? No doubt, the end of boxes promises to end many of the popular perspectives and approaches in intercultural communication studies. However, the end of boxes in no way means the end of diversity. It simply means the rise of a new diversity, what Cory Booker, the mayor of Newark, New Jersey, nicely refers to as a "delicious diversity."

Complexity is the hallmark of this new diversity. It is global, multicultural, and evangelical (generously drawing on all kinds of influences and resources). This new diversity is even redefining what diversity means. Whereas the current approach views diversity in terms of attributes that allow for boxes, this new diversity views diversity as a perspective, as a way of looking at the world. It is determined to revision our view of the world by changing our ways of defining ourselves. It foregrounds our common heritages as well as our common fates. Our diversity is an expression of our identity rather than the creation of our identity. In this way, our diversity is open to the world. It is always changing, moving, and mixing. This new diversity respects traditions and customs, yet is also unwilling to be bound by traditions and customs. We enter the world as citizens of the world rather than as citizens of boxes.

But the mentality of viewing diversity in terms of boxes persists. As a way of preserving this view of diversity, the focus is on increasing the number of boxes available to us. That is, by viewing diversity in terms of boxes, many view the solution to our diversity problems from the perspective of boxes. However, when in 2000 the U.S. government allowed people to identify themselves as more than one race on the U.S. Census, the result, according to demographer William Frey of the Milken Institute in Santa Monica, California, was "a statistical mess." People could now choose from six racial categories, which present a matrix of 63 possible racial choices, compared with 5 a decade ago. The census found that there were nearly 7 million multiracial people living in the country. Moreover, multiracial children are one of the fastest-growing segments of the U.S. population. About two million children have parents of different races. Also, the number of mixed-race families in United States is steadily increasing, due to a rise in interracial marriages and relationships, as well as an increase in transracial and international adoptions. Adam Pertman, director of the Evan B. Donaldson Adoption Institute, estimates that the number of U.S. adoptions from abroad has tripled in the past decade. "When you look at the number of people adopting from Asia, from Latin America—more than half are adopting from countries where the kids aren't going to look anything like their parents. That's starting to make a difference in the way people think of families, of inheritance, of nurture versus nature, you name it."

Census analysts estimate that the mixed-race population grew by about 25% from 2000 to 2006. Analysts expect this trend to continue. According to Nicholas Jones of the Census Bureau, "The multiracial population is much younger than the total population." Other census data show that more than 1 in 6 adopted kids is of a different race from their parents. Indeed, according to the U.S. Census, the number of interracial marriages in the United States has been on the rise since such unions became legal in the United States in 1967: from 310,000 in 1970, to 651,000 in 1980, and 1,161,000 in 1992. Interracial marriages represented 0.7% of all marriages in 1970, rising to 1.3% in 1980 and 2.2% in 1992. In the United States, marriages between blacks and whites increased 400% in the last 30 years, with a 1,000% increase in marriages between whites and Asians. With the introduction of the mixed-race category, the 2000 U.S. Census found interracial marriage to be even more widespread, with 2,669,558 interracial marriages recorded, or 4.9% of all marriages. There were 1.5 million Hispanic–white marriages in the United States, a half million Asian–white marriages, and more than a quarter million black–white marriages.

Wendy Roth, a sociologist at the University of British Columbia, believes that interracial marriages serve as a litmus test of social relations between different groups. "If this is a sign of anything bigger, it's a sign of the fact that those barriers, those social barriers between racial groups are being chipped away at a little bit." In a recent survey, 47% of white teens, 60% of black teens, and 90% of Hispanic teens said they had dated someone of another race. Moreover, according to the Pew Research Center, "More than one-fifth of all American adults (22%) say that they have a close relative who is married to someone of a different race." Attitudes toward interracial relationships have also grown more tolerant. In 2003, more than three quarters of all adults (77%) said it is "all right for blacks and whites to date each other," up from 48% who felt this way in 1987. Acceptance of interracial dating is greatest among the young. In surveys conducted in 2002 and 2003, fully 91% of respondents born after 1976 said that interracial dating is acceptable, compared with 50% of the oldest generation (those reaching adulthood during World War II) who expressed this view. Also, blacks (91%) and Hispanics (90%) are more accepting of interracial dating than are non-Hispanic whites (71%).

Data from the 2000 census also reveal that nearly two million African Americans claim to belong to many races. Census analysts had no explanation as to why 5% of African Americans, or about double what had been expected, saw themselves as multiracial. About half of that group, or 784,000 people, saw themselves as white and black. According to Claudette Bennett, the chief of the racial statistics branch at the Census Bureau, "We really didn't expect that number. We just don't really have a good handle on it right now." Many civil rights groups are concerned that multiple race choices will undermine the integrity of such groups. During the 2000 Census, the NAACP and other minority organizations encouraged people of color to stick to one race. "We wanted to make sure that all the very important anti-discrimination laws, voting rights laws and anti-hate laws . . . could still be enforced," the NAACP's Hilary Shelton says. "So make sure you put down what you're perceived as."

But a person's identity is also shaped by how a person perceives himself or herself. As seen in the latest U.S. census findings, increasing numbers of persons perceive themselves in ways that exceed any one box, or two boxes, or three boxes, or any number of boxes. Yet this social evolution is in no way a threat to the many important gains of the civil rights movement. We are merely evolving to new ways of experiencing race, ethnicity, and sexuality. With boxes increasingly losing currency, race, ethnicity, sexuality, and religion are becoming unbound, meaning that our ability to avoid persons of different races, ethnicities, sexualities, and religions will become increasingly impossible.

REPORT TAKES AIM AT 'MODEL MINORITY' STEREOTYPE OF ASIAN-AMERICAN STUDENTS

Tamar Lewin

The image of Asian-Americans as a homogeneous group of high achievers taking over the campuses of the nation's most selective colleges came under assault in a report issued Monday.

The report, by New York University, the College Board and a commission of mostly Asian-American educators and community leaders, largely avoids the debates over both affirmative action and the heavy representation of Asian-Americans at the most selective colleges.

But it pokes holes in stereotypes about Asian-Americans and Pacific Islanders, including the perception that they cluster in science, technology, engineering and math. And it points out that the term "Asian-American" is extraordinarily broad, embracing members of many ethnic groups.

"Certainly there's a lot of Asians doing well, at the top of the curve, and that's a point of pride, but there are just as many struggling at the bottom of the curve, and we wanted to draw attention to that," said Robert T. Teranishi, the N.Y.U. education professor who wrote the report, "Facts, Not Fiction: Setting the Record Straight."

"Our goal," Professor Teranishi added, "is to have people understand that the population is very diverse."

The report, based on federal education, immigration and census data, as well as statistics from the College Board, noted that the federally defined categories of Asian-American and Pacific Islander included dozens of groups, each with its own language and culture, as varied as the Hmong, Samoans, Bengalis and Sri Lankans.

Their educational backgrounds, the report said, vary widely: while most of the nation's Hmong and Cambodian adults have never finished high school, most Pakistanis and Indians have at least a bachelor's degree.

The SAT scores of Asian-Americans, it said, like those of other Americans, tend to correlate with the income and educational level of their parents.

"The notion of lumping all people into a single category and assuming they have no needs is wrong," said Alma R. Clayton-Pederson, vice president of the Association of American Colleges and Universities, who was a member of the commission the College Board financed to produce the report.

"Our backgrounds are very different," added Dr. Clayton-Pederson, who is black, "but it's almost like the reverse of what happened to African-Americans."

The report found that contrary to stereotype, most of the bachelor's degrees that Asian-Americans and Pacific Islanders received in 2003 were in business, management, social sciences or humanities, not in the STEM fields: science, technology, engineering or math. And while Asians earned 32 percent of the nation's STEM doctorates that year, within that 32 percent more than four of five degree recipients were international students from Asia, not Asian-Americans.

The report also said that more Asian-Americans and Pacific Islanders were enrolled in community colleges than in either public or private four-year colleges. But the idea that Asian-American "model minority" students are edging out all others is so ubiquitous that quips like "U.C.L.A. really stands for United Caucasians Lost Among Asians" or "M.I.T. means Made in Taiwan" have become common, the report said.

Asian-Americans make up about 5 percent of the nation's population but 10 percent or more—considerably more in California—of the undergraduates at many of the most selective colleges, according to data reported by colleges. But the new report suggested that some such statistics combined campus populations of Asian-Americans with those of international students from Asian countries.

The report quotes the opening to W. E. B. Du Bois's 1903 classic "The Souls of Black Folk"—"How does it feel to be a problem?"—and says that for Asian-Americans, seen as the "good minority that seeks advancement through quiet diligence in study and work and by not making waves," the question is, "How does it feel to be a solution?"

That question, too, is problematic, the report said, because it diverts attention from systemic failings of K-to-12 schools, shifting responsibility for educational success to individual students. In addition, it said, lumping together all Asian groups masks the poverty and academic difficulties of some subgroups.

The report said the model-minority perception pitted Asian-Americans against African-Americans. With the drop in black and Latino enrollment at selective public universities that are not allowed to consider race in admissions, Asian-Americans have been turned into buffers, the report said, "middlemen in the cost-benefit analysis of wins and losses."

Some have suggested that Asian-Americans are held to higher admissions standards at the most selective colleges. In 2006, Jian Li, the New Jersey-born son of Chinese immigrants, filed a complaint with the Office for Civil Rights at the Education Department, saying he had been rejected by Princeton because he is Asian. Princeton's admission policies are under review, the department says.

The report also notes the underrepresentation of Asian-Americans in administrative jobs at colleges. Only 33 of the nation's college presidents, fewer than 1 percent, are Asian-Americans or Pacific Islanders.

LOVE THAT DARE NOT SQUEAK ITS NAME
Dinitia Smith

Roy and Silo, two chinstrap penguins at the Central Park Zoo in Manhattan, are completely devoted to each other. For nearly six years now, they have been inseparable. They exhibit what in penguin parlance is called "ecstatic behavior" that is, they entwine their necks, they vocalize to each other, they have sex. Silo and Roy are, to anthropomorphize a bit, gay penguins. When offered female companionship, they have adamantly refused it. And the females aren't interested in them, either.

At one time, the two seemed so desperate to incubate an egg together that they put a rock in their nest and sat on it, keeping it warm in the folds of their abdomens, said their chief keeper, Rob Gramzay. Finally, he gave them a fertile egg that needed care to hatch. Things went perfectly. Roy and Silo sat on it for the typical 34 days until a chick, Tango, was born. For the next two and a half months they raised Tango, keeping her warm and feeding her food from their beaks until she could go out into the world on her own. Mr. Gramzay is full of praise for them.

"They did a great job," he said. He was standing inside the glassed-in penguin exhibit, where Roy and Silo had just finished lunch. Penguins usually like a swim after they eat, and Silo was in the water. Roy had finished his dip and was up on the beach.

Roy and Silo are hardly unusual. Milou and Squawk, two young males, are also beginning to exhibit courtship behavior, hanging out with each other, billing and bowing. Before them, the Central Park Zoo had Georgey and Mickey, two female Gentoo penguins who tried to incubate eggs together. And Wendell and Cass, a devoted male African penguin pair, live at the New York Aquarium in Coney Island. Indeed, scientists have found homosexual behavior throughout the animal world.

This growing body of science has been increasingly drawn into charged debates about homosexuality in American society, on subjects from gay marriage to sodomy laws, despite reluctance from experts in the field to extrapolate from animals to humans. Gay groups argue that if homosexual behavior occurs in animals, it is natural, and therefore the rights of homosexuals should be protected. On the other hand, some conservative religious groups have condemned the same practices in the past, calling them "animalistic."

But if homosexuality occurs among animals, does that necessarily mean that it is natural for humans, too? And that raises a familiar question: if homosexuality is not a choice, but a result of natural forces that cannot be controlled, can it be immoral?

The open discussion of homosexual behavior in animals is relatively new. "There has been a certain cultural shyness about admitting it," said Frans de Waal, whose 1997 book, "Bonobo: The Forgotten Ape" (University of California Press), unleashed a torrent of discussion about animal sexuality. Bonobos, apes closely related to humans, are wildly energetic sexually. Studies show that whether observed in the wild or in captivity, nearly all are bisexual, and nearly half their sexual interactions are with the same sex. Female bonobos have been observed to engage in homosexual activity almost hourly.

Before his own book, "American scientists who investigated bonobos never discussed sex at all," said Mr. de Waal, director of the Living Links Center of the Yerkes Primate Center at Emory University in Atlanta. "Or they sometimes would show two females having sex together, and would say, 'The females are very affectionate.'"

Then in 1999, Bruce Bagemihl published "Biological Exuberance: Animal Homosexuality and Natural Diversity" (St. Martin's Press), one of the first books of its kind to provide an overview of scholarly studies of same-sex behavior in animals. Mr. Bagemihl said homosexual behavior had been documented in some 450 species. (Homosexuality, he says, refers to any of these behaviors between members of the same sex: long-term bonding, sexual contact, courtship displays or the rearing of young.) Last summer the book was cited by the American Psychiatric Association and other groups in a "friend of the court" brief submitted to the Supreme Court in Lawrence v. Texas, a case challenging a Texas anti-sodomy law. The court struck down the law.

"Sexual Exuberance" was also cited in 2000 by gay rights groups opposed to Ballot Measure 9, a proposed Oregon statute prohibiting teaching about homosexuality or bisexuality in public schools. The measure lost.

In his book Mr. Bagemihl describes homosexual activity in a broad spectrum of animals. He asserts that while same-sex behavior is sometimes found in captivity, it is actually seen more frequently in studies of animals in the wild.

Among birds, for instance, studies show that 10 to 15 percent of female western gulls in some populations in the wild are homosexual. Females perform courtship rituals, like tossing their heads at each other or offering small gifts of food to each other, and they establish nests together. Occasionally they mate with males and produce fertile eggs but then return to their original same-sex partners. Their bonds, too, may persist for years.

Among mammals, male and female bottlenose dolphins frequently engage in homosexual activity, both in captivity and in the wild. Homosexuality is particularly common among young male dolphin calves. One male may protect another that is resting or healing from wounds inflicted by a predator. When one partner dies, the other may search for a new male mate. Researchers have noted that in some cases same-sex behavior is more common for dolphins in captivity.

Male and female rhesus macaques, a type of monkey, also exhibit homosexuality in captivity and in the wild. Males are affectionate to each other, touching, holding and embracing. Females smack their lips at each other and play games like hide-and-seek, peek-a-boo and follow the leader. And both sexes mount members of their own sex.

Paul L. Vasey, a professor of psychology and neuroscience at the University of Lethbridge in Canada, who studies homosexual behavior in Japanese macaques, is editing a new book on homosexual behavior in animals, to be published by Cambridge University Press. This kind of behavior among animals has been observed by scientists as far back as the 1700's, but Mr. Vasey said one reason there had been few books on the topic was that "people don't want to do the research because they don't want to have suspicions raised about their sexuality."

Some scientists say homosexual behavior in animals is not necessarily about sex. Marlene Zuk, a professor of biology at the University of California at Riverside and author of "Sexual Selections: What We Can and Can't Learn About Sex From Animals" (University of California Press, 2002), notes that scientists have speculated that homosexuality may have an evolutionary purpose, ensuring the survival of the species. By not producing their own offspring, homosexuals may help support or nurture their relatives' young. "That is a contribution to the gene pool," she said.

For Janet Mann, a professor of biology and psychology at Georgetown University, who has studied same-sex behavior in dolphin calves, their homosexuality "is about bond formation," she said, "not about being sexual for life."

She said that studies showed that adult male dolphins formed long-term alliances, sometimes in large groups. As adults, they cooperate to entice a single female and keep other males from her. Sometimes they share the female, or they may cooperate to help one male. "Male-male cooperation is extremely important," Ms. Mann said. The homosexual behavior of the young calves "could be practicing" for that later, crucial adult period, she added.

But, scientists say, just because homosexuality is observed in animals doesn't mean that it is only genetically based. "Homosexuality is extraordinarily complex and variable," Mr. Bagemihl said. "We look at animals as pure biology and pure genetics, and they are not." He noted that "the occurrence of same-sex behavior in animals provides support for the nurture side as well." He cited as an example the ruff, a type of Arctic sandpiper. There are four different classes of male ruffs, each differing from the others genetically. The two that differ most from each other are most similar in their homosexual behaviors.

Ms. Zuk said, "You have inclinations that are more or less supported by our genes and in some environmental circumstances get expressed." She used the analogy of right- or left-handedness, thought to be genetically based. "But you can teach naturally left-handed children to use their right hand," she pointed out.

Still, scientists warn about drawing conclusions about humans. "For some people, what animals do is a yardstick of what is and isn't natural," Mr. Vasey said. "They make a leap from saying if it's natural, it's morally and ethically desirable."

But he added: "Infanticide is widespread in the animal kingdom. To jump from that to say it is desirable makes no sense. We shouldn't be using animals to craft moral and social policies for the kinds of human societies we want to live in. Animals don't take care of the elderly. I don't particularly think that should be a platform for closing down nursing homes."

Mr. Bagemihl is also wary of extrapolating. "In Nazi Germany, one very common interpretation of homosexuality was that it was animalistic behavior, subhuman," he said.

What the animal studies do show, Ms. Zuk observed, is that "sexuality is a lot broader term than people want to think."

"You have this idea that the animal kingdom is strict, old-fashioned Roman Catholic," she said, "that they have sex just to procreate."

In bonobos, she noted, "you see expressions of sex outside the period when females are fertile. Suddenly you are beginning to see that sex is not necessarily about reproduction."

"Sexual expression means more than making babies," Ms. Zuk said. "Why are we surprised? People are animals."

By viewing our diversity in terms of race, ethnicity, gender, disability, sexual orientation, and religion, most intercultural texts and discourses perpetuate the commonly held notion that our differences can be found in these attributes. As such, the goal is always on managing, tolerating, and bridging these differences and identifying the communication practices that can help us achieve these goals. On the other hand, intercultural communication problems are often seen in terms of our failure to properly navigate our differences, such as using a wrong word or phrase, seeming to lack sensitivity to something, failing to do something, or simply doing something wrong.

The problem with looking at differences in terms of categories of race, ethnicity, nationality, sexual orientation, disability, gender, civilization, and religion is that our differences are seen as residing within these concepts. This practice promotes stereotyping. It fosters the impression that all persons of a certain persuasion or category share a common sensibility, a common rationality, a common morality, a common spirituality. That is, that all persons of a certain category share a common set of experiences. But all groups, regardless of how homogenous such groups pretend or are perceived to be, are laden with diversity, tension, and even conflict. This, again, can be seen in the many different denominations of Christianity or any other religion.

Using race, ethnicity, sexuality, disability, civilization, and religion to guide our behavior toward others will consistently bring confusion, distortion, and conflict as these notions mask the diversity found among supposedly homogenous peoples. Any person's identity, as Nobel Laureate Amartya Sen (2006) nicely explains in an essay entitled *What Clash of Civilizations?*, is enormously complex and cannot provide clean and tidy categorizations that make boxes possible. According to Sen, "Religious categories . . . cannot be presumed to obliterate other distinctions, and even less can they be seen as the only relevant system of classifying people across the globe." In bracketing peoples into those belonging to "the Islamic world," "the Western world," "the Hindu world," and "the Buddhist world," Sen claims that "the divisive power of classificatory priority is implicitly used" to place peoples "firmly inside a unique set of rigid boxes."

In reality, every person determines who is different, what certain differences mean, and, ultimately, and how to treat these differences, such as who will be friend or foe. Our differences also reside in our relation to each other. For instance, according to the Bible, both Judaism and Islam are born from the children of Abraham. Thus a Muslim can choose to treat a Jew as a brother, a fellow U.S. citizen, a fellow human being, or a sworn enemy. Every treatment, of course, comes with a different set of consequences and implications. The point being that perception matters a lot in communication, and the power of perception belongs to us. How we perceive and situate (friend or foe) others influences how we relate and communicate with others. In fact, how we perceive, situate, relate, and communicate with others is inseparable. We cannot alter one realm without affecting the other realms. Just as well, by altering one realm we alter the other realms.

THE PROBLEM WITH MEANING

We have all heard calls for the banning of certain words, symbols, and language. Presumably, certain words and symbols are simply offensive or hostile to various minority groups. What usually results is the institution of various speech codes in organizations that prohibits the use of certain words and language. We are also encouraged to be extremely sensitive when using certain words and language that can seem to be offensive.

The problem with this popular sentiment to ban certain words and language for fear of offending various minority groups is that meaning is found within human beings rather than in words and symbols. We assign meanings to words, symbols, and language. That one person is assigning an offensive meaning to certain words in no way means that another person will assign that same meaning to those words. We all retain the power to assign our own meanings to our language and symbols. That our life experiences will always be different, regardless of our race, gender, ethnicity, and sexual orientation being common, also means that our meanings will always be different. The point being that words, symbols, and language come with no set meanings. Even within groups of a common ancestry, meaning is always fluid, always slipping, sliding, and shifting over language. Neither can meaning be imposed on us by simply exposing us to certain words and symbols again and again. In an increasingly global, plural, and multicultural word, one should always remember to ask, "What do you mean by that?" This is the most constructive way of reminding ourselves that meaning resides within us rather than in words, symbols, and language.

The other problem with this popular sentiment to ban certain words and language is that this practice promotes stereotyping. It does so by perpetuating the notion that persons of a certain persuasion are of the same worldview and thereby will have the same reaction to certain words and symbols. As is, "This is offensive to African Americans!" or "This is offensive to homosexuals!" No doubt, many words and symbols are offensive to many members of a certain persuasion. But no group is a monolith. Within all groups, there is always diversity and dissent, conflict and tension, which means that many different meanings and reactions are always in play. That some meanings are in the minority in no way means that these meanings are less important.

CRIME AND PUNISHMENT AT NOTRE DAME UNIVERSITY

It all began with simply reading a book. Keith John Sampson is a janitor at Indiana University–Purdue University Indianapolis (IUPUI). He is also nearing completion of a degree in communications studies. Sampson has a habit bringing books to work so that he can read in the break room during breaks. Sampson was recently reading a scholarly book he checked out from the public library, and which was also available at the university library. *Notre Dame vs. the Klan: How the Fighting Irish Defeated the Ku Klux Klan,* was published in 2004 by Loyola Press of Loyola University Press and authored by Todd Tucker. The book tells the story of a 1924 street fight between Notre Dame University students and Klansmen, who had gathered in South Bend purposely to terrorize the university's Catholic students. The clash lasted two days, during which the Notre Dame students prevailed, and is recognized as a turning point in Klan history.

The book was a *Notre Dame Magazine* "Pick of the Week." In its review, *The Indiana Magazine of History* noted that Todd Tucker "succeeds in placing the event in a broad framework that includes the origins and development of both the Klan and Notre Dame."

However, on the basis of the cover alone, a co-worker sitting across from Sampson complained that the book was offensive. The cover shows the Notre Dame dome and two burning crosses amid a crowd of robed and hooded Klansmen. In fact, the cover art was deemed traumatizing enough to prompt the shop steward to reprimand Sampson, saying that reading a book about the Klan was comparable to bringing pornography into the workplace. On both occasions, that is, with the co-worker and shop steward, Sampson tried to explain what the book was really about. However, both times, neither individual was willing to listen.

Sampson was eventually ordered to report to Marguerite Watkins at the IUPUI Affirmative Action Office. He was told a co-worker had filed a racial harassment complaint against him for reading *Notre Dame vs. the Klan* in the break room. Once again Sampson sought to explain to Watkins what the book was about. He even tried to show her the book, but according to Sampson, she showed no interest in seeing it. In a November 2007 letter, affirmative action officer Lillian Charleston told Sampson that "your conduct constitutes racial harassment in that you demonstrated disdain and insensitivity to your co-workers who repeatedly requested that you refrain from reading the book which has such an inflammatory and offensive topic in their presence." The letter also stated that Sampson "used extremely poor judgment by insisting on openly reading the book" in the presence of his black co-workers.

After a few weeks of relatively quiet controversy and a bit of media reports, Sampson received a second letter from the affirmative action office saying that no determination could be made as to whether his reading choice was intentionally hostile. Thus no disciplinary action would be taken.

But the matter was yet to be over for Sampson. He learned that the incident was now being investigated by IUPUI Human Resources Department. However, after five months, and the involvement of the ACLU, Sampson's record was finally cleared of the racial harassment finding. Charles Bantz, IUPUI's chancellor, publicly admitted the university mishandled the case.

Still, many persons were outraged by how the university dealt with Sampson for simply reading a scholarly book on a university campus. A columnist for the *Washington Post* wrote, "Mind reading was the crux of this case and scores of others where the interpretation of speech codes hinges on unanswerable questions that require the power of divination: What was he thinking? What was she feeling? And who decides what thoughts are acceptable and which feelings are sacrosanct?"

But as regards to other speech code cases on U.S. college campuses, Sampson's case is by no means extraordinary.

THE PROBLEM WITH RELIGION

In *Worlds at War: The 2,500-Year Struggle between East and West,* Anthony Pagden (2008) writes, "I believe that the myths perpetrated by all monotheistic religions—all religions indeed—have caused more lasting harm to the human race than any other single set of beliefs" (p. xix). This sentiment, in many ways, pervades intercultural communication literatures and discourses. That is, most intercultural texts and discourses seem to want nothing to do with our religious differences. Even intercultural communication course descriptions make no mention of religion. Diversity is commonly defined in terms of race, gender, ethnicity, sexual orientation, and increasingly, disability. As always, the emphasis is on how best to navigate, tolerate, bridge, and celebrate these differences. Complaints by religious groups of being violated by the language and behaviors of others tend to attract less attention and are often even ignored. Religious groups complain again and again about our unwillingness to treat religion as equal to race, ethnicity, gender, and sexual orientation and to condemn religious bigotry and prejudice as aggressively as other kinds of bigotry.

Indeed, most intercultural communication texts and discourses do seem to want nothing to do with our religious diversity. But any cursory look at how our religious differences are playing out in the world plainly shows that these differences are trumping other kinds of differences. Religion is increasingly prominent in many of the world's most persistent and violent conflicts.

The problem that many intercultural texts and discourses have with recognizing and embracing our religious diversity is that religion seems determined to defy our ambitions to tolerate, bridge, and celebrate our differences. It tends to give the impression that our differences, even our religious differences, will always be contradictory. Supposedly, every religion demands deep convictions to a set of beliefs that are simply nonnegotiable. For example, many persons of certain religious persuasions and denominations believe that homosexuality is an abomination before God and, as a result, can never be tolerated, bridged, embraced, or celebrated. Moreover, many religions openly claim that all religions are by no means morally and spiritually equal. Many clergy openly expressed this sentiment after the horrendous events of September 11, 2001. For example, Reverend Jerry Falwell said that "[The Prophet] Mohammed was a terrorist . . . a violent man, a man of war."

But whereas many view religion and our religious diversity as obstacles to harmony, Jonathan Sacks (2003), author of *The Dignity of Difference: How to Avoid the Clash of Civilizations,* believes that the world's great religions contain the frameworks that best allow us to find harmony in an increasingly global, plural, and multicultural world. He wants us to recover those religious traditions that speak of "human solidarity, of justice and compassion, and the non-negotiation dignity of individual lives" (p. 12). Sacks believes that

> there is much a religious voice—more precisely a range of religious voices—can add to the collective conversation on where we are, or should be, going. Faced with fateful choices, humanity needs wisdom, and religious traditions, alongside the great philosophies, are our richest resources of wisdom. They are sustained reflections on humanity's place in nature and what constitute the proper goals of society and individual life. They build communities, shape lives and tell the stories that explain ourselves to ourselves. They frame the rituals that express our aspirations and identities. In uncharted territory one needs a compass, and the great faiths have been the compass of mankind.

Sacks also believes that in an age of uncertainty, the world's great religions "remind us that we are not alone, nor are we bereft of guidance from the past. The sheer tenacity of the great faiths—so much longer-lived than political systems and ideologies—suggest that they speak to something enduring in human character. Above all, it was religion that first taught human beings to look beyond the city–state, the tribe and the nation to humanity as a whole" (p. 12).

Sacks also claims that the world's great religions contain explicit instructions about treating *strangers*—persons of different creeds, faiths, and cultures. In numerous places, the Hebrew Bible commands us to "love the stranger," as the following examples show.

- You shall love your neighbor as yourself.
- You shall not oppress a stranger, for you know the heart of the stranger—you yourselves were strangers in the land of Egypt.

- Thou shalt not oppress a hired servant that is poor and needy, whether he be of thy brethren, or of thy strangers that are in thy land within thy gates.
- For the LORD your God, He is God of gods, and Lord of lords, the great God, the mighty, and the awful, who regardeth not persons, nor taketh reward. He doth execute justice for the fatherless and widow, and loveth the stranger, in giving him food and raiment. Love ye therefore the stranger; for ye were strangers in the land of Egypt.
- When a stranger lives with you in your land, do not ill-treat him. The stranger who lives with you shall be treated like the native-born. Love him as yourself, for you were strangers in the land of Egypt. I am the Lord your God.

Sacks also believes that only the world's great religions promote the virtues, such as forgiveness, justice, and restraint, that are vital to creating harmony in a global, plural, and multicultural world. These virtues allow us to get beyond the grievances of the past that can make for too many cycles of revenge. Finally, Sacks claims that the world's abundant diversity, which is God's creation, reminds us that God loves diversity. This is why the world has many different religions. There are many paths to redemption and salvation. According to Sacks, to proclaim that only our religion offers the only path to God, is to reduce God to our image, and this is contrary to us being made in the image God. We honor God by honoring our diversity. Being open to the paths other creeds, religions, and cultures offer enlarges our faith. For Sacks,

> The test of faith is whether I can make space for difference. Can I recognize God's image in someone who is not in my image, whose language, faith, ideals, and different from mine. If I cannot, then I have made God in my image instead of allowing him to remake me in his. Can Jews, Muslims, Hindus, Sikhs, Confucians, Orthodox, Catholics, and Protestants make space for one another in the Middle East, India, Sri Lanka, Chechnya, Kosovo and the dozens of other places in which ethnic and religious groups exist in close proximity? Can we create a paradigm shift through which we come to recognize that we are enlarged, not diminished, by difference, just as we are enlarged, not diminished, by the 6,000 languages that exist today, each with its unique sensibilities, art forms and literary expressions? (2003, p. 201)

Sacks believes that the cultivation of this faith, which all the great religions stress, is absolutely vital for the creation of the harmony that strangers need to prosper together. Thus in the end, whereas many call for the downplaying and sequestering of religion, viewing religion as an obstacle to harmony, Sacks calls for the embracing and promoting of our best religious and spiritual virtues.

Evidently, religion presents many problems for intercultural communication. But these problems can be managed and even resolved. We merely have to be ready to acquire a new set of tools—that is, new ways of framing and defining diversity. Yes, our religious diversity does reflect different convictions and passions. But such diversity is in no way the cause of our tensions and conflicts with others of different persuasions and denominations. These tensions and conflicts come from our unwillingness to exercise the necessary empathy and compassion to recognize our humanity in each other. Without this empathy and compassion, any kind of diversity will put us at each other's throats.

THE PROBLEM WITH INEQUALITY

In *The Trouble with Diversity: How we Learned to Love Identity but Ignore Inequality,* Walter Benn Michaels (2006) criticizes advocates of multiculturalism for being complicit in masking how inequality sustains the ordering of our society. He claims that the mainstream success of identity politics and multiculturalism is due to the fact that both engage in this complicity and thereby actually block any rigorous scrutiny of inequality. For instance, Michaels claims that affirmative action programs promote a false sense of diversity and equity. He is referring to the compelling correlation between standardized test scores and social class background. "The problem with affirmative action is not (as it is often said) that it violates the principles of meritocracy; the problem is that it produces the illusion that we actually have a meritocracy" (p. 84). Moreover, in failing to attend to inequality, Michels claims that advocates of multiculturalism downplay the economic disparities within racial and ethnic groups that make for different social, political, and economic realities. Indeed, the figures on inequality in the U.S. are striking:

- The top 1% of households received 21.8% of all pretax income in 2005, more than double what that figure was in the 1970s. This is the greatest concentration of income since 1928, when 23.9% of all income went to the richest 1%.
- Between 1979 and 2005, the top 5% of U.S. families saw their real incomes increase 81%. Over the same period, the lowest-income fifth saw their real incomes decline 1%.
- In 1962, the wealth of the richest 1% of U.S. households was roughly 125 times greater than that of the typical household. By 2004, it was 190 times.
- The richest 1% of U.S. households now owns 34.3% of the nation's private wealth, more than the combined wealth of the bottom 90%. The top 1% also owns 36.9% of all corporate stock.
- U.S. CEOs earned 411 times as much as average workers in 2005, up from 107 times in 1990.

In a recent Harvard University faculty roundtable discussion, Robert Putnam said that many "social scientists believe this sudden rebirth of economic inequality is the biggest news of the last half-century . . . on class segregation, the numbers are moving in the wrong direction. Interracial marriages are increasing, but inter-class marriages are decreasing."

Michaels wants to move beyond "diversity . . . and to help put inequality back on the national agenda" (2006, p.16). Michaels contends "that the least important thing about us—our identity—is the thing that we have become most committed to talking about, and that this commitment is, especially from the standpoint of left politics, a profound mistake" (p.19). He believes that advocates of multicultural-ism tend to make believe that our real problem is cultural difference rather than economic difference. Also, Michaels claims that these folks, by enfolding race and ethnicity into culture, help perpetuate the ideology of race and ethnicity that the status quo thrives on. Thus "culture is now being used as a virtual synonym for racial identity . . . and to some extent it's also being used as a replacement for racial identity" (p. 40).

But an "immediate objection to this way of thinking about culture instead of race, of course, is that it just takes the old practice of racial stereotyping and reno-vates it in the form of cultural stereotyping" (p. 41). Michaels contends that race and culture continue to seduce us by the promise of a politics that poses no threat to the status quo. For instance, whereas progressives urge us to preserve the differ-ences between groups, conservatives contend that preserving such differences pro-motes discrimination and fosters social division. "The problem with this debate (or, looked at another way, the virtue of this debate) is that, from the standpoint of economic inequality, it doesn't matter which side you're on, and it doesn't matter who wins. Either way, economic inequality is absolutely untouched" (p. 75).

THE PROBLEM WITH TOLERANCE

Most intercultural communication readings and discourses promote tolerance. We are encouraged to tolerate each other's differences. As Neuliep (2000) writes about the benefits of intercultural communication, "Communicating and establishing re-lationships with people of different cultures can lead to a host of benefits, includ-ing healthier communities; increased international, national, and local commerce; reduced conflict; and personal growth through increased tolerance" (p. 2). Simi-larly, Michael Walzer (1997), author of *On Toleration,* writes:

> I begin with the proposition that peaceful coexistence (of a certain sort: I am not writing here about the existence of masters and slaves) is always a good thing. Not because people always in fact value it—they obviously don't. The sign of its goodness is that they are so strongly inclined to say that they value it: they can't justify themselves, to themselves or to one another, without endorsing the value of peaceful coexistence and of the life and liberty it serves. This is a fact about the moral world—at least in the limited sense that the burden of the argument falls on those who would reject these values. (p. 2)

But tolerance, as even the staunchest proponents of toleration acknowledge, is a morally and theoretically tenuous notion on which to build a diversity politics. Even Walzer acknowledged as much. As Horton observed, "What is clear though is that any liberal theory in which toleration has a central place must offer some account of why it is valuable. It is not an obvious or uncontroversial good." Indeed, for persons to tolerate differences that they believe are morally abominable is always a difficult and tenuous proposition. Stanley Fish (1997), another proponent of tolerance, also acknowledged the difficulty of sustaining and even promoting tolerance:

> [T]he trouble with stipulating tolerance as your first principle is that you cannot possibly be faithful to it because sooner or later the culture whose core values you are tolerating will reveal itself to be intolerant at the same core. (pp. 382–383)

History bears sufficient testimony to this point. Toleration is seen to demand too much of us and for no apparent benefit, and as a result, when the opportunity appears, dominant groups seek to oppress minority groups. On the other hand, Walzer offers no objective framework that speaks to what differences should be tolerated. He is slippery on this point. He acknowledges that "to argue that different groups and/or individuals should be allowed to coexist in peace is not to argue that every actual or imaginable difference should be tolerated . . . The toleration of problematic practices varies across the different regimes in a complex way, and the judgments we make of the variance are likely to be similarly complex" (1997, p. 6). But who would call for tolerance of slavery and ethnic cleansing? These are no doubt easy examples. What about homosexuality?

In an essay titled *The Difficulty of Tolerance,* Scanlon (1996) wrote, "Tolerance involves a more attractive and appealing relation between opposing groups. Any society, no matter how homogenous, will include people who disagree about how to live and about what they want their society to be like . . . Given that there must be disagreement, and that those who disagree must live together, is it not better, if possible, to have these disagreements contained within a framework of mutual respect?" (p. 230). Moreover, Nick Fotion and Gerard Elfstrom (1992), authors of *Toleration,* admit, "It [toleration] is not a morally pivotal concept in the sense that no moral principle is generated and no moral system created simply by understanding it. Instead, engaging in normative ethics on any level . . . requires appeal to moral principles that apparently have little or nothing directly to do with toleration" (p. 151).

The fact that proponents of toleration admit that nothing is fundamentally moral about toleration raises a moral paradox. On one hand, toleration demands that what is being asked to be tolerated must at least be tolerable, which means that our capacity for toleration must be enlarged to become tolerant so as to cover everything that is potentially tolerable. Thus to become tolerant, and thus presumably less bigoted, narrow-minded persons must become less judgmental and biased, which is to say, must relax their convictions to their own morals, beliefs, and truths. However, doing so undermines *differences,* for our morals, beliefs, and truths are diluted without any deep conviction. What become the virtues of such morals, truths, and beliefs to begin with? Yet, on the other hand, toleration demands the highest levels of toleration—a superseding belief that toleration is decent, good, and moral. In this way, toleration encourages moral relativism—all is good except that which is abominable.

Robert Weissberg (1998), author of *Political Tolerance,* wants to rescue toleration from multiculturalism. Though a proponent of toleration, Weissberg wants less toleration. He argues that calls for unrestricted toleration are based on faulty premises, foremost of which is that unlimited toleration is politically and morally virtuous, and that our society has a low threshold for diversity. Weissberg contends that toleration must be grounded in a fixed set of guiding principles that simply forbids certain practices that threaten the common good. He wrote, "The forceful repression of political ideas and groups, even if not an immediate physical threat or a clear violation of criminal law, can be reasonably defended, even in a democracy . . . We are not talking of mere rebuke or condemnation, we are vindicating state *coercion*" (p. 77). Yet, "There is no neat formula, nor can one be furnished. Searching for an effortless, logical, abstract way to establish the point at which a democratic group crosses the line and transforms itself into a subversive conspiracy is foolhardy" (p. 108).

Weissberg contends that his guiding principles offer no guarantees of full legitimacy for homosexuals. He believes that society possesses the obligation to govern public morality and decorum. He also believes that the majority of the citizens should determine the standards for moral, civil, and decent behavior. Weissberg contends that what makes full legitimacy for homosexuals tenuous is that the majority—as seen in opposition to gay marriage—currently rejects this kind of legitimacy. After all, "Being gay could be viewed as no different from indulging in a risky weakness, a predilection akin to alcoholism and drug addiction. Forced therapy to cure those apprehended for succumbing to the temptation of risky homosexual eroticism is conceivable, just as drug addicts caught in criminal acts are occasionally forced into therapy" (p. 174). However, Weissberg seems to have forgotten that this political formulation is responsible for institutionalizing all kinds of horrendous actions and programs against minority groups with no political capital.

CONCLUSION

The various problems that were outlined in this chapter are by no means really problems. These problems are windows—places that allow us to look at the world anew. These supposed problems remind us that our current ways of looking at the world are deficient, leaving us with ways of framing diversity and communication that are no less deficient. In many ways, these supposed problems point to the possibility of other theoretical frameworks and approaches that can provide much more constructive, generative, and expansive understandings of intercultural communication. These frameworks and approaches can allow us to move past the confusion and dread that now surround our dealings with persons who seem most different to us. Indeed, besides giving us a different way of looking at the world, new frameworks give us new ways of experiencing the world.

Introducing an Ecological Model

INTRODUCTION

Most intercultural communication readings offer different approaches on which to view intercultural relations. For instance, Klopf and McCroskey (2007) offer a functional approach, Neuliep (2000) offers a contextual approach, and Martin and Nakayama (2007) offer a dialectical approach. In the functional approach, the goal is to understand how different cultures make for different communication behaviors. The contextual approach aims to understand the cultural, microcultural, environmental, perceptual, and sociorelational contexts in which intercultural communication occurs. According to Neuliep (2000), "A context is a complex combination of a variety of factors, including the setting, circumstances, background, and overall framework within which communication occurs" (pp. 18–19). The dialectical approach "emphasizes the processual, relational, and contradictory nature of intercultural communication, which encompasses many different kinds of intercultural knowledge" (Martin & Nakayama, 2007, p. 69).

The goal of these intercultural communication approaches is to help us better understand and appreciate each other's differences. Although all differences are by no means morally comparable, such as slavery being comparable to freedom, most intercultural communication readings refrain in every possible way from broaching this politically perilous matter. One result is an orientation to intercultural communication matters in most readings that never engages the most contentious issues—such as women's seemingly subordinated and even oppressed positions in many cultures—that currently surround discussions of diversity and culture. A next result is an impression that these sensitive issues stand outside the realm of theory—that is, beyond any kind of rigorous understanding.

We believe that intercultural communication studies need a framework that is beyond the goal of merely accommodating, tolerating, and bridging differences. Such a framework should be able to reliably help us know what differences should be encouraged and which ones should be discouraged. On the other hand, intercultural communication studies can also benefit immensely from a framework that moves discussions of diversity away from a perspective of utility and necessity, such as when most intercultural communication readings begin with how being interculturally proficient is necessary for business success in a global economy, or when support of immigration (and affirmative action) is cast as being economically good. We believe that intercultural communication studies need a theoretical framework that can fundamentally expand our understanding of the relation between diversity, communication, and the human condition.

We believe an ecological framework can enlarge intercultural communication studies' understanding and framing of diversity. This framework begins on the assumption that social, cultural, and communicational processes are inherently ecological—relationships between organisms sharing an environment. In our view, this framework gives us a rigorous moral and theoretical calculus to understand diversity, as every ecology must abide by the same algorithms or simply perish. One such algorithm is that ecologies are either evolving or devolving, that is, either promoting or undermining life. No ecology is ever morally neutral. On the other hand, though the proclivity of every ecology is to affirm life, evolution is difficult, even perilous. It requires an embracing of ambiguity, mystery, and complexity, and thereby an unwillingness to be seduced by the illusion of certainty and simplicity. In other words, evolution requires ecologies to develop the resiliency to deal with high levels of ambiguity, as in our openness to new ways of understanding and experiencing the world. In this way, social, cultural, and communicational processes that cultivate, promote, and promise certainty, besides undermining innovation and evolution, promote crippling fears and illusions about issues that seem most unknown, different, and complex.

Cultures also undercut ambiguity, mystery, and complexity by insisting on rigid and redundant structures. On the other hand, such structures, by promoting conformity and homogeneity, only heighten our fear of what is different. Simply put, such structures heighten our fear of our own humanity. So when such structures are pervasive, dysfunctionality lurks, communication ends, and diversity is undercut. Thus cultures in states and modes of evolution have flexible arrangements, meaning that such ecologies function through relationships rather than structures. It is these relationships that allow ecologies to change, innovate, and evolve. Ecologies also evolve by promoting relationships with many different kinds of ecologies. This is the notion of ***embeddedness.*** Ecologies survive and flourish by being embedded within as many ecologies as is physically possible. In fact, embeddedness undercuts the notion that "because [our] view of the world is shaped by the perspective of [our] culture, it is often difficult to understand and appreciate many of the actions originating in other people, groups, and nations" (Samovar, Porter, & McDaniel, 2006, p. v). It does so by showing that cultures and peoples who are evolving, innovating, and changing, and thereby highly embedded, are so highly influenced by other cultures and peoples that assuming cultural boundaries is all but meaningless. High levels of embeddedness make for a belonging and understanding of multiple ecologies. In this way, embeddedness enlarges our humanity and also quilts our humanity with other peoples and cultures. On the other hand, the relational promiscuity that promotes embeddedness also promotes permeability, which is also a reliable measure of ecological prosperity. Permeability allows for the back and forth movement of resources, knowledge, and expertise between ecologies.

Our point is that distinct attributes and processes distinguish a flourishing ecology from a dying ecology. Ultimately, the latter is afraid of the world's ambiguity, mystery, and complexity. It is beholden to the past and bent on promoting isolation to avoid supposed contamination from outside influences. It is also hostile to other ecologies, especially those that supposedly threaten pollution, contamination, and chaos. In contrast, ecologies on the evolving side of the continuum move courageously into the world's ambiguity, mystery, and complexity. These ecologies look toward the future with hope and possibility and aim to maintain harmony with other ecologies by sharing resources and expertise. In short, these ecologies recognize that the virtues of cooperation exceed those of competition.

To look at cultures as ecologies is to recognize that all cultures are bound by a common set of rules. Cultures that promote ways of being that undermine evolution and innovation by disrupting learning will always face decline and ruin. However, cultures that promote evolution and innovation will always survive and flourish. The notion that a culture can be preserved by religiously holding on to the ways of the past is simply contrary to what is necessary for preservation. But preservation is by no means the only notion that this emergent framework changes. Again, most intercultural communication readings focus on the need to understand our many differences, the origins of our differences, the implications of our differences, the need to respect our differences, and how best to navigate, negotiate, and bridge our differences. The assumption is that our differences are what ultimately make for strife and conflict. Our differences are cast as a set of dangerous and perilous rapids that demand vigilant and sensitive navigation. Any wrong act, movement, behavior, or word can presumably send us crashing into the rocks and currents of discord. But framing cultures as ecologies moves us away from this popular intercultural cookbook approach by emphasizing diversity rather than difference and thereby reminding us that only communication ends aggression. Also, many intercultural communication readings and discourses tend to assume that cultures are relatively stable and homogenous. However, all human ecologies, even those that seem the most homogenous, have tensions, conflicts, and dissent.

ABUSE AND GERMANY'S MUSLIM WOMEN
Rachel Elbaum

BERLIN—Imagine a home with so much pressure to cook, clean and take care of younger siblings that you don't have enough time to do homework. Imagine your parents forbidding you from going out to socialize with friends from school. Imagine running away from home at 17.

This was Leyla's life. Born in Turkey near the Syrian border, Leyla* came to Germany at the age of six with her mother and siblings to join her father, one of the many so-called "guest workers" invited by the German government during the 1960s and 1970s. (*The women interviewed for this story spoke on condition of anonymity for reasons of safety.)

Leyla excelled in German schools, but life at home was overshadowed by her parents' loveless marriage, verbal abuse from her father and few demonstrations of affection. It got worse when her older sister was married off and left home, and Leyla was suddenly thrust into the role of housekeeper and babysitter.

Then, after years of cleaning floors, cooking dinners and finding just enough time to finish a bit of homework, Leyla had enough of feeling like a slave and went to live in a shared house set up specifically for Turkish girls with troubled family lives.

Life away from her family was better, but it turned out her nightmare was only beginning. Leyla would shortly become one of hundreds of immigrant women in Germany—many from Muslim backgrounds—subjected to abuse, forced marriages and other violent family situations against their will.

VIRGINITY CHECK

After months of living on her own—and a chance to concentrate on school work and even have a social life—Leyla's parents asked her to join them on a trip back to Turkey. "Your grandparents are sick," they told her. "Come to see them one last time."

Against the advice of friends and her social workers, Leyla acceded and joined her parents on the long drive to Turkey.

"As soon as we left my mother took away my passport," said Leyla, recounting her story at a café in one of Berlin's Turkish neighborhoods. "They told me Germany was now dead to me."

But the most frightening part of the drive was when her parents said she would be going to a gynecologist to find out if she was still a virgin.

"I just wanted five minutes alone with the doctor, to give him a little money and get him to lie for me," said Leyla, who at that time had slept with a boyfriend in Germany. But her plan didn't work and the doctor confirmed her parents' worst nightmare. Her mother went into hysterics, wailing in the doctor's office, while her father stood there, unable to speak.

"It wasn't until then that I realized what a shame I had brought on them," she said.

Quickly, they arranged a marriage with a cousin, explaining to the family that she wouldn't bleed on her wedding night as a result of a sports injury.

"He wanted to marry me. It was a good deal for him, he wanted to come to Germany," she said of her cousin, whom she met just once.

Her distress at the whole situation was magnified when during the meeting he attempted to kiss and touch her.

It turned out to be a blessing in disguise. Hoping to avoid a marriage like her parents', she told her father of the cousin's unwelcome advances and he agreed to call off the match.

Eventually, with the help of her social worker in Berlin, Leyla managed to get back to Germany, and her place in what was the first shelter established for immigrant girls, enabled to her get a degree in early education and become a caregiver/counselor in a women's shelter for immigrant girls stuck in family situations similar to her own. Now 42, she has managed to build a new life and is married to a German man.

Religion, Culture, Tradition

While Leyla managed to avoid a fate preordained by her family, it is impossible to know how many others are left in violent situations with few means of escape. An editor for the Turkish newspaper Hurriyet has estimated that 50 percent of Muslim women in Germany have been victims of domestic violence. In addition, forced marriages often turn into violent homes.

At the heart of the matter is a complicated dance between Germany's inability to fully embrace immigrants, many of whom were invited from Turkey to fill labor shortages, and the immigrants' unwillingness to let go of behaviors and traditions that appear brutal to mainstream Western Europeans.

Critics of Germany's record with guest workers say the country has been standoffish with the new residents, leaving them clinging to their homeland's culture for a sense of familiarity and belonging, a phenomenon particularly true among Muslim immigrants. Many Germans, meanwhile, blame the immigrants for holding on to their old ways and say the responsibility for their poor situation lies mostly with the guest workers for not making more efforts to adapt to German norms and customs.

"You can't say [these attitudes against women are] because of one specific thing," said Seyran Ates, a Berlin lawyer of Turkish descent who focuses on women's rights. "Many families, who marry their children off early, want to prevent sex outside of marriage. Some are worried that here in Germany their kids will take a German partner or a partner of another nationality so they marry their kids very quickly with another immigrant or a person here they know."

"It is an absolute mix of religion, culture and tradition," said Ates, who was born into a Muslim family.

In part because of several highly publicized murders of Muslim women by family members for "dishonorable" behavior—along with the murder of the controversial Dutch filmmaker Theodore Van Gogh, who often spoke out about the abuse of women—there is a new willingness to discuss forced marriage and spousal violence against women taking place in Turkish and other immigrant communities.

There are about a dozen shelters around Germany that cater specifically to immigrant women, and several organizations that provide support and advice for those seeking to get out of abusive relationships. The majority of these organizations receive government support or funds in one form or another.

Two-Year Nightmare

At one of these shelters, the Interkulturelles Frauenhaus (Intercultural Women's House) in Berlin, an Iranian woman, Shabnam, is still trying to recover from a two-year nightmare marriage.

The well-dressed 24-year-old originally came to Germany after marrying a former neighbor who lured her with promises of a better life than the one she could have in Iran.

He had a good job and a nice apartment in Hanover, he told her at the meeting their parents arranged in Turkey. With strong pressure from her parents to accept his proposal, and her own desire to have a husband, Shabnam found herself married at the end of his visit.

Only after her arrival in Germany did she find out her new spouse's promises were all lies. He had no job and few plans to find one. Eventually he started drinking. And then the beatings started. If she asked why he didn't look for work, he hit her.

Ambitious and wanting to learn German so she could get a job, she instead was trapped at home, cooking Persian food for his friends and taking care of the house.

"I couldn't talk to him," Shabnam said. "I was unhappy, I slept a lot, I had a lot of problems, I couldn't think."

After a breakdown caused by her husband's revelation that he was moving to the United States, Shabnam landed in the hospital for a month. A friend then encouraged her to seek help through the Interkulturelles Frauenhaus. Shabnam is now learning German, and hopes to soon begin a degree course in computer science.

EARLY INTERVENTION

In some ways, Shabnam is a success story. She got the help she needed. And so have the nearly 200 other women and children the Interkulturelles Frauenhaus has assisted this year.

Advocates and caregivers agree that the best way to end these problems is to start educating children early that these attitudes are wrong.

"We need to work with all people and not just with the victims when it's too late and they're getting divorced," Ates said. "We must start much earlier, in kindergarten." But to make this possible, "we need more government support and institutionalized support. Help costs money."

Although there are still hundreds of women across Germany seeking help from shelters, and countless more who suffer in silence, advocates are hopeful that the recent public focus on women's issues is helping more women find help and even avoid forced and abusive relationships.

"I have a feeling that it is getting better, now there is more openness," said Leyla. "Parents are more willing to listen to their children. Not for everyone, but slowly . . ."

IN EUROPE, DEBATE OVER ISLAM AND VIRGINITY

Elaine Sciolino and Souad Mekhennet

PARIS—The operation in the private clinic off the Champs-Élysées involved one semicircular cut, 10 dissolving stitches and a discounted fee of $2,900.

But for the patient, a 23-year-old French student of Moroccan descent from Montpellier, the 30-minute procedure represented the key to a new life: the illusion of virginity.

Like an increasing number of Muslim women in Europe, she had a hymenoplasty, a restoration of her hymen, the vaginal membrane that normally breaks in the first act of intercourse.

"In my culture, not to be a virgin is to be dirt," said the student, perched on a hospital bed as she awaited surgery on Thursday. "Right now, virginity is more important to me than life."

As Europe's Muslim population grows, many young Muslim women are caught between the freedoms that European society affords and the deep-rooted traditions of their parents' and grandparents' generations.

Gynecologists say that in the past few years, more Muslim women are seeking certificates of virginity to provide proof to others. That in turn has created a demand among cosmetic surgeons for hymen replacements, which, if done properly, they say, will not be detected and will produce tell-tale vaginal bleeding on the wedding night. The service is widely advertised on the Internet; medical tourism packages are available to countries like Tunisia where it is less expensive.

"If you're a Muslim woman growing up in more open societies in Europe, you can easily end up having sex before marriage," said Dr. Hicham Mouallem, who is based in London and performs the operation. "So if you're looking to marry a Muslim and don't want to have problems, you'll try to recapture your virginity."

No reliable statistics are available, because the procedure is mostly done in private clinics and in most cases not covered by tax-financed insurance plans.

But hymen repair is talked about so much that it is the subject of a film comedy that opens in Italy this week. "Women's Hearts," as the film's title is translated in English, tells the story of a Moroccan-born woman living in Italy who goes to Casablanca for the operation.

One character jokes that she wants to bring her odometer count back down to "zero."

"We realized that what we thought was a sporadic practice was actually pretty common," said Davide Sordella, the film's director. "These women can live in Italy, adopt our mentality and wear jeans. But in the moments that matter, they don't always have the strength to go against their culture."

The issue has been particularly charged in France, where a renewed and fierce debate has occurred about a prejudice that was supposed to have been buried with the country's sexual revolution 40 years ago: the importance of a woman's virginity.

The furor followed the revelation two weeks ago that a court in Lille, in northern France, had annulled the 2006 marriage of two French Muslims because the groom found his bride was not the virgin she had claimed to be.

The domestic drama has gripped France. The groom, an unidentified engineer in his 30s, left the nuptial bed and announced to the still partying wedding guests that his bride had lied. She was delivered that night to her parents' doorstep.

The next day, he approached a lawyer about annulling the marriage. The bride, then a nursing student in her 20s, confessed and agreed to an annulment.

The court ruling did not mention religion. Rather, it cited breach of contract, concluding that the engineer had married her after "she was presented to him as single and chaste." In secular, republican France, the case touches on several delicate subjects: the intrusion of religion into daily life; the grounds for dissolution of a marriage; and the equality of the sexes.

There were calls in Parliament this week for the resignation of Rachida Dati, France's justice minister, after she initially upheld the ruling. Ms. Dati, who is a Muslim, backed down and ordered an appeal.

Some feminists, lawyers and doctors warned that the court's acceptance of the centrality of virginity in marriage would encourage more Frenchwomen from Arab and African Muslim backgrounds to have their hymens restored. But there is much debate about whether the procedure is an act of liberation or repression.

"The judgment was a betrayal of France's Muslim women," said Elisabeth Badinter, the feminist writer. "It sends these women a message of despair by saying that virginity is important in the eyes of the law. More women are going to say to themselves, 'My God, I'm not going to take that risk. I'll recreate my virginity.'"

The plight of the rejected bride persuaded the Montpellier student to have the operation.

She insisted that she had never had intercourse and only discovered her hymen was torn when she tried to obtain a certificate of virginity to present to her boyfriend and his family. She says she bled after an accident on a horse when she was 10.

The trauma from realizing that she could not prove her virginity was so intense, she said, that she quietly borrowed money to pay for the procedure.

"All of a sudden, virginity is important in France," she said. "I realized that I could be seen like that woman everyone is talking about on television."

Those who perform the procedure say they are empowering patients by giving them a viable future and preventing them from being abused—or even killed—by their fathers or brothers.

"Who am I to judge?" asked Dr. Marc Abecassis, who restored the Montpellier student's hymen. "I have colleagues in the United States whose patients do this as a Valentine's present to their husbands. What I do is different. This is not for amusement. My patients don't have a choice if they want to find serenity—and husbands."

A specialist in what he calls "intimate" surgery, including penile enhancement, Dr. Abecassis says he performs two to four hymen restorations per week.

The French College of Gynecologists and Obstetricians opposes the procedure on moral, cultural and health grounds.

"We had a revolution in France to win equality; we had a sexual revolution in 1968 when women fought for contraception and abortion," said Dr. Jacques Lansac, the group's leader. "Attaching so much importance to the hymen is regression, submission to the intolerance of the past."

But the stories of the women who have had the surgery convey the complexity and raw emotion behind their decisions.

One Muslim born in Macedonia said she opted for the operation to avoid being punished by her father after an eight-year relationship with her boyfriend.

"I was afraid that my father would take me to a doctor and see whether I was still a virgin," said the woman, 32, who owns a small business and lives on her own in Frankfurt. "He told me, 'I will forgive everything but not if you have thrown dirt on my honor.' I wasn't afraid he would kill me, but I was sure he would have beaten me."

In other cases, the woman and her partner decide for her to have the operation. A 26-year-old French woman of Moroccan descent said she lost her virginity four years ago when she fell in love with the man she now plans to marry. But she and her fiancé decided to share the cost of her $3,400 operation in Paris.

She said his conservative extended family in Morocco was requiring that a gynecologist—and family friend—there examine her for proof of virginity before the wedding.

"It doesn't matter for my fiancé that I am not a virgin—but it would pose a huge problem for his family," she said. "They know that you can pour blood on the sheets on the wedding night, so I have to have better proof."

The lives of the French couple whose marriage was annulled are on hold. The Justice Ministry has sought an appeal, arguing that the decision has "provoked a heated social debate" that "touched all citizens of our country and especially women."

At the Islamic Center of Roubaix, the Lille suburb where the wedding took place, there is sympathy for the woman.

"The man is the biggest of all the donkeys," said Abdelkibir Errami, the center's vice president. "Even if the woman was no longer a virgin, he had no right to expose her honor. This is not what Islam teaches. It teaches forgiveness."

IDENTIFYING FOUR ECOLOGICAL AXIOMS

Our supposedly intercultural problems are really ecological problems—problems that stem from the undermining of evolution. Put differently, our supposed diversity problems are fundamentally ecological in origin, meaning that such problems reflect a lack of permeability, diversity, embeddedness, and harmony in our social, cultural, and communicational processes. No amount of sensitivity or respect for each other's differences can save us from the anguish that promise to come from cultures that disrupt learning. The hostility that is always pervasive to that which is different, complex, and unknown will always ferment strife and discord. In this way, such cultures, and the differences that come from these cultures, should neither be tolerated nor accommodated. To look at cultures as ecologies is to look at diversity in terms of evolution, and evolution involves disruption, transformation, and even revolution. It is about promoting emergent models of communication that can push us to evolve, innovate, and change, rather than merely accommodate, tolerate, and bridge. For regardless of our differences, only evolution, and by that models of communication that promote evolution, will ultimately save us from ourselves and each other.

An axiom is a self-evident truth. It requires no experimentation to be proven true. Does the sun rise in one direction and set in another? Yes, that is an axiom. Do objects fall to the ground? Yes, that is an axiom. On the other hand, axioms are also parameters, meaning that any attempt to violate an axiom comes with serious consequences and implications. In an ecological framework, there are four major axioms—*permeability, diversity, embeddedness,* and *vulnerability.*

The Axiom of Permeability

There are no walls, no barricades, and no fences around rivers, forests, deserts, lakes, savannahs, and oceans. In other words, there are no walls of separation be-tween ecologies. Streams flow into lakes, lakes flow into rivers, and rivers flow into forests and oceans. Ecologies share relationships with other ecologies. This is how ecologies survive and flourish. In sharing relationships with other ecologies, ecologies acquire new capabilities and new resources. Ecologies therefore survive and flourish by maintaining permeable boundaries—boundaries that allow ecolo-gies to share resources with other ecologies. History affirms this reality. The most culturally, artistically, technologically, and educationally advanced civilizations have always been the most permeable and, as a result, did the most trading and ex-changing with other civilizations. This is the case of the United States, where im-migrants continue to make invaluable contributions to arts, sciences, politics, eco-nomics, and education. Without a relatively permeable immigration policy, the United States would lack this vital contribution.

Yet no ecology is without boundaries. Any ecology can only share relation-ships with so many other ecologies. But permeability is fundamentally an orienta-tion to the world. It is about being open to new ways of doing things, new ways of understanding, perceiving, and experiencing the world. It is about being willing to learn from others and sharing resources and talents with others. In this way, by giving us access to other worlds, permeability enlarges our own worlds.

U.S. UNIVERSITIES RUSH TO SET UP OUTPOSTS ABROAD

Tamar Lewin

When John Sexton, the president of New York University, first met Omar Saif Ghobash, an investor trying to entice him to open a branch campus in the United Arab Emirates, Mr. Sexton was not sure what to make of the proposal—so he asked for a $50 million gift.

"It's like earnest money: if you're a $50 million donor, I'll take you seriously," Mr. Sexton said. "It's a way to test their bona fides." In the end, the money material-ized from the government of Abu Dhabi, one of the seven emirates.

Mr. Sexton has long been committed to building N.Y.U.'s international presence, increasing study-abroad sites, opening programs in Singapore, and exploring new partnerships in France. But the plans for a comprehensive liberal-arts branch campus in the Persian Gulf, set to open in 2010, are in a class by themselves, and Mr. Sexton is already talking about the flow of professors and students he envisions between New York and Abu Dhabi.

The American system of higher education, long the envy of the world, is becoming an important export as more universities take their programs overseas.

In a kind of educational gold rush, American universities are competing to set up outposts in countries with limited higher education opportunities. American universities—not to mention Australian and British ones, which also offer instruction in English, the lingua franca of academia—are starting, or expanding, hundreds of programs and partnerships in booming markets like China, India and Singapore.

And many are now considering full-fledged foreign branch campuses, particularly in the oil-rich Middle East. Already, students in the Persian Gulf state of Qatar can attend an American university without the expense, culture shock or post-9/11 visa problems of traveling to America.

At Education City in Doha, Qatar's capital, they can study medicine at Weill Medical College of Cornell University, international affairs at Georgetown, computer science and business at Carnegie Mellon, fine arts at Virginia Commonwealth, engineering at Texas A&M, and soon, journalism at Northwestern.

In Dubai, another emirate, Michigan State University and Rochester Institute of Technology will offer classes this fall.

"Where universities are heading now is toward becoming global universities," said Howard Rollins, the former director of international programs at Georgia Tech, which has degree programs in France, Singapore, Italy, South Africa and China, and plans for India. "We'll have more and more universities competing internationally for resources, faculty and the best students."

Since the terrorist attacks of Sept. 11, 2001, internationalization has moved high on the agenda at most universities, to prepare students for a globalized world, and to help faculty members stay up-to-date in their disciplines.

Overseas programs can help American universities raise their profile, build international relationships, attract top research talent who, in turn, may attract grants and produce patents, and gain access to a new pool of tuition-paying students, just as the number of college-age Americans is about to decline.

Even public universities, whose primary mission is to educate in-state students, are trying to establish a global brand in an era of limited state financing.

Partly, it is about prestige. American universities have long worried about their ratings in U.S. News and World Report. These days, they are also mindful of the international rankings published in Britain, by the Times Higher Education Supplement, and in China, by Shanghai Jiao Tong University.

The demand from overseas is huge. At the University of Washington, the administrator in charge of overseas programs said she received about a proposal a week. "It's almost like spam," said the official, Susan Jeffords, whose position as vice provost for global affairs was created just two years ago.

Traditionally, top universities built their international presence through study-abroad sites, research partnerships, faculty exchanges and joint degree programs offered with foreign universities. Yale has dozens of research collaborations with Chinese universities. Overseas branches, with the same requirements and degrees as the home campuses, are a newer—and riskier—phenomenon.

"I still think the downside is lower than the upside is high," said Amy Gutmann, president of the University of Pennsylvania. "The risk is that we couldn't deliver the same quality education that we do here, and that it would mean diluting our faculty strength at home."

While universities with overseas branches insist that the education equals what is offered in the United States, much of the faculty is hired locally, on a short-term basis. And certainly overseas branches raise fundamental questions:

Will the programs reflect American values and culture, or the host country's? Will American taxpayers end up footing part of the bill for overseas students? What happens if relations between the United States and the host country deteriorate? And will foreign branches that spread American know-how hurt American competitiveness?

"A lot of these educators are trying to present themselves as benevolent and altruistic, when in reality, their programs are aimed at making money," said Representative Dana Rohrabacher, a California Republican who has criticized the rush overseas.

David J. Skorton, the president of Cornell, on the other hand, said the global drive benefited the United States. "Higher education is the most important diplomatic asset we have," he said. "I believe these programs can actually reduce friction between countries and cultures."

Tempering Expectations

While the Persian Gulf campus of N.Y.U. is on the horizon, George Mason University is up and running—though not at full speed—in Ras al Khaymah, another one of the emirates.

George Mason, a public university in Fairfax, Va., arrived in the gulf in 2005 with a tiny language program intended to help students achieve college-level English skills and meet the university's admission standards for the degree programs that were beginning the next year.

George Mason expected to have 200 undergraduates in 2006, and grow from there. But it enrolled nowhere near that many, then or now. It had just 57 degree students—3 in biology, 27 in business and 27 in engineering—at the start of this academic year, joined by a few more students and programs this semester.

The project, an hour north of Dubai's skyscrapers and 7,000 miles from Virginia, is still finding its way. "I will freely confess that it's all been more complicated than I expected," said Peter Stearns, George Mason's provost.

The Ras al Khaymah campus has had a succession of deans. Simple tasks like ordering books take months, in part because of government censors. Local licensing, still not complete, has been far more rigorous than expected. And it has not been easy to find interested students with the SAT scores and English skills that George Mason requires for admissions.

"I'm optimistic, but if you look at it as a business, you can only take losses for so long," said Dr. Abul R. Hasan, the academic dean, who is from the South Dakota School of Mines and Technology. "Our goal is to have 2,000 students five years from now. What makes it difficult is that if you're giving the George Mason degree, you cannot lower your standards."

Aisha Ravindran, a professor from India with no previous connection to George Mason, teaches students the same communications class required for business majors at the Virginia campus—but in the Arabian desert, it lands differently.

Dr. Ravindran uses the same slides, showing emoticons and lists of nonverbal taboos to spread the American business ideal of diversity and inclusiveness. She emphasizes the need to use language that includes all listeners.

And suddenly, there is an odd mismatch between the American curriculum and the local culture. In a country where homosexual acts are illegal, Dr. Ravindran's slide show suggests using "partner" or "life partner," since "husband" or "wife" might exclude some listeners. And in a country where mosques are ubiquitous, the slides counsel students to avoid the word "church" and substitute "place of worship."

The Ras al Khaymah students include Bangladeshis, Palestinians, Egyptians, Indians, Iraqis, Lebanese, Syrians and more, most from families that can afford the $5,400-a-semester tuition. But George Mason has attracted few citizens of the emirates.

The students say they love the small classes, diversity and camaraderie. Their dorm feels much like an American fraternity house, without the haze of alcohol. Some praise George Mason's pedagogy, which they say differs substantially from the rote learning of their high schools.

"At my local school in Abu Dhabi, it was all what the teachers told you, what was in the book," said Mona Bar Houm, a Palestinian student who grew up in Abu Dhabi. "Here you're asked to come up with your personal ideas."

But what matters most, they say, is getting an American degree. "It means something if I go home to Bangladesh with an American degree," said Abdul Mukit, a business student. "It doesn't need to be Harvard. It's good enough to be just an American degree."

Whether that degree really reflects George Mason is open to question. None of the faculty members came from George Mason, although that is likely to change next year. The money is not from George Mason, either: Ras al Khaymah bears all the costs.

Nonetheless, Sharon Siverts, the vice president in charge of the campus, said: "What's George Mason is everything we do. The admissions are done at George Mason, by George Mason standards. The degree programs are Mason programs."

Seeking a Partnership

Three years ago, Mr. Ghobash, the Oxford-educated investor from the United Arab Emirates, heard a presentation by a private company, American Higher Education Inc., trying to broker a partnership between Kuwait and an American university.

Mr. Ghobash, wanting to bring liberal arts to his country, hired the company to submit a proposal for a gulf campus run by a well-regarded American university. American Higher Education officials said they introduced him to N.Y.U. Mr. Ghobash spent hundreds of thousands of dollars on the company's fees, talked with many N.Y.U. officials and paid for a delegation to visit the emirates before meeting Mr. Sexton, the university president, in June 2005.

Mr. Sexton said he solicited the $50 million gift to emphasize that he was not interested in a business-model deal and that academic excellence was expensive. Mr. Ghobash declined to be interviewed. But according to American Higher Education officials, $50 million was more than Mr. Ghobash could handle.

So when the agreement for the Abu Dhabi campus New York University was signed last fall, Mr. Ghobash and the company were out of the picture, and the government of Abu Dhabi—the richest of the emirates—was the partner to build and operate the N.Y.U. campus. The Executive Affairs Authority of Abu Dhabi made the gift in November 2007.

"The crown prince shares our vision of Abu Dhabi becoming an idea capital for the whole region," Mr. Sexton said. "We're going to be a global network university. This is central to what N.Y.U. is going to be in the future. There's a commitment, on both sides, to have both campuses grow together, so that by 2020, both N.Y.U. and N.Y.U.-Abu Dhabi will in the world's top 10 universities."

Neither side will put a price tag on the plan. But both emphasize their shared ambition to create an entity central to the intellectual life not just of the Persian Gulf but also of South Asia and the Middle East.

"We totally buy into John's view of idea capitals," said Khaldoon al-Mubarak, chairman of the Executive Affairs Authority. "This is not a commercially driven relationship. It's a commitment to generations to come, to research. We see eye to eye. We see this as a Catholic marriage. It's forever."

It is also, for New York University, a chance to grow, given Abu Dhabi's promise to replace whatever the New York campus loses to the gulf.

"If, say, 10 percent of the physics department goes there, they will pay to expand the physics department here by 10 percent," Mr. Sexton said. "That's a wonderful opportunity, and we think our faculty will see it that way and step up."

Mr. Sexton is leading the way: next fall, even before the campus is built, he plans to teach a course in Abu Dhabi, leaving New York every other Friday evening, getting to Abu Dhabi on Saturday, teaching Sunday and returning to his New York office Monday morning.

"The crown prince loved the idea and said he wanted to take the class," Mr. Sexton said. "But I said, 'No, think how that would be for the other students.'"

UNCHARTED TERRITORY

While the gulf's wealth has drawn many American universities, others dream of China's enormous population.

In October, the New York Institute of Technology, a private university offering career-oriented training, opened a Nanjing campus in collaboration with Nanjing University of Posts and Telecommunications, and dozens of American universities offer joint or dual degrees through Chinese universities.

Kean University, a public university in New Jersey, had hoped mightily to be the first with a freestanding undergraduate campus in China. Two years ago, Kean announced its agreement to open a branch of the university in Wenzhou in September 2007. Whether the campus will materialize remains to be seen. Kean is still awaiting final approval from China, which prefers programs run through local universities.

"I'm optimistic," said Dawood Farahi, Kean's president. "I'm Lewis and Clark, looking for the Northwest Passage."

In fact, his negotiations have been much like uncharted exploration. "It's very cumbersome negotiating with the Chinese," he said. "The deal you struck yesterday is not necessarily good today. The Chinese sign an agreement, and then the next day, you get a fax saying they want an amendment." Still, he persists, noting, "One out of every five humans on the planet is Chinese."

Beyond the geopolitical, there are other reasons, pedagogic and economic.

"A lot of our students are internationally illiterate," Dr. Farahi said. "It would be very good for them to have professors who've taught in China, to be able to study in China, and to have more awareness of the rest of the world. And I think I can make a few bucks there." Under the accord, he said, up to 8 percent of the Wenzhou revenues could be used to support New Jersey.

With state support for public universities a constant challenge, new financing sources are vital, especially for lesser-known universities. "It's precisely because we're third tier that I have to find things that jettison us out of our orbit and into something spectacular," Dr. Farahi said.

POSSIBILITIES AND ALARMS

Most overseas campuses offer only a narrow slice of American higher education, most often programs in business, science, engineering and computers.

Schools of technology have the most cachet. So although the New York Institute of Technology may not be one of America's leading universities, it is a leading globalizer, with programs in Bahrain, Jordan, Abu Dhabi, Canada, Brazil and China.

"We're leveraging what we've got, which is the New York in our first name and the Technology in our last name," said Edward Guiliano, the institute's president. "I believe that in the 21st century, there will be a new class of truly global universities. There isn't one yet, but we're as close as anybody."

Some huge universities get a toehold in the gulf with tiny programs. At a villa in Abu Dhabi, the University of Washington, a research colossus, offers short courses to citizens of the emirates, mostly women, in a government job-training program.

"We're very eager to have a presence here," said Marisa Nickle, who runs the program. "In the gulf, it's not what's here now, it's what's coming. Everybody's on the way."

Some lawmakers are wondering how that rush overseas will affect the United States. In July, the House Science and Technology subcommittee on research and science education held a hearing on university globalization.

Mr. Rohrabacher, the California lawmaker, raises alarms. "I'm someone who believes that Americans should watch out for Americans first," he said. "It's one thing for universities here to send professors overseas and do exchange programs, which do make sense, but it's another thing to have us running educational programs overseas."

The subcommittee chairman, Representative Brian Baird, a Washington Democrat, disagrees. "If the U.S. universities aren't doing this, someone else likely will," he said. "I think it's better that we be invited in than that we be left out."

Still, he said he worried that the foreign branches could undermine an important American asset—the number of world leaders who were students in the United States.

"I do wonder," he said, "if we establish many of these campuses overseas, do we lose some of that cross-pollination?"

Permeability is also about seduction. It is about an ecology being ready and open to be seduced by other ecologies. From an ecological standpoint, seduction is vital. We have to be ready to be culturally and linguistically seduced by persons of other cultures, other languages. Without seduction, cross-pollination, a vital life-affirming processes, is impossible. In sum, without seduction, life is impossible. Seduction is about permeability, being open to the influences of other ecologies. But seduction is also about the recognition that no ecology possesses all the resources it needs to flourish. Other resources belong to other ecologies. Indeed, seduction constitutes the most efficient means to acquire resources and build stable and durable relationships. In the case of global classrooms, seduction is about persuasion, which means a willingness to temper our convictions, to suspend our truths, and even to abandon our positions. All this is difficult to do. So Representative Rohrabacher wants less permeability, and Representative Brian Baird is afraid about the loss of cross-pollination. But increasing permeability between U.S. universities and colleges and other countries will actually increase cross-pollination between these ecologies and ultimately increase our understanding of each other.

TRANSWORLD IDENTITY

The term *transworld identity* is often discussed in the discipline of philosophy as an individual's identity across possible worlds. It is rooted in the idea that a person's identity exists in more than one possible world, including the world in which they currently live, which is referred to as the actual world. According to the philosopher David Lewis (1986), there is no objective difference in status between an "actual world" and "a possible world." The "possible world" is a place similarly "real" to an actual world, and the difference in one's identity in either world is one of interpretation. Lewis, for instance, suggests that the playwright Bertrand Russell could be a playwright in his actual world, but a philosopher in a possible world. Russell could simultaneously inhabit the identity of a playwright and a philosopher, depending on when, where, and by whom he was being perceived.

Many scholars are interested in transworld identity because it implies an understanding of identity as dynamic, unstable, and constantly in emergence in temporally distinct spaces and geographies. Recently, academic discourse on identity has shifted from discussions about the self as a stable entity to the self as a socially produced subject, which, as Hall (1991) points out, is neither simple nor stable. Referring to it as a structure that is split, Hall suggests that it can be many things at many different times as a process of identification. Our selves are influenced to a great degree by people with whom we choose to identify, and this can mean that we can simultaneously reside in different worlds (Sen, 2006). Such approaches to identity have become commonplace in postcolonial studies, where scholars have focused their attention on transworld identity.

Postcolonial theory is a term that refers to cultures in the Americas, Africa, and Asia affected by the imperial process from the moment of colonization to the present. Postcolonial theorists are interested in examining how colonialism affected education, language, geographic borders, religion, institutional and governmental structures, and cultural values and how these influences are lived and indeed embodied by individuals in the present. This theory makes complex any simplistic understanding of identity, especially among individuals born and raised in postcolonized countries or those who moved to the colonial metropoles after decolonization movements. Hybridity and liminality are two identity specific concepts that are central to postcolonialism. Homi Bhabha (1994) defined hybridity as the condition of identity of persons who live between colonial pasts and postcolonial presents. For Bhabha there are three spaces along which a postcolonial identity may be understood. The first space is the identity of the colonizer, the second space is the identity of the colonized, the third space is the identity of the postcolonial who cannot belong to either and so resides in between in a liminal or third space. For instance, for a person from India, which is a former British colony, identity could reside in between Englishness and Indianness—a third space that is neither here nor there but in between. In this way, hybridity represents the complex and multiple ways that people are located within and between different worlds with different affiliations. Hybridity can refer to most individuals, rather than just persons from postcolonized nations, because the world is witnessing a period of constant dislocation driven by powerful forces of globalization, capitalism, wars, and so on. There is now less of a binary opposition between colonial subjugation and domination.

Given these trends, contemporary scholars within the area of cosmopolitan studies have been proposing the idea of the *cosmopolitan*—a person who views himself or herself as belonging to the world and thereby of obligations that exceed any one community, religion, ethnicity, or nationality. Cosmopolitanism dates back to the Cynics of the 4th century BC, who are credited with coining the expression that means "citizen of the cosmos" (Appiah, 2006). The movement was a rejection of the conventional view that human beings belong to one community among communities. Instead, a cosmopolitan was a person who straddled many communities within the universe; thus, his/her identity was spread across worlds. Although, cosmopolitanism as a movement went in and out of popularity, it is now seeing resurgence in the humanities and social sciences. For those interested in understanding identity in complex ways, it entails universality plus difference. It suggests that we can and do belong to various worlds and so have disparate identity affiliations; albeit, but we are all universally connected and have obligations to each other. It is opposed to the "solitarist" approach to identity, which implies that human beings are members of merely one group (Sen, 2006). Such an approach is unable to capture the complexity of alliances and choices that a person encounters contemporary life. A cosmopolitan approach to identity is a transworld identity, as it entails a self that belongs many groups, even those who may or may not agree with each other yet still include the person in their midst.

The Axiom of Diversity

As seen in the rich diversity that can be found in lakes, rivers, savannas, forests, streams, and oceans, all ecologies are rich in diversity. Also, all ecologies are always adding and generating new species and, as a result, always becoming more and more diverse. Diversity is therefore the measure of all ecologies, which means that ecologies survive and flourish by nurturing, adding, and generating diversity. As Nobel Laureate Freeman Dyson (2000) observed, "I do not claim any ability to read God's mind. I am sure of only one thing. When we look at the glory of stars and galaxies in the sky and the glory of forests and flowers in the living world around us, it is evident that God loves diversity."

Diversity gives ecologies new capabilities and, in so doing, access to new resources. In this way, diversity allows ecologies to adapt and take advantage of new and changing conditions. This axiom is aptly seen in sports, as in the case of Juan Pablo Montoya, Yao Ming, Tiger Woods, and most important, Jackie Robinson.

MAJOR LEAGUE BASEBALL

In 1941 Jackie Robinson gained national recognition by becoming the first athlete in the history of UCLA to earn a letter in four different sports in the same year (football, basketball, track, and baseball). He also became the first African-American major league baseball player of the modern era in 1947. His major league debut with the Brooklyn Dodgers ended approximately 80 years of baseball segregation, also commonly known as the baseball color line. Robinson was a member of six World Series teams, earned six consecutive All-Star Game nominations, and won numerous awards during his career. In 1947, Robinson won The Sporting News Rookie of the Year Award and was the first Rookie of the Year Award. In 1949, Robinson was awarded the National League MVP Award. He was inducted into the Baseball Hall of Fame in 1962.

Unfortunately, Robinson always had to deal with a tremendous amount of harassment and physical threats from both players and fans. Players on opposing teams often heckled him with racist slurs. He was even abused by his own teammates, some of whom threatened to sit out the 1947 season rather than play with Robinson. Apparently, the brewing mutiny subsided when Leo Durocher, manager of the Dodgers, told the team, "I don't care if the guy is yellow or black, or if he has stripes like a . . . zebra. I'm the manager of this team, and I say he plays. What's more, I say he can make us all rich. And if any of you can't use the money, I'll see that you are all traded." When other teams threatened to sit out the season to protest the entry of Robinson to major league baseball, National League President Ford Frick promised to suspend them.

No one now disputes the fact that Robinson ultimately made baseball a better sport. The prosperity and diversity that baseball now boasts can be traced directly to Robinson. Without Robinson, there would be no Derek Jeter, Alex Rodriguez, Barry Bonds, Reggie Jackson, Ken Griffey, Jr., Hank Aaron, Willie Mays, Roberto Clemente, Juan Marichal, Roy Campanella, and other great baseball players who have made tremendous contributions in growing the sport. In fact, without Robinson, there would be no Juan Pablo Montoya, Tiger Woods, Michael Jordan, and Yao Ming. In this way, Robinson reminds us of the power of diversity to expand ecologies, as well as the difficulties that often come with promoting diversity.

NASCAR

Ecologies survive by finding new ways to acquire new resources. NASCAR now faces this reality. To find new sponsors and advertisers and acquire more revenue from advertisers and sponsors, NASCAR must find new fans and patrons. Thus, for NASCAR to survive and flourish, it must grow, which means that it must be open and willing to change and evolve.

Through such initiatives as Drive for Diversity, NASCAR has long been seeking to attract minority drivers to the second-most-popular professional sport (in terms of television ratings) and fastest-growing sport in the United States. Although NASCAR does employ many members of diversity groups in various behind the scenes positions, the public face of NASCAR—such as the drivers, the fans, and the patrons—remains devoid of members of diversity groups. In fact, as of 2007, NASCAR's Drive for Diversity has yet to produce elite minority and female drivers who compete regularly in either the NEXTEL or Busch Series.

In comparison, Formula One Racing, one of NASCAR's competitors, is much more diverse, with many Latino and even a few women drivers. Also, Formula One events take place all over the world, which many claim helps the organization attract drivers from around the world. Most of NASCAR's events occur in the United States, and only certain regions of the United States.

NASCAR is excited about the prospects of Juan Pablo Montoya, who joined NASCAR in 2006. Montoya comes to NASCAR with a large following in North America and a record that includes a victory in the IRL's 2000 Indianapolis 500, a title in the rival Champ Car World Series, and seven F1 wins.

As the largest U.S. minority group (42.7 million), Hispanics represent one of NASCAR's best hopes for growth. According to the U.S. Census Bureau, Hispanics will number 102.6 million, or a quarter of the population, by 2050.

Indeed, TV ratings were down for 2006 and 2007, and NASCAR is reportedly moving quickly to add minority drivers and team members. According to NASCAR CEO Brian France, "If we don't get diversity right, this sport will not achieve what it needs to achieve from a popularity standpoint."

Richard Lapchick, director of the University of Central Florida's Institute for Diversity and Ethics in Sports, is encouraged by NASCAR's commitment to diversity. "I'm encouraged by what they're trying to do, and I think the effort is genuine. They understand it's not only the right thing to do but a business imperative."

PGA

Tiger Woods is also a compelling example of the promise of diversity. His achievements to date rank him among the most successful golfers of all time. He was the highest paid professional athlete in 2006, having earned an estimated $100 million from winnings and endorsements.

As of 2008, Woods has won 14 professional major golf championships, the second most of any male player, and 62 PGA Tour events, tied for the fourth most of all time. He has more career major wins and career PGA Tour wins than any other active golfer. He is the youngest player to achieve the Career Grand Slam and the youngest and fastest to win 50 tournaments on Tour. Woods has held the number one position in the world rankings for the most consecutive weeks and for the greatest total number of weeks. He has been awarded PGA Player of the Year a record nine times, has won the Byron Nelson Award for lowest adjusted scoring average a record eight times, and has tied Jack Nicklaus's record of leading the money in eight different seasons. He has been named Associated Press Male Athlete of the Year four times, a record he shares with Lance Armstrong.

Woods is no doubt responsible for a major surge of interest in the game of golf. He has dramatically increased attendance at golf tournaments and boosted TV ratings to record levels. In fact, ratings tend to drop a lot when Woods is out of contention in a tournament. Woods is also responsible for generating tremendous interest in the sport among multicultural audiences. For example, according to the National Golf Foundation, the number of African Americans who played golf at least once climbed from 431,000 in 1991 to 800,000 last year. This accounted for a significant portion of the game's overall growth, from 24 million golfers in 1991 to 26.5 million in 1997. The number of juniors, ages 12 to 17, playing golf went from 1.8 million in 1996 to 2.4 million in 1997. Thus golf programs and tournaments have exploded across the United States.

In response to the exploding interest in golf by members of minority groups, the PGA established the National Minority Golf Foundation in 1995 to create more opportunities for minorities in golf. It provides grants to juniors, the physically disabled, the financially disadvantaged, and others traditionally excluded from the game. Funding for the program, which includes clinics and the building of urban golf facilities, continues to increase exponentially. According to Lew Horne, president of the National Minority Golf Foundation, "Tiger has kicked open the door of opportunity. He's playing an important role in stimulating the growth of golf, particularly among more diverse demographic groups … Tiger has given golf a chance to do what it should have done 50 years ago."

NATIONAL BASKETBALL ASSOCIATION

The National Basketball Association (NBA) consistently receives high marks for promoting diversity in sports. In league offices, the number of women and members of minority groups remains high. The NBA has one black owner, Robert Johnson, of the Charlotte Bobcats. Also, as of 2007, the league has three black CEOs/presidents, five black general managers, and 12 black coaches. On the 30 team rosters, 76% of the players were black and 2% Latino and Asian. In fact, the NBA continues to set records for members of minority groups in the positions of league office professionals, team vice presidents, and assistant coaches, as well as senior administrative and team professional positions.

The influx of players from around the world has also affected the game on many levels. As Luke Peterson observed in an article entitled *The Globalized Association,* "as the NBA acquires more international talent, global citizens from regions that nurtured this new talent become ardent fans." This increased international interest translates to league games now being shown in 212 countries. In fact, many of the game's most dominant players—Steve Nash, Jose Calderon, Tony Parker, Dirk Nowitski, and Tim Duncan—were born outside of the United States. Overall, 85 players from overseas were on NBA rosters for the 2007 season, and only two teams had an all-U.S. roster. In addition, the majority of the MVP titles are now going to players born outside the United States.

But as the NBA goes global, and NBA scouts continue to actively recruit foreign talent, the popularity of the game continues to grow dramatically in the United States. In 1981, the NBA commanded an average of $19 million per year for their U.S. television deals. In 2001, this number exceeded $660 million. Moreover, of the 1,000 media members who came to New Orleans for the 2008 All-Star Game,

285 hailed from 33 foreign countries and territories. The game was also broadcast by 123 international telecasters to 215 countries and territories in 44 different languages. Among the countries were China, Spain, Italy, France, Taiwan, Hong Kong, Ukraine, Germany, and England. This high level of media attention is no doubt due to the fact that the NBA now boasts 77 international players, and a record 12 of those players took part in the All-Star festivities.

The NBA has begun playing preseason games overseas and is reportedly considering expanding the league with a five-team European division. Places like London, Berlin, Rome, Paris, and Madrid either already have or are in the process of constructing NBA-ready arenas, and the NBA believes the expansion could come within a decade.

But is there such a thing as too much diversity? Indeed, is all diversity positive? From an ecological perspective, diversity only constitutes the generation and addition of those practices that allow an ecology to adapt and flourish. So, as in the case of Juan Pablo Montoya, Tiger Woods, Yao Ming, Tony Parker, and so forth, the outcome must ultimately be positive and constructive for the whole ecology.

The Axiom of Embeddedness

Every ecology is located or embedded within other ecologies. So a lake is embedded within a forest, a coral reef is embedded within an ocean, and so forth. The notion of embeddedness means that ecologies are always being influenced by other ecologies. That is, every human ecology is located within a cultural, historical, and political context that shapes the behavior of that ecology. No ecology functions in a vacuum. Thus no ecology can avoid being influenced by other ecologies. This reality is seen in the distinct version of Islam that is emerging in the United States.

FOR MUSLIM STUDENTS, A DEBATE ON INCLUSION
Neil MacFarquhar

SAN JOSE—Amir Mertaban vividly recalls sitting at his university's recruitment table for the Muslim Students Association a few years ago when an attractive undergraduate flounced up in a decidedly un-Islamic miniskirt, saying "Salamu aleykum," or "Peace be upon you," a standard Arabic greeting, and asked to sign up.

Mr. Mertaban also recalls that his fellow recruiter surveyed the young woman with disdain, arguing later that she should not be admitted because her skirt clearly signaled that she would corrupt the Islamic values of the other members.

"I knew that brother, I knew him very well; he used to smoke weed on a regular basis," said Mr. Mertaban, now 25, who was president of the Muslim student group at California State Polytechnic University, Pomona, from 2003 to 2005.

Pointing out the hypocrisy, Mr. Mertaban won the argument that the group could no longer reject potential members based on rigid standards of Islamic practice.

The intense debate over whether organizations for Muslim students should be inclusive or strict is playing out on college campuses across the United States, where there are now more than 200 Muslim Students Association chapters.

Gender issues, specifically the extent to which men and women should mingle, are the most fraught topic as Muslim students wrestle with the yawning gap between American college traditions and those of Islam.

"There is this constant tension between becoming a mainstream student organization versus appealing to students who have a more conservative or stricter interpretation of Islam," said Hadia Mubarak, the first woman to serve as president of the national association, from 2004 to 2005.

Each chapter enjoys relative autonomy in setting its rules. Broadly, those at private colleges tend to be more liberal because they draw from a more geographically dispersed population, and the smaller numbers prompt Muslim students to play down their differences.

Chapters at state colleges, on the other hand, often pull from the community, attracting students from conservative families who do not want their children too far afield.

At Yale, for example, Sunnis and Shiites mix easily and male and female students shocked parents in the audience by kissing during the annual awards ceremony. Contrast that with the University of California, Irvine, which has the reputation for being the most conservative chapter in the country, its president saying that to an outsider its ranks of bearded young men and veiled women might come across as "way Muslim" or even extremist.

But arguments erupt virtually everywhere. At the University of California, Davis, last year, in their effort to make the Muslim association more "cool," board members organized a large alcohol-free barbecue. Men and women ate separately, but mingled in a mock jail for a charity drive.

The next day the chapter president, Khalida Fazel, said she fielded complaints that unmarried men and women were physically bumping into one other. Ms. Fazel now calls the event a mistake.

At George Washington University, a dodge ball game pitting men against women after Friday prayers drew such protests from Muslim alumni and a few members that the board felt compelled to seek a religious ruling stating that Islamic traditions accept such an event.

Members acknowledge that the tone of the Muslim associations often drives away students. Several presidents said that if they thought members were being too lax, guest imams would deliver prayer sermons about the evils of alcohol or premarital sex.

Judgment can also come swiftly. Ghayth Adhami, a graduate of the University of California, Los Angeles, recalled how a young student who showed up at a university recruitment meeting in a Budweiser T-shirt faced a few comments about un-Islamic dress. The student never came back.

Some members push against the rigidity. Fatima Hassan, 22, a senior at the Davis campus, organized a co-ed road trip to Reno, Nevada, two hours away, to play the slot machines last Halloween. In Islam, Ms. Hassan concedes, gambling is "really bad," but it was men and women sharing the same car that shocked some fellow association members.

"We didn't do anything wrong," Ms. Hassan said. "I am chill about that whole co-ed thing. I understand that in a Muslim context we are not supposed to hang out with the opposite sex, but it just happens and there is nothing you can do."

Khalida Fazel, center, a chapter president, said she received complaints after an event with unmarried men and women.

But as Saif Inam, the vice president of the chapter at George Washington put it, "At the end of the day, I don't want God asking me, 'O.K. Saif, why did you organize events in which people could do un-Islamic things in big numbers?'"

The debate boils down to whether upholding gender segregation is forcing something artificial and vaguely hypocritical in an American context.

"As American Islam gets its own identity, it is going to have to shed some of these notions that are distant from American culture," said Rafia Zakaria, a student at Indiana University. "The tension is between what forms of tradition are essential and what forms are open to innovation."

American law says men and women are equal, whereas Muslim religious texts say they "complement" each other, Ms. Zakaria said. "If the law says they are equal, it's hard to see how in their spiritual lives they will accept a whole different identity."

The entire shift of the association from a foreign-run organization to an American one took place over arguments like this.

The Americans won out partly because the number of Muslim American college students hit a critical mass in the late 1990s, and then, after the Sept. 11 terrorist attacks, foreign students, fearful of their visas being revoked, started avoiding a group that was increasingly political.

Some critics view strict interpretation of the faith as part of the association's DNA. Organized in the 1960s by foreign students who wanted collective prayers where there were no mosques, the associations were basically little slices of Saudi Arabia. Women were banned. Only Muslim men who prayed, fasted and avoided alcohol and dating were welcomed. Meetings, even idle conversations, were in Arabic.

Donations from Saudi Arabia largely financed the group, and its leaders pushed the kingdom's puritan, Wahhabi strain of Islam. Prof. Hamid Algar of the University of California, Berkeley, said that in the 1960s and 1970s, chapters advocated theological and political positions derived from radical Islamist organizations and would brook no criticism of Saudi Arabia.

That past has given the associations a reputation in some official quarters as a possible font of extremism, but experts in American Islam believe college campuses have become too diverse and are under too much scrutiny for the groups to foster radicals.

Zareena Grewal, a professor of religion and American studies at Yale, pointed to several things that would repel extremists. Members are trying to become more involved in the American political system, Professor Grewal said, and the heavy presence of women in the leadership would also deter them. Members "are not sitting around reading 'How to Bomb Your Campus for Dummies,'" she said.

Its leaders think the organization is gradually relaxing a bit as it seeks to maintain its status as the main player for Muslim students.

"There were drunkards in the Prophet Muhammad's community; there were fornicators and people who committed adultery in his community, and he didn't reject them," Mr. Mertaban said. "I think M.S.A.'s are beginning to understand this point that every person has ups and downs."

That every ecology is embedded within other ecologies means that every ecology can either be polluted/contaminated by another ecology or nourished/nurtured by another ecology. How do we therefore distinguish a positive influence from a negative one? As all ecologies need to generate diversity to survive and flourish, influences can either aid diversity or diminish it. A negative influence does the latter. Thus, in regard to the Islam emerging in the United States, a level of diversity is emerging that is significant. Of course, many conservatives are afraid of this diversity and want Islam to be beyond the reach of local influences. But this is ecologically impossible. Ecologies must either adapt to new environs or simply perish.

There is no version of anything that is devoid of local influences—that is, devoid of a larger historical, cultural, and political context. Yet there is nothing inherently wrong about this reality. By being embedded, ecologies nourish each other and also gain access to new resources. Ecologies therefore survive and flourish by being embedded within other ecologies, and naturally, those that achieve the most embeddedness will prosper the most. In this way, those ecologies that the most embedded, and recognize the need to be embedded, will also be the ones that are most permeable.

Embeddedness is also about being willing to draw direction and inspiration from other systems, other nations, other cultures, and other peoples. Take the case of law. As Aharon Barak, president of the Supreme Court of Israel, observed in a paper in the *Harvard Law Review,* "The law of a society is a living organism . . . when social reality changes, the law must change too. Just as change in social reality is the law of life, responsiveness to change in social reality is the life of the law." To help deal with these legal changes, many nations have constitutions and legal systems that encourage judges to look to other constitutions and legal systems for direction and inspiration. South Africa's Constitution contains the following provision: "When interpreting the Bill of Rights, a court . . . must consider international law; and may consider foreign law." The result is a lot of cross-fertilization and cross-pollination between many legal systems.

In remarks before the Southern Center for International Studies, Sandra Day O'Connor, who recently retired from the U.S. Supreme Court, claimed that no legal system can avoid the reality of globalization.

> No institution of government can afford any longer to ignore the rest of the world. Globalization also represents a greater awareness of, and access to, peoples and places far different from our own. The fates of nations are more closely intertwined than ever before, and are more acutely aware of the connections.

Ruth Bader Ginsburg, a current member of the U.S. Supreme Court, also believes that the U.S. "judicial system will be poorer . . . if we do not both share our experience with, and learn from, legal systems with values and a commitment to democracy similar to our own." However, as both O'Connor and Ginsburg pointed out, U.S. courts are far from developing a transnational legal philosophy. Anthony Kennedy, another member of the U.S. Supreme Court, believes that "There is a kind of know-nothing quality to the debate . . . of being suspicious of foreign things." Aharon Barak also laments the fact that U.S. courts seem to have no interest in foreign law. "Many countries derive inspiration from the United States Supreme Court, particularly in its interpretation of the U.S. Constitution. By contrast, most Justices of the United Sates Supreme Court never cite foreign case law in their judgments. They fail to make use of an important source of inspiration, one that enriches legal thinking, makes law more creative, and strengthens the democratic ties and foundations of different legal systems." Indeed, many judges and legal scholars in the United States stridently oppose U.S. judges looking to other legal systems for direction and inspiration. Seventh Circuit U.S. Court of Appeals Judge Richard Posner wrote, "To cite foreign law as authority is to flirt with the discredited . . . idea of a universal natural law; or to suppose fantastically that the world's judges constitute a single, elite community of wisdom and conscience."

Antonin Scalia, a member of the U.S. Supreme Court, believes that the notion that U.S. law "should conform to the laws of the rest of the world—ought to be rejected out of hand." The Court should also "cease putting forth foreigners' views as part of the reasoned basis of its decisions. To invoke alien law when it agrees with one's own thinking, and ignore it otherwise, is not reasoned decision-making, but sophistry." For Steven Calabresi, a professor of constitutional law at Northwestern University, the fact that the United States "is an exceptional nation, with an exceptional people and an exceptional role to play in the world," means that U.S. courts have nothing much to learn from foreign law. In a recent paper in the *Boston Law Review,* Calabresi wrote, "Americans are more individualistic, more religious, more patriotic, more egalitarian, and more hostile to unions and Marxism than are the people of any other advanced democracy."

But is this hostility and unwillingness to consider the legal practices and discourses of other nations the most constructive position in an increasingly global, plural, and multicultural world—a world that increasingly requires trust, cooperation, and generosity between nations so as to deal with problems vital to our well-being? Ultimately, in such a world, what matters is whether persons are willing and open to learn from others and much less about what exactly is to be learned. It is the willingness to learn and to be open to the perspectives of others that matter most in the building of relationships between different peoples. This is what embeddedness means.

The Axiom of Vulnerability and Equity

All ecologies are laden with diverse species with diverse capabilities. Yet the well-being of any ecology is ultimately dependent on the condition of the most vulnerable species in that ecology. If the most vulnerable species in any ecology are in peril, all the other species, regardless of how strong, fast, or large, are also in peril. The fates of all species in an ecology are intertwined. Thus, besides promoting a diversity of species, every ecology must also nurture the most vulnerable species. This is the ecological axiom of vulnerability and equity.

This axiom suggests that every community and society has an ecological obligation to nurture the most vulnerable peoples among us, such as those who have been historically marginalized, disenfranchised, and brutalized. Our survival and prosperity depend on our proper treatment of these peoples. We therefore cannot separate diversity and equity. Attending to diversity also involves attending to the needs of those who have been marginalized, disenfranchised, and brutalized.

But what is ultimately the moral of the story? Why should those who seem to be the fittest, strongest, and brightest care about the condition of those who seem to be the most vulnerable? The answer is empathy and compassion. This is what attending to the most vulnerable among us cultivates and propagates. It pushes us to develop empathy and compassion—the means to understand and experience the world from the perspective of the others, especially those who seem to be most different to us, such as being of a different religious or sexual orientation. Empathy and compassion undercut the formation of a narrow and rigid view of the world.

WHEN GIRLS WILL BE BOYS
Alissa Quart

It was late on a rainy fall day, and a college freshman named Rey was showing me the new tattoo on his arm. It commemorated his 500-mile hike through Europe the previous summer, which happened also to be, he said, the last time he was happy. We sat together for a while in his room talking, his tattoo of a piece with his spiky brown hair, oversize tribal earrings and very baggy jeans. He showed me a photo of himself and his girlfriend kissing, pointed out his small drum kit, a bass guitar that lay next to his rumpled clothes and towels and empty bottles of green tea, one full of dried flowers, and the ink self-portraits and drawings of nudes that he had tacked to the walls. Thick jasmine incense competed with his cigarette smoke. He changed the music on his laptop with the melancholy, slightly startled air of a college boy on his own for the first time.

Rey's story, though, had some unusual dimensions. The elite college he began attending last year in New York City, with its academically competitive, fresh-faced students, happened to be a women's school, Barnard. That's because when Rey first entered the freshman class, he was a woman.

Rey, who asked that neither his last name nor his given name be used to protect his and his family's privacy, grew up in Chappaqua, the affluent Westchester suburb that is home to the Clintons, and had a relatively ordinary, middle-class Jewish childhood. Rey, as he now calls himself, loved his younger brother, his parents were together and he was a good student, excelling in English and history. But he always had the distinct feeling that he wasn't the sex he was supposed to be. As a kid, he was often mistaken for a boy, which was "mostly cool," Rey said. "When I was 5, I told my parents not to correct people when strangers thought I was a boy. I was never a girl, really—I questioned my own gender, and other people also questioned my gender for me." When Rey entered puberty, he felt the loss of the "tomboy" sobriquet acutely.

"My body changed in freshman year of high school, and it made me depressed," Rey said. That year, he started to wonder whether he was really meant to become a woman. His friends in high school were almost all skater boys and musicians, and he related to them as if he were one of them. He began to define himself as "omnisexual," although he was mostly attracted to women.

The idea that he might actually want to transition from female to male began to take shape for Rey when he was 14 or 15; he can't quite remember when exactly. "A transmale speaker guy" gave a talk at a meeting of his high school's Gay Straight Alliance, and Rey was inspired. Then he took a typical step for someone going to high school in the first years of this century. He went home and typed "transgender" into Google.

At the end of his freshman year in high school, he met Melissa, a student at Smith College who was back in Westchester for summer break and later became his girlfriend. During one of their days together, Melissa, who was immersed in campus gender activism, mentioned the concept of being a "transman" and spoke of her transmale friends. Rey confided his questions about his gender identity to her, and she encouraged him to explore them further. For most of high school, Rey spent hours online reading about transgendered people and their lives. "The Internet is the best thing for trans people," he said. "Living in the suburbs, online groups were an access point." He also started reading memoirs of transgendered people. He asked Melissa to explain the gender theory she was learning in college.

In his senior year, he took on the name Rey. At 17, he finally felt ready to come out as trans to his family, who according to Rey struggled to understand his new identity. Around that time, he also visited a clinic in Manhattan, hoping to start hormone therapy. He was told that unless he wanted his parents involved in the process, he'd have to wait until he was 18. In the meantime, Rey began to apply to colleges. He wanted to go to "a hippie school," as he put it, yet he felt pressure to choose a school like Barnard that hewed to an Ivy League profile. Though he decided on Barnard, he still planned to start on testosterone as soon as he turned 18. When I asked him why he wanted to start hormone therapy so soon, he replied simply, "You live your life and you feel like a boy." Of course, living life like a boy is not what an elite women's college has historically been about.

At 18, Rey is part of a growing population of transgender students at the nation's colleges and universities. While still a rarity, young women who become men in college, also known as transmen or transmales, have grown in number over the last 10 years. According to Brett-Genny Janiczek Beemyn, director of the Stonewall Center at the University of Massachusetts, Amherst, who has studied trans students on college campuses, adults who wished to transition historically did so in middle age. Today a larger percentage of transitions occur in adolescence or young adulthood. The National Center for Transgender Equality estimates that between a quarter of a percent and 1 percent of the U.S. population is transgender—up to three million Americans—though other estimates are lower and precise figures are difficult to come by. Still, the growing number of young people who transition when they are teenagers or very young adults has placed a new pressure on colleges, especially women's colleges, to accommodate them.

The number of young people who openly identify as transgendered has grown for a few reasons. Some parents of young children who are "gender nonconforming"—usually children who identify psychologically with the opposite sex but also children who have hermaphroditic traits, like indeterminate sex organs—now allow their kids to choose whether they are referred to as "he" or "she" and whether to wear boys' or girls' clothing. And some of these parents, under a doctor's supervision, have even begun to administer hormone blockers to prevent the arrival of secondary sex characteristics until a "gender variant" child is old enough to make permanent choices. The Internet also offers greater access to information about transmale and gender-variant identities.

In addition, 147 colleges and universities nationwide now include "gender identity and expression" in their nondiscrimination policies, and students will often use gender-neutral pronouns like "ze" and "hir"—especially if they post on campus message boards. At Wesleyan last year, students initiated a survey of bathrooms, checking to see if they were transgender-friendly—open to all sexes. Many colleges now have Transgender Days of Remembrance in memory of victims of gender-identity-related hate crimes. Students at the University of Vermont hold a yearly "Translating Identity Conference" for trans college students that draws hundreds of people from around the country. The increasing number of trans college students has even given rise to a surprisingly deft reality television show, "Transgeneration," on the Sundance Channel, which featured a transmale student at Smith College.

The conventional thinking is that trans people feel they are "born in the wrong body." But today many students who identify as trans are seeking not simply to change their sex but to create an identity outside or between established genders—they may refuse to use any gender pronouns whatsoever or take a gender-neutral name but never modify their bodies chemically or surgically. These students are also considered part of the trans community, though they are known as either gender nonconforming or genderqueer rather than transmen or transmale.

At many of America's first-tier women's colleges, the growth of the trans community has led to campus workshops on transgender identity. According to students at Smith, a good number of restrooms have been made over as "gender neutral." And some professors make sure to ask students to fill out slips indicating their preferred names and pronouns. Students at several women's colleges have also created trans groups to reflect their experiences and political views. According to one transmale student I talked to at Wellesley, there are at least 15 gender-nonconforming students at the college, ranging from full-on trans to genderqueer, who have formed their own group. Other women's colleges, like Smith, have in the last few years had on-campus gender-nonconforming groups with up to 30 members, more than 1 percent of that school's population.

Which doesn't mean it isn't sometimes a struggle to be trans or gender-nonconforming on campus. Many trans students feel themselves to be excluded or isolated at women's schools and at coed colleges. Some talk of being razzed or insulted by fellow students. And even within a college's gender-nonconforming population, students are often divided among those who define themselves as men but don't transition medically, those who do and those who prefer not to define themselves as either male or female.

These difficulties are a natural part of being a minority that is still fighting for acceptance. But trans students' problems can also be institutional. The presence of trans students at women's colleges can't help raising the question of whether—or to what degree—these colleges can serve students who no longer see themselves as women.

From his first week at Barnard, Rey told me, he felt he was struggling. The women on campus seemed to Rey to be socially conservative and archly feminine, and he felt he had to seek solace elsewhere. At the Callen-Lorde Community Health Center in downtown Manhattan—the medical facility for gay, lesbian, bisexual and transgender people that he visited while he was still in high school—he began to get biweekly testosterone "T" shots (he turned 18 in September). Rey had psychological counseling elsewhere first; typically a letter of referral from a mental-health professional is required before anyone between 18 and 24 can receive hormone therapy. Rey also began to bind his breasts. But binding hurt, he said; it made it hard for him to breathe. He especially hated "having to alter your body every morning so you can go through the world and people will accept you."

But as a transmale student in a sea of women at Barnard, he felt alone. He longed to be with his girlfriend, Melissa, and with transmale friends, some of whom, like Rey, were attending women's colleges. Even as he sought to adopt a more conventionally male appearance, he wanted to maintain his ties with his former self. "I am all for not rubbing out my past as female," he told me.

But it was not to be that simple. As a transmale college student, he was something of a pioneer. And he began to hit some walls.

In the first week of September, he found out that his roommates had complained to the college's freshman housing director about being asked to share their rooms with a man. They wanted Rey to find somewhere else to live. According to Dorothy Denburg, the dean who spoke to Rey about the situation, these young women were disturbed when Rey told them on the first day "that he was a transboy and wanted to be referred to by male pronouns." Rey's roommates had, after all, chosen to attend a women's college in order to live and be educated in the company of other women. Barnard doesn't have singles for freshmen. As Rey saw it, he was simply shut out by his two roommates—and by the rest of the school. A week after learning of his roommates' disapproval, Rey, together with the dean and his parents, decided that Rey should transfer to Columbia's School of General Studies.

Rey felt lost. He slept on people's couches and stayed with one friend, a Columbia student and fellow trans activist, for a week. The story of his rooming travails ultimately wound up on the gossip pages of The New York Post. The Post squib cast Rey as an infiltrator in one of the last girls-with-pearls bastions.

"They were very typical feminine girls," explained Rey. "I didn't fit in. It's why I didn't hang out with straight girls for most of high school—I hung out with queer women. Around the Barnard women, I felt extremely other."

Rey described the days that followed as "the worst semester ever." As his new hormone regime began to take effect, he started to go through male puberty, which meant increased bone mass and a deepening voice and facial hair. He struggled to lead the normal life of an arty college student: eating vegan, going to clubs, keeping his grades up. Only recently, Rey says, has his life brightened. Indeed the transformation from the person he was to who he has become is startling. The second time we met, on a street corner near Columbia in Upper Manhattan, was a cold but sunny day in January, and Rey was aglow, smiling and laughing. Accompanied by his girlfriend, Melissa, now a graceful college senior, he greeted me with a hug.

The reason for this cheer, he said, was that he finally felt on the way to becoming who he really is. The testosterone shots he had received every other week since October had lowered his voice a few octaves. He was in the process of legally changing his name to a male name, although he couldn't decide whether to go casual (Rey) or Old Testament (Asher). And in December Rey underwent what he called "chest reconstruction surgery," also known as "top surgery," which he paid for out of pocket.

Melissa helped Rey through it, feeding him antibiotics and massaging his postsurgery chest with arnica cream. He joined a campus trans organization, GendeRevolution. In a few short months, he had become a full-blown activist. He quit smoking. To cap it off, he was bar-mitzvahed in Israel in January. He'd had his bat mitzvah at 13, but as Rey put it, he didn't feel "connected to the experience." He was bar-mitzvahed without his parents in attendance, but he took the rite of passage to heart. After all, at 13 he'd become a woman. Now, at 18, he was a man.

Despite the seriousness of the issues Rey has dealt with, all in such a short time, he often seemed like a giddy teenager, probably because he still was one. Clad in his usual uniform of baggy pants and a B-Boy cap covered with images of euros, he gossiped about his friends, music, sex and food, from time to time throwing his arm around Melissa, who is pixielike, slim and Rey's height—a little over five feet. She was wearing skinny jeans and ballet flats. She was so supportive of Rey's transformation that she was taken aback when I asked if his period of postoperative recovery had been hard for her.

"He's so much happier now," she said. Even though Melissa always defined herself as a lesbian, she said her partner's transition made sense to her. Part of the couple's sangfroid is generational—she and Rey see themselves as genderqueer rather than gay. For them, sexual orientation is fluid. Like some of their peers, Melissa and Rey want to be—and sometimes imagine they already are—part of the first generation to transcend gender.

On the face of it, it's not surprising that students like Rey would choose to attend a women's college. Same-sex colleges have always been test beds for transformations among American women. Set up as places where women could flourish without men, colleges like Barnard, Wellesley, Smith and Mount Holyoke have always had dual personalities, serving both as finishing schools and as incubators of American feminism. Smith College's alumnae include not only Barbara Bush and Nancy Reagan but also Betty Friedan, Gloria Steinem and Catharine MacKinnon.

The schools that decided to remain single-sex in the 1970s, when many colleges around the country went coed, represented a significant and even controversial challenge to liberal ideas about gender equality. And in refashioning their identities for the time, many became loci for the interrogation of gender roles. It was, after all, at all-female schools that many young women first began to question the very notion of femininity. And this questioning found echoes in the curriculum. Scholars like Esther Newton, Gayle Rubin, Anne Fausto-Sterling and Judith Butler ushered in an era that reconceived gender as a social construct, distinct from both a person's sex and sexuality. For Butler and others, femaleness did not automatically produce femininity and maleness did not produce masculinity: gender was fluid and variable, something to be fashioned, and could shift in character depending on the culture or the time period. As some see it, the presence of trans students at single-sex colleges is simply a logical extension of this intellectual tradition.

Indeed, as one transmale student I spoke to at Wellesley pointed out, women's colleges are uniquely suited to transgender students. "There's no safer place for transmen to be than a women's college because there's no actual physical threat to us," he told me, adding, "I have more in common with women because of that shared experience than I do with men." And even though Rey chose to leave Barnard for a coed school, he also says that women's schools can—and should—act as havens for transmale students, that they are, in fact, natural beacons for trans people, because "feminists and trans activists are both interested in gender."

In a sense, transgender and genderqueer students could be said merely to be holding women's colleges to their word: to fully support women's exploration of gender, even if that exploration ends with students no longer being female-identified. As Judith Halberstam, a professor of English and gender studies at the University of Southern California and the author of "Female Masculinity," put it, feminist theory offers students a way to think about gender as performance, to create a trans self or a genderqueer one—and give that self contours, definition—in a way that was simply unavailable 30 years ago. Indeed, Rey discovered his own trans identity reading queer theory, and even transitioning to be a man hasn't changed his core sense of himself. "I'm still queer even though I am a man now—it's the beauty of the term," Rey said.

"I think gender is a spectrum—gender is more complicated than sex," Rey continued. He sees everyone, and not just transmen, as having "their own gender," just as they might have their own personality or temperament. Rey's point isn't merely academic. A good number of gender nonconforming students I spoke to at women's colleges agreed with him. Most did not have operations but rather defined gender simply by how they experienced it, seeing themselves as existing on a "gender continuum" with their more conventionally feminine college friends. I met with one such student, Jordan Akerley, a 22-year-old senior at Wellesley. As we sat in the student-run on-campus cafe where Akerley works, Akerely explained what it is like to live out a theory of identity that doesn't exactly conform to one gender or the other.

"I find pronouns cumbersome and self-limiting," Akerley told me, which is why friends use the name Jordan, a name that Akerley says she intends to make official this year. Akerley, a co-captain of the school's soccer team, takes no hormones and has no plans to have an operation. Akerley's look and entire manner is quite unremarkable, even conservative: hair combed in a modified Tin Tin do, sporty, plain cotton shirt, jeans and sneakers. The only sign of an "alternative" or outsider identity—other than appearing masculine enough to be frequently mistaken on campus for a female student's boyfriend—is Akerley's eyebrow ring. Akerley's affect could be that of an aspiring politician: amiable, physically attractive, clean cut, inoffensive and articulate.

"My identity is fluid; it may evolve and fluctuate," Akerley explained. "My preference is not to use gender pronouns. My work is not always grammatically correct because of the lack of pronouns."

Though women's colleges may seem a haven for trans or gender-nonconforming students, accommodating such students requires balancing a complex set of needs and expectations—inside and outside the college. Barnard, like many women's colleges, has an admissions policy of accepting only "legal" women. The college's president, Judith Shapiro, who wrote an article on transsexualism in the 1980s, is clearly sympathetic to the trans population in general, but when I spoke to her she wondered aloud why a transmale or male-identified student "would want to be in a woman's college." She went on to explain her position this way: "Having been very involved in second-wave feminism, I am interested in gender revolutionaries, but I still think gender is a major category in our society." In many ways, Shapiro could be said to represent the position women's colleges now find themselves in: caught between wanting to embrace a campus minority that their own interrogation of gender roles has helped to shape and defending the value of institutions centered on the distinct experience of being female.

Colleges must also navigate the attitudes and expectations of their alumnae. While some alumnae have readily accepted the presence of trans students on their campuses, others, like Suzanne Corriell and Regis Ahern, graduates of Mount Holyoke, see it as a betrayal of the foundational principles of their alma mater. Corriell and Ahern recently wrote an angry letter to The Mount Holyoke Alumnae Quarterly, charging that admitting transmale students was, in effect, a way of "passively going coed" and that the "lifestyle choices" of these students was a bald negation of a women's college charter. Trans students, they wrote, were simply "men seeking to take advantage of Mount Holyoke's liberal and accepting atmosphere."

When I called Corriell, who is 28, at the law library at the University of Richmond, where she works, she explained her feelings to me this way: "I am a strong believer in women's education, and I think the colleges are a dying breed that need protection. I respect their agenda, which is educating women." She paused, then said: "Educating trans students in a same-sex residential community produces difficulty—when a student no longer identifies as a woman, the privilege to attend these schools is lost. Men have lots of schools they can go to—why must transmen go to women's schools?"

Of course, many trans students identify first as women—as lesbians or feminist activists. They are attracted to women's schools precisely because of their reputation as safe harbors for exploring these identities. As a result, many transmale students apply to women's schools and attend them before they have fully come out as "gender nonconforming"—and this is likely to be the case for years to come.

Denburg, the Barnard dean, acknowledges that women's colleges have always been places "where women can explore definitions and dimensions of gender." But it is only in the last five years of her tenure as dean, she says, that she has encountered transmale students. She had, she said, no objection to Rey's attending Barnard. The school has helped other gender-nonconforming students, among them a resident adviser in his senior year, who had to inform his female dorm mates about his gender transition over the summer. Denburg described her work with these students "as an educational journey for me as well, that has helped me to better understand the drive of someone who feels they are in the wrong body."

That said, Barnard does not have the kind of groups for trans students or awareness campaigns and gender-neutral bathrooms that some of the other women's colleges do. And it has not been as affiliated with women's and gender activism as some of its sister schools. Rey's case, as Denburg put it, "caught us off guard," mostly because administrators had never encountered a student who wanted to transition physically at such a young age. To Denburg, 18 still seems very young for such a decision.

Many people would agree that going on hormones carries risks: there are few studies on the long-term effects of hormone therapies on transmen. Some transmen in their 20s and 30s have told me they worry about the hormones' potential side effects—an increase in "bad" cholesterol and the risk of heart disease and stroke. For transmen, finding appropriate health care is complicated by the fact that student health services typically need to refer such students to outside clinics or hospitals for their care—and transmen may need additional insurance or be required to bear at least some of the medical costs themselves.

Rey always expected to go off-campus for his transition. He wound up being operated on by a private surgeon in New York City. (He received no "bottom surgery," as it is known—few transmen do, in part because the operation is thought to be too rudimentary and in part because many transmen view it as unnecessary.) While many gender-nonconforming students don't have "top surgery" in their freshman years, they may still struggle with their colleges' medical services, not because they want specialized treatments but because they want health care that is sensitive to their new identities. As one gender-noncomforming student complained to me, he hated that health services insisted on treating him "like a girl."

Colleges, trans activists and advocates say, are even less prepared for advising students on how their gender-variant identities may affect their futures, including their professional lives. After all, many states don't have protection for gender-nonconforming people in the workplace, and "gender identity" was recently dropped from the 2007 Employment Non-Discrimination Act, or ENDA. "There's no professional development for trans kids at colleges," said Shannon Sennott, a founder of Translate, a Brooklyn-based nonprofit group that holds workshops on trans awareness at women's colleges. "The majority disappear into big cities, working as bartenders with advanced degrees because there's real prejudice against trans workers." Hadley Smith, a recent Wellesley graduate and a Translate founder who describes himself as gender-nonconforming, said that unemployment or limited employment is par for the course for many transgendered people, but those limits may seem starker when high-achieving graduates from educationally competitive schools like Smith College feel, out of fear of discriminating employers, that they have to abandon, at least temporarily, their professional aspirations.

Some transmale students ultimately go "stealth" after graduation, not mentioning their earlier lives as women. When I asked Rey how he hoped to handle it, he said he had no intention of hiding and was planning to be out as a transman for the rest of his life. With all the bravado of youth, he said: "I won't get a career that I can't be out and trans in. I'm not planning to go into business.

"I've learned not to try to see my future—to do the best I can in the space I am in," he continued, and then added shyly, "I would like to, you know, make public art."

On a winter afternoon, I visited Rey at his new workplace at Columbia University's Office of Multicultural Affairs, where he was organizing a series of trans awareness events on campus. Rey was being paid by the college to create the series, and at the moment he had two chores on his list: booking a transmale photographer as a speaker and creating signage for gender-neutral bathrooms. To achieve the latter, Rey was busy sketching possible new symbols. Melissa, his girlfriend, was helping him. First they turned the familiar female stick figure into a rocket ship, making her legs into a flame. Rey created a few variations of the sign with a ballpoint pen. Then he drew a confused-looking person standing in front of both a male and a female bathroom, not knowing which one to pick. Next, he tried a single circle with the male and female symbols attached to it. Melissa laughed mockingly at the drawing of the confused man, but she nodded her head in approval at the two other symbols.

The dynamic between the two is often like this—teasingly supportive. Earlier at lunch, Melissa joked about whether they were even in a relationship, "I'm not sure: Rey doesn't do labels." Then she told Rey, "I've saved 20 voice mails of your voice changing over the last four months." He looked at her adoringly as they ate

French fries in sync: Melissa was not only his girlfriend but also the historian of his identity.

"Before I was on hormones, people would get confused when I spoke over the phone—they thought I was male, and then they'd start asking questions about how old I was," Rey said. "I didn't want to stay a prepubescent boy."

When talk turned to the couple's plans for the future, Melissa was more concerned about Rey leaving "wet towels on the floor," she said, and "tracking mud in the house" than about his medical transition. His lack of housekeeping skills was particularly on her mind, since the two are planning to move in together over the summer. "We'll stay together," Melissa said. "That's unless you go gay . . . again." She laughed. She was talking about the possibility of Rey's coming out a second time—going from being a woman who loves women to a man who loves women to a man who loves men. The remark was meant lightly, but nonetheless it got to the heart of the radical gender leaps both she and Rey were making in their every-day lives.

Then Rey grew more serious.

"Some transmen want to be seen as men—they want to be accepted as born men," he said. "I want to be accepted as a transman—my brain is not gendered. There's this crazy gender binary that's built into all of life, that there are just two genders that are acceptable. I don't want to have to fit into that."

CONCLUSION

There are many ways to assess the value of a framework. It must be *heuristic*—give us new insights and understandings. In other words, a framework should give us a new understanding or simply a better understanding. Also, a framework should have *parsimony.* It should give us elegant understandings. Moreover, a framework should possess *rigor.* It should be able to withstand punishing scrutiny by elegantly accounting for many different variables and scenarios. Further, a framework should give us *scope.* It should allow us to look into the future and forecast. We should be able to reliably anticipate what will happen when certain forces are set in motion. Finally, a framework should be *generative.* It should allow us to look at the world anew and, in so doing, reimagine what is possible. In our view, this emergent ecological framework meets all these requirements. We will showcase in the remaining sections of this book how this framework allows us to revision all the components, such as language, culture, diversity, and communication, that come into play in dealing with those who seem most different to us.

CHAPTER 3

Intercultural Communication: Redefining Language

INTRODUCTION

Many intercultural communication discourses and literatures focus on language. Intercultural communication is presumably about our ability to understand peoples of different cultures. We generally tend to believe that a common language is necessary for this occur. For instance, according to Mary Fong (2003), "Spoken language is a vehicle for people to communicate in social interaction by expressing their experience and creating experience. Words reflect the sender's attitude, beliefs, and points of view. Language expresses, symbolizes, and embodies reality . . . Communication cannot exist without language, and language needs the process of communication to engage people in social interaction" (p. 198). In *Who We Are,* Samuel Huntington assumes an inseparable relationship between language commonality and unity.

> Without a common language, communication becomes difficult if not impossible, and the nation becomes the arena for two or more language communities whose members communicate far more intensely with the members of

their group than with those of the other group. Countries where almost everyone speaks the same language, such as France, Germany, and Japan, differ significantly from countries with two or more linguistic communities, such as Switzerland, Belgium, and Canada. In the latter countries divorce is always a possibility, and historically these countries have in large part held together by fear of more powerful neighbors. Efforts to make each group fluent in the other's language seldom succeed. Few Anglo-Canadians have been fluent in French. Few Flemish and Walloons are at home in the other's language. German-speaking and French-speaking Swiss communicate with each other in English." (p. 159)

Likewise, Gary Imhoff (1987) asserts, "Language diversity has been a major cause of conflict . . . Any honest student of the sociology of language should admit that multilingual societies have been less united and internally peaceful than single-language societies" (p. 40). Rusty Butler, a member of Ronald Reagan's Department of Education, claims that without English being the official language of the United States, "the language situation could feed and guide terrorism" and that bilingual education has "serious implications for national security." President George W. Bush also believes that "we must honor the great American tradition of the melting pot by helping newcomers assimilate into our society. Americans are bound together by our shared ideals, an appreciation of our history, respect for our flag, and the ability to speak and write in English."

Indeed, many surveys and opinion polls in the United States consistently find overwhelming support for the promotion of a common language, in this case, English.

- 87% of Americans support making English the official language of the United States.
- 77% of Latinos believe English should be the official language of government operations.
- 82% of Americans support legislation that would require the federal government to conduct business solely in English.
- 74% of Americans support all election ballots and other government documents being printed in English.
- 83% of Americans believe new immigrants should learn English.
- 85% of Americans believe it is very hard or somewhat hard for immigrants to get a good job or be successful in this country without learning English.
- 79% of Republicans and 59% of Democrats reject the idea that all Americans should know multiple languages.
- 92% of Americans believe that preserving English as our common language is vital to maintaining our unity; 69% agree that the United States is at risk of becoming "disunited" by language.
- 79% of Americans believe immigrants should be required to learn English before they are granted citizenship.

- 68% of Americans oppose bilingual or multilingual election ballots.
- 91% of foreign-born Latino immigrants agree that learning English is essential to succeed in the United States, according to a 2002 Kaiser Family Foundation poll.
- By more than a 2 to 1 margin, immigrants themselves say the United States should expect new immigrants to learn English.
- 73% of immigrants believe schools should teach English as quickly as possible.
- 63% of immigrants believe that all teaching should be done in English.
- Nearly two thirds of Latino adults—65%—favor making English the nation's official language.
- 68% of Latinos say that the goal of bilingual education programs should be to make sure that students learn English well.
- 72% of young adults favor a law making English the official language of the United States.

These results show that many of us assume that sharing a common language reflects a common set of beliefs, values, and truths. We also seem to assume that language commonality reflects cultural similarity. In this way, accents and dialects matter a lot to many of us. Rosina Lippi-Green (1997), professor of linguistics and Germanic linguistics at the University of Michigan, and author of *English with an Accent: Language, Ideology, and Discrimination in the United States,* writes, "Accent serves as the first point of gate-keeping because we are forbidden by law and social custom, and perhaps by a prevailing sense of what is morally and ethnically right, from using race, ethnicity, homeland or economics more directly. We have no such compunctions about language, however. Thus, accent becomes a litmus test for exclusion, an excuse to turn away, to refuse to recognize the other" (p. 64).

In many ways language allows us to distinguish ourselves from others. It locates us in the world. It tells us who is like us, who shares our values, beliefs, traditions, and so forth. It also tells us who is different to us, who has different values, beliefs, traditions, and so forth. In other words, language diversity sets off various fears. In assuming that that communication is impossible, and thereby understanding unattainable, language diversity heightens our fear of chaos, confusion, and disunity. We therefore tend to believe that unity, progress, and social evolution require that we either remove or lessen our language diversity. We must linguistically assimilate.

Our fear of language diversity is seen in our determination to pass endless propositions and amendments making English the official language of the United States and ending bilingual educational programs. Of course the United States is by no means the only country determined to end language diversity. Many persons claim that language commonality is necessary to maintain the historical, political, social, and cultural integrity of a country. It promotes a common identity. It binds us to each other. It allows for shared experiences. It cultivates a common consciousness—a common set of values, beliefs, truths, assumptions, and expectations. For example, Peter Salins (1997), professor of urban affairs and planning at Hunter College of the City University of New York, contends that assimilation is at the foundation of United States' "unsurpassed prosperity," social cohesion, and superior social evolution. He is surprised that many persons, such as those who support bilingual educational programs, are ready to tinker with a process that has supposedly spared the United States disunity and chaos, and made for our "greatness."

> How could America's intellectual and political leaders be so short-sighted as to cast away thoughtlessly the paradigm of assimilation that had proved invaluable in unifying the nation for over a century and a half? . . .
>
> The history of the past thirty years has shown that America's opinion and policy elites made a terrible mistake by turning away from assimilation and negating the assimilation contract. And it has, indeed, been the country's leaders—the media, in education, in government, and in corporate America—who have been specifically responsible. The rank and file of ordinary Americans were never consulted, and if they had been, they would have rejected the abandonment of the assimilation paradigm. But regardless of where the fault lies, if ever there was a time to promote assimilation, it is today . . . The United States' two-hundred year history of maintaining national unity while accommodating ethnic diversity may be robust enough to withstand a temporary defection from the ethos and practice of assimilation, but it cannot withstand it for long before a host of unhappy consequences is unleashed. (pp. 15–16)

Salins warns of the dangers of cultural and racial disunity and chaos that can result from our abandonment of assimilation.

> In the end, though, the greatest danger looming for the United States is interethnic conflict, the scourge of almost all other nations with ethnically diverse populations. Assimilation has been our country's secret weapon in diffusing such conflict before it occurs, and without a strong assimilationist ethos, we leave ourselves open for such misfortune. Assimilation is not really about people of different racial, religious, linguistic, or cultural backgrounds becoming alike; it is about people of different . . . backgrounds believing they are irrevocably part of the same national family. It is this belief that allows them to transcend their narrow ethnic loyalties and that blunts, to the point of insignificance, the spurs of ethnic conflict and discord. (p. 17)

Salins believes that the future of the United States depends on a modern assimilation project that begins and ends with language commonality. The tenets of this assimilation project are: "(1) everything that the U.S. Constitution espouses; (2) a commitment to market capitalism; (3) the density and redundancy of institutional life; and (4) a commitment to modernity and progress that permeates all of society" (p. 51). These would be instilled in us through an educational system that demands proficiency in Standard English. "American culture does have a distinctive base, and that base, from the nation's beginning, has been English . . . Because of its importance, language is the one feature of American culture that is not optional, even under America's flexible rules of assimilation . . . On this point, social commentators across the spectrum of cultural ideology . . . agree" (p. 86).

FOR ENGLISH STUDIES, KOREANS SAY GOODBYE TO DAD
Norimitsu Onishi

AUCKLAND, New Zealand—On a sunny afternoon recently, half a dozen South Korean mothers came to pick up their children at the Remuera Primary School here, greeting one another warmly in a schoolyard filled with New Zealanders.

The mothers, members of the largest group of foreigners at the public school, were part of what are known in South Korea as "wild geese," families living separately, sometimes for years, to school their children in English-speaking countries like New Zealand and the United States. The mothers and children live overseas while the fathers live and work in South Korea, flying over to visit a couple of times a year.

Driven by a shared dissatisfaction with South Korea's rigid educational system, parents in rapidly expanding numbers are seeking to give their children an edge by helping them become fluent in English while sparing them, and themselves, the stress of South Korea's notorious educational pressure cooker.

More than 40,000 South Korean schoolchildren are believed to be living outside South Korea with their mothers in what experts say is an outgrowth of a new era of globalized education.

The phenomenon is the first time that South Korean parents' famous focus on education has split wives from husbands and children from fathers. It has also upended traditional migration patterns by which men went overseas temporarily while their wives and children stayed home, straining marriages and the Confucian ideal of the traditional Korean family. The cost of maintaining two households has stretched family budgets since most wives cannot work outside South Korea because of visa restrictions.

In 2006, 29,511 children from elementary through high school level left South Korea, nearly double the number in 2004 and almost seven times the figure in 2000, according to the Korean Educational Development Institute, a research group that tracks the figures for the Ministry of Education. The figures, the latest available, did not include children accompanying parents who left South Korea to work or emigrate, and who could also be partly motivated by educational goals.

South Koreans now make up the largest group of foreign students in the United States (more than 103,000) and the second largest in New Zealand after Chinese students, according to American and New Zealand government statistics. Yet, unlike other foreign students, South Koreans tend to go overseas starting in elementary school—in the belief that they will absorb English more easily at that age.

In New Zealand, there were 6,579 South Koreans in the country's elementary and secondary schools in 2007, accounting for 38 percent of all foreign students.

"We talked about coming here for two years before we finally did it," said Kim Soo-in, 39, who landed here 16 months ago with her two sons. "It was never a question of whether to do it, but when. We knew we had to do it at some point."

Wild geese fathers were initially relatively wealthy and tended to send their families to the United States. But in the last few years, more middle-class families have been heading to less expensive destinations like Canada, Australia and New Zealand.

Now, there are also "eagle fathers," who visit their families several times a year because they have the time and money. Those with neither, who are stuck in South Korea, are known as "penguin fathers."

The national experience is considered enough of a social problem that an aide to South Korea's president recently singled out the plight of the penguin fathers.

President Lee Myung-bak said he would start to address the problem by hiring 10,000 English teachers. "This is unprecedented," he said. "Korea is actually the only country in the world undergoing such a phenomenon, which is very unfortunate."

South Korean students routinely score at the top in international academic tests. But unhappiness over education's financial and psychological costs is so widespread that it is often cited as a reason for the country's low birthrate, which, at 1.26 in 2007, was one of the world's lowest.

South Korean parents say that the schools are failing to teach not only English but also other skills crucial in an era of globalization, like creative thinking. That resonates among South Koreans, whose economy has slowed after decades of high growth and who believe they are increasingly being squeezed between the larger economies of Japan and China.

It could take years to see how well this wave of children will fare back in South Korea, especially since they are now going overseas at the elementary level. But earlier this decade, when the wild geese children tended to be high school students, many succeeded in plying their improved English scores to get into colleges in the United States or other English-speaking countries, education experts said. For others, their years overseas was a roundabout way to get into top South Korean colleges, like Yonsei University in Seoul, which increasingly offer courses or entire programs in English.

For New Zealand's public schools, which charge foreign students annual tuition of $8,700, South Koreans provide an important source of revenue. The economic benefits have helped offset resentment toward an Asian influx that has remade many schools in Auckland, the country's largest city, lending an Asian character to the business district and raising home prices in the wealthier suburbs.

At Remuera Primary, Ms. Kim said she believed that English fluency would increase her sons' chances of gaining admission to selective secondary schools in South Korea and ultimately to a leading university in Seoul. Her husband, Park Il-ryang, 43, graduated from a little-known Korean university, and he said that the resulting lack of connections had hampered his own career.

Before coming here, the parents had sent one son, Jun-sung, now 10, to evening cram schools and their other son, Jun-woo, now 8, to an English preschool. Parents in their apartment building talked incessantly about their children's education.

Even so, the sons were not making sufficient progress in English, the parents said. They hired a private English tutor to supplement the supplementary cram schools. "We didn't think the cram schools were doing any good, but we were too insecure to stop sending them, because the other parents were sending their children," Ms. Kim said.

At their house recently, the sons peeked through the living-room blinds to see whether their neighbor, Charles Price, was free to play. In no time, the boys were coming and going, barefoot, between the houses, carrying "Bionicle" action figures.

The parents were pleased that their sons had integrated well into the neighborhood and school, and were now even speaking English to each other. But Ms. Kim was worried that her younger son was making shockingly simple mistakes in his spoken Korean and might not form a solid "Korean identity."

Striking the right balance would be critical to the brothers' re-entry into South Korea, with its fierce competition to get into the best schools.

South Korean women's rising social status and growing economic power have fueled the wild geese migration, according to education experts like Oh Ook-whan, a professor at Ehwa Womans University who has studied the separated families. Conservatives have criticized the wild geese mothers for being obsessed about their children's education at the risk of destroying their marriages. The women's real intention, they say, is to get as far away as possible from their mothers-in-law.

The mothers say they are the modern-day successors to one of the most famous mothers in East Asia: the mother of Mencius, the fourth-century Chinese Confucian philosopher. In a story known in South Korea, as well as China and Japan, Mencius's mother moved to three neighborhoods before finding the environment most favorable to her son's education.

"I don't know why Mencius's mother is so revered and why we wild geese mothers are so criticized," said Chang Soo-jin, 37, who moved here with her two children nearly two years ago. "Our coming out here is exactly the same as what she did."

Here, the English skills of her 6-year-old daughter, Amy, have improved so much that she now has the reading abilities of an 8-year-old, said her teacher at Sunderland, a small private school where all 16 foreign students come from South Korea.

Yet Amy's father, Kevin Park, 41, was not totally convinced that the benefits had been worth splitting up the family. He had reluctantly agreed with his wife's decision to come here with the children and then extend their stay, twice.

After his family left Seoul, Mr. Park, an engineer, moved into what South Koreans call an "officetel," a building with small units that can be used as apartments or offices. Hearing about wild geese fathers becoming dissolute living by themselves, he stopped drinking at home.

"I'm alone, I miss my family," Mr. Park said grimly in an interview in Seoul. "Families should live together."

Living apart for years strains marriages and undermines the role of a father, traditionally the center of the family in South Korea's Confucian culture, education experts and psychologists said. Some spouses have affairs; some marriages end in divorce.

"Even if there are problems, some couples choose to ignore them for the sake of their children's education," said Choi Yang-suk, a psychologist at Yonsei who has studied wild geese families in the United States and Canada.

Here, Park Jeong-won, 40, and her husband, Kim Yoon-seok, 45, an ophthalmologist who was here on a visit, said their marriage had grown stronger despite living apart for four and a half years. Every reunion, they said, was like a honeymoon.

But while Ms. Park said she talked to her husband a couple of hours daily by phone, she said her son and daughter never asked to talk to their father. He, in turn, never asked to talk to his children, the couple said.

"We may be a strange family," Ms. Park said.

Dr. Kim said his own father had always been too busy with work to spend much time with the family, and on weekends woke up at 4 a.m. to play golf.

"Maybe that's why, now that I'm a father, I have a similar relationship with my son," he said.

Asked whether she missed her father, Ellin, 11, said: "I don't miss him that much. I see him every year."

"Do you think that's enough?" her mother asked, a little surprised.

Ellin corrected herself and said she saw him twice a year.

THE POWER OF WORLDVIEWS

A *worldview* is commonly defined as "a framework of ideas and attitudes about the world, ourselves, and life, a comprehensive system of beliefs—with answers for a wide range of questions." Indeed, every worldview comes with a set of foundational beliefs—beliefs that give rise to other beliefs. For us in the Western world, a foundational belief is that the world is divided between opposing forces that are in conflict with each other—such as order versus chaos, meaning versus ambiguity, life versus death, homogeneity versus diversity, or harmony versus noise. We tend to believe that progress, unity, and social evolution require that the forces of order, meaning, life, health, homogeneity, and harmony prevail over the forces of chaos, ambiguity, death, diversity, disease, and noise. We therefore tend to believe that the forces of order, meaning, life, health, homogeneity, and harmony are morally superior to the forces of chaos, ambiguity, death, diversity, disease, and noise. Naturally, what emerges is a determination in the Western world to promote those forces that are supposedly morally superior and subdue the other forces. What also emerges is a natural suspicion and fear of anything, any person, or any action that is seen as promoting chaos, ambiguity, death, diversity, and so forth. This is the origin of our fear and suspicion of language diversity.

We also tend to define communication in terms of commonality. Communication is presumably about us using a common set of linguistic and symbolic codes to create a common reality. We also tend to perceive communication as a linguistic and symbolic activity. But is language diversity really a threat to unity, progress, and social evolution? Does language diversity undercut communication? Is linguistic and symbolic convergence necessary for communication? Should persons who are linguistically different be forced to linguistically assimilate?

LEGISLATION, COERCION, AND ASSIMILATION

Since 1981, over 50 bills have been introduced in the U.S. Congress supporting English as the official language of the United States. On August 13, 1982, Sen. S. I. Hayakawa of California introduced an amendment in support of English as the official language of the United States. The amendment required that the English language be recognized as the official language of the United States, and that no language other than the English language be recognized as the official language of the United States. Speaking before the U.S. Congress in favor of the proposal, Hayakawa said,

> Language is a unifying instrument which binds people together. When people speak one language they become as one, they become a society.
>
> In the Book of Genesis, it says when the Lord saw that mankind spoke one universal language, He said, "Behold, they are one people, and they all have the same language and nothing which they propose to do will be impossible for them."
>
> If you will recall the Bible story, God destroyed this power by giving mankind many languages rather than the one. So you had proliferation of language breaking up human pride and, therefore, human power.

But there are more recent political lessons to be drawn on the subject of language when you think that right here in this U.S. Senate and the Congress we have descendants of speakers of at least 250 to 350 languages. If you go back to the grandparents of just the Members of Congress, you have speakers of, I would say, at least 350 languages. But we meet here as speakers of one language. We may disagree when we argue, but at least we understand each other when we argue. Because we can argue with each other, we can also come to agreements and we can create societies. That is how societies work.

Take in contrast to this the situation in, for example, Belgium, where a small country is sharply divided because half of the population speaks French and the other half Flemish. Those who speak Flemish do not like the people who speak French and those who speak French do not want to speak Flemish.

Think of Canada, just to the north of us, where the French-speaking people feel paranoid about the fact that they are a minority and feel that they are being picked upon and abused by the English-speaking majority.

Think about Ceylon, right now, of course, known as Sri Lanka. Sri Lanka is sharply divided right to this day because the speakers of Sinhalese, which is the language of Sri Lanka, and the speakers of Tamil, which as the language of India. A number of people moved from India into Sri Lanka, and they created a language bloc thus the two are fighting each other.

Think of the recent history of India. Between 1957 and 1968, something like 1 million were killed in what were essentially language riots. They were riots about other things as well, about cultural difference, but essentially those cultural differences could not be resolved because there were a hundred languages dividing those people. So they could not understand each other and they could not come to the resolutions we arrive at daily in a Chamber like this or in the House of Representatives.

So, Mr. President, the fact that we have a common language, one language, is one of the most important things we have tying us together. . .

Mr. President, the United States, a land of immigrants from every corner of the world, has been strengthened and unified because its newcomers have historically chosen ultimately to forgo their native language for the English language. We have all benefited from the sharing of ideas, of cultures and beliefs, made possible by a common language. We have all enriched each other.

The Italians are better for having lived next door to the Jews; the Jews are better for having socialized with the Chinese; the Chinese are better for having mixed with the Italians, and so on. All around, we are better Americans because we have all melded our cultures together into this wonderful cultural symphony which is the United States of America.

There are those who want separatism, who want bilingual balance, who want bilingual education. I am all in favor of bilingual education only insofar as it accelerates the learning of English. I do not believe that the taxpayer should be taxed to promote an enclave of speakers of Yiddish, speakers of Japanese, speakers of Spanish, speakers of Bulgarian, speakers of Russian, of Tibetan, or any other language. Essentially, the taxpayers' responsibility is to see it that we all speak English together no matter where we come from. That cultural unity which we ultimately achieve—that is the United States.

Mr. President, that is what I want to preserve when I say I want an amendment that says the English language shall be the official language of the United States.

I thank the Chair.

A vote on the issue was taken on August 17, 1982. The senators supported the amendment by better than a three-to-one margin, with the final result being 78 ayes and 21 nays.

RESOLUTIONS AND LANGUAGE

The resolution was heard around the world. On December 18, 1996, Oakland School District of California passed a resolution granting legitimacy to a language commonly referred to as Black English or Ebonics. The resolution directed the school district's superintendent to "immediately devise and implement the best possible academic program for imparting instruction to African-American students in their primary language for the combined purposes of maintaining the legitimacy and richness of such language . . . and to facilitate their acquisition and mastery of English language skills."

Reaction to the Resolution

The public reaction to this resolution by the Oakland School District was overwhelmingly negative. There was almost unanimous protest against the resolution. The school board was accused of being ignorant, irresponsible, and incompetent. Although the school board released a clarifying statement to quell the uproar, especially within the Black community, the attacks continued.

> Elevating black English to the status of a language is not the way to raise standards of achievement in our schools and for our students.
>
> Education Secretary Richard Riley

> I understand the attempt to reach out to these children, but this is an unacceptable surrender, borderlining on disgrace. It's teaching down to our children and it must never happen. I appeal to that board to please reverse that decision because they're becoming really, unfortunately, the laughingstock of the nation.
>
> Rev. Jesse Jackson, Founder & President Rainbow Coalition

Ebonics . . . is a cruel joke . . . There is, within the larger African American community, and in other communities, various dialects. They're not languages, they are dialects . . . We have to find ways to bridge out of that into proper English.

Kweisi Mfume, President, NAACP

I am strongly opposed to bilingual education. I believe it divides the country . . . There are already enough divisions between blacks and whites.

Peter King, R–New York

Multiculturalism of the strident sort that the Oakland board has espoused is no favor to American subcultures. In the short, it may enliven everyone's appreciation of the variety of American styles, but in the long run it can only turn that variety into mainstream mush.

Louis Menand, New Yorker Magazine

This [The Oakland School Board Resolution] is multiculturalism gone a little haywire.

William Bennett, Education Secretary (Ronald Reagan Administration)

The school board . . . blundered badly . . . when it declared that black slang is a distinct language that warrants a place of respect in the classroom . . . the new policy will . . . stigmatize African-American children.

The New York Times, Editorial

The nationwide roar of laughter over Ebonics is a very good sign . . . [A] big reason for all the chuckling over Ebonics is the decreasing public tolerance for the politically correct notions lurking in the shadows of this debate—identity politics, victimization and self-esteem theory.

John Leo, Columnist, U.S. News & World Report

Those probably best qualified to comment on the teaching merit of the ruling, specifically linguists, somehow never had equal access to the popular media forums that opponents to the ruling had. So only few heard that *The Linguistic Society of*

America, the representing body for linguists, unanimously endorsed the Oakland School Board resolution with a statement that concluded, "In fact, all human linguistic systems—spoken, signed, and written—are fundamentally regular . . . [T]he Oakland School Board's decision to recognize the vernacular of African-American students in teaching them Standard English is linguistically and pedagogically sound." According to Steven Pinker (1994), Harvard College Professor and Johnstone Family Professor in the Department of Psychology at Harvard University,

> Many prescriptive rules of grammar are just plain dumb and should be deleted from the usage handbooks. And most of standard English is just that, standard, in the same sense that certain units of currency or household voltages are said to be standard. It is just common sense that people should be given every encouragement and opportunity to learn the dialect that has become standard in their society and to employ it in many formal settings. But there is no need to use terms like "bad grammar," "fractured syntax," and incorrect usage" when referring to rural and black dialects . . . using terms like "bad grammar" for "nonstandard" is both insulting and scientifically inaccurate. (p. 400)

Simply put, nothing is linguistically or grammatically wrong or deficient about Ebonics. The school board's resolution was linguistically and scientifically sound.

> People used to believe that African American English was illogical, poorly constructed and inadequate for any cognitive or linguistic growth . . . But while it is certainly different from Standard English, it is not inferior.
>
> John R. Rickford, Linguist, Department of Linguistics, Stanford University

> What makes standard English standard is a matter of social attitudes and the political power of those who speak the standard dialect . . . Because standard English speakers control education, commerce, government, and other powerful institutions, the standard dialect is firmly associated with public life.
>
> Carolyn Temple Adger, Center for Applied Linguistics

> The Ebonics controversy is, finally and most importantly, a fight . . . about language . . . as an instrument of influence and social control . . . who controls language . . . [and] the words that can be used for public discourse . . . determines . . . what can and should be listened to and taken seriously.
>
> Robin Lakoff, Professor of Linguistics, University of California, Berkeley

In an essay entitled *Communication, Conflict, and Culture,* Mortensen (1991) posits that language, communication, and culture coevolved to end the violent conflict that is supposedly of our endowed capacity for strife and conflict. He also sees communication and language as products of necessity. Supposedly, both evolved from the need for coordination to help our evolutionary ancestors establish relations with others—either for protection or acquisition of resources, alliances, and mates—that are necessary for our survival. Both also evolved from the need for manipulation to increase our chances of survival. Mortensen (1991) believes that probably "our ancestors acted under communal pressures to devise primitive codes that worked well enough (in a communal sense) to insure a measure of territorial control required to gather food and capture objects of prey as well as facilitate the evasion of other predators" (p. 286). Daniel Dennett (1995), Distinguished Arts and Sciences Professor and Director of the Center for Cognitive Studies at Tufts University, also views communication, language, and culture as products of natural selection forces. He writes, "What is preserved and transmitted in cultural evolution is informational—in a media-neutral, language-neutral sense" (pp. 353–354). Dennett adopts a transmission view of communication, language, and culture. That is, the primary function of communication, language, and culture is to transmit information. This is the common view in different scholarly literatures. Kenichi Aoki (1991) also traces the origins of cultural transmission to our evolutionary development. He defines cultural transmission as "the transfer of information between individuals by social learning" (p. 439). Moreover, "cultural transmission is not limited to the human (e.g., the songs of most perching birds are culturally transmitted), but it is particularly important in our species. Without it, there would be no language(s); there would be no tool-making tradition(s); civilization as we know it would not exist" (p. 440).

However, Noam Chomsky, professor of linguistics and philosophy, Massachusetts Institute of Technology, undoubtedly the most distinguished linguist of the 20th century, contends that language is uniquely human. He forcefully rejects the natural selection theory view on the origin of language. He sees human beings as being uniquely programmed and equipped for language. In *Language and Mind,* Chomsky (1968) wrote, "Anyone concerned with the study of human nature and human capacities must somehow come to grips with the fact that all normal human beings acquire language, whereas acquisition of even its barest rudiments is quite beyond the capacities of an otherwise intelligent ape . . . It is widely thought that the extensive modern studies of animal communication challenge this classical view; and it is almost universally taken for granted that there exists a problem of explaining the evolution of language from systems of animal communication" (p. 59).

According to Chomsky, "A careful look at recent studies of animal communication" provides little support for these assumptions. Rather, "these studies bring out even more clearly the extent to which human language appears to be a unique phenomenon, without significant analogue in the animal world. If this is so, it is quite senseless to raise the problem of explaining the evolution of human language from more primitive systems of communication that appear at lower levels of cognitive capacity" (p. 59).

Chomsky (1988) contends all languages follow a fixed set of universal principles of language structure that are biologically determined. As a result, language differences are cultural rather than biological. Chomsky wrote, "My own work leads me to the conclusion that there are far reaching, deep-seated universal principles of language structure. I think we tend to be unaware of them and pay attention only to differentiation of languages because of a very natural response to variety as distinct from the essential shared properties on mankind . . . I think we will discover that language structures really are uniform. The uniformity results from the existence of fixed, immutable, biologically determined principles, which provide the schematism which makes a child capable of organizing and coming to terms with his rather restricted experiences of everyday life and creating complex intellectual structures on that basis" (pp. 151–152).

Chomsky labels this underlying calculus a *Universal Grammar.* This calculus could also be described as an attractor—a self-organizing calculus that exists within all living systems. Attractors give systems symmetry and diversity. They noncoercively allow the system to take on endless possible variations. In this way, rather than limiting, attractors enable. According to Chomsky, "I think in a general way we can say that a person's knowledge of his language is based on a system of rules and principles. If you look carefully at these rules, you will discover that the rules themselves are of a narrow range. There are certain kinds of rules that are permissible; there are other kinds of rules that are not permissible. There are also strict conditions on their application" (1988, p. 152).

David Lightfoot (1999), professor of linguistics, University of Maryland, wrote, "There seems to be nothing in other species remotely comparable to the kind of computations and compositionality made available by the human UG [Universal Grammar]" (p. 229). He also forcefully reported that the historical record offers no proof of languages being anything but enormously complex. Derek Bickerton (1995) is equally adamant about the equality of languages, "If there were any link between cultural complexity and linguistic complexity, we would expect to find that the most complex societies had the most complex languages while simpler societies had simpler languages. We do not find any such thing . . . When you take all aspects into account, languages are roughly equal in complexity" (p. 35). In short, no language has ever been shown to be less complex than others.

In *Language and Human Behavior,* Derek Bickerton (1995) put the matter well, "The claim that we are just another species ignores the range as well as the power of human behavior. The range of behavior in other creatures does not extend much beyond seeking food, seeking sex, rearing and protecting young, resisting predation, grooming, fighting rivals, exploring and defending territory, and unstructured play. Human beings do all these things, of course, but they also do math, tap dance, engage in commerce, build boats, play chess, invent novel artifacts, drive vehicles, litigate, draw representationally, and do countless other things that no other species ever did. As such any theory that would account for human behavior has to explain why the behavior of all other species is, relatively speaking, so limited, while that of one single species should be so broad. Why is there not a continuum of behaviors, growing gradually from amoeba to human? Why don't chimpanzees build boats, why can't orangutans tap dance?" (p. 6).

In a book titled *The Menace of Multiculturalism,* Alvin Schmidt (1997), a professor of sociology at Illinois College, argued that the English language reflects the unparalleled greatest of Western civilization. It is supposedly the language of freedom and liberty. According to Schmidt (1997), "English, like no other language, has been the medium by which the British and their descendants, the Americans, fashioned a culture of freedom and liberty that other societies with different languages have not even come close to equaling" (pp. 122–123). He echoes J. R. Joelson's claim that "the world's greatest articles and documents of human rights and freedom were first written in the English language" (p. 123). Schmidt then rhetorically asked, "Without being a linguistic determinist, one is nevertheless moved to ask: Why has no other language inspired such monumental hallmarks of freedom? This question is all the more significant when one considers that these documents did not arise in just one culture or in one century . . . Obviously, this is not a popular position to take today when more and more people have accepted multiculturalism and its contrary-to-fact propaganda that argues all cultures are equal or of equal value" (p. 123).

Schmidt (1997) contends that the lack of democracy and freedom in Latin America is directly related to the Spanish language being devoid of concepts related to democracy and freedom. Consequently, "making the United States a bilingual country with Spanish the second language and status equal to English would rupture the nation's social and political stability, similar to Canada's present state of affairs. It would have disastrous effects on the existing American institutions of liberty and human rights. Along with accepting the Spanish language, the United States would receive huge loads of cultural baggage that would greatly deteriorate American culture" (p. 124).

But Universal Grammar releases us from the belief that language reflects social evolution, as Schmidt claims. It also releases us from the notion that the condition of our language reflects our cognitive and moral capacity. As Lippi-Green (1997) observed, "The myth of standard language persists because it is carefully tended and propagated. Individuals acting for a larger social group take it upon themselves to control and limit spoken language variation, the most basic and fundamental of human socialization tools. The term standard itself does much to promote this idea: we speak of one standard and in opposition, non-standard, or substandard. This is the core of an ideology of standardization which empowers certain individuals and institutions to make these decisions" (p. 59).

LANGUAGE DIVERSITY AND COMMUNICATION

It would seem that the lessening and ending of the world's language diversity is ultimately good for intercultural communication. The reason is that sharing a common language supposedly facilitates communication and, as a result, is necessary for diverse peoples to trade, share resources, and cultivate good relations. It would also seem that the move away from oral-based languages to writing-based languages is a positive trend as the latter seems *more* stable and reliable as a mode of communication. Indeed, many opinion polls show again and again that many of us believe a common and standardized language is necessary for diverse peoples to build a prosperous future together. This is why, as the United States becomes more racially and ethnically diverse, many are advocating for Standard English to be the official language of the country. No organization is probably more committed to realizing this goal than English First. With over 150,000 members, English First is a national nonprofit lobbying organization founded in 1986. It aims to make Standard English the United States' official language, to give every child the opportunity to learn Standard English, and to eliminate bilingual and multilingual policies and programs. But as Richard Rodriguez (2002), author of *Brown: The Last Discovery of America,* noted, "Nativists who want to declare English the official language of the United States do not understand the omnivorous appetite of the language they wish to protect. Neither do they understand that their protection would harm our tongue . . . Those Americans who would build a fence around American English to forestall the Trojan burrito would turn American into a frightened tongue, a shrinking little oyster tongue" (p. 112).

The erasing of the world's language diversity should concern us all. When languages disappear, cultures, knowledge systems, and histories also disappear. The world becomes less and less diverse. On the other hand, no language can be preserved like a piece of sculpture. Languages are ecologies. Thus languages change, evolve, devolve, and even die. What, therefore, does the end of the world's rich language diversity mean for all of us? We know from an ecological perspective that diversity is the order of all ecologies, meaning that all ecologies always become more and more diverse. This is why, again, there is no one species of birds, or fish, or plants, or flowers, and so forth. Diversity is vital for ecologies to flourish and prosper. It also gives ecologies access to different capabilities and capacities. It also increases the resources that ecologies possess, thereby enlarging the ability of any ecology to survive and prosper. These realities are compellingly seen in the vital and invaluable role that many Native American communities played in helping the United States and other nations prevail in World Wars I and II.

CODE TALKERS

Code talkers were Native Americans who served in the U.S. military and whose primary job was the transmission of secret tactical messages. The code talkers transmitted these messages over military telephone or radio communication nets using formal or informally developed code built on their native languages.

The name code talkers is associated with bilingual Navajo speakers specially recruited during World II by the marines to serve in their standard communications units in the Pacific Theater. Other Native American code talkers were used by the U.S. Army in both World War I and World War II, using Choctaw and Comanche soldiers on a smaller scale.

Native American languages were chosen by the U.S. military for various reasons. Most important, speakers of these languages were only found inside the United States and were virtually unknown elsewhere. As Marder (1945) explained, "Transmitting messages that the enemy cannot decode is a vital military factor in any engagement, especially where combat units are operating over a wide area in which communications must be maintained by radio. Throughout the history of warfare, military leaders have sought the perfect code—a code that the enemy could not break down, no matter how able his intelligence staff." According to analysts, "most codes are based on the codist's native language. If the language is a widely used one, it will also be familiar to the enemy and, no matter how good your code may be, the enemy eventually can master it. Navajo, however, is one of the world's "hidden" languages; it is termed "hidden" along with other Indian languages, as no alphabet or other symbols of it exist in the original form."

Even the ability to speak Navajo fluently would in no way guarantee that an enemy can decode a military message, as there is no Navajo dictionary that lists military terms, and words used for "jeep," "emplacement," "battery," "radar," "antiaircraft," and other military things were improvised by Navajos in the field.

Indeed, an unusual spoken human language is much harder to crack than a code based on a common language. That the chosen Native American languages had no written literature also made researching them difficult. In testimony on behalf of The Choctaw Nation of Oklahoma before The Committee on Indian Affairs of The Senate of the United States, Chief Gregory Pyle (2004) made this point, "As we know, there are hundreds of Native American languages spoken throughout our Country. What was only realized under the stress of War is that such languages were useful as codes. Since the language of Native Americans is based on a different linguistic root and syntax than Teutonic/European or Romance languages, it was not susceptible to being broken through common code-breaking means, such as repetition or substitution of characters. Also, since these languages were only spoken by a relatively small number of people, and since there were few, if any, dictionaries and textbooks for such languages, they were essentially a mystery for any non-Native American code breaker. You couldn't go anywhere to learn about them, since they were oral languages. In fact, they were the perfect languages for transmission of secrets (p. 53).

Also, many grammatical structures in Native American languages are fundamentally different from other languages, adding another layer of incomprehensibility. Nonspeakers would find it extremely difficult to accurately distinguish unfamiliar sounds used in these languages. Moreover, a person who uses a language all his or her life sounds distinctly different from a person who learned the same language as an adult, thereby reducing the chance of good imposters sending false messages. Finally, "the additional layer of an alphabet cypher was added to prevent interception by native speakers who had no training as code talkers, in the event of their capture by the Japanese."

In the end, Japan Imperial Army and Navy never cracked the Navajo code, and high-ranking military officers have stated that the United States would never have won the Battle of Iwo Jima without the code talkers. The Navajo code talkers were also deployed in the Korean War.

The code talkers received no recognition until the declassification of the operation in 1968. In 1982, the code talkers were given a Certificate of Recognition by President Ronald Reagan, who also named August 14th "National Code Talkers Day." On December 21, 2000, the U.S. Congress passed, and President Bill Clinton signed, Public Law 106–554, 114 Statute 2763, which awarded the Congressional Gold Medal to 29 World War II Navajo code talkers. In July 2001, U.S. President George W. Bush presented the medal to four surviving code talkers (the fifth living code talker was not able to attend) at a ceremony held in the Capitol Rotunda in Washington, DC.

COGNITIVE ERGONOMICS

In a report titled *Towards Knowledge Societies*, United Nations Education and Scientific Organization (UNESCO; 2005) focuses on "the need to recognize that linguistic diversity is a treasure contributing to human knowledge and to the many different ways of gaining access to knowledge" (p. 154). Acknowledging the fact that many persons view linguistic diversity as an obstacle to development, the report contends, "It is crucial to recognize that linguistic diversity is a source of enrichment for humanity and cannot be seen as a handicap when it is combined with cultural diversity" (p. 154). As such, "the disappearance of a language is a loss for all human beings for it generally means the disappearance not only of a way of life and a culture, but also a representation of the world and of an often unique form of access to knowledge and to the mind" (p. 154).

The UNESCO report discusses various reasons why preserving and promoting linguistic diversity is vital. For instance, such diversity is important for cognitive ergonomics. "Indeed to set limits on linguistic diversity in knowledge societies would be tantamount to reducing the paths of access to knowledge, since their capacity to adapt technically, cognitively and culturally to the needs of their actual or potential users would be diminished. Preserving the plurality of languages translates into enabling the largest number to have access to the media of knowledge" (p. 153). Moreover, linguistic diversity preserves indigenous languages, which "play an essential role in national construction." The report claims, "Indigenous languages continue to be the main medium of expression of aspirations, intimate desires, feelings, and local life. They are indeed the repositories of cultures" (p. 152).

To preserve and promote linguistic diversity, UNESCO recommends that school systems throughout the world "encourage the expansion, within pluralistic education communities, of a multilingual culture, reconciling the requirements of the teaching of a mother tongue and of several other languages" (p. 154). It also calls for educational systems that are bilingual, and where resources permit, even trilingual. "This policy could be facilitated by massive exchanges of teachers and language assistants within the region of the world, or indeed between regions" (p. 154). Besides introducing peoples to different knowledge systems, UNESCO also points to the fact "that bilingual persons usually possess a greater cognitive malleability and flexibility than do monolingual persons." In this way, all peoples stand to gain from the preservation and promotion of linguistic diversity. According to UNESCO, "Reducing the erosion of linguistic diversity, discovering ways to prevent the fast extinction of indigenous languages or promoting the wide use of several common languages, does not mean championing a lost cause for the sake of nostalgia. It means, rather, an acknowledgement that languages are at once cognitive media, vehicles of culture and an enabling environment for knowledge societies, for which diversity and pluralism and synonymous with enrichment and the future" (p. 155). On this matter, Hans George Gadamer (2005), who has written extensively on the relation between language and being, would agree completely:

> We must learn more languages. That is the main point. English will naturally become the worldwide language of commerce, but there will be mother tongues everywhere. And that is what we must fight for. Every language has a new point of view, and one will become more tolerant when one permits the way the other speaks. I believe that by learning more foreign languages, one will be educated in the end to a greater self-critique. That is also a possible way to achieve world peace. We will also have to learn, to say, that all religions have their partiality and therefore may justify their recognition of the others. I don't know, but I suspect that this must happen if we wish to survive . . . [T]here is no last, definitive word.

That is given to no one. If the other misunderstands me, then I must speak differently until he understands me. We are all always only underway.

The UNESCO report is particularly sensitive to the loss of oral-based languages. These languages are most susceptible to linguistic erosion because modern technology favors writing-based languages. Moreover, these languages can only be learned communally. Thus when these languages die, the communities that sustain these languages also die. In *Literacy and Orality,* Walter Ong discusses the distinguishing features of oral-based cultures. Ong contends that writing-based cultures tend to foster "abstractions that disengage knowledge from the [environment] where human beings struggle with one another." However, "by keeping knowledge embedded in the life world, orality situates knowledge within a context of struggle" (1988, p. 43). According to Ong, "Primary orality fosters personality structures that in certain ways are more communal and externalized, and less introspective than those common among literates. Oral communication unites people in groups. Writing and reading are solitary activities that throw the psyche back on itself" (p. 68). Moreover, "Oral cultures tend to be devoid of cognitive structures that promote geometrical figures, abstract categorization, formal logical reasoning processes, definitions, comprehensive descriptions, and articulated self analysis" (p. 54). Finally, "Persons whose worldview has been formed by high literacy need to remind themselves that in functionally oral cultures the past is not felt as a . . . terrain, laden with verifiable facts and bits of information. It is the domain of the ancestors, a resource for renewing awareness of present existence . . . orality knows no lists or charts or figures."

HOUSE OF WORDS

The Dogon are a people found in Mali, West Africa. Within the Dogon culture there is a meeting place in the center of the village that plays a vital role for the community. It is called a *Togu Na* or *House of Words*. It is also known as the *House of the Mother*, although women are forbidden from entering its walls. One of the first places constructed when a Dogon settlement is founded, much discussion takes place in the Togu Na, "where people learn the art of rhetorical persuasion through the use of logical reasoning." All manner of business and social issues are discussed in the Togu Na. Rites of passage are also performed in the Togu Na. According to Tito Spini, "The Togu Na is also used for teaching purposes where the spoken word is the seed of knowledge for each type of manual work and for numerous spiritual initiations too." The Togu Na is open on all sides, usually round in shape, and normally consist of a millet-stalk gently curved thatched roof supported by either stone or wooden pillars carved to look like human beings, with the arms and head supporting the roof and the trunk extending down to the stone floor. The low ceiling is deliberately designed to prevent overzealous discussions from escalating into fights.

THE NATURE OF SYMBOLS

Although meaning resides within and between human beings, language and symbols still matter. We use language and symbols to reflect and convey our truths, our beliefs, our values, and hopes, and our fears. We find the use of such symbols in a lot of religious symbolism. We also use symbols to identity and distinguish ourselves from others. This is what emblems, flags, logos, and various tattoos are commonly about. We also use symbols to show our solidarity with different movements and various causes and projects. This is why many of us wear different color ribbons. Symbols allow us to identity and position ourselves in the world. Symbols make us visible to each other. Thus symbols are important to the human experience. However, just as much as our symbols make us visible, our symbols can also threaten and torment. Such is the case with Old Glory—the flag the Ku Klux Klan uses. Many who support this flag claim that the Ku Klux Klan is misappropriating this symbol. Supposedly, the flag has nothing to do with supporting racism. But again, because of the fact that meaning resides within us, how does one know when a symbol is being used to harass or torment? Moreover, who gets to own a symbol and thereby control who gets permission to use that symbol and control what meanings are attached to that symbol?

A tremendous amount of controversy and conflict surround the use of Native American mascots by schools and colleges in the United States. As a way of finally resolving the matter, the National Collegiate Athletic Association (NCAA) decided recently to study the controversy.

The overwhelming majority of the comments received by NCAA supported the elimination of American Indian mascots, nicknames, images, and logos in intercollegiate athletics. Persons who offered comments were both native and nonnative. The committee noted five major themes among those who want to eliminate the mascots: (a) American Indian mascots and the images create a negative atmosphere; (b) American Indian mascots are disrespectful, oppressive, and insulting; (c) the stereotypes damage self-esteem and are psychologically destructive; (d) American Indians are in the minority and therefore lack the power to fight against those in the majority; and (e) those claiming to honor American Indians know little or nothing about American Indian culture.

The NCAA found that persons who support retaining the use of American Indian mascots noted the need for institutional decision making, rights of member schools, and the ability of mascots to honor the courage and strength of American Indian people. In fact, the NCAA found that the "primary argument for American Indian mascots is that they are "intended to honor" American Indians. This argument, which is asserted by nearly every proponent of American Indian mascots, notes that by using the mascot, universities and colleges are keeping alive the image of the American Indian and all its good traits, and highlighting the dignity, persistence, and bravery of Indians, particularly in battle. Proponents also claim that the dances, war chants, and other activities are meant to convey the idea that the American Indian has traits that colleges and universities wish to take on for the purposes of competition. In the end, the NCAA decided to prohibit all sports teams, including cheerleaders and band members, from using Native American images, nicknames, and logos on team uniforms and as team mascots in postseason events. It ruled that such representation of native culture was "hostile and offensive."

The new policy made national headlines. Florida Governor Jeb Bush called the NCAA ruling ridiculous and said such representation honors native cultures. "We're still a little surprised at how this all came out and how the NCAA described what we do [in using the Ute as a symbol]," Utah athletics director Chris Hill said. "We know we have the support of the Ute Nation, and we anticipate that we will appeal." Rep. Tom Feeney, R–Fla., who sits on the House Judiciary Committee, was also upset by the new policy and promised to seek redress for the affected schools and colleges in Congress. "There's no end to this . . . I really believe the NCAA is imposing the thought police on sports teams." Florida State University was eventually exempted from the new policy because the Seminole tribe officially sanctions the school's use of Seminoles as a nickname and Chief Osceola as a mascot. Max Osceola, the chief and general council president of the Seminole Tribe of Florida, said that it was an "honor" to be associated with the school.

Many who oppose the NCAA new policy often point to a Peter Harris poll published in *Sports Illustrated* that showed that 81% of Native Americans support the use of Indian nicknames in high school and college sports, and 83% of Native Americans support the use of Indian mascots and symbols in professional sports. *Sports Illustrated* concluded that the "poll suggests that although Native American activists are virtually united in opposition to the use of Indian nicknames and mascots, the Native American population sees the issue far differently." However, a paper published in the *Journal of Sport & Social Issues* claims that the article in *Sports Illustrated* "provides a flawed and biased account of pseudo-Indian mascots that misconstrues their history as well as significance to Native and non-Native peoples." For instance, dissent does exist within the Seminole Nation of Oklahoma. Although the council has yet to take a decision on the exemption for Florida State University, David Narcomey, a general council member, is "deeply appalled, incredulously disappointed." "I am nauseated that the NCAA is allowing this minstrel show to carry on this form of racism in the 21st century."

Human beings will always be in the business of creating, using, and even misusing symbols. What is also a fact is that meaning will always reside within us rather than in symbols. There is nothing inherently wrong with any of these truths. But these truths do present us with certain challenges. We do have to always remind ourselves that symbols matter to human beings. We therefore need to treat all symbols with sufficient understanding and compassion. On the other hand, no symbol can be confined to only a certain meaning, regardless of our most strenuous efforts. Thus both sides need understanding and compassion. Yet this in no way means that any symbol should be spared conflict, protest, and even contempt. Neither does this mean that any society can avoid tensions, struggles, and conflicts over our certain symbols. It merely means that all of us have to enter these processes carefully, respectfully, and compassionately.

CLASH OF CULTURES: THE SCREAMING MINARETS OF OXFORD
Andy McSmith

A small metal cross in Oxford's Broad Street marks the spot where one of the worst acts of religious bigotry in English history was perpetrated: the burning of bishops Latimer and Ridley—the Oxford Martyrs—during the reign of Mary I, Bloody Mary, the last Catholic ruler of England.

Four hundred and fifty years on, a row has now flared in the city which threatens to pitch Muslims and a few Christian allies against an outraged coalition of both secular and non-secular figures. The issue in question is whether the cry of Muslims being summoned to prayer should be allowed to resound over Oxford's dreaming spires.

The row blew up after the Oxford Central Mosque said it would apply to the city council for permission to broadcast the call to prayer from loudspeakers in the minaret in a newly built mosque, three times a day. The sound is familiar to anyone who has visited any part of the Muslim world, but in Britain it is rare, even in those cities with a high concentration of Muslims.

Some people might think that it would add a beautiful new sound to the already rich cultural diversity of the nation's premier university town, but that is not a view shared by people living within earshot of the minaret, who face having their lunchtimes, early afternoons and early evenings punctuated by the sound of the muezzin calling "hasten to prayer".

The proposal has attracted so much opposition that it has prompted the Bishop of Oxford, the Rt Rev John Pritchard, to issue a plea for tolerance, in one of his first public statements since taking up his new office.

For the moment, the Oxford Central Mosque has said it is going to delay the request for planning permission. The new mosque, in Manzil Way, east Oxford, is still under construction, and will not be finished until the end of the year.

Muslims are summoned to prayer five times a day: at dawn, at midday, in mid-afternoon, just after sunset, and at night about two hours after sunset.

There is no suggestion that the call is going to be sounded at dawn or at night in Oxford, but the mosque will ask to be allowed to broadcast the three daytime calls, though their spokesman, Sarder Rana, said they will be "happy" if they get permission to make the call to Friday prayers only.

Allan Chapman, a devout Christian who is leading the campaign against the call to prayer, was relieved by the delay, which he attributed to the opposition from local residents.

"If there hadn't been hell and fury we would have had this place wailing away already," he said. "The opposition to this brings together people who on paper are totally apart. It links true blue Tories who go to church with ex-Marxists who don't believe in God. We see it as naked Islamic imperialism. The community around the mosque is very Christian and European.

"The call to prayer is a sound many people find menacing. It's redolent of things they don't want to think about. It's also a form of preaching. It will destroy the cohesion of a very well integrated community."

He added: "What has angered people—and it has absolutely screamingly angered many people—is when we see Anglican clergymen overtly supporting Islam. We're totally staggered. It's being a traitor to the job description of their employment."

Opponents of the call to prayer believe they have a natural ally in the Bishop of Rochester, the Right Rev Nazir Ali, who has not commented directly on the Oxford row, but who alleged in a newspaper article this month that parts of Britain were being turned into "no-go" areas for non-Muslims.

He said: "Attempts have been made to impose an 'Islamic' character on certain areas, for example, by insisting on artificial amplification for the Adhan, the call to prayer. Such amplification was, of course, unknown throughout most of history and its use raises all sorts of questions about noise levels and whether non-Muslims wish to be told the creed of a particular faith five times a day on the loudspeaker."

The new Bishop of Oxford has implied that people are getting worked up for no good reason.

"I would say to anyone who has concerns about the call to prayer to relax and enjoy our community diversity and be as respectful to others as you would hope they would be to you," he told the Oxford Mail.

"I sympathise with those who find any kind of expression of public faith intrusive, but I think part of living in a tolerant society is saying, 'I don't agree with this but I accept it as part of my responsibility as being part of a diverse community.'"

Mr Rana denied that Oxford's Muslims wanted to force their religion on anyone. He said: "In Spain, Muslims ruled for 800 years, but they didn't make everybody Muslims. Islam doesn't allow us to force anybody [to convert].

"In Pakistan, the bell rings in Christian churches. We never object. There is a tradition in Islam that we issue a call to prayers. It's a very beautiful sound. I don't believe most people will object."

"Clash of Cultures: The Screaming Minarets of Oxford" by Andy McSmith, *The Independent, January 25, 2008.* Reprinted by permission of The Independent.

AS A SCULPTURE TAKES SHAPE IN MEXICO, OPPOSITION TAKES SHAPE IN THE U.S.
Ginger Thompson

MEXICO CITY—In a tumbledown studio here barely big enough for his work and far too small for the magnitude of his crusade, the sculptor John Houser is putting finishing touches on an American monument that he hopes will break records and uphold tradition.

The son of a sculptor who worked on Mount Rushmore, Mr. Houser, 63, envisions his monument—a 36-foot bronze equestrian statue of a Spanish colonizer who founded the first European settlements in the Southwestern United States—one day towering over the border between the United States and Mexico with the power of the Statue of Liberty.

But in a time when popes and presidents apologize for past crimes against humanity, the project faces hostile questions over how to honor the contributions of a founding father without dishonoring the descendants of those he brutalized—the Spaniard, Don Juan de Oñate, is said to have once cut off the right feet of Indians who opposed him. Plans for the monument have sparked demonstrations and angry letters to newspapers by those who argue that the monument glorifies a man of privilege who maimed Indians and snubs the life-and-death struggles of minorities and women in the establishment of the American West.

The monument, set to be completed by the end of this year and dedicated in 2003 in the Southwest capital of El Paso, was designed to memorialize the first European explorations of a region called El Paso del Rio del Norte. It depicts Oñate astride a rearing horse as he claimed the land north of the Rio Grande for Spain.

Oñate, the Mexican-born scion of some of Spain's wealthiest families, blazed the Pass of the North in 1598, more than two decades before English Pilgrims arrived at Plymouth Rock. And the celebrations of the arrival of Oñate's convoy of some 500 settlers and 7,000 animals are considered the United States' first Thanksgiving.

When it is completed, the Oñate monument will be the largest bronze equestrian statue in the world and an engineering marvel. Oñate's horse—an Andalusian that is as powerful a figure in the monument as its rider—will be defiantly rearing on its hind legs. It is a pose that has confounded the world's great monumental sculptors.

During treatments for a failed kidney about five years ago, Mr. Houser sat in a dialysis chair and worked out the vexing physics of erecting a 10-ton statue of a man astride a rearing steed. "Even da Vinci had a hard time doing a horse like this," he said.

Its size, he explained, conveys the impact of Oñate's arrival in the region and the explorer's influence in the development of Hispanic culture.

"Size is an aesthetic quality to me," Mr. Houser said during an interview. "When you see a monument like Mount Rushmore, the first thing that comes to your mind is a sense of wonder. It's awe-inspiring, like the history I am trying to portray."

But there are always two sides to history. Indian people throughout Texas and New Mexico revile Oñate for an incident in 1599 when, according to most scholars, he terrorized the rebellious Acoma tribe by cutting off the right feet of dozens of young warriors. Though evidence of the account is sketchy, historians generally accept that Oñate ordered the brutal punishment and that his orders were probably carried out. In the wake of growing protests over the Oñate monument, at least two El Paso City Council members have rescinded their support for the project, though one has said he may reconsider.

Historians like Oscar Martinez at the University of Arizona argue that erecting a statue to Oñate—particularly the largest statue of its kind—is a lot like flying the Confederate flag over the South Carolina state capital.

"The Pueblo people have never gotten over the cruel treatment and oppression they endured under Oñate," Mr. Martinez wrote in a letter to the El Paso City Council. "Oñate's behavior can actually be compared to Nazi officers who directed campaigns against the Jews in the 1930's and 1940's, including extermination drives."

"Who would ever consider building a statue to some Nazi personage and placing it the town square?"

Mr. Houser rejects accusations that he has a "white man's view" of history. He says he developed into an artist by living among circus performers in Italy, Lacandon Indians in the rain forest of southern Mexico, the Appalachian mountain people of North Carolina and the Gullah people of the sea islands. The first five years of Mr. Houser's life were spent at the foot of Mount Rushmore, where his father, Ivan, worked as chief assistant to the sculptor Gutzon Borglum, helping to carve faces some six stories high into the side of a cliff.

To Mr. Houser, comments about Nazis and Indian butchers sound like a lot of new-age babble. If monuments were erected only to honor saints, he argues, then there would be no monuments to Jefferson or Lincoln. There would be no Mount Rushmore or Vietnam Memorial. Mr. Houser said his goal with the Oñate monument was to commemorate a human struggle, one characterized by great hardship and even greater cruelties, but one that indisputably and indelibly marks the culture of the New World.

"The difference with this project," he said, "is that it honors history, not heroes. We are not telling people to look at the statue and ignore all the bad sides of the individual. We are hoping this monument will get people interested in history and encourage them to explore all sides."

"To ignore Oñate's influence," Mr. Houser added, "would be to falsify history."

Simmering resentment over Don Juan de Oñate erupted several years ago when cities across the Southwest celebrated the 400th anniversary of the explorer's arrival at the Rio Grande, mirroring Mexican protests over Hernando Cortés. Vandals cut off the right foot of an Oñate statue in Alcalde, N. M. And city officials in Albuquerque were forced to abandon plans to erect a statue of the rugged colonizer in favor of a memorial that depicts Spain's positive contributions to the region, including horses, cattle, irrigation and fruit trees.

Marc Simmons, a historian who has written three dozen books on New Mexico, said that last year residents of that state were mired in a debate over whether to erect a statue of an Indian leader named Popé in Statuary Hall in the Capitol in Washington. Historians say that in 1680, Popé negotiated treaties among several Indian tribes and led a massacre of some 500 Spanish settlers that temporarily ended the colonizing of New Mexico. (The statue has since won approval.)

"With all the fuss, we might as well just forget history," Mr. Simmons said. "People are stuck with Hollywood images of the West, where Indians lived peacefully in some kind of Garden of Eden until white men came along. The truth is, those times were rough and bloody. And violence came from both sides. We may regret it, but we can't ignore it."

Still, Mr. Houser said he was "thunderstruck" by the conflict over his project. He began work on it in 1988 when the El Paso City Council began seeking proposals for urban beautification projects to dress up its colorless downtown. El Paso is a largely poor city of blue-collar laborers and government workers in the West Texas desert, and its main attractions are discount megastores that draw thousands of shoppers from its sister city in Mexico, Ciudad Juárez. There is little public art, except for a cross that looks down on the city from a peak of the Franklin Mountains. A fiberglass sculpture of alligators was commissioned for San Jacinto Plaza after the city removed a decades-old live exhibit.

Mr. Houser proposed creating a sculpture walk through downtown El Paso that would include larger-than-life statues of the region's first explorers. Together, the statues would enshrine the epic achievements of some 500 years of travel on the old trade route between Mexico City and Santa Fe that was known as the Camino Real, or Royal Road.

The project was named "The XII Travelers Memorial of the Southwest." Its name is a modified version of the title of a 1946 book of illustrations by Tom Lea, an El Paso author and painter.

In 1996, the first statue, a 14-foot sculpture of Fray García de San Francisco, who opened the first mission of the Pass of the North and is considered the founder of El Paso and Ciudad Juárez, was dedicated in the predominantly Roman Catholic, immigrant-filled city without much fuss. But there was an immediate storm of protest over other figures Mr. Houser had offered to immortalize in bronze, including the gunfighter John Wesley Hardin and the Mexican revolutionary Pancho Villa.

The project has also won support from important cultural figures, including the late James Michener and the sculptor Walker Hancock, who created the statue of MacArthur at West Point and took over carvings at Stone Mountain, Ga. Mr. Houser's project has also received the support of Don Manuel Gullon y de Oñate, a descendant of the Spanish explorer. And the late Alex Haley was interested in Mr. Houser's plans to erect a statue of Estevanico the Moor, a slave who arrived in the Pass of the North with a shipwrecked expedition from Portugal.

The Oñate statue was conceived as the centerpiece of the project. Next to a monument of the Sioux chief Crazy Horse being carved into the side of a 600-foot ridge in the Black Hills of South Dakota, Mr. Houser's Oñate would look like a toy action figure. But the monument will be a dominating figure in downtown El Paso, a giant addition to a series of urban restorations and gallery openings.

Protests have not deterred Mr. Houser from his work. Four years ago he moved to Mexico, where he believed costs for a studio, a crew and a foundry would be cheaper than in the United States. With the help of a committee of supporters in El Paso, he has raised 90 percent of the $1.2 million needed for the statue. His son, Ethan, works as chief assistant on the project.

"Whether they like it or not," said Ethan Houser, taking a break from his work on Oñate's sleeve, "we are going to give El Paso a gorgeous statue."

Mr. Houser, whose kidney problems gave him a frightening glimpse of death, said he hoped the project would give him a kind of immortality.

"The main challenge for us is to create something powerful enough and of such artistic quality that people want to keep it around," Mr. Houser said. "The bronze will endure over thousands of years. All the political squabbles will perish."

THE FUTURE OF LANGUAGE DIVERSITY

The displacing and erasing of the world's language diversity is fundamentally being driven by the belief that this diversity undermines communication, cooperation, and development. But this diversity is in no way an obstacle to these ambitions. We can share a common language and still have conflict, turmoil, and even genocide. History makes no case in favor of language commonality. In fact, genocide can be found in places where different peoples shared a common language. What a diverse world foremost needs is empathy—the promotion of communication practices that encourage us to understand and experience the world from the perspective of others. We can exercise empathy without sharing a common language. It is apathy rather than language diversity that ultimately puts us at each other's throats. Still, Lee Chong-Yeong (2003) claims, "Linguistic politics is increasingly becoming a destabilizing factor of world peace and justice" (p. 58). He blames "linguistic hegemonism and linguistic egoism" for causing conflicts throughout the world and for promoting linguistic incommunicability, linguistic injustice, and linguistic injustice, all of which undermine justice and world peace. The solution to all of these problems, according to Chong-Yeong, lies in the promotion of an ethnically neutral auxiliary language, such as Esperanto.

But linguistic hegemonism and linguistic egoism are merely expressions and symptoms of larger forces that torment linguistic diversity and, by that, world peace and justice. In other words, linguistic hegemonism and linguistic egoism are products of ideological hegemonism, egoism, and chauvinism. Ending this kind hegemonism, egoism, and chauvinism involves changing our relation to language and how we embody language rather than merely changing the words and sounds that come out of our mouths. But ultimately, ending this kind of hegemonism, egoism, and chauvinism involves ridding ourselves of the belief that diversity is a threat to all that is good, decent, and civil. Without doing this, our fear of language diversity will persist.

LANGUAGE AND DISABILITY

Language plays an integral role in shaping our social worlds, our relations to each other, and our understanding of our identity and humanity. Simply put, language matters. Few persons better understand this reality than persons who have been historically marginalized, disenfranchised, and brutalized. Reason being that a lot of this marginalizing, disenfranchising, and brutalizing occurs through language. For historically disenfranchised peoples, the struggle for inclusion and emancipation is a struggle for language, such as changing the language, words, and symbols that make for various discourses. It is also involves changing the language that describes historically marginalized and disenfranchised peoples. In most cases, this involves inventing a new language, a new vocabulary, a new grammar, a new syn-

Negative Language	Positive Language
• Disabled person	• Person with (who has) a disability
• Defective child	• Child with a congenital disability
	• Child with a birth impairment
• Mentally ill person	• Person with mental illness or psychiatric disability
• Schizophrenics	• People who have schizophrenia
• Epileptics	• Individuals with epilepsy
• Amputee	• Person with an amputation
• Paraplegics	• Individuals with paraplegia
• The disabled	• People with disabilities
• The retarded	• Children with mental retardation
• The mentally ill	• People with a mental illness
• The physically disabled	• Individuals with a physical disability
• The learning disabled	• Children with specific learning disabilities
• Retarded adult	• Adult with mental retardation
• Chronic mental illness	• Person with persistent mental illness or psychiatric disability
• Confined to a wheelchair	• Uses a wheelchair
• Homebound	• Child who is taught at home

tax. The goal is to create new social worlds—ones that complement the aspirations and ambitions of historically marginalized and disenfranchised peoples. It is also about creating social worlds that end the ideological, material, and physical practices that harm the humanity of marginalized and disenfranchised peoples.

These are the language struggles that occupy the disabled rights movement. "Often, persons with disabilities are viewed as being afflicted with, or being victims of, a disability. In focusing on the disability, an individual's strengths, abilities, skills, and resources are often ignored. In many instances, persons with disabilities are viewed neither as having the capacity or right to express their goals and preferences nor as being resourceful and contributing members of society. Many words and phrases commonly used when discussing persons with disabilities reflect these biases."

Writing style manuals now recommend "that the word *disability* be used to refer to an attribute of a person, and *handicap* to the *source* of limitations." For instance, Patricia Bauer, a prominent advocate for disability rights, advises that "people with Down syndrome are just that—people—and should be referred to as such." We should therefore say that a person "has Down syndrome," or is a "child with Down syndrome." We should refrain from saying that people "suffer" from Down syndrome, or are "afflicted" by Down syndrome. "Down syndrome is a chromosomal condition that doesn't interfere with a person's ability to lead a happy, satisfying and productive life, and to contribute to their family and community." According to Bauer, "Using language that puts the person first sends a strong message that people should not be defined by their disabilities."

Writing style manuals also advise that the terms *nondisabled* or *persons without disabilities* be used rather than the term *normal* when comparing persons with disabilities to others. "Usage of *normal* makes the unconscious comparison of *abnormal,* thus stigmatizing those individuals with differences." Ultimately, the guiding principle for "non handicapping language is to maintain the integrity of individuals as whole human beings by avoiding language that (a) implies that a person as a whole is disabled (e.g., disabled person), (b) equates persons with their condition (e.g., epileptics), (c) has superfluous, negative overtones (e.g., stroke victim), or (d) is regarded as a slur (e.g., cripple)."

GIRL SCOUTS REJECT GIRL WITH AUTISM
Susan Donaldson James

For two years, Magi Klages, despite having autism, thrived in the Girl Scouts—an organization that pledges to "help people at all times" and to be "honest and fair, considerate and caring."

But when Magi's Brownie troop grew too large and her parents moved her to a smaller one for children with special needs, they never imagined their 8-year-old would be kicked out.

Michele and Kevin Klages of Oconomowoc, Wis., were told their daughter was a "danger" to the new group's four other children who are all physically disabled.

"We don't get it," said Michele Klages, who always accompanies Magi to Brownie meetings. "She's 30 pounds and we were there. We were told she was scaring the other girls."

When the troop sat down for a mat-weaving project, Magi threw a fit, Michele Klages said, biting herself and running out of the circle.

HAVING AN 'AUTISTIC MOMENT'

"She was having moments as most autistic children do," the 42-year-old mother told ABCNews.com. "We pulled her out of the circle and let her have her moment. At one point she got up and ran away and her father got her."

Michele Klages said they felt the Nov. 13 meeting had gone "fairly well" for an autistic child thrust into a new situation. But four days later she got the call that Magi would not be welcome in the new troop.

"To feel like someone doesn't want your child around, it rips your heart out," said Michele Klages, who is also raising a 10-year-old son and holds a part-time office job. "I never expected my child to be discriminated against. Never in a million years."

She said they had been up-front with the group leader about Magi, who is mostly nonverbal and relies on sign language to communicate. They were especially upset to learn the leader has a child with special needs.

"It's terrible," said Michelle Tompkins, a spokeswoman for the Girl Scouts of the United States of America, who said she had received a "courtesy call" from the local council about the incident. "We are very inclusive and have a national policy against all forms of discrimination."

Anita Rodrigues, spokeswoman for the Girl Scouts of Wisconsin Southeast, did not return several phone calls from ABCNews.com. But Michele Klages says the council contacted her about the possibility of finding another troop for Magi to join.

Even the Autism Society of America admits that the Girl Scouts do "wonderful work" with children with disabilities and has often contributed volunteers to help children with this neurological disorder.

It says that children with autism are rarely dangerous to others and that the incident illustrates the need for more support and training in organizations like the Girl Scouts.

"These children are so misunderstood," said Michele Klages. "We need to educate ourselves that these kids can be loving and fun. They should be given a chance like any other child."

CONFRONTATIONS SOMETIMES HAPPEN

But while social confrontations like the ones experienced by the Klageses are not common, they happen.

Earlier this year, 13-year-old Adam Race, who is also autistic, was banished from his Minnesota Catholic church. His priest issued a restraining order, saying the teen—who was 6 feet tall and weighed more than 225 pounds—hit a child, nearly knocked over an elderly parishioner and spit and urinated in the church.

"My son is not dangerous," Carol Race told The Associated Press. "The church's action is a certain community's fears of him. Fears of danger versus actual danger."

Autism is a complex developmental disability that strikes one in 150 children—one in 94 boys—usually before the age of 3, according to the Centers for Disease Control and Prevention. The disorder takes its greatest toll on a child's social interaction and communication skills.

The numbers of children with autism have dramatically increased in the last decade, but it is not clear if the disease has become more prevalent or if doctors are just getting better at diagnosing.

"Fortunately, we are seeing increased awareness and a greater willingness to understand autism," said Marguerite Colston, spokeswoman for the Autism Society of America, who has an autistic son the same age as Magi.

But with few support services outside the schools, "parents and communities have to figure things out for themselves," Colston told ABCNews.com.

The autism society recently published a booklet—"Growing Up Together"—to help children better understand the disorder. It describes "unusual" behaviors, such as difficulty talking or not talking at all, flapping hands, avoiding eye contact and trouble reading facial expressions.

The sound of a school bell may hurt their ears; some have trouble eating food because of taste and smell sensitivities. "On the other hand," according to the booklet, "things that bother most of us, like a bee sting, may not appear to be as painful to them."

Integration and modeling typical children is important, according to Colston. "When children with autism become more and more isolated, the stranger they will be."

Autistic Children Rarely Hurt Others

Like Magi, other children with autism are much more likely to show self-injury and property destruction than hurt others, according to Wayne Fisher, director for the Center for Autism Spectrum Disorders at the University of Nebraska Medical Center.

"We don't see a lot of danger when they integrate," he told ABCNews.com. "These are unusual cases."

"They are likely to display strong emotional reactions to new situations and changes in environment," Fisher said.

Magi might well have adapted to her new Girl Scout troop after several more visits, as routine is important, he said.

"But their behaviors are not well understood by the general public and it makes them uncomfortable."

And research shows that typical children also benefit from interacting with autistic children, showing improvements in patience, social skills and communication.

Michael Alessandri, executive director of University of Miami's Center for Autism and Related Disorders, called the Klages' incident "shocking."

Scouts: Including Autistic Children

"There is no reason a child with autism or any disability couldn't be meaningfully included in Girl Scouts or any other experience like this," Alessandri told ABCNews.com.

"Children with autism are often excluded because of lack of understanding of their needs and because their special needs have not been appropriately accommodated," he said. "We hear of this far too often."

In May, a mother in Port St. Lucie, Fla., considered legal action after her son's kindergarten teacher led his classmates to vote him out of class. Alex Barton, 5, was being evaluated for autism.

"No one is served by this action," said Alessandri. "The child with autism misses out on an opportunity that is rightfully theirs. And others miss out on the joy of learning about people with autism who are always remarkable in so many ways."

Under law, the Girl Scouts—if it receives federal funding—is required to make a "reasonable accommodation" for Magi under the Americans With Disabilities Act, according to Alison Barnes, a law professor at Marquette University in Milwaukee, Wis.

Asking Magi to travel a long distance for another troop would not meet the letter of the law, Barnes said.

"What happened here instead is [Magi] got a troop that said, 'OK, we'll try it.' Then after one day they said, 'Never mind, we don't want to do it,'" Barnes told ABCNews.com.

But in a similar case in 2006, a California court struck down a suit filed by parents who claimed their teenage son—who had a form of autism—was not allowed to attend a weeklong Boy Scout camp.

Lawyers for the troop argued that the boy, "spits, kicks and swears at the other children."

The court dismissed the case, ruling that Boy Scouts—which also openly discriminates against gays and atheists—is a private club.

But the Girl Scouts has been historically open to anyone and prides itself on its anti-discrimination policies.

The Klageses say the local council called them this week to help find another troop for Magi.

"They want to work with us and we'll continue to work with them," said Michele Klages. "Magi really wants to be a Girl Scout, but it's important to find a troop that's a good fit for her."

But Magi won't go back to the troop that kicked her out. "These leaders need to be educated and they can't pick which disabilities they want in the troop," her mother said. "It's not their call."

"Every child needs more than one chance in a new situation," she said. "I'm a mother protecting my child. I want people to know this is not something to fear."

Advocates are increasingly even challenging the language of disability, as this language connotes a condition that is inferior to be abled. In fact, many advocates are dropping the language of disability and disabled altogether. The new language is *differences*, as in differences in physical and psychological functioning. Thus persons with autism and Down syndrome now call for the recognition of neurodiversity, just as how women call for gender diversity, gays for sexual orientation diversity, and Latinos and Blacks for racial diversity. The goal is to expand our understanding and appreciation of human diversity by recognizing the fact that language plays an integral role in shaping our social worlds and our position in these worlds.

The language of disability comes from a worldview that possesses a set of beliefs, values, assumptions, and truths that creates a distinction between human beings who are presumably disabled and those who are presumably abled. However, this distinction is a **social construction**—something purely created by human beings. Race, ethnicity, and gender are also examples of social constructions. But social constructions eventually become social positions, as to view a person a certain way is ultimately to treat that person a certain way. No social construct is politically neutral. That is, social constructs come with different implications and consequences. To perceive a person as disabled is to treat that person as disabled. The only way to change this reality is for us to move toward a worldview that fosters no distinction among human beings. However, to change our social worlds and our positions in these worlds, a new language must come forth. In this case, by promoting a language of differences and dropping the language of disability, advocates are reaching for a language that finally achieves equality.

THE RELATION BETWEEN LANGUAGE AND COMMUNICATION

The Ebonics controversy captures and reflects our many assumptions and beliefs about language. We believe that the role of language is to convey our thoughts and emotions to each other. We believe that in doing so language allows us to organize and coordinate our actions. Therefore without language, organization and coordination would be impossible, meaning that language is supposedly vital for the making of a civil and modern society. Within this perspective of language all of us have an obligation to keep the language of society secure and stable. We must guard against any form of linguistic pollution and contamination. But as the notion of Universal Grammar makes plain, no language needs such protection. All languages are syntactically, grammatically, and structurally sound. The distinction between a language and a dialect is purely political—those without power and privilege we describe as speaking a dialect and those who have power and privilege we describe as speaking a language. It is all privilege politics.

Languages in being ecologies fertilize and influence other languages. In fact, languages thrive by being ecologically promiscuous. This is why so many other languages are found within English. For what would be the beauty of English without such foreign words and phrases as *trek, slim, apartheid, admiral, albatross, average, cheque, garbage, hazard, magazine, mattress, racket, syrup, zero, soda, sheriff, ream, monkey,* and *sofa?* Who would call for the expunging of such foreign words and phrases from English, or even believe that such expunging is possible? (By last count, English draws from 146 other languages) Evidently, such cross-pollination enriches our languages. It gives us access to other worlds. It also makes our languages inclusive and, ultimately, makes us inclusive.

Still, the Ebonics controversy, as with nearly all other language controversies, captures our many fears about language diversity. Our primary fear is that without a standardized language—that is, one that is supposedly stable and secure by our doing—human beings will descend into anarchy and disunity. But such fear is without any basis in theory, history, or reality. Language diversity is no obstacle to communication between different peoples. As Jonathan Sacks (2003) explains, "Cultures are like languages. The world they describe is the same but the ways they do so are almost infinitely varied. English is not French. Italian is not German. Urdu is not Ugaritic. Each language is the product of a specific community and its history, its shared experiences and sensibilities. There is no universal language. There is no way we can speak, communicate or even think without placing ourselves within the constraints of a particular language whose contours were shaped by hundreds of generations of speakers, storytellers, artists and visionaries who came before us, whose legacy we inherit and of whose story we become a part. Within any language we can say something new. No language is fixed, unalterable, complete. What we cannot do is place ourselves outside the particularities of language to arrive at a truth, a way of understanding and responding to the world that applies to everyone at all times. That is not the essence of humanity but an attempt to escape reality" (pp. 54–55).

Communication problems are fundamentally problems of understanding, specifically the lack thereof. It is about the unwillingness to understand and exerting the necessary effort to understand. Yes, language facilitates understanding. But understanding exceeds language. With the necessary determination and effort, different peoples, in the face of language diversity, can achieve understanding. We can celebrate our language diversity without fostering any suspicion and distrust of each other. We can even understand things that language will never allow us to fully understand. The reason is that meaning resides within human beings and our relationships to each other rather than in language and symbols. We attach meanings to language and symbols. But because all human beings have different life experiences, our meanings will always differ. We are reminded of this reality when a person says, "I thought you meant," or, "What do you mean by that, exactly?"

Yet there is nothing fundamentally wrong about the diversity of our experiences. Neither is there anything wrong about the fact that language is always about interpretation—one person using language to mean and the other person trying to interpret what the other person means. That human beings retain the power to control what things linguistically and symbolically mean allows us to control language rather than to be controlled by language. In a world where language controls meaning, human beings would be limited to only those meanings that our language affords. In such a world, language would rule over us. It would have the power to control what we experience and what we can imagine. In such a world, language would stop us from understanding and experiencing that which is beyond language. In such a world, new words and phrases would never enter our consciousness. There would be no catalyst to create new words, new phrases, new metaphors that reflect new experiences and understandings. In a world where meanings reside within language, human beings would have no capacity to create, innovate, and imagine. Such a world would make us less human. For what would be the possibility of poetry in such a world? What would be the possibility of great literatures and scriptures in such a world? Where would our diversity come from? That there are numerous denominations of all the world's great religions is a compelling reminder that even meaning resides within us rather than in language.

Languages do have the ability to convey our meanings and even set off new meanings within us. The power of language, words, and symbols is great and thereby should always be used with empathy and sensitivity to avoid inflicting unnecessary pain and misery on others, especially the most vulnerable among us. The promotion of this practice is vital in a world that is increasingly plural, global, and multicultural. However, the power of human beings to mean and to use language is no less extraordinary. It is through this power that diversity enters the world. It is also through this power that human beings retain the power to imagine and realize new worlds.

JAPAN AND CHINA: NATIONAL CHARACTER WRIT LARGE
Norimitsu Onishi

TOKYO—Of all languages in the world, Japanese is the only one that has an entirely different set of written characters to express foreign words and names. Just seeing these characters automatically tells the Japanese that they are dealing with something or someone non-Japanese.

So foreign names, from George Bush to Saddam Hussein, are depicted in these characters, called katakana. What's more, the names of foreign citizens of Japanese ancestry are also written in this set of characters, indicating that while they may have Japanese names, they are not, well, really Japanese.

By contrast, in Chinese, no such distinction is made. There, non-Chinese names are depicted, sometimes with great difficulty, entirely in Chinese characters. Foreigners are, in effect, made Chinese.

At bottom, the differences reflect each country's diverging worldview. In contrast to the inner-looking island nation of Japan, China has traditionally viewed itself as the Middle Kingdom of its name, the center of the world. If it is natural for

Japan to identify things or people as foreign, viewing them with some degree of caution, it may be equally natural for China to take "Coca-Cola" or "George Bush," and find the most suitable Chinese characters to express them.

In Japan, the rigid division between the inside and outside in the language underscores this country's enduring ambivalence toward the non-Japanese. The contrast with China is stark, and speaks also to the future prospects of Asia's two economic giants as they compete for influence in a world of increasingly fluid borders.

While today's Japanese travel overseas with an ease and confidence that would have been unimaginable only two generations ago, they remain uneasy about foreign things and people coming here. Safer to label them clearly as foreign.

Not so China.

"China is a big continent and has an inclination to think that it is No. 1 and that others are uncivilized," said Minoru Shibata, a researcher at NHK, Japan's public broadcast network. "Therefore, they feel that giving Chinese names to foreigners is doing them a favor."

China and Japan represent the two nations that still widely use Chinese characters in their writing. The Chinese, as the creators of this system, still use them exclusively.

Come to Japan, and things get extremely complicated. In their everyday lives, the Japanese use three different sets of characters in writing—four if the widely used Roman alphabet is also included.

First are the Chinese characters, called kanji here. Japanese names are written in kanji. Currently, the number of kanji permitted for names stands at 2,230, and selecting a character outside this list is illegal. Parents have been pressing for an expanded list, though, and so the justice ministry said recently that it is considering adding between 500 and 1,000 characters.

Second is a set of phonetic characters used for Japanese words. Third are the katakana, the set of phonetic characters for foreign words.

"There is no other language that has three sets of characters—only Japanese," said Muturo Kai, president of the National Institute for Japanese Language.

In the United States, parents' freedom to name their children may be absolute. Here the government and the media set the boundaries of names and the way they are written, thereby also setting the boundaries of Japanese identity.

In the media, the names of George Bush and Saddam Hussein are written in the characters reserved for foreign names. But so are the names of people of Japanese ancestry, like Alberto Fujimori, Peru's deposed president, or Kazuo Ishiguro, the author of "Remains of the Day," who left Japan at the age of 5 and is a British citizen. Their names could be written in kanji, but are instead written in katakana, in an established custom indicating that they are not truly Japanese.

The distinctions are sometimes difficult to draw, as they touch upon the difficult question of who is Japanese, or, rather, when does someone stop being

Japanese. If Mr. Ishiguro had kept his Japanese citizenship all these years, would his name be written differently here? Why is the name of Mr. Fujimori, who holds Japanese citizenship and now lives in exile here, not written in kanji like the names of other Japanese? The media have no set criteria.

Are the criteria citizenship, blood, mastery of the Japanese language or customs? Or, in this island nation where leaving Japan has always meant leaving the village, does one start becoming non-Japanese the minute one steps off Japanese soil?

There is a strong argument to be made for that. Children of Japanese business families stationed overseas for a few years invariably encounter problems returning here. Schoolmates often pick on them and call them gaijin, meaning foreigner or outsider. That problem has decreased in recent years, as more and more Japanese have spent time abroad. But those children are still considered to have suffered from their years overseas, in contrast to, say, an American child whose experience living abroad would usually be considered a plus.

Chinese identity is a different matter. Whether you are a fourth-generation Chinese-American student at Berkeley, or the children of Chinese operating a restaurant in Lagos, Nigeria, you are considered Chinese, or an insider, upon returning to China. Your name will be written in the same way as everybody else's. Unlike Japan's, Chinese identity transcends borders.

"Chinese people have a strong feeling of comradeship toward overseas Chinese," said Naokazu Hiruma, who is in charge of language use at the daily Asahi Shimbun and studied in China. "Overseas Chinese have a long tradition, and they remain Chinese even after generations have passed. Japanese regard second- or third-generation overseas Japanese, even though they are of Japanese origin, as 'people from that country over there.'"

Many contend that communication between peoples of different languages and cultures is impossible because our different languages supposedly reflect different worldviews. No doubt, different languages do reflect different worldviews and thereby point to things in one world that may be absent in other worlds. For instance,

> Among the Wintu Indians of California, the principle of the inviolate integrity of the individual is basic to the very morphology of the language. Many of the verbs which express coercion in our language—such as take a baby to (the shade), or to change the baby—are formed in such a way that they express a cooperative effort instead. For example, the Wintu would say, "I went with the baby," instead of, "I took the baby." They never say, and in fact cannot say, as we do, "I have a sister,"

or a "son," or "husband." Instead, they say, "I am sistered," or "I live with my sister." (Lee, 1987, p. 8)

But languages are also fundamentally ecological—always changing, evolving, and adapting to new experiences and influences.

We can create new languages that reflect our determination to bridge our different worlds and understand each other. Even without a common language between different peoples, communication is always possible. That meaning resides within us means that the possibility for understanding also resides within us. As such, the responsibility for communication also belongs to us. To view language diversity as the fault of our intercultural communication problems with others releases us of this responsibility. It puts the fault on language diversity and on those who are promoting this diversity by supposedly refusing to speak English, and our own version of English. In other words, the fault is with those who are linguistically and culturally different. It also creates the impression that resolving our intercultural communication problems merely requires of us the promotion of English and the elimination of language diversity. But this solution will do nothing to promote understanding between different peoples. The fact that understanding exceeds language also means that the demands of understanding exceed language. In short, understanding is hard work. It requires a great obligation from us in terms of effort and resources. We have to be focused and committed to the task. We have to be ready to suspend our worldview and try earnestly to look and even experience the world from the perspective of the other person. We have to acknowledge our biases, prejudices, and stereotypes. All of this is difficult to do. Yet without a commitment and determination to do all this, achieving understanding is impossible, even in a world that is linguistically and culturally homogenous.

CONCLUSION

The United States is by no means the only nation that seems determined to impose language commonality. In fact, many nations are equally determined to do so. Understandably, language plays an integral role in the formation of our identity. It situates us in the world. It connects us to our community, our history, our environment. It allows us to make sense of ourselves, each other, and the world. As such, the loss of our language, or any threats to our language, brings much anxiety. Such loss is seen as the beginning of the end of our identity, community, and history. On the other hand, language diversity can be daunting, even overwhelming. It immediately gives us the sense that communication is impossible, that the alien sounds coming out of mouth of the person means that the person is of a world alien to us. We can therefore anticipate that many communities will continue to stridently oppose language diversity. But in a world that is increasingly global, plural, and multicultural, such opposition is futile, as well as unnecessary.

CHAPTER 4

Intercultural Communication: Redefining Communication

KEY TERMS

Frozen Conflicts

Noise

INTRODUCTION

Intercultural communication begins on the premise that through communication our differences can be bridged, managed, and even resolved. On the other hand, without communication, our differences are distorted, aggravated, and even demonized. Thus the goal of intercultural communication is always to promote, facilitate, and encourage communication. But this is never easy to do, as our many differences do present many challenges. Communication requires a willingness to suspend our truths so that one person can genuinely experience and understand the world from the position of another person. Simply put, communication requires the nurturing of doubt, a willingness to view even our most sacred truths as fallible. In *The Meaning of It All: Thoughts of a Citizen-Scientist,* Nobel Prize recipient Richard Feynman (1998) elaborates on the virtues of promoting and cultivating doubt. "Scientists . . . are used to dealing with doubt and uncertainty. All scientific knowledge is uncertain. This experience with doubt and uncertainty is important. I believe that it is of very great value, and one that extends beyond the sciences. I believe that to solve any problem that has never been solved before, you have to leave the door to the unknown ajar. You have to permit the possibility that you do not have it exactly right. Otherwise, if you have made up your mind already, you might not solve it" (p. 28). Moreover,

> If we were not able or did not desire to look in any new direction, if we did not have a doubt or recognize ignorance, we would not get any new ideas. There would be nothing worth checking, because we would know what is true. So what we call scientific knowledge today is a body of statements of varying degrees of certainty. Some of them are most unsure; some of them are nearly sure; but none is absolutely certain. Scientists are used to this. We know that it is consistent to be able to live and not know. Some people say, "How can you live without knowing?" I do not know what they mean. I always live without knowing. That is easy. How you get to know is what I want to know.

According to Feynman,

> This freedom to doubt is an important matter in the sciences and, I believe, in other fields. It was born of a struggle. It was a struggle to be permitted to doubt, to be unsure. And I do not want us to forget the importance of the struggle and, by default, to let the thing fall away. I feel a responsibility as a scientist who knows the great value of a satisfactory philosophy of ignorance, and the progress made possible by such a philosophy, progress which is the fruit of freedom of thought. I feel a responsibility to proclaim the value of this freedom and to teach that doubt is not to be feared, but that it is to be welcomed as the possibility of a new potential for human beings. If you know that you are not sure, you have a chance to improve the situation. I want to demand this freedom for future generations.

But doubt is difficult to promote, as the seductive and attractive pull of certainty is always lurking. In relation to doubt, certainty requires less of us. It requires no reflecting, no contemplating, no probing, no questioning, no challenging, no contesting, no grappling. In this way, certainty undermines communication. It heightens the possibility, intensity, and negativity of conflict between different peoples. It puts us at each other's throats by convincing us that our differences are the cause of our conflicts with others rather than our own unwillingness to maintain doubt.

What should always be of concern to us is the lack of open, honest, and vibrant communication between different peoples that have to share spaces and resources with each other. The lack of such communication is rarely a positive sign in such instances. It nearly always signals that various perspectives are suppressed, or that various sides are being silenced out of fear of retribution. Indeed, intercultural communication rarely ever occurs in a context where all sides have equal power and privilege. In most cases, one side has the power—as in the case of media ownership and control—to ridicule, blame, and demonize the other side. This reality often makes open, honest, and vibrant communication impossible. It pushes marginalized and disenfranchised peoples to the margins—spaces and places that promise anonymity and thereby a way to avoid the retribution that dominant groups often use against marginalized and disenfranchised groups. This is often the reality that makes for all kinds of writings on bathroom walls.

GRAFFITI AS INTERCULTURAL COMMUNICATION

Graffiti frequently reflect tensions and conflicts among diverse groups (e.g., Bruner & Kelso, 1980; Cole, 1991; Scheibel, 1994; Vervort & Lievens, 1989; Warakowski, 1991). D'Angelo (1976) views graffiti as a reflection of contemporary customs and moral values that reveals details about everyday life. Kostka (1974) and Bushnell (1990) consider graffiti a highly structured communication medium. Newall (1986–1987) contends that graffiti functions to vent hostilities, express fantasies, communicate triumphs, declare rebellion, and promote propaganda. As such, graffiti provides an outlet for people to express their attitudes with regard to race, gender, and sexual orientation. Anonymous drawings and writings on walls and other surfaces represent a communicative opportunity to gain insights into how different peoples treat each other through anonymous text. What distinguishes this opportunity from others is the fact that it functions both personally and openly. Personally, graffiti allows the key benefit of anonymity, that is, protection against any form of retribution. Any person can say whatever, however, and whenever, to whomever. In fact, graffitists often acknowledge this benefit in graffiti: "It's a chance to vent frustrations—to say things you wouldn't dare speak up about . . . because sometimes you feel like letting the whole world know how you're feeling w/out [sic] giving yourself away" (Fraser, 1980, pp. 258, 260).

Further, the lack of explicit rules and protocols allows people to express themselves without the fear of social punishment that arises from any kind of violation. Accordingly, graffiti levels the playing field by getting past all the factors—such as social status, hierarchical position, education, access, familiarity with rules, expertise, communication competence—that advantageously privilege and benefit certain members against others. It is the only rhetorical form that affords such virtues. Consequently, graffiti represents an equal opportunity communicational form—perhaps, the only rhetorical form that affords such equality for all discussants.

Graffiti also invites participation. It aptly follows Kenneth Burke's (1969) notion that certain "formal patterns can readily awaken an attitude of collaborative expectancy in us" (p. 58). In addition, the open nature of graffiti matches its personal nature. According to Bruner and Kelso (1980), "although written in the privacy of a toilet stall, the writing of graffiti is an essentially social act . . . To write graffiti is to communicate; one never finds graffiti where they cannot be seen by others" (p. 241). Indeed, along with the benefits of anonymity, graffitists explicitly posit that visibility is a key attraction (Fraser, 1980). As Burke (1969) suggests, "You are drawn to the form, not in your capacity as a partisan, but because of some universal appeal in it" (p. 58). On the other hand, Burke also cautions that meanings are not always subordinate to form. For example, Burke (1969) claims that "the more violent your original resistance to the proposition, the weaker will be your degree of surrender by collaborating with the form" (p. 58).

Many scholars also contend that dominant groups use the open nature of graffiti to intimidate and "discipline" minority groups (Bruner & Kelso, 1980; Cole, 1991). Moreover, graffiti often functions as a symbolic system of visual and nonverbal communication within a political arena. The bathroom constitutes the political arena because it is where the presence of groups is noted and where the tensions and conflicts between them are revealed and made visible. The contention is that graffiti allows for open discourses (sexist, racist, and homophobic speech) that organizations and societies cannot sanction, but that may also act to establish or reinforce the privileging aspects of patriarchal practices, thus supporting the hegemonic order. On the other hand, when government officials officially and oppressively mute various public discourses, graffitists consistently resort to public walls to hold such discourses (Chaffee, 1989). Thus, graffiti allows all conflicts and concerns to be equally visible and known to all who pass by. In so doing, all members of a cultural group, by way of accessibility, are equally potential participants and discussants in such discourses. In short, what is meant to be seen is eventually seen, especially so when dealing with captured audiences. As regards what is known and by whom, all members of all cultural groups are thus equally privileged.

Graffitists regularly search for virgin wall and use winding arrows to pinpoint their involvement and participation when lack of space prohibits the placement of a response close to the interaction unit. Besides the arrows, graffitists regularly refer to the particular wall inscription to indicate their participation. As Bruner and Kelso (1980) point out, "a new person . . . who chooses to write a graffito must take account of what has previously been written, even in the minimal sense of choosing an appropriate location on the wall" (p. 241). Chain responses often target other chain responses in a discourse unit. Graffitists also return and offer responses to other inscriptions that target their original inscription. In sum, the discourse features, the scolding and correcting, and the use of winding arrows are empirical evidences of social interaction and derivation of meaning among graffitists.

The absence of both social punishment and retribution allows graffiti to serve as text that is attractive to individuals who want to transgress and upset organizational and societal norms. This transgression will be found in both content and manner of the text. The literature reveals that this transgression is used both negatively and positively. Graffiti is used to intimidate disenfranchised groups seeking to contest the hegemony of dominant groups. Minority groups are increasingly targeted with derogatory graffiti (Higgins, 1989; Kirk, 1990; Taylor, 1990). For instance, the level of racist graffiti increased at Wellesley College during a period marked by intermittent tensions over race and sexual orientation (Flint, 1992).

Jones (1991) posits that the proliferation of racially insulting graffiti on U.S. campuses in recent years reflects a genuine conflict between and among ethnic groups, particularly between blacks and whites, resulting from the impact of economic, political, and social factors. On the other hand, various persons use graffiti to contest the dominant relations of power and the various social devices that are meant to sanction only certain kinds of discourses and actions. Indeed, members in a variety of institutions use graffiti to facilitate the communication of ideas and concerns that their organizations explicitly or implicitly sanction. For example, women students at Brown University recently resorted to graffiti to address issues of rape and sexual harassment. Names of men began to appear on women's bathroom walls after someone wrote the name of a male student and accused him of rape. The graffito also invited others to: "Compile a list of other men to watch out for" (Starr, 1990, p. 64). According to Lisa Billowitz, a student representative on Brown's Sexual Assault Task Force, "the bathroom list arose out of frustration, anger and pain. Many of the women have tried to go through proper channels and have been thwarted" (quoted in Starr, 1990, p. 64). These actions by women resulted in the implementation of many new programs and services to address issues of rape and sexual harassment on campus. Also, on noticing the sizeable amount of lesbian-related graffiti in a university's female bathrooms, a member of the editorial board of the school's newspaper wrote a graffito asking lesbians to do an article about being gay on campus. The following were responses to the editor's graffito:

(A) *I think all homosexuals should get together and contact me to write about it [homosexuality] for "Campus" section of [students' newspaper]. It's a start. Contact Campus Editor! TM*

(B) *Can you promise confidentiality? I am not ashamed of my love for other women, but I would hate to open myself up to the ridicule of sexual bigots. Take a look at the poorly stated but strongly felt comments written here and try to imagine what a can of worms such disclosure in your medium would open up for me and other women like me on campus.*

(C) *Please put an article in the [paper] on you dykes 'cause I really want to understand what makes you tick. OK. "Inquiring minds want to know."*

The hostility that is being referred to above is clearly evidenced in the following exchanges found in the same female bathroom:

(A) *One point only, lesbianism is unnatural. Two women cannot produce life. You all are sick but you are looking for companionship beyond female friendship. A love/sex relationship between two women defies nature itself.*

(B) *Fear of [sister] power. Don't impose your own insecurity and confusion on other [sisters]!*

(C) *Black women are life!!!*

(D) *Lesbianism is unnatural because God says its so.*

(E) I really don't understand how a woman could be attracted to another woman and I agree with the sister girl to the left of me. Homosexuality is very unnatural and since God says it's wrong in the bible I don't [think] he would create a human being that way. It's a learned behavior.

(F) You have to learn to interpret the bible. King James was a racist woman hater. Reading is Fundamental. You also think God is a HE. Question everything that contradicts your Freedom and liberty.

In other women's bathroom on this campus, the following exchanges were found:

(A) Dikes Suck!
(B) Bigoted Black women keep us all enslaved

(A) Repressed homosexuals make me ill
(B) Suck [expletive] Bitch!

(A) Sharon Loves TINA
(B) TINA LOVES Sharon. The Gay 90s Are Here
(C) [Fags] Are Bitches
(D) To Me Homosexuality Is Truly Unnatural And I Believe It is a Mental Disorder
(E) Can I get an AMEN

(A) Kill FAGS! I am Homophobic And Proud of it!
(B) KILL GAYS!! Gays will take over the University! Put an end to the Gay Movement! Men, stand up for your [expletive] Woman, stand up for your [expletive] Kill Gays! . . .
(C) Don't Tempt me . . .

Such exchanges among lesbians, and between lesbians and heterosexual women, are particularly common in women's bathrooms (e.g., Alexander, 1978; Bruner & Kelso, 1980; Cole, 1991; Reich, Buss, Fein, & Kurtz, 1977). Most of the exchanges found in women's bathrooms are often lengthy, are carefully crafted, and involve many discussants. Several scholars (Bruner & Kelso, 1980; Cole, 1991; Hentschel, 1987) posit that women use the bathrooms to build a community that is without the aggressive and hostile features that patriarchy fosters. "The underlying meaning of female graffiti is that they express the co-operation of the dominated and reflect the strategy of mutual help employed by those in a subordinate status" (Bruner & Kelso, 1980, pp. 249–250). Similarly, Cole (1991) contends that women use graffiti to counter their subordinated position in a patriarchal society: "Because womyn are free to choose the topics [of discussion] . . . womyn are able to share interests and experiences they may not generally share with men. As a result, womyn's . . . graffiti open avenues that call male dominance into question" (p. 403). This is seen in the following graffiti found in a women's bathroom stall:

(A) African American women. Look! Don't judge people. You don't understand homosexuality at all! If it was a choice I wouldn't choose it because of all this abuse. Why can't I just be myself in this world.

(B) Be yourself [sister]. I got your back.
(C) Goddess power forever!
(D) Dykes and lesbians do what you please.

No doubt, graffiti functions for both men and women to provide a forum for forbidden topics. Both males and females talk about race, gender, and sexual orientation. Evidently, anonymity allows graffitists to express themselves without fear of retribution. The manner—particularly the language—of the expressions tends to go beyond normative bounds. In other words, the anonymity of graffiti allows for a kind of passion that seldom characterizes face-to-face communication among individuals on this campus. Graffitists are frequently visceral and vulgar. Many graffitists seem to revel in the freedom that the context offers, purging themselves of thoughts and ideas that the normative bounds of society constrain and prohibit.

(A) Jews have big noses because the air is free.
(B) And little [expletive] because whores cost so much.

(A) Getting a Jap [Japanese] Bitch to [expletive] is like squeezing water out of a rock!!!
(B) Why are Jap chicks bowlegged?
(C) From squatting to piss in the gutter!

(A) [Expletive] Bush and all those White Bastards. Signed an aware . . . student.
(B) Do you think all white men are the enemy?
(C) Can't we all just get along? Rodney King
(D) [Expletive] Rodney King. He needs to get his ass bust again.
(E) Lighten up pal.

(A) I hate all [you] West Indians. [Expletive] them Africans and other foreign diaspora blacks who look down on African Americans. I love my own. To hell with Pan Africanism.

(A) Why don't you Jamaicans learn to write and speak proper English?
(B) Listen up. The language is our culture fool.
(C) That is why Jamaicans are so poor and ignorant.

Indeed, many exchanges reflect a willingness and openness to address forbidden concerns that rarely characterizes other contexts for interaction on campus. The freedom that graffiti offers thus makes for a visceral passion, which is often reflected in the vulgar and racist language, the explicit subject matter, and the hostile and threatening manner of the exchanges.

What is evident in graffiti is that dominant relations of power are suppressing certain discourses and thereby certain groups. As the dominant relations of power sequester public discussions of various subjects to bathroom walls, exchanges within the bathrooms reflect the same practices. Any mention of these subjects is met with hostility. The contestation of power relations found on the bathroom walls is, then, representative of a conflict that a dominant group seeks to suppress by making discussions of various subjects unwelcomed through social punishment and threats of violence. As Stanley Deetz (1992) observed, "When discussion is thwarted, a particular view of reality is maintained at the expense of equally plausible ones, usually to someone's advantage. It should not be surprising that systems of domination are protected from careful exploration and political advantage is protected and extended. Their continuation provides both security and advantage" (p. 188).

THE PURSUIT OF DIALOGUE

Only few discourses about diversity make no mention of dialogue. Dialogue is nearly always proposed as the solution to our problems with diversity, implying that the lack of dialogue—rather than the nature of our differences—is responsible for our problems with diversity. Many intercultural communication programs promote dialogue circles. We are encouraged in these circles to share openly and honestly our beliefs and truths, our pains and humiliations, our biases and prejudices. Presumably, through dialogue common ground will be found. We will thereby get beyond our differences and find the common ground that will save us from strife and conflict. That is, finding this common ground will supposedly save us from our differences. But what happens when finding common ground seems impossible? This is the matter that David Lochhead (1989) takes up in *The Dialogical Imperative: A Christian Reflection on Interfaith Encounter.*

Lochhead claims that what most persons define and describe as dialogue is really monologue. Dialogue involves no quest for common ground. To strive for common ground presumes that our differences are obstacles to harmony. It also presumes that dialogue requires a lessening of our convictions and passions. We must be flexible. But dialogue requires no such compromise.

> A truly dialogical relationship has no other purpose than itself. Dialogue is the end of dialogue. It is common to justify dialogue as something that helps us understand ourselves better, as something that contributes to our own growth and maturity. Whereas change in the form of growth is something that one might well hope and expect from a dialogical relationship, it cannot be its prime purpose. If the dialogue partner is viewed primarily as the instrument of my growth, then he or she is a means for my fulfillment rather than one who is loved for his or her own sake ... A relationship that is entered into for the results it will bring, whether it be the conversion of the other or our own growth, is still in the realm of monologue. (p. 79)

According to Lochhead, dialogue is about loving our neighbor as Jesus Christ loved us. This is the dialogical imperative. The promise of dialogue resides in the activity rather than the result. In this case, the process is about loving our neighbor as Jesus Christ loved us. Dialogue is "first and foremost, a fundamental relationship into which we are called with our neighbor. Unless dialogue is selective—that is, unless we are called into dialogical relationships with some people but not with others (which could only be the case if dialogue were not universally binding)—we must say further that dialogue is a fundamental relationship with the world to which we are called" (1989, p. 85).

Lochhead believes that achieving genuine harmony—especially among peoples of different religious traditions—requires a focus on a theology of dialogue. That is, how can we love our neighbor as Jesus Christ loved us? What are the obstacles to us doing so? For instance, "As a Christian, I am likely to persist in my belief that Buddhists are wrong about God. I am not likely to adopt their belief that the existence or nonexistence of God is irrelevant to the spiritual quest. Nevertheless, the Buddhist critique of theism will inevitably cause me to examine and reexamine my own theistic assumptions. As a result of coming to understand reality as seen by Buddhists, my doctrine of God will be transformed" (1989, p. 93). In loving our neighbor as Jesus Christ loved us, our hearts and minds open. Dialogue enlarges our ways of experiencing and perceiving each other and, ultimately, enlarges our view of the world and God. But these are the consequences of dialogue, which Lochhead warns should never be mistaken for the activity of dialogue.

This distinction is important as, again, most discourses about dialogue view dialogue as a way of changing the thoughts and sentiments of others to find either commonality or common ground. But this is monologue. This is about using others as a means to an end. This is about dialogue as a strategy to achieving conversion and imposing our reality and sensibility on others. Ultimately, this kind of dialogue undermines the formation of genuine understanding among peoples of different traditions, especially religious traditions. Peoples who suspect that conversion is being subtly cultivated will eventually opt out and most likely become suspicious of those pushing the conversion under the pretext of dialogue. But according to Lochhead, a theology of dialogue invites no such suspicion and distrust. Regardless of our neighbor's convictions and passions, the burden is purely on us to love our neighbor as Jesus Christ loved us. However, Lochhead never tells us what is the Muslim to do, or the Hindu, or the Buddhist, or the Jain.

REDEFINING COMMUNICATION

As always, definitions matter. There are many interesting definitions of communication that pervade intercultural communication literatures and discourses.

- Communication is the interaction between people. It is the exchange of information, ideas, or beliefs.

- Communication is the expression of a thought, be it concrete or abstract.
- Communication is the process of transmitting any type of verbal or nonverbal message through a medium.
- Communication is the process of receiving and sending messages with others.

In most cases, the definitions of communication found in intercultural communication literatures and discourses share a striking similarity—communication is consistently seen as fundamentally a linguistic and symbolic activity that involves the transaction of messages. The primary assumption is that this activity occurs between separate human beings. In the case of intercultural communication, communication presumably occurs between peoples of different cultures, and communication competency is about being able to navigate our differences so that the different persons can achieve a level of understanding. This process involves acquiring knowledge of different cultures so that our messages never violate or bring us into conflict with the differences of others. This approach to communication is the status quo in intercultural communication studies—learning about each other's differences and how best to communicatively navigate these differences to achieve a common understanding. But is this the most constructive way to approach communication in an increasingly global, plural, and multicultural world— a world of differences that increasingly defy the bounds of race, ethnicity, gender, sexual orientation, nationality, and religion? These differences can neither be forecasted nor anticipated. In this emerging plural, global, and multicultural world, our differences foremost reside in our different histories, rationalities, sensibilities, emotionalities, spiritualities, and modalities, rather than in our different ethnicities, nationalities, sexualities, geographies, and religions.

In *The Community of Those Who Have Nothing in Common,* Alphonso Lingis claims that our commonly conceived definitions of communication erode our natural diversity by pitting us in a violent struggle against **noise**. For these definitions, communication is achieved by conquering, suppressing, and limiting noise. Noise is presumably confusion resulting from lack of knowledge of each other, from the lack of linguistic and symbolic commonality, from us coming from different interpretive environs, and from our different accents and dialects. As such, many of us tend to believe that the goal of communication should be to vanquish noise, either through ending bilingual education, promoting the assimilation of different cultures, norming our different sensualities, rationalities, sensibilities, spiritualities, and modalities (especially through the institution of speech codes), downplaying our different histories, by insisting on allegiance to country rather than the world, or cultivating linguistic and symbolic convergence (such as making English the official language of the United States).

What emerges is violence as noise is an integral element in human affairs. It is inextricable and inescapable. It reflects what Lingis refers to as the natural murmur of the world. To silence noise is to silence our own diversity—the diversity that comes naturally with the world. According to Lingis (1994), "Entering into communication means extracting the message from the background noise and from the noise that is internal to the message. Communication [becomes] a struggle against interference and confusion. It is a struggle against the irrelevant and ambiguous signals which must be pushed back into the background and against the cacophony in the signals the interlocutors address to one another—the regional accents, mispronunciations, inaudible pronunciations, stammerings, coughs, ejaculations, words started and then cancelled, and ungrammatical formulations" (p. 70). In this way, communication becomes an effort to silence—and eventually marginalize—those expressions, experiences, and understandings that reflect different ways of being in the world. Communication homogenizes us.

To approach communication as a struggle against noise is to ultimately create communities and societies that are hostile to diversity. In these communities and societies, diversity can only be tolerated. But this tolerance is always precarious. Persons who are perceived as different must promise again and again to never threaten the order of things. There must also be a promise to share a common language, to lose thick accents that supposedly make communication difficult, and to adhere to prevailing traditions and customs. Still, those who are perceived as different are always seen as a threat and thereby deserving of suspicion. But what is the possibility of intercultural communication when the goal is ultimately assimilation? That is, why should the promise of intercultural communication merely be about working, socializing, and getting along with peoples of different cultures? What other ways are there to define communication that allow us to embrace linguistic convergence and divergence, meaning and ambiguity, clarity and confusion? Moreover, what other ways to define communication that make for communities and societies never heighten our distrust and suspicion of our differences? In fact, what other ways can we define communication that can put us in harmony with the world's natural diversity rhythms?

NEW DEFINITIONS OF COMMUNICATION

Communication is a powerful tool in resolving even the most profound tensions and conflicts with peoples of different persuasions and even different religions. But all definitions of communication are by no means theoretically equal. We now introduce a new definition of communication. This definition locates the origins of communication in our capacity to be vulnerable. *Communication is about our being vulnerable to the humanity of others.*

Being vulnerable means being open to the interpretations, experiences, understandings, and even confusions and frustration of others. It also means recognizing that our own meanings, interpretations, and understandings will never exceed the world's ambiguity, complexity, and mystery. So being vulnerable also means embracing human fallibility and thereby recognizing that oftentimes our actions will conflict with our best intentions and motives. Being vulnerable also means recognizing that many times life's complexity, ambiguity, and mystery will often exceed us. Confusion is a common human experience that demands compassion, patience, and even forgiveness. As such, being vulnerable also means being tolerant of the anxiety and chaos that come with being human. Finally, being vulnerable means, as Bishop Desmond Tutu (1999) wrote in *No Future Without Forgiveness,* being "generous in our judgments of others, for we can never really know all there is to know about another" (p. 169). Compassion, mercy, and forgiveness are integral to being and becoming vulnerable. As Jonathan Sacks (2003) explains, "Truth in heaven transcends space and time, but human perception is bounded by space and time. When two propositions conflict it is not necessarily because one is true the other false. It may be, and often is, that each represents a different perspective on reality, an alternative way of structuring order, no more and no less commensurable than a Shakespeare sonnet, a Michelangelo painting or a Schubert sonata" (p. 64).

IMPLICATIONS AND DEFINITIONS

To define communication in terms of vulnerability foregrounds the human component in the study and teaching of communication by shifting communication away from expressing and understanding to a focus of experiencing and embodying. Communication no longer becomes something one does to another, but rather something one is to another. This emergent definition thereby moves notions of communication competency beyond that of skills, techniques, and strategies, to one of capacity and resiliency. It makes for the natural and organic entry of compassion, mercy, and forgiveness into communication studies, as such notions are vital to being vulnerable. It also pushes us to attend to the larger discourses, worldviews, and institutions that situate and permeate our humanity. Do such discourses, worldviews, and institutions promote our reaching and searching for mutual understanding, which is to say, do such discourses, worldviews, and institutions promote trust, openness, and compassion? Moreover, in foregrounding the notion of vulnerability, this emergent definition of communication places the burden of communication on us. It obligates us to help each other understand our interpretations and orientations, regardless of the differences that seem to hopelessly divide us. We have to own our own ways of encountering others. It also pushes us to examine the larger social, political, and cultural arrangements that situate communication by looking at how different arrangements bear on our ability to be vulnerable to each other. But most important, this emergent definition of communication elevates the study of communication by showing our own potentiality to create and shape our worlds. Communication is no longer reduced to merely an expression or product of various mental, psychological, biological, social, or even historical forces. Rather, communication constitutes our capacity to help with the completion of the world. It expands our humanity and enlarges our worlds by constantly demanding of us new meanings, new understandings, new experiences, and ultimately, new modes of being in the world with others. In this way, this emergent model of communication commits us to identify and support only those arrangements that promote communication.

Thus in contending that the origins of communication reside in our vulnerability, this emerging definition of communication is pushing us to look anew at what being human means and to imagine new ways of being in the world. If the origins of communication reside in our symbolic and linguistic capacity, as is commonly assumed in communication studies, then our moral capacity is in no way fundamentally larger than that found in apes, chimpanzees, and bonobos. It therefore makes sense to continue to look to these animals for moral direction. If, however, our communication capacity resides in our vulnerability, then we have to look beyond these animals for moral direction. We thereby gain the opportunity to imagine new worlds. We also acquire a larger sense of what is moral. In this regard, what arguably makes this emergent definition of communication most constructive is that it stretches our notions of what it means to be humane and decent and, in so doing, disrupts relations of power that sustain the most hideous systems of discrimination by assuming that our communication capacity—and ultimately our worth—is an expression of our cognitive capacity.

WALLS, FENCES, AND COMMUNICATION

Without communication, distortion happens. Without communication, aggression happens. In short, without communication, no opportunity exists for peoples to understand each other. We are devoid of any means to demystify and become less afraid of each other. All that remains is our misperception and distortion of each other. The lack of communication ferments suspicion, distrust, and ultimately, hostility. As such, what is the value of devices, practices, structures, and arrangements that limit and even end communication between different peoples? For instance, what is the value of walls and fences in an increasingly plural, global, and multicultural world? What is the value of the walls in Iraq to separate Shiite and Sunni neighborhoods? What is the value of the wall that the United States is building on the border with Mexico? What is the value of the wall that the Israelis are constructing between Israel and Palestine? What is the value of the wall Thailand is proposing to build on its border with Malaysia? What is the value of the fence that the United Arab Emirates is building on its border with Oman? What is the value of the wall that Saudi Arabia is building on its border with Yemen? Or the wall that Botswana is building on its border with Zimbabwe? Or the fence Brunei is building on its border with Limbang? Or the wall Iran is building on its border with Pakistan? Or the wall Russia is proposing to build on its border with Chechnya? Or the wall Thailand is proposing to build on its border with Malaysia? Indeed, over 20 countries are either constructing or proposing to construct new border walls. But with the construction of all these different walls and fences, how will the peoples on different sides of these walls and fences demystify each other, understand each other, and ultimately, become less afraid of each other? How would cooperation be possible when communication is impossible? Our future depends, as Rabbi Jonathan Sacks reminds us in the *Dignity of Difference: How to Avoid the Clash of Civilizations,* on "our ability to understand and be understood by people whose cultures, creeds, and values and interests conflict with ours and to whom . . . we must speak and listen" (2003, p. 3). This involves being "ready to hear of their pain, humiliation and resentment and discover that their image of us is anything but our image of ourselves" (p. 23). It also involves "letting our world be enlarged by the presence of others who think, act, and interpret reality in ways radically different from our own" (p. 23).

There is a physical dimension to communication—human beings have to be physically available to each other for communication to occur. Walls deny this availability. However, when communication is undercut, perception reigns, as without communication, there is no way to verify or disqualify our various perceptions of each other. The result is most often distortion, which makes for the justification for the erection of new walls and fences. So, yes, walls and fences can immediately lessen the quantity and intensity of conflict between different peoples. But ultimately, walls and fences compound the gravity of the conflict by hardening the distortions and misperceptions that both sides harbor. This reality is seen well in Northern Ireland. After the Roman Catholics and Protestants signed a peace treaty over a decade ago, the walls separating the different factions show no signs of ever coming down.

INTERCULTURAL COMMUNICATION AND FOREIGN POLICY

In foreign policy circles, especially in the United States, there is a position that opposes any communication, much less any negotiation, with certain countries and entities. Doing so is seen as legitimizing and even appeasing these countries and entities. Thus President George W. Bush recently declared, "No nation can negotiate with terrorists. For there is no way to make peace with those whose only goal is death." Moreover, in a speech in Israel addressing the Knesset, President Bush said, "Some seem to believe we should negotiate with terrorists and radicals, as if some ingenious argument will persuade them they have been wrong all along. We have heard this foolish delusion before. . .We have an obligation to call this what it is—the false comfort of appeasement, which has been repeatedly discredited by history."

Robert Kaufman, professor of public policy at Pepperdine University, believes that there "are . . . categories of regimes . . . [and] categories of entities . . . where their goals are so implacable that negotiating with them actually is more dangerous than not negotiating, because you legitimize them if you do negotiate." Peter R. Neumann, Director of the Centre for Defence Studies at King's College, also believes that democracies should never negotiate with violent nonstate actors. "Democracies must never give in to violence, and terrorists must never be rewarded for using it. Negotiations grant legitimacy to terrorists and their methods and undermine actors who have pursued political change through peaceful means. Negotiations can destabilise the negotiating governments' political system, undercut international efforts to outlaw terrorism, and set a dangerous precedent."

Instead, many call for the isolation of these supposedly rogue countries and entities or the laying down of a long list of preconditions before any communication or negotiation can begin. But is a foreign policy based on promoting the isolation of those who fundamentally oppose or are even hostile to our interests constructive? Does such a policy diffuse tension and the possibility of violent conflict? Does such a policy lessen misunderstanding? Does such a policy lessen distrust and suspicion? Historically, no such case can be made. The reason is that isolation exaggerates our distortions and misperceptions of each other. It undercuts any opportunity or occasion to adjust and correct our misperceptions of each other. On the other hand, isolation hardens our misperceptions of each other. In denying communication, isolation prevents any challenges to our perceptions and positions. We are never challenged to look differently at the world. The result, again, is a hardening of our perceptions and positions, and with this the loss of flexibility that is vital to finding common ground.

But should the United States negotiate with every country and entity? According to Cris M. Currie (2002),

> We simply need to make it clear that a decision to negotiate does not mean acceptance of the other side's behavior. (p. 1)

What about preconditions for negotiations? Foreign policy is all about contradiction, opposition, and even propagating illusions and fabrications. In foreign policy, one person's liberator is usually another person's conqueror; just as much as one person's ally in the global war against terror is another person's enemy of Islam. In foreign policy, nothing is ever constant—everything is open to different interpretations and perceptions. Yet foreign policy is also about making believe that your side owns the moral high ground. All sides employ this strategy. But such moral posturing has no effect on the other side. It is merely for local consumption, such as getting your citizenry to rally around your position and making whatever sacrifices are necessary to uphold your foreign policy position. Without the threat of aggression, no side will accept preconditions. To accept preconditions is comparable to allowing the other side to determine the rules of the game, choose the referees and umpires, and decide what outcomes win the game. The side that must accept the preconditions is obviously disadvantaged before the negotiations begin.

Yet the fact that the threat of aggression is necessary to force the other side to accept preconditions compromises any negotiation between the sides. It releases the side that is threatening force of any responsibility to genuinely look at the world from the position of the other side. After all, by having the other side accept the preconditions, the outcome of any negotiation is already determined. But for the side that must accept the preconditions, the humiliation lingers and ferments. It is never forgotten and often passed down from one generation to the next. In short, the conflict is never genuinely resolved. In foreign policy circles, these are called **frozen conflicts**, which promise to eventually thaw out and cause all kind of problems.

In foreign policy no absolute outcome will fully satisfy all sides. Negotiation requires a willingness to compromise, and communication is about finding moments of understanding that can allow us to get to other moments of understanding. There is never a *final* understanding in communication. But with any negotiation, what is vital to success is both sides negotiating in good faith. As Cris M. Currie explains,

> We need not accept their values or their conduct. What we do accept is the humanity underneath as deserving of due process . . . (p. 1)

Or, as Secretary of State James Baker recently noted, "talking to an enemy is not, in my view, appeasement."

Aggression is always possible when negotiation is impossible, just as much as misperception is always possible when communication is impossible. As such, the side that has the military means to impose preconditions on the other side is nearly always the side that is unwilling to negotiate or comes with the longest list of preconditions. Negotiation is merely seen as another option rather than the path to resolution. But this mentality merely forces the other side to find comparable means of retaliation so as to avoid the humiliation of having to accept all manner of preconditions. Any foreign policy that favors isolating other nations and setting long lists of preconditions is ultimately encouraging those nations to acquire weapons of mass destruction.

Of course, many nations need no encouragement in trying to acquire such weapons. But no policy should push these nations further to do so. Thus, how constructive is any foreign policy that encourages a new arms race? With both sides increasingly possessing weapons of mass destruction, negotiation is actually becoming the only rational foreign policy position. Indeed, South African President Nelson Mandela once pointedly told President Clinton at an international conference to follow his lead and negotiate face-to-face with his enemies to solve conflicts peacefully. "The United States as the leader of the world should set an example to all of us to help eliminate tensions throughout the world. And the best way of doing so is to call upon its enemies to say, 'Let's sit down and talk peace.'" Mandela conceded that negotiating with enemies can be difficult. "We had a government which had slaughtered our people, massacred them like flies. It was repugnant to think that we could sit down and talk with these people." But Mandela said that bridging differences was necessary to bring peace to South Africa.

CONCLUSION

We are in a parallel world. In one realm, the world is becoming increasingly global, plural, and multicultural. However, in the other, an increasing number of nations now have weapons of mass destruction. Even neighboring nations now threaten each other with weapons of mass destruction. Yet no nation will ever win a war involving weapons of mass destruction. The promise of communication can never guarantee the end of aggression as an option in resolving conflict. It only promises the possibility of such a reality. It reminds us that such a possibility is within our grasp. We are by no means of a world that condemns us to death and destruction. Within communication resides the possibility of peace and prosperity. But as much as possibility is laden with power, such as the power to reimagine the world, possibility is also fragile. Therefore possibility must always be nurtured and encouraged, as the demise of possibility constitutes our demise. After all, what is the worth of a world without any possibility of harmony between different peoples? We attend to our well-being by attending to possibility. Thus by attending to communication, the womb of possibility, we attend to the condition of the world.

CHAPTER 5

Intercultural Communication: Redefining Diversity

KEY TERMS

Intergroup Contact Theory

Scapegoating

Self-expansion model

INTRODUCTION

We commonly define diversity in terms of race, ethnicity, sexuality, disability, and religion. But in an increasingly global, plural, and multicultural world, does this remain the most constructive method? Do these groupings capture and reflect our diversity—what is principally different about us? Does the addition of persons from these groupings really bring diversity? Is diversity merely the compilation of different perspectives? If so, should all perspectives and persuasions be equally embraced, valued, and celebrated? That is, are all perspectives morally equal? If, however, this is in no way the case, who determines which differences should be valued and which should be devalued—or even persecuted? On the other hand, many definitions of diversity exclude religion, others exclude sexuality, others exclude disability, and still others exclude social class.

The problem with looking at diversity in terms of race, gender, ethnicity, sexuality, disability, and so forth is that this perspective locates diversity in our physical attributes. We assume that a person of a different ethnicity constitutes a different way of understanding the world. But this practice fosters stereotyping. We are by no means the sum of our race, ethnicity, disability, or religion. We are also mothers

127

and daughters, fathers and sons, brothers and sisters, aunts and uncles, friends and neighbors, teachers and students, comrades and colleagues, conservatives and progressives. Moreover, race, ethnicity, disability, and religion are often bundled with each other. There is the homosexual Latino woman who is also a devout Christian and the bisexual African-American man who is a devout Buddhist and whose mother is Jewish. In such cases, as with most cases, an Asian man who is a devout Christian and believes that homosexuality is an abomination before God should value or privilege what differences?

We currently understand diversity as a noun. We believe that human beings possess diversity as a result of possessing certain attributes, such as a certain race, ethnicity, gender, disability, nationality, and so on. To look at diversity this way naturally lends for the grouping and sorting of human beings by various attributes. However, an ecological approach makes plain that diversity is always changing and evolving, and trying to neatly group and sort us is increasingly impossible and often counts for nothing much. Case in point—a person could be of a certain ethnicity but be of a different political, cultural, social, or sexual orientation from another person of the same ethnicity, so to assume that a person's ethnicity can be a reliable measure of what is different between two human beings is really a distortion. Yet this distortion happens by downplaying the complexity and diversity between these people. As such, reducing us to a category reduces our own diversity and complexity.

An ecological approach gives us a framework that ends this kind of distortion. So let us look now at what this approach gives us in terms of redefining and expanding our understanding of diversity.

- It presents diversity as a *process that is ever changing, ever moving, ever evolving.*
- It defines diversity as a *relational process*—diversity happens between human beings.
- It positions diversity as a *moral undertaking.* The prosperity of any community is dependent on the ability of that group to *generate* diversity.

To view diversity from an ecological perspective is to understand intercultural communication in terms of practices and habits of being that allow for the generation of and the creation of diversity. Intercultural communication is an *enabling* process—enabling new ways of understanding and experiencing the world that affirm life. In this way, *an intercultural experience is any experience or encounter that enables new ways of being and understanding the world.*

So whereas mainstream approaches to intercultural communication focus on lessening the tension and friction between human beings by encouraging us to better understanding our differences, an ecological approach to intercultural communication focuses on expanding and enlarging our experiencing and understanding of each other. Mainstream approaches focus on equipping us with knowledge of our differences and how to navigate these differences, whereas an ecological approach focuses on creating new differences and sustaining this process. But these approaches are by no means mutually exclusive. We do encounter each other with our differences, and appreciating these differences is important, as differences often reflect a lot that matters to us. We should never trivialize each other's differences. But as all relationships are fundamentally ecological, the prosperity and even survival of these relationships depend on them changing and evolving. This means that these relationships have to abide by all the ecological practices that allow ecologies to change, evolve, and flourish, such as promoting permeability, vulnerability, flexibility, diversity, and equity. When these relationships change and evolve, new ways of being and understanding emerge. It is within the evolution of these new modes of being and understanding that contain the possibility of harmony and peace between different peoples.

INTERGROUP CONTACT THEORY

We are increasingly sharing our social worlds with peoples of all manner of ethnicities, nationalities, spiritualities, sexualities, abilities, and histories. This trend only promises to continue as this new century unfolds. Intergroup contact is inevitable. Of course, many persons, such as Samuel Huntington and Pat Buchanan, believe that this contact will only bring strife and war. However, *intergroup contact theory* gives us a different vision of what can potentially come from this increasing contact between different peoples.

Originally formulated by Gordon Willard Allport (1954) in a book entitled *The Nature of Prejudice,* intergroup contact theory claims that contact between groups under optimal conditions can effectively reduce intergroup prejudice. Specifically, Allport held that reduced prejudice will result when four features of the contact situation are present:

1. equal status between the groups in the situation;
2. common goals;
3. intergroup cooperation; and
4. the support of authorities, law, or custom.

Allport's formulation of intergroup contact theory "has inspired extensive research over the past half century." This research spans a variety of groups, situations, and societies.

In a rigorous analysis of more than 500 studies, Pettigrew and Tropp (2008) found that intergroup contact typically reduces prejudices of many types by "(1) enhancing knowledge about the outgroup, (2) reducing anxiety about intergroup contact, and (3) increasing empathy and perspective taking" (p. 922). For instance, various researches have found that "Whites who have had contact with members of other racial and ethnic groups show lower levels of physiological stress and self-reported anxiety than Whites without such contact experiences."

Many investigations have found that "intergroup anxiety mediates the relationships between intergroup contact and prejudice," that positive intergroup contact "outcomes can be achieved to the extent that anxiety is reduced," and that "reducing negative feelings such as anxiety and threat represents an important means by which intergroup contact diminishes prejudice." Intergroup anxiety refers to "feelings of threat and uncertainty that people experience in intergroup contexts." Typically, these feelings "grow out of concerns about how they should act, how they might be perceived, and whether they will be accepted."

IN BRONX SCHOOL, CULTURE SHOCK, THEN REVIVAL
Elissa Gootman

Junior High School 22, in the South Bronx, had run through six principals in just over two years when Shimon Waronker was named the seventh.

On his first visit, in October 2004, he found a police officer arresting a student and calling for backup to handle the swelling crowd. Students roamed the hallways with abandon; in one class of 30, only 5 students had bothered to show up. "It was chaos," Mr. Waronker recalled. "I was like, this can't be real."

Teachers, parents and students at the school, which is mostly Hispanic and black, were equally taken aback by the sight of their new leader: A member of the Chabad-Lubavitch sect of Hasidic Judaism with a beard, a black hat and a velvet yarmulke.

"The talk was, 'You're not going to believe who's running the show,'" said Lisa DeBonis, now an assistant principal.

At a time when the Bloomberg administration has put principals at the center of its efforts to overhaul schools, making the search for great school leaders more pressing than ever, the tale of Mr. Waronker shows that sometimes, the most unlikely of candidates can produce surprising results.

Despite warnings from some in the school system that Mr. Waronker was a cultural mismatch for a predominantly minority school, he has outlasted his predecessors, and test scores have risen enough to earn J.H.S. 22 an A on its new school report card. The school, once on the city's list of the 12 most dangerous, has since been removed.

Attendance among the 670 students is above 93 percent, and some of the offerings seem positively elite, like a new French dual-language program, one of only three in the city.

"It's an entirely different place," Schools Chancellor Joel I. Klein said in a recent interview. "If I could clone Shimon Waronker, I would do that immediately."

Not everyone would.

Mr. Waronker has replaced half the school's teachers, and some of his fiercest critics are teachers who say he interprets healthy dissent as disloyalty and is more concerned with creating flashy new programs than with ensuring they survive. Critics note that the school is far from perfect; it is one of 32 in the city that the state lists as failing and at risk of closing. Even his critics, though, acknowledge the scope of his challenge.

"I don't agree with a lot of what he's done, but I actually recognize that he has a beast in front of him," said Lauren Bassi, a teacher who has since left. "I'm not sure there's enough money in the world you could pay me to tackle this job."

Mr. Waronker, 39, a former public school teacher, was in the first graduating class of the New York City Leadership Academy, which Mayor Michael R. Bloomberg created in 2003 to groom promising principal candidates. Considered one of the stars, he was among the last to get a job, as school officials deemed him "not a fit" in a city where the tensions between blacks and Hasidic Jews that erupted in Crown Heights, Brooklyn, in 1991 are not forgotten.

"They just said he may be terrific, but not the right person for that school," Chancellor Klein said.

Some parents at J.H.S. 22, also called Jordan L. Mott, were suspicious, viewing Mr. Waronker as too much an outsider. In fact, one parent, Angie Vazquez, 37, acknowledged that her upbringing had led her to wonder: "Wow, we're going to have a Jewish person, what's going to happen? Are the kids going to have to pay for lunch?"

Ms. Vazquez was won over by Mr. Waronker's swift response after her daughter was bullied, saying, "I never had no principal tell me, 'Let's file a report, let's call the other student's parent and have a meeting.'"

For many students and parents, the real surprise was that like them, Mr. Waronker speaks Spanish; he grew up in South America, the son of a Chilean mother and an American father, and when he moved to Maryland at age 11, he spoke no English.

"I was like, 'You speak Spanish?'" recalled Nathalie Reyes, 12, dropping her jaw at the memory.

He also has a background in the military. Mr. Waronker joined R.O.T.C. during college and served on active duty for two years, including six months studying tactical intelligence. After becoming an increasingly observant Jew, he began studying at a yeshiva, thinking he was leaving his military training behind.

"You become a Hasid, you don't think, 'Oh my God, I'm going to suppress revolutions,'" Mr. Waronker said. But, he said, he drew on his military training as he tackled a school where a cluster of girls identifying themselves as Bloods stormed the main office one day looking for a classmate, calling, "We're going to get you, you Crip." He focused relentlessly on hallway patrols, labeling one rowdy passageway the "fall of Saigon." In an effort to eliminate gang colors, he instituted a student uniform policy.

He even tried to send home the students who flouted it, a violation of city policy that drew television news cameras. In his first year, he suspended so many students that a deputy chancellor whispered in his ear, "You'd better cool it."

In trying times—when a seventh grader was beaten so badly that he nearly lost his eyesight, when another student's arm was broken in an attack in the school gym, when the state listed J.H.S. 22 as a failing school—Mr. Waronker gathered his teachers and had them hold hands and pray. Some teachers winced with discomfort.

At first Mr. Waronker worked such long hours that his wife, a lawyer, gently suggested he get a cot at school to save himself the commute from their home in Crown Heights.

He also asked a lot from his teachers, and often they delivered. One longtime teacher, Roy Naraine, said, "I like people who are visionaries."

Sometimes teachers balked, as when Mr. Waronker asked them to take to rooftops with walkie-talkies before Halloween in 2006. He wanted to avoid a repetition of the previous year's troubles, when students had been pelted with potatoes and frozen eggs.

"You control the heights, you control the terrain," he explained.

"I said, if you go on a roof, you're not covered," said Jacqueline Williams, the leader of the teachers' union chapter, referring to teachers' insurance coverage.

Mr. Waronker has also courted his teachers; one of his first acts as principal was to meet with each individually, inviting them to discuss their perspective and goals. He says he was inspired by a story of how the late Rabbi Menachem Mendel Schneerson, the Lubavitch spiritual leader, met with an Army general, then inquired after his driver.

"That's leadership," he said, "when you're sensitive about the driver."

Lynne Bourke-Johnson, now an assistant principal, said: "His first question was, 'Well, how can I help you, Lynne?' I'm like, 'Excuse me?' No principal had ever asked me that."

The principal enlisted teachers in an effort to "take back the hallways" from students who seemed to have no fear of authority. He enlisted the students, too, by creating a democratically elected student congress.

"It's just textbook counterinsurgency," he said. "The first thing you have to do is you have to invite the insurgents into the government." He added, "I wanted to have influence over the popular kids."

These days, the congress gathers in Mr. Waronker's office for leadership lessons. One recent afternoon, two dozen students listened intently as Mr. Waronker played President Franklin D. Roosevelt's address after the bombing of Pearl Harbor, then opened a discussion on leadership and responsibility.

When an etiquette expert, Lyudmila Bloch, first approached principals about training sessions she runs at a Manhattan restaurant, most declined to send students. Mr. Waronker, who happened to be reading her book, "The Golden Rules of Etiquette at the Plaza," to his own children (he has six), has since dispatched most of the school for training at a cost of $40 a head.

Flipper Bautista, 10, loved the trip, saying, "It's this place where you go and eat, and they teach you how to be first-class."

In a school where many children lack basic reading and math skills, though, such programs are not universally applauded. When Mr. Waronker spent $8,000 in school money to give students a copy of "The Code: The 5 Secrets of Teen Success" and to invite the writer to give a motivational speech, it outraged Marietta Synodis, a teacher who has since left.

"My kids could much better benefit from math workbooks," Ms. Synodis said.

Mr. Waronker counters that key elements of his leadership are dreaming big and offering children a taste of worlds beyond their own. "Those experiences can be life-transforming," he said.

So when Emmanuel Bruntson, 14, a cut-up in whom Mr. Waronker saw potential, started getting into fights, he met with him daily and gave him a copy of Jane Austen's "Emma."

"I wanted to get him out of his environment so he could see a different world," Mr. Waronker said.

Mr. Waronker has divided the school into eight academies, a process that has led to some venomous staff meetings, as teachers sparred over who got what resources and which students. The new system has allowed for more personalized environments and pockets of excellence, like an honors program that one parent, Nadine Rosado, whose daughter graduated last year, called "wonderful."

"It was always said that the children are the ones that run that school," she said, "so it was very shocking all the changes he put in place, that they actually went along with it." Students agree, if sometimes grudgingly, that the school is now a different place.

"It's like they figured out our game," groused Brian Roman, 15, an eighth grader with a ponytail.

Back in Crown Heights, Mr. Waronker says he occasionally finds himself on the other side of a quizzical look, with his Hasidic neighbors wondering why he is devoting himself to a Bronx public school instead of a Brooklyn yeshiva.

"We're all connected," he responds.

Gesturing in his school at a class full of students, he said, "I feel the hand of the Lord here all the time."

THE SELF-EXPANSION MODEL

The *self-expansion model* is another framework that is increasingly playing an integral role in enriching our understanding of intercultural communication (Aron & Aron, 1986; Aron, Mashek, & Aron, 2004; Brody, Wright, Aron, & McLaughlin-Volpe, in press; Wright, Brody, & Aron, 2005). The model claims to provide a framework for understanding the motivation behind and psychological consequences of forming relationships with persons of different groups. The model makes the following claims:

- First, human beings are motivated to self-expand to increase our ability to achieve the resources vital for meeting future challenges. Self-expansion involves incorporating the perspectives, experiences, and identities of persons of other groups into our own identity to increase feelings of efficacy (our capacity to prevail in the face of adversity). This process is commonly referred to as the self-expansion motive. According to Brody and colleagues (in press), "self-expansion may represent a basic human process that would, at times, lead to an appetitive interest in other groups. The logic follows directly from the basic premise of the model—people seek to expand the self by building relationships with others who can increase their current complement of resources, perspectives, and identities. Someone who shares most of what we currently are will offer little opportunity for self-expansion, while forming a relationship with someone who has a different set of perspectives and identities provides a much greater potential for expansion of the self . . . Thus, if we are not too afraid of being rejected or that a relationship simply could not work out, we should be drawn to others quite different from ourselves, making members of other groups particularly appealing" (pp. 19–20).
- Second, the self-expansion model claims that the process of self-expansion is affectively positive. It makes us feel good. It also leads us to have positive feelings and behaviors to other members of the other group. For example, one study found that "participants who had more friends in a particular group had more positive attitudes towards that group" and that "the closer the participant was to their closest friend in a group, the more positive they felt to that group." Also, "When closeness to their closest friend in a group was high, the more interactions participants had with members of that group, the more positive attitudes they had towards the group" (p. 22, From Brody, Wright, Aron, & McLaughlin-Volpe, in press).
- Third, the model claims that self-expansion is also self-transformation. Taking on the perspectives, experiences, and identities of persons of other groups changes our worldview. The process leads us to perceive and experience the world from the perspective of the other group. It also leads us to treat persons from the other groups like ourselves. In this way, the process promotes empathy and equity.

Proponents of the self-expansion model claim that the model allows us to look at intercultural communication in ways that exceed merely tolerating our differences with members of other groups. It allows us to look at others positively rather than suspiciously. The model encourages us to view members of other groups as resources rather than threats. Without such resources, our ability to survive and flourish becomes difficult. Thus the self-expansion motive makes for a natural rather than contrived inclination to seek out and form relationships with persons who seem most different to us. That the process is affectively positive only lubricates the process.

Proponents of the self-expansion model also believe that intercultural communication programs and initiatives should focus on promoting rapid friendship between members of different groups. We should do so by promoting initiatives that pair persons of different groups and then asking each person "to reciprocally disclose increasingly intimate thoughts, feelings and past experiences, to compliment and support each other, and to find and describe similarities between themselves" (p. 29, From Brody, Wright, Aron, & McLaughlin-Volpe, in press). Other initiatives should focus on cultivating cooperation in meeting a joint goal and developing trust between members of different groups. In the end, Brody and colleagues believe,

> People's self-expansion motives may provide the basic fuel that will motivate us to cross the spaces that divide us, but it will be those who structure social situations to cultivate and support meaningful cross-group relationships who may be most influential, not only in closing the spaces between us as individuals, but in building the bridges that will cross the spaces that divide our groups. By creating small changes in everyday life situations, there is the potential to create large changes in our social world, and to move the rhetoric and the reality of intergroup relations from talk of tolerance to feelings of genuine respect, admiration, and perhaps—even compassionate love. (in press, p. 33)

THE PROBLEM WITH BLASPHEMY

The human species is inherently diverse. We encounter each other with our different rationalities, sensibilities, spiritualities, modalities, and ultimately, different histories. These differences are inevitable, unpredictable, and uncontrollable. There is simply no way to anticipate consistently how any person will perceive or experience anything. We therefore tend to perceive and experience things differently. We assign different meanings to things. Even persons who share the same ethnicity, gender, nationality, religion, and disability assign different meanings to things. We will always have to negotiate meaning—trying to understand what others mean and are trying to mean. We can never assume what others mean or the meanings people assign to things. We must always attend to meaning, including where our different meanings come from. Intercultural communication is about recognizing and engaging our different meanings. What do you mean? What are you trying to mean? But contrary to popular perception, meaning resides within human beings and our relationships with each other, rather than in language and symbols. In this way, intercultural communication problems are really problems of meaning, such as our mistaking the meaning of others, missing the meaning of others, failing to understand the meaning of others, confusing the meaning of others, misinterpreting the meaning of others, being unwilling to consider the meaning of others, or simply having no interest in the meaning of others. These situations often present many kinds of intercultural communication problems and set off many unpleasant consequences, such as being accused of being offensive, seditious, or blasphemous. In many places, to be merely accused of blasphemy or sedition is a death sentence.

According to Feroza Jussawalla (1996),

> Rushdie is the victim not only of the condition of postmodernity, where meaning is wrenched from the author's hands to rest in the hands of readers like the Ayatollah Khomeini, but of the indeterminacy of meaning outside certain cultural contexts.

In Search of Meaning

The fact that meaning which resides within human beings presents many challenges. There is no way to exercise total control over our meanings. Our meanings can be misconstrued, misinterpreted, and even missed by others. Also, meanings are always bound by context. To understand what a person means requires understanding or knowing the context in which the meaning is emerging. No meaning is ever devoid of a political, historical, cultural, and social context. But every context is always changing, as life is always changing. So our meanings are also always changing.

That meaning resides within us also means that there is no way to ever know for certain what others mean. Mistaking, misinterpreting, and even missing each other's meanings are natural human experiences. We can certainly do much to lessen these practices, but completely ending these practices is simply impossible. Yet these practices are by no means responsible for our intercultural communication problems. These problems spring from our own unwillingness to explore, nurture, and even encourage the rise of new and different meanings. No doubt, various meanings can cause much pain and distress. But to coercively suppress such meanings does nothing to end the motives and forces that make for these meanings. The sentiment will still persist. Regardless of how difficult the process is, meanings have to be engaged. What do you mean? What are you trying to mean? Where is this meaning coming from? Do you understand the pain or hurt this meaning is causing? In a plural, global, and multicultural world, where meanings will always be diverse, meanings demand deliberation, negotiation, and compassion. For just as much as the meanings of others can be misconstrued, our meanings can also be misconstrued.

AUTHOR FACING DEATH THREATS BREAKS SILENCE TO DEFEND PLAY
Vikram Dodd

The author of the play cancelled last month after violent protests by Sikhs has broken her silence, saying she still wants her work to be staged and telling of the effect death threats had on her and her family.

Writing in the Guardian today, Gurpreet Kaur Bhatti says it was not fear that kept her silent but "practical issues" about her own safety and that of those closest to her.

"My play, Behzti, has been cancelled, I've been physically threatened and verbally abused by people who don't know me. My family has been harassed and I've had to leave my home. I have been deeply angered by the upset caused to my family and I ask people to see sense and leave them alone."

Bhatti says she "wholeheartedly" stands by the play, adding that the threats and hate mail have "stirred only tolerance and courage within me". The play was closed by the Birmingham Repertory theatre after windows were smashed and its doors stormed by some Sikhs who said the play insulted their religion.

The row sparked protests that artistic freedom of expression was under threat, while others claimed that right did not allow gratuitous offence to people's faith.

Death threats forced Bhatti into hiding. The writer says she was "very saddened" by the decision to cancel the production, but accepts the theatre had no choice because of the danger of more violence.

Behzti, or Dishonour, was set in a gurdwara, a Sikh temple, and included scenes of murder and rape.

Bhatti denies a claim by one theatre boss that she blocked plans to stage her play after it was cancelled. She denies changing any part of the play because of pressure and says she wants the play to be performed again: "I will, when the time is right, discuss the play's future with relevant parties."

In today's article Bhatti, herself a Sikh, says her faith in God remains strong and condemns people who used the row over her play to condemn Sikhism.

"There can never be any excuse for the demonisation of a religion or its followers. The Sikh heritage is one of valour and victory over adversity."

She continues: "I am proud to come from this remarkable people and do not fear the disdain of some, because I know my work is rooted in honesty and passion.

"I hope bridges can be built, but whether this prodigal daughter can ever return home remains to be seen."

Bhatti says the play was taken out of context by some people and was not intended to offend, saying that it was meant to "to explore how human frailties can lead people into a prison of hypocrisy."

Sikh leaders initially called for the setting of the play to be moved out of the gurdwara, but Bhatti rejects this option: "I feel that the choice of setting was crucial and valid for the story I wanted to tell and, in my view, the production was respectful to Sikhism.

"It is only a shame that others have not had the chance to see it and judge for themselves."

Artists and writers in Britain and around the world expressed their support for Bhatti.

The issue of freedom of speech was highlighted again this week when Christian groups demanded that the BBC drop a programme, Jerry Springer—The Opera, which they claimed was blasphemous.

Bhatti says the artist's right to free expression is vital. "I believe that it is my right as a human being and my role as a writer to think, create and challenge. The dramatists who I admire are brave. They tell us life is ferocious and terrifying, that we are imperfect and only when we face our imperfections truthfully can we have hope.

"Theatre is not necessarily a cosy space, designed to make us feel good about ourselves. It is a place where the most basic human expression—that of the imagination—must be allowed to flourish."

From *The Guardian London, January 13, 2005.* Copyright © Guardian News & Media Ltd. 2005.

HATE SPEECH OR FREE SPEECH? WHAT MUCH OF WEST BANS IS PROTECTED IN U.S.
Adam Liptak

VANCOUVER, British Columbia—A couple of years ago, a Canadian magazine published an article arguing that the rise of Islam threatened Western values. The article's tone was mocking and biting, but it said nothing that conservative magazines and blogs in the United States did not say every day without fear of legal reprisal.

Things are different here. The magazine is on trial.

Under Canadian law, there is a serious argument that the article contained hate speech and that its publisher, Maclean's magazine, the nation's leading newsweekly, should be forbidden from saying similar things, forced to publish a rebuttal and made to compensate Muslims for injuring their "dignity, feelings and self respect."

The British Columbia Human Rights Tribunal, which held five days of hearings on those questions in Vancouver last week, will soon rule on whether Maclean's violated a provincial hate speech law by stirring up animosity toward Muslims.

As spectators lined up for the afternoon session last week, an argument broke out.

"It's hate speech!" yelled one man.

"It's free speech!" yelled another.

In the United States, that debate has been settled. Under the First Amendment, newspapers and magazines can say what they like about minority groups and religions—even false, provocative or hateful things—without legal consequence.

The Maclean's article, "The Future Belongs to Islam," was an excerpt from a book by Mark Steyn called "America Alone." The title was fitting: The United States, in its treatment of hate speech, as in so many areas of the law, takes a distinctive legal path.

"In much of the developed world, one uses racial epithets at one's legal peril, one displays Nazi regalia and the other trappings of ethnic hatred at significant legal risk and one urges discrimination against religious minorities under threat of fine or imprisonment," Frederick Schauer, a professor at the John F. Kennedy School of Government at Harvard, wrote in a recent essay called "The Exceptional First Amendment."

"But in the United States," Schauer continued, "all such speech remains constitutionally protected."

Canada, Britain, France, Germany, the Netherlands, South Africa, Australia and India all have laws or have signed international conventions banning hate speech. Israel and France forbid the sale of Nazi items like swastikas and flags. It is a crime to deny the Holocaust in Canada, Germany and France.

Last week, the actress Brigitte Bardot, an animal rights activist, was fined €15,000, or $23,000, in France for provoking racial hatred by criticizing a Muslim ceremony involving the slaughter of sheep.

By contrast, U.S. courts would not stop the American Nazi Party from marching in Skokie, Illinois, in 1977, though the march was deeply distressing to the many Holocaust survivors there.

Six years later, a state court judge in New York dismissed a libel case brought by several Puerto Rican groups against a business executive who had called food stamps "basically a Puerto Rican program." The First Amendment, Justice Eve Preminger wrote, does not allow even false statements about racial or ethnic groups to be suppressed or punished just because they may increase "the general level of prejudice."

Some prominent legal scholars say the United States should reconsider its position on hate speech.

"It is not clear to me that the Europeans are mistaken," Jeremy Waldron, a legal philosopher, wrote in The New York Review of Books last month, "when they say that a liberal democracy must take affirmative responsibility for protecting the atmosphere of mutual respect against certain forms of vicious attack."

Waldron was reviewing "Freedom for the Thought That We Hate: A Biography of the First Amendment" by Anthony Lewis, the former New York Times columnist. Lewis has been critical of attempts to use the law to limit hate speech.

But even Lewis, a liberal, wrote in his book that he was inclined to relax some of the most stringent First Amendment protections "in an age when words have inspired acts of mass murder and terrorism." In particular, he called for a re-examination of the Supreme Court's insistence that there is only one justification for making incitement a criminal offense: the likelihood of imminent violence.

INTERPRETING MEANINGS

But what happens when our meanings are misconstrued? In fact, our meanings will always be misconstrued. This is the reality of a multicultural, plural, and global world. We are always engaging each other with different rationalities, sensibilities, spiritualities, and modalities. In a multicultural, plural, and global world, the challenge is to find the most constructive ways to deal with misunderstanding and lack of understanding. In such a world, misunderstanding is the norm. Sheila McNamee and Kenneth Gergen (1999) explained this point well in *Relational Responsibility: Resources for Sustainable Dialogue.*

> Disruptions, and even wrenching upheavals within any relationship should not be considered unusual or deeply problematic deviations from the normal; they are the warp and woof of cultural life. Given the person's existence in multitude of relationships, each itself is a pastiche of sundry traditions, and given the presence of these varied and incoherent vocabularies within any particular interchange, complete harmony is bought at the price of vast suppression. Although all action is intelligible and warranted within some form of relationship, local idioms do not always leap their boundaries with ease. Felicitous in their local context, they may elsewhere constitute egregious breaches. Furthermore, because we bring to bear on any action multiple voices of evaluation (many ways of visioning the true and the good), there is virtually no behavior that cannot be faulted by at least one available standard. At any point in an otherwise harmonious relationship, because of failures of understanding, in achieving mutual agreement, or running smoothly is, to a degree, unwarranted. Such glitches are the normal order of things. From the present standpoint, so-called good understandings are always partial, mutual agreement is precariously situated, and smooth interchange is often the result of habit. Not every demands a culprit. (p. 24)

Thus nothing is fundamentally wrong or unnatural with being misunderstood. In fact, misunderstanding can enliven communication. We must simply commit to understanding the reasons for our misunderstanding and lack of understanding. We must also commit to removing the abstractions that often impede understanding. The reality of misunderstanding keeps communication vibrant. It stops us from being complacent and thereby too rigid in our ways. To expect misunderstanding is to be committed to overcoming misunderstanding. Misunderstanding and understanding are of complementary union that requires harmony between the opposing sides. There is no understanding that is ever devoid of the possibility of misunderstanding. On the other hand, misunderstanding invites understanding. A world devoid of misunderstanding would have no reason for understanding.

Harmony is about recognizing the virtues that both understanding and misunderstanding bring. It is also about recognizing that both sides need each other. This means that misunderstanding in no way impedes communication, and understanding in no way means the end of misunderstanding. Both will always dwell within each other. Harmony is about embracing both forces, which means that the challenge of a multicultural, plural, and global world will in no way end the possibility of misunderstanding. This is a fool's errand. Instead, the challenge of communication is to find harmony between understanding and misunderstanding.

LEGISLATING MEANING

The Racial and Religious Hatred Act of 2006 is an Act of the Parliament of the United Kingdom that creates an offence of inciting (or "stirring up") hatred against a person on the grounds of their religion. In the act,

- A person who uses threatening words or behaviour, or displays any written material which is threatening, is guilty of an offence if he intends thereby to stir up religious hatred.
- A person who publishes or distributes written material which is threatening is guilty of an offence if he intends thereby to stir up religious hatred.
- If a public performance of a play is given which involves the use of threatening words or behaviour, any person who presents or directs the performance is guilty of an offence if he intends thereby to stir up religious hatred.
- A person who distributes, or shows or plays, a recording of visual images or sounds which are threatening is guilty of an offence if he intends thereby to stir up religious hatred.
- A person who has in his possession written material which is threatening, or a recording of visual images or sounds which are threatening, with a view to— (a) in the case of written material, its being displayed, published, distributed, or included in a programme service whether by himself or another, or (b) in the case of a recording, its being distributed, shown, played, or included in a programme service, whether by himself or another, is guilty of an offence if he intends religious hatred to be stirred up thereby.

The maximum penalty for anybody convicted of any of these offences is seven years imprisonment.

Government officials claim that the aim of the new legislation is to protect people from incitement to hatred against them because of their faith. It will still allow artists to offend, criticize, and ridicule faiths. According to Home Office Minister Paul Goggins, "It is about protecting the believer, not the belief." It is also about Parliament sending a clear message. "This will be a line in the sand which indicates to people a line beyond which they cannot go . . . People of all backgrounds and faiths have a right to live free from hatred, racism, and extremism." However, David Davis, a prominent Conservative member of Parliament, believes that the law seriously undermines freedom of speech and is "massively counterproductive." "Religion, unlike race, is a matter of personal choice and therefore appropriate for open debate." Liberal Democrat Evan Harris believes that the act jeopardizes freedom of expression. "The government's measure would stifle religious debate and feed an increasing climate of censorship."

Alan Thornett claims that the new law "is a serious threat to free speech and civil liberties and is an integral part of the wider attack on civil rights launched by new Labour . . . Effectively it expands the arcane blasphemy laws, which already exist in Britain, and will promote intolerance and bigotry, further divide religious communities, and raise the spectre of censorship." Polly Toynbee, writing in the *Guardian* just before the passage of the act, contends that

> What's at stake here is the right to be insulting and cause offence. Many Muslim groups think it will protect their religious sensitivities—and so it will, by shifting the cultural balance away from free speech towards a sanctimonious right to feel offended.

But what happens when our meanings are properly interpreted? That is, what happens when a person has no qualms about offending others, or believes that the exercise of certain speech exceeds the concerns of any group sensibility? Also, what happens when a person claims that trying to avoid offending others constitutes a violation of free speech and the open exchange of ideas? That is, what happens when a person is simply unwilling to submit to a certain sensibility or expectation of appropriate behavior? Does our submission to the sensibility of others threaten democracy? Should the protection of every sensibility by every community be equal? In a multicultural, plural, and global world, how does any society decide which sensibility should be respected and which others left exposed to be violated? In fact, should any modern society be in the business—either through legislation, policy, or convention—of protecting the sensibility of any community? Understandably, promoting our sensibility to the differences of others is a noble pursuit. But is the promotion of such a sensibility through legislation, policy, or convention necessary for the moral evolution of a society that values diversity?

BISHOP OFFERS APOLOGY
FOR HOLOCAUST REMARKS

Rachel Donadio

ROME—A bishop whose recent rehabilitation by Pope Benedict XVI provoked global outrage has apologized for remarks in which he denied the Holocaust, a Catholic news agency reported on Thursday.

The bishop, Richard Williamson, was one of four traditionalist bishops whose excommunications Pope Benedict revoked last month. In an interview broadcast on Swedish television several days before that, Bishop Williamson denied the existence of the Nazi gas chambers and the scope of the Holocaust.

In a statement published by the Zenit news agency on Thursday, Bishop Williamson said, "I can truthfully say that I regret having made such remarks, and that if I had known beforehand the full harm and hurt to which they would give rise, especially to the church, but also to survivors and relatives of victims of injustice under the Third Reich, I would not have made them."

He added, "To all souls that took honest scandal from what I said, before God I apologize."

His statement did not address the content of his televised remarks, in which he said that no more than 300,000 people died in the Holocaust and none in gas chambers. In recent weeks, he has said in interviews that he needs more time to study documentation about the Holocaust.

In his statement on Thursday, he said that the views he expressed on Swedish television were those of "a nonhistorian," and that his perspective was formed "20 years ago on the basis of evidence then available, and rarely expressed in public since."

The impact of a German pope pardoning a Holocaust denier prompted widespread criticism, engulfing the Vatican in an international political crisis. Many local churches were sent scrambling to reassure parishioners worried about the Vatican's moral authority.

In an effort to control the damage in recent weeks, the pope has repeatedly condemned Holocaust denial. This month, in a rare instance of the Vatican's expanding on comments by the pope himself, the church said that Bishop Williamson must distance himself from his statements on the Holocaust or he would not be allowed to serve as a bishop in the Roman Catholic Church. The Vatican also said that Benedict was not aware of Bishop Williamson's remarks when he decided to revoke his excommunication.

Bishop Williamson said Thursday that he had been asked "to reconsider" his remarks by the pope and Bishop Bernard Fellay, the superior general of the traditionalist Society of St. Pius X to which Bishop Williamson belongs, "because their consequences have been so heavy."

Jesús Colina, the director of the Rome-based Zenit news agency, said he had received Bishop Williamson's statement from the Vatican committee that oversees relations with the Society of St. Pius X, and had confirmed its veracity with Cardinal Darío Castrillón Hoyos, who oversees the committee.

Attempts to reach the cardinal were unsuccessful. The Vatican spokesman, the Rev. Federico Lombardi, said he had no comment on the report of Bishop Williamson's statement.

Some outside observers were not convinced by Bishop Williamson's statement. "He does everything except confront the central issue of this whole crisis," said Rabbi Marvin Hier, the founder of the Simon Wiesenthal Center in Los Angeles. "Has he changed his mind about the Holocaust, and does he believe that the Holocaust is a historic fact?"

He said he did not think that Bishop Williamson should be accepted as a bishop in the Catholic Church until his apology included recognition of the Holocaust.

The Society of St. Pius X is an ultraconservative group founded in opposition to the liberalizing reforms of the Second Vatican Council.

The four rehabilitated bishops were ordained by their schismatic leader in 1988 without papal approval; they were then excommunicated by Pope John Paul II. Last month Pope Benedict revoked the excommunications to heal a schism in the church.

In later statements, the Vatican has said that the society must accept the teachings of Vatican II before it can be brought in full communion with the church. It remains to be seen how Bishop Williamson's statement on Thursday will affect negotiations between the Vatican and the Society of St. Pius X.

This week, Bishop Williamson was expelled by Argentina, where he directed a seminary, and traveled to Britain.

On Thursday, the Pope John Paul II Cultural Center and the Anti-Defamation League announced that they were starting a renewed Catholic-Jewish dialogue in the United States.

The problem with officially and legally promoting a certain sensibility to the differences of others is that the practice promotes stereotyping. There is diversity within all groups, meaning that no group possesses a common sensibility. So how is a person to know when a sensibility will be violated? It is seen in the fact that the playwright Gurpreet Kaur is also a Sikh. It is also seen in the different reactions within the Sikh community. Moreover, speech is never exercised in a moral vacuum. To prohibit certain speech in no way stops the thoughts and emotions that bring forth such speech. It merely makes for the creation of new kinds of speech, or pushes such speech in the shadows, like bathroom walls. Also, coercively promoting a certain sensibility to the differences of others undermines the makings of an ecologically vibrant society. The making of such a society often requires the expression and consideration of thoughts that most persons at the moment consider acts of sedition, heresy, or blasphemy. Yet history shows us again and again that such thoughts eventually become status quo. Such was the case of Galileo, Charles Darwin, Jesus Christ, Elizabeth Cady Stanton, Thomas Jefferson, Frederick Douglass, and many others. Further, coercively promoting a certain sensitivity to the differences of others undermines diversity by removing the diversity of our sensibilities. We are being coerced into a common sensibility. We are forcing others to act like us, to look at the world like us, to feel about things like us. Finally, coercively promoting a certain sensitivity to the differences of others is simply unnecessary. Again, no speech occurs in a moral vacuum. Speech always occurs in a moral, historical, and political context. We can best control speech by scrutinizing and changing the moral context that gives rise and legitimacy to certain speech. Thus rather than focusing on limiting speech, our focus should be on examining and altering the context that is giving rise to certain kinds of speech, specifically speech that is devoid of empathy and compassion. That is, what context promotes empathy and compassion in our speech? How best could such a context be cultivated? Obviously, such a context begins with encouraging empathy and compassion. As always, empathy in no way means agreement with the position of others. It merely means a willingness to look and even experience the world from the position of others. Thus empathy promises no end to conflict. It merely promises the lessening of our conflicts and the intensity of such conflicts.

SCAPEGOATING

Intercultural communication is always difficult when resources and opportunities are scarce or are perceived to be so. Thus the phenomenon known as *scapegoating*—accusing, blaming, and even attacking other peoples for supposedly taking away our resources and privileges—is formed. The Scapegoat Society describes scapegoating as "a hostile socialpsychological discrediting routine by which people move blame and responsibility away from themselves and towards a target person or group. It is also a practice by which angry feelings and feelings of hostility may be projected, via inappropriate accusation, towards others. The target feels wrongly persecuted and receives misplaced vilification, blame and criticism." In many instances, scapegoating tends to happen when resources and privileges are scarce. It deflects attention from the forces and arrangements that are *really* responsible for the plight of the group that is doing the scapegoating. It also allows us to deny responsibility for our own complicity in creating the status quo that now seems to be conspiring against us. Finally, scapegoating promises us an easy solution to what are in most cases difficult problems. We merely have to rid ourselves of the peoples—usually a minority—who are supposedly taking away our resources and privileges. In this way, the peoples who are most susceptible to be scapegoated and negatively stereotyped are those already with the least power and privilege among us. Such is often the case with immigrants.

Recently, *The New York Times* published a pair of articles that gives us a compelling account of the horrors of scapegoating. On May 19, 2008, this is how the first story (Bearak, 2008) began.

ANTI-IMMIGRANT VIOLENCE IN JOHANNESBURG
Barry Bearak

JOHANNESBURG—Violence against immigrants, like some windswept fire, spread across one neighborhood after another here in one of South Africa's main cities this weekend, and the police said the mayhem left at least 12 people dead—beaten by mobs, shot, stabbed or burned alive.

Thousands of panicked foreigners—many of them Zimbabweans who have fled their own country's economic collapse—have now deserted their ramshackle dwellings and tin-walled squatter hovels to take refuge in churches and police stations.

This latest outbreak of xenophobia began a week ago in the historic township of Alexandra and has since spread to other areas in and around Johannesburg, including Cleveland, Diepsloot, Hilbrow, Tembisa, Primrose, Ivory Park and Thokoza.

Amid so much violence, the police were spread thin, sending in squads of officers in armored vehicles. "We are using all available resources and will call in reinforcements if the need arises," a police spokesman, Govindswamy Mariemuthoo, told reporters.

President Thabo Mbeki said Sunday that he would set up a panel of experts to investigate the causes of the violence. Jacob Zuma, the president of the governing African National Congress and the man presumed to succeed Mr. Mbeki next year, called the attacks on foreigners a matter of national shame.

"We should be the last people to have this problem of having a negative attitude towards our brothers and sisters who come from outside," Mr. Zuma said.

Many of South Africa's current leaders sought shelter in neighboring countries during the apartheid years and were deeply embarrassed by the violence.

Newspaper editorials have called the outbursts a matter of using immigrants as scapegoats for South Africa's problems. The official unemployment rate is

23 percent. Food prices have risen sharply. The crime rate is among the highest in the world.

And yet South Africa, with the most prosperous economy in the region, is a magnet that draws a continuing stream of job seekers from Malawi, Mozambique and elsewhere. An estimated three million Zimbabweans have sought refuge in their neighbor to the south, many of them fleeing here in recent months as Zimbabwe's economy has utterly collapsed and political violence has intensified.

Mobs of South Africans shout: "Who are you? Where are you from?" as they maraud through the narrow streets they share with immigrants. They order people from their homes, steal their belongings and put padlocks on the houses.

Shops and businesses—many of them owned by Zimbabweans, Somalis and Pakistanis—have been looted. Many victims are legal residents with all the proper immigration documents. Some are being assaulted by neighbors they have known for years. However genuine the rage against immigrants, criminals have also made crafty use of the opportunity.

The police said they arrested more than 200 people over the weekend.

CONCLUSION

Dealing with diversity will never be easy. We will always by psychologically seduced by homogeneity, stability, commonality, and certainty. But defining and viewing diversity in terms of physical attributes that lend for our grouping into a set of boxes only undercut our ability to deal with our differences. This common approach to defining diversity promotes stereotyping by assuming that these boxes reflect and capture our differences, and that persons who are of a certain box look at the world similarly and thereby share a common set of beliefs, values, fears, norms, truths, expectations, and experiences. Of course, nothing could be further from the truth. As such, this popular approach to defining diversity actually limits diversity by downplaying the diversity and complexity found within peoples who are supposedly of a certain box. On the other hand, this approach downplays the commonality and similarity found between peoples of supposedly different boxes. As McPhail (1996) observed, our "belief in separatedness has . . . made us strangers, and has created a language of negative difference which manifests itself in the social and symbolic spaces of race, gender, and rhetoric" (p. 66). Moreover, as Mary Catherine Bateson explained, this approach underestimates "the possibility of getting along without completely sharing, and the self-organizing properties of human communication. We assume that patterning must come from the past, underestimating the way in which a group of strangers can learn not only to interact with harmony but also to generate new regularities, which come to be treasured" (1994, p. 176).

Defining diversity in terms of boxes also limits communication by producing the conditions that naturally lead to the banning and prosecuting of various discourses, words, symbols, images, and kinds of meanings. We are to believe that all persons of a certain persuasion (box) possess a common rationality, sensibility, modality, and spirituality and thereby will be equally offended or react similarly to various words, meanings, symbols, and discourses. Thus the rise of speech codes on U.S. college campuses. Now many persons are simply afraid of saying or writing anything that can be deemed offensive by a member of a certain persuasion (box). An aggrieved person merely has to proclaim, "This is offensive to . . . !" and the consequences can be profound for the accused. Yes, certain words, images, symbols, meanings, and discourses can cause many of us pain, distress, and even torment. There is also a lack of empathy that can be distressing. But limiting communication does nothing to end the sentiments, motives, and apathy that produce the offending discourses, images, words, meanings, and so forth. It merely creates a fragile and false civility. We are, out of fear of condemnation, retribution, and prosecution, pretending to be nice to each other and accepting of each other's differences. But eventually this tenuous arrangement collapses, and our illusion of progress becomes apparent to all. The lack of progress frustrates us. We are often disillusioned and convinced that achieving diversity is all but impossible. But such problems spring from the lack of communication rather than the nature of our differences. Achieving diversity requires all the communication human beings can muster. We should always be encouraging and promoting communication, always challenging ourselves and each other to be vulnerable to the humanity of others. Just as much as dolphins need water, human beings need communication.

To view diversity from an ecological perspective is to view diversity as a changing, evolving process that happens between human beings. We evolve our way out of our diversity problems. By promoting permeability, vulnerability, and equity, any problem between human beings, regardless of our differences, can be managed. These processes contain the possibility of harmony. However, these processes are really communication processes. In other words, promoting these vital ecological processes requires setting off or embodying a definition of communication that promotes empathy, compassion, mercy, and forgiveness. Without such a definition of communication, achieving diversity is impossible. Thus an ecological approach views diversity as an expression of communication. When communication flourishes, diversity flourishes.

CHAPTER 6

Intercultural Communication: Redefining Culture

INTRODUCTION

The language in popular intercultural communication discourses suggests that intercultural communication involves communication between peoples of different cultures. Such discourses often begin with defining what is culture and outlining different attributes of different cultures. Indeed, many definitions of culture are found in intercultural communication discourses.

- Culture embraces all the manifestations of social habits of a community, the reactions of the individual as affected by the habits of the group in which he lives, and the products of human activities as determined by these habits.
- Culture . . . refers to that part of the total setting [of human existence] which includes the material objects of human manufacture, techniques, social orientations, points of view, and sanctioned ends that are the immediate conditioning factors underlying behavior.
- Culture is essentially a construct that describes the total body of belief, behavior, knowledge, sanctions, values, and goals that mark the way of life of any people.
- Culture . . . consists in those patterns relative to behavior and the products of human action that may be

inherited, that is, passed on from generation to generation independent of the biological genes.

- Culture is the sum total of the ways of doing and thinking, past and present, of a social group. It is the sum of the traditions, or handed-down beliefs, and of customs, or handed-down procedures.
- The customs, traditions, attitudes, ideas, and symbols that govern social behavior show a wide variety. Each group, each society has a set of behavior patterns (overt and covert) that are more or less common to the members, which are passed down from generation to generation and taught to the children and that are constantly liable to change. These common patterns we call the culture . . .
- The culture of a society is the way of life of its members; the collection of ideas and habits that they learn, share, and transmit from generation to generation.
- Culture is . . . a set of ready-made definitions of the situation that each participant only slightly retailors in his own idiomatic way.
- A culture is the way of life of a people, whereas a society is the organized aggregate of individuals who follow a given way of life. In still simpler terms a society is composed of people; the way they behave is their culture.
- [Culture is] the material and social values of any group of people, whether savage or civilized (their institutions, customs, attitudes, behavior reactions).
- A culture consists of the acquired or cultivated behavior and thought of individuals within a society, as well as of the intellectual, artistic, and social ideals that the members of the society profess and to which they strive to conform.
- Culture is those habits that humans have because they have been learned from other humans.
- Culture consists of patterned and functionally interrelated customs common to specifiable human beings composing specifiable social groups or categories.

But there are a few problems that attend to popular definitions of culture. These definitions tend to create and reinforce the notion that commonality is what defines cultures, such as commonality of language, commonality of history and ancestry, commonality of ethnicity, commonality of values, beliefs, and truths, and commonality of traditions and customs. Presumably, diversity is found between cultures. There is no doubt commonality among peoples. But popular definitions of culture overplay this commonality and downplay the diversity, tension, and even conflict among peoples. Also, popular definitions tend to foster the impression that cultures are stable. But cultures are always moving, changing, and even rumbling. Sometimes, cultures are even on the brink of exploding. Finally, popular definitions of culture give the impression that human beings are passive products and subjects of culture. Presumably, cultures give us our identities. No doubt, many of our fears, values, beliefs, and truths do come from the peoples that surround us.

But many of our beliefs, values, and so forth also come from other places and influences. Natural disasters and changing ecological conditions often do push us to develop new values, new beliefs, new truths, and new ways of being. There is also the power of imagination and inspiration—or what many peoples refer to as the power of Eros. But most important, there is the power of ambiguity—the great unknown that comes with the world. Ambiguity pervades everything. However, by pervading everything, ambiguity disrupts everything. Yet without ambiguity, meaning would be impossible. Diversity would also be impossible. In fact, life would be impossible. Ambiguity allows for the creation of meaning. It makes interpretation possible. This is why all peoples eventually develop new fables, new traditions, new customs, narratives, and so forth. Ambiguity is also conspiring against the status quo. Just as much as human beings are products of cultures, just as much cultures are products of us.

Thus an emergent view in intercultural communication studies is challenging the commonly held view that cultures are stable and homogenous (Belay, 1993; Casmir, 1993; Dervin, 1991; Martin & Nakayama, 1999; McPhail, 1996; Rodriguez, 2003; Said, 2000; Shutter, 1993; Starosta, 1991). Again, the common criticism is that popular definitions of culture—by assuming that cultures are stable and homogeneous—mask the many points of conflict, dissent, and diversity that permeate all cultures and thereby also mask the full complexity that cultures possess and even create. Also, in exaggerating (really distorting) our perceptions of stability and homogeneity, such definitions force us to adopt dichotomous stances that stop us from "moving toward multiple perspectives that might inform each other in a dialogue of differences" (Dervin, 1991, p. 50). As Edward Said (2001) noted, "There isn't a single Islam: there are Islams, just as there are Americas. This diversity is true of all traditions, religions or nations even though some of their adherents have futilely tried to draw boundaries around themselves and pin their creeds down neatly."

We are now articulating new understandings of culture that highlight the complexity, diversity, and discontinuity found in all cultures. These new understandings tend to look at culture in terms of processes rather than attributes. The focus is movements, rhythms, and tensions. Cultures are always in flux. Movement is status quo. In other words, new understandings are viewing cultures in terms of verbs rather than nouns. We push forward this emergent verb trend by viewing human beings as *culturing* beings. We define culturing as our proclivity to construct new and different meanings, understandings, and practices to reckon with the world's ambiguity and ever-changing nature that constantly subvert current meanings, understandings, and practices. We are always constructing new and different ways of being and understanding the world, which is to say that cultures are always reckoning with change. This is why cultures are always in flux. Culturing is born of our uniquely human need to bring meaning to bear on the world's ambiguity. It represents the various tensions and rhythms that come with our trying to find and hold onto meanings in a world that is constantly changing and moving and thereby will never lend for *one* meaning, *one* interpretation, *one* truth, *one* vision.

Culturing begins on the premise that cultures are always negotiating the interplay between ambiguity and meaning, chaos and order, homogeneity and diversity, equilibrium and disequilibrium, agency and structure, and other such seemingly contradictory tensions. In this way, cultures are always experiencing tensions, stresses, and conflicts. Culturing allows us to look anew at what being human means and expands our understanding of moral action by locating our humanity within a potentially moral world. It answers the call for "a way to acknowledge and accept those aspects of dialectical inquiry that contribute to self-reflection and the appreciation of Otherness, and at the same time cultivate an awareness of those aspects that perpetuate symbolic violence" (McPhail, 1996, p. 150). It also gives us a theoretical and political way "to step back from the imaginary thresholds that separate people from each other" by releasing us from the dichotomous labels and positionalities that come with such thresholds (Said, 2001).

THE RELATION BETWEEN AMBIGUITY AND MEANING

In being ecological, all cultures have points of homogeneity and diversity, continuity and discontinuity, order and chaos, center and periphery, rigidity and flexibility, volatility and stability, agency and structure (Bohm, 1980; Capra, 1983; Gribbin, 1984; Herbert, 1987; Jantsch, 1980). However, being ecological in nature also means that cultures can only survive and flourish by promoting the forces and practices that make for change and evolution. Integral to the promotion of such change and evolution is the nurturing of ambiguity (Bohm, 1980; Prigogine & Stengers, 1984).

Meaning and ambiguity share an inseparable relationship (Janstch, 1980; Prigogine & Stengers, 1984). A world devoid of ambiguity is one devoid of meaning. Each defines the other by providing for the existence of each other. So there is always meaning in ambiguity and ambiguity in meaning. No meaning is ever completely stable, ever beyond the reach of a new and different interpretation. Yet there is much that is valuable about this inseparable relation between ambiguity and meaning. Ambiguity challenges us to look at the world anew. It expands our humanity by forcing us to develop new meanings, new ways of experiencing and being in the world. In this way, ambiguity fosters diversity and evolution. It is a life catalyst or, according to Mary Catherine Bateson (1994), "the warp of life." Systems that focus deterministically on eliminating ambiguity allow for no growth, no evolution, and ironically, no order (Bohm, 1980). Ambiguity makes for open and vibrant systems—the only systems that change, evolve, and strive.

Ambiguity makes for new experiences, new understandings, new ways of being, and new kinds of relations with each other by keeping meaning open and fluid. Regardless of our most strenuous efforts, no meaning is ever absolute, ever devoid of ambiguity, ever devoid of the possibility of a different interpretation. The ambiguity of the world keeps meaning in a constant state of flux and openness (Bateson, 1994). There is always the occasion for a new and different interpretation. Meaning is always multivocal and incomplete (Bohm, 1980; Lee, Wang, Chung, & Hertel, 1995). In this way, ambiguity poses a constant threat to the status quo. It pushes us to look at the world anew. Ultimately, ambiguity makes our worlds and cultures permeable by promoting the evolution of new ways of being and understanding the world. When ambiguity flourishes, life evolves through the constant evolution of new and different meanings. Abdulkarim Soroush, who is seen by many scholars as Iran's boldest scholar, and who faces constant persecution from Iran's religious autocracy for offering a fundamentally different vision of Islam, makes this point well:

> The essence of religion will always be sacred, but its interpretation by fallible human beings is not sacred—and therefore can be criticized, modified, refined, and redefined. What single person can say what God meant? Any fixed version would effectively smother religion. It would block the rich exploration of the sacred readings. (quoted in Wright, 1999, pp. 46–47)

Indeed, all ecologies have points of disequilibrium that constantly disrupt the status quo. These points reflect different interpretations, meanings, and truths that make for conflict and dissent. Forests fires resulting from natural forces represent points of disequilibrium. Yet such fires are vital for the well-being of forests by allowing for the burning of underbrush and old trees that encumber forests' ecosystems from evolving and flourishing. Points of disequilibrium perform a vital life-affirming function by blocking natural systems from becoming completely homogeneous, that is, from becoming beholden to one understanding of the world. Moreover, such points undercut the reifying and deifying of certain ways of being and, in so doing, act as catalysts for evolution and transformation. Conversely, through the suppression of such points, cultures lose the ability to respond flexibly and creatively to new situations.

So all cultures possess a striving to evolve and through such evolution find prosperity. But such evolution is dependent on cultures promoting the rich interplay between meaning and ambiguity. This involves cultures promoting understandings of communication that stress interpretation rather than transmission. As McPhail observed (1996), "Communication, as it has been practiced and continues to be practiced in Western culture, is geared towards social control and the maintenance of existing ideological and epistemological structures" (p. 138). Such an understanding of communication pervades mainstream intercultural communication discourses (Martin & Nakayama, 1999; McPhail, 1996). We tend to view communication as a medium phenomenon—communication conveys and articulates culture. Communication emerges as a representational phenomenon, a way of representing and reflecting our worlds. In persisting in looking at communication in terms of transmission, such an understanding perpetuates the view that cultures lend for methods that strive to make neat and tidy claims that allow us to distinguish cultures.

Viewing communication as transmission also assumes that human beings are passive to the world. We are supposedly molded by our different cultures, and as a result, cultural patterns can supposedly predict behavior (Martin & Nakayama, 1999). Accordingly, exaggerated notions of stability and homogeneity permeate many popular definitions of culture (Dervin, 1991; Martin & Nakayama, 1999; Moon, 1996). Deetz (1995) contends that viewing communication as transmission misses the politics of self-construction. It depoliticizes communication by masking issues of identity formation and blocking scrutiny of the deep ideological structures that constrict meaning creation processes. For Deetz (1995), "Communication is about dialogic, collaborative constructions of self, other, and world in the process of making collective decisions. This includes the production and reproduction of personal identities, social knowledge, and social structures" (p. 107). Communication places and displaces us. It simultaneously gives us an understanding of the world while simultaneously undercutting that understanding of the world. For instance, we never mirror our experiences or our thoughts. Each retelling creates new experiences, new meanings, new understandings, and often, even new truths. In this way, communication enables us by affording us constant access to new experiences, new meanings, new understandings (Arthos, 2000; Gordon, 2000).

A quantum world needs understandings of communication that can speak to its quantum proclivity. Such understandings can be found in emergent definitions of communication that assume no separation between communication and the world (e.g., Bohm, 1980; Thayer, 1995). Such definitions stress a consequential rather than referential understanding of communication (Thayer, 1995). That is, emergent definitions of communication hold to the quantum notion that we and the world are embedded within each other. Communication situates us in the world rather than is the means to represent the world. As Thayer (1995) noted, "In naming the world, we name ourselves; in explaining the world, we explain ourselves; in defining the world, we define ourselves" (p. 9). Through communication we construct as well as embody our worlds. However, such constructing and embodying is by no means arbitrary. Some communication practices are more humane than others. Those practices that embrace ambiguity pull us toward the center of the world and put us in harmony with the world's ever-changing rhythms. Meaning remains open and fluid, allowing us to also remain open and fluid. On the other hand, many practices threaten the rich interplay between ambiguity and meaning.

Arguably, one of the most serious and insidious is that of ***reification.*** Reification is when processes become structures. It is about the loss of flexibility, fluidity, and spontaneity. Reification can be seen in rituals, customs, and practices that allow for no innovation or disruption. As such, reification limits agency by limiting ambiguity. It seduces us by limiting the anxiety that comes with ambiguity. In limiting agency, however, reification limits our obligation to each other. It promotes separation and fragmentation. Reification also encumbers the evolution of new and different ways of being and understanding the world by promoting rigidity rather than flexibility. It does so by turning us away from the world's ambiguity. We thereby lose the courage to fully embrace the ambiguity that is vital for new thoughts, ideas, experiences, understandings, and meanings to enter the world. In this way, reification also undercuts diversity and plurality. Finally, reification blocks the formation of the deep and complex human relations that flow from vibrant meaning creation and interpretive processes. In *Developing Through Relationships,* Alan Fogel (1993) wrote about how reification harms the evolution of such relations:

> When relationships evolve into patterns in which participants perceive them as sequences of discrete exchanges or reward and cost it is quite likely that the creativity has gone out of them. They are no longer dynamic systems in which individuals grow, they have become prisons of the soul. Repeated encounters, therefore, can sometimes dull the senses and produce hatred, anger, and boredom. It is not mere repetition that leads to creative elaboration, it is one's stance toward the other, one's openness to change and desire to create new meaning through the relationship. (p. 90)

Fogel also believes that "relationships must have . . . something that may never be understood or even articulated, something that entices the mind and body and that renews the meaning in the relationship" (p. 90). Cultures also need this mystery that only ambiguity promotes. Diversity evolves from this mystery. Thus the end of mystery is always a sign of diversity being in peril.

Cultivating and nurturing ambiguity demand a certain kind of communication sensibility. Such a sensibility assumes that our becoming is intertwined with that of the world. Practices that harm our becoming also harm the becoming of the world. As such, this kind of communication sensibility encourages us to be open, sensitive, and tolerant of new ways of understanding and experiencing the world (Czubaroff & Friedman, 2000; Pearce & Littlejohn, 1997; Rodriguez, 2006).

SPANGLISH AS CULTURING

We are increasingly bending and stretching identity in ways that are unparalleled in human history. "Movement is [indeed] status quo," and the movement that Ed Morales (2002) is referring to in *Living in Spanglish: The Search for Latino*

Identity in America is what many Latinos throughout the United States are fondly calling Spanglish. "At the root of Spanglish is a very universal state of being. It is a displacement from one place, home, to another place, home, in which one feels at home in both places, yet at home in neither place. It is a kind of banging-one's-head-against-the-wall state, and the only choice you have left is to embrace the transitory (read transnational) state of in-between" (Morales, 2002, p. 7).

Spanglish is a "forward-looking race that obliterates all races" by embracing all races. In other words, it is "a call to end race" as we commonly understand race. "But in order to face down race, we must first immerse ourselves in it. In all of them" (Morales, 2002, p. 14). Moreover, Spanglish is "a space where multiple levels of identification is possible" (Morales, 2002, p. 17), akin, Morales believes, to what Michel Foucault calls a heterotopic space—a kind of effectively enacted utopia in which all the other real sites that can be found within the culture are simultaneously represented, contested, and inverted" (quoted in Morales, 2002, p. 17). Spanglish is also akin to what Pico Iyer (2000) described in *The Global Soul: Jet Lag, Shopping Malls, and the Search for Home* as the global soul—a person who "has grown up in many cultures all at once—and so lived in the cracks between them" (p. 18).

Spanglish is about the evolution of an identity that is finally disconnected from one race, one place, one space, one language, one vision, one history. "There is no prescribed form, no cultural norms involved in being Spanglish—the world of Spanglish is the world of the multiracial individual" (Morales, 2002, p. 9). It is the culture of the future. Moreover, Spanglish is the triumph of heterogeneity, multi-subjectivity, and multiplicity and celebrates a "permanently evolving, and rapidly expanding difference" (Morales, 2002, p. 26). In this way, Spanglish is about the end of culture as a noun. It is about culturing. In other words, Spanglish demonstrates that no culture, no race, no ethnicity, no language, is inherently stable and homogenous.

In disconnecting identity from space, Spanglish finally allows us to imagine a world devoid of such conflict and strife. Also, in releasing identity from space, Spanglish allows us to imagine more expansive and inclusive models of identity and, thereby, more expansive and inclusive models of space. As such, releasing identity from geography in no way weakens identity. Identity, as with any other ecology, must also change and evolve to survive and prosper, and such change is only possible when our models of identity remain fluid and permeable. This is what Spanglish is about. Spanglish represents the fullest expression of identity in terms of social evolution.

Spanglish is also increasingly making us global souls. It frees us from the rigid confines of one race, one ethnicity, one language, one geography, one people, one culture, one history, one reality, one worldview, one god. Such confines only serve to distort and limit what we can become. The evolution of Spanglish also signals that increasing numbers of us are refusing to be confined to one race, one ethnicity, one culture, one geography, and no one probably understood this better than Eddie Figueroa, a New York conceptual artist, who Ed Morales discussed in *Living in Spanglish.*

Morales wrote that Figueroa was thoroughly obsessed with Latinos being a "multicultural people and that there was no space for us in the conventional world, and we had to invent an imaginary space to allow us to gel" (p. 90). He believed this imaginary space could be found in the concept of the Puerto Rican Embassy, which evolved later into the Spirit Republic of Greater Puerto Rico. For Figueroa, "The Puerto Rican Embassy is a concept, it's an idea, it's not a physical location . . . We are dealing with concepts that are beyond geography, beyond three dimensions. With the Puerto Rican Embassy, we're declaring our independence. The spirit republic is a free place. To win this fight we don't need weapons, this is the weapon that's going to win [points to heart]. The revolution is here, man" (quoted in Morales, 2002, p. 91). Morales (2002) claims Figueroa made "it a little easier for Puerto Ricans to be several people at once, in several places, looking backward from the future into the past . . . It is an idea that is no longer as bizarre as it seemed" (p. 92).

Pico Iyer (2000) wonders about whether there is a migratory striving that is making us global souls. He quoted Simone Weil ("We must take the feeling of being at home into exile. We must be rooted in the absence of place."), Thomas Paine ("My country is the world, and my religion is to do good."), and Ralph Waldo Emerson ("What is man but a congress of nations?"). He seems uncertain as to what to make exactly of this global soul phenomenon. On one hand, Iyer (2000) believes that "our shrinking world gave more and more of us the chance to see, in palpable, unanswerable ways, how much we [have] in common, and how much we could live . . . beyond petty allegiances and labels, out-side the reach of nation-states" (p. 17). He also writes, "I have grown up, too, with a keen sense of the blessings of being unaffiliated, it has meant that almost everywhere is new and strange to me (as I am new and strange to it), and nearly everywhere allows me to keep alive a sense of wonder and detachment" (Iyer, 2000, p. 24). On the other hand, Iyer (2000) fears that "a lack of affiliation may mean a lack of accountability, and forming a sense of commitment can be hard without a sense of community" (p. 25). Moreover, "Displacement can encourage the wrong kinds of distance, and if the nationalism we see sparking up around the globe arises from too narrow and fixed sense of loyalty, the internationalism that's coming to birth may reflect too roaming and undefined sense of belonging" (Iyer, 2000, p. 25). Further, "the Global Soul may see so many sides of every question that he never settles on a firm conviction; he may grow so used to giving back a different self according to his environment that he loses sight of who he is when nobody's around" (Iyer, 2000, p. 25). Yet Iyer (2000) used the phrase *global soul,* never global citizen, global people, nor even global being. But the reality is that increasing numbers of persons are living between home and exile and struggling to escape the confines of one race, one gender, one sexuality, one nationality, one ethnicity, one geography. As the half-English, half-Japanese, Malaysian man says to Iyer, "One country is not enough." Others would add, "One race is not enough." "One ethnicity is not enough." "One culture is not enough." "One cosmology is not enough." "One religion is not enough." "One language is not enough." "One sexuality is not enough." The fact is, as Richard Rodriguez observed, borders are collapsing. "Our borders do not hold. National borders do not hold. Ethnic borders. Religious borders. Aesthetics borders, certainly. Sexual borders. Allergenic borders. We live in the 'Age of diversity,' in a city of diversity—I do, anyway—so we see what we do not necessarily choose to see: People listing according to internal weathers. We hear what we do not want to hear: Confessions we refuse to absolve" (2000, p. 213).

Iyer wonders whether human beings have a migratory impulse. We have, after all, always been moving from place to place. But this movement is in no way purely migratory. It also exceeds the fact that increasing numbers of persons have multiple passports, live in airports, and travel all over the planet like nomads. The global soul, as seen in Spanglish, represents the highest evolutionary point so far in human history. Unfortunately, many critics are yet to understand this reality. Nobel Laureate Octavio Paz describes Spanglish as an abomination ("Ni es bueno ni es malo, sino abominable.") (quoted in Stavans, 2000a, p. 555). Moreover, besides finding Spanglish offensive, Roberto González Echevarría (1997), Sterling Professor of Hispanic and Comparative Literature at Yale University, believes that "it is naïve to think that we [U.S. Latinos] could create a new language that would be functional and culturally rich" as Spanish. He believes that Spanglish "poses a grave danger to Hispanic culture and to the advancement of Hispanics in mainstream America" (Gonzalez Echevarría, 1997, p. A.29). "Spanglish is an invasion of Spanish by English" (Gonzalez Echevarría, 1997, p. A.29). Gonzalez Echevarría (1997) also believes "that people should learn languages well and that learning English should be the priority for Hispanics, if they aspire, as they should, to influential positions" (p. A.29). Those who practice Spanglish "are doomed to writing not a minority literature but a minor literature." Indeed, Gonzalez Echevarría believes that "Spanish is our strongest bond, and it is vital that we preserve it" (p. A.29). Likewise, Antonio Garrido, director of the Instituto Cervantes in New York, an organization created by the Spanish government to promote Spanish and Hispanic-American culture, believes that Latinos should strive for good English and good Spanish so as "to have a future" in the United States. "Spanglish has no future" (quoted in Kong, 2003). For Claudio Véliz (1994):

> There is irony in the choice of this ghastly but accurate descriptive name for what passes for Spanish in many … regions. "Spanglish" is, pseudonationalistic protestations notwithstanding, an unseemly, scarcely literate linguistic hodge-podge that would not be tolerated in any country within hearing distance of the Real Academia. The irony is that the admixture of extraneous bits of flotsam, the adulteration of spelling and syntaxes, and the virtual abandonment of all gram-

matical decorum are only possible because this patois found shelter in the ambit of the Gothic fox. Every time they open their mouths, the users of "Spanglish" proclaim urbi et orbi that they have embraced the "mental habits," the cultural dispositions, and the customs of the English-speaking host nation with enthusiasm, and to prove it, they present their listeners with the tattered, pitiful remains of the language they inherited from Nebrija. (p. 125)

However, in defense of Spanglish, Illan Stavans (2000b) recounted that Yiddish was never a unified tongue, but rather a series of regional varieties drawn from Hebrew, German, Russian, and other Slavic languages. In fact, such was the contempt for Yiddish that rabbis and the Jewish intelligentsia saw Yiddish as unworthy of biblical dialogue. In 1978, however, the Yiddish author Isaac Bashevis Singer was awarded the Nobel Prize in Literature.

Evidently, Spanglish's critics view Spanglish as a dirty dialect that threatens to pollute Spanish and English. Spanglish emerges as a debased language form—a product of backward and primitive peoples. This is why critics like Gonzalez Echevarría (1997), of Yale University, have no qualms about harping on social class issues. "The sad reality is that Spanglish is primarily the language of poor Hispanics, many barely literate in either language. They incorporate English words and constructions into their daily speech because they lack the vocabulary and education in Spanish to adapt to the changing culture around them" (p. A.29). He also fears Spanglish "creating a Babel of hybrid tongues" (p. A.29). But the story of Babel has nothing to do with language diversity. Language is merely a dimension of communication. It is by no means the sum of communication or even the primary constitution of communication. In other words, communication is possible without language. The hallmark of communication is compassion rather than language. Without compassion, our capacity to genuinely understand each other is impossible. Thus the story of Babel is really about the problems that come with the lack of compassion.

But when was any language ever pure? Linguistic purity, as even Gonzalez Echevarría (1997) acknowledges, is an illusion. All languages are promiscuous— a promiscuity that reflects us constantly bending and twisting and recreating language to speak to new and different experiences and influences. This is why any language can be so different from one place to the next. Linguistic hybridity speaks to the ever evolving and changing nature of language to be inclusive rather than exclusive. As long as human beings use language, linguistic hybridity will be the order of language. To attempt to keep any language pure is simply to promote the demise of that language. But more than that, language purity is really about clinging to racial purity and ideological stability. It is about the promotion of exclusion and preservation of the status quo. We can always settle for bilingualism. But bilingualism is merely about access to different spaces. Spanglish takes us much further. It represents the mutual joining and sharing of spaces and places. As Morales (2002) noted, "The mixing of language that occurs in Spanglish is a metaphor for the mixture of race; it allows for races to have different voices in the same language, eliminating the need to structure language, or thinking in terms of racial category" (p. 48).

Spanglish shows us linguistically and communicatively forging of the means to find harmony in this ever-changing world. This is why Spanglish is emerging and blossoming in the most heterogeneous spaces and places in the world, like New York and Los Angeles. Exclusion is an option only for those persons who are economically privileged. But exclusion is also death. Inclusion is the order of every ecology. It represents interconnectedness and embeddedness. It also represents the end of isolation and rejection. Spanglish is about the rise of inclusion in a world where exclusion is increasingly status quo. Spanglish reminds us that inclusion has always been the order of the world. We have always been connected and interconnected. Buddhists, Hindus, and Jains have been teaching this reality for hundreds of years. Our quest for exclusion, either racially, linguistically, ethnically, or spatially, is illusory. We will always be interconnected.

No doubt, the United States is browning, and this change will significantly affect U.S. society. But to reduce this browning to a racial phenomenon is to downplay what this browning really means for the United States. Brown is the color of creation. The rise of brown is evolutionary. It represents the end of old biases, prejudices, and suspicions. Besides racially, as seen in President Barack Obama, the United States is also browning culturally and ideologically. Spanglish captures this browning.

CULTURING NEW WORLDS

Understandably, intercultural communication theory has a deep tradition against claims of different cultures being morally superior to others. Much good has come from upholding this tradition. But emergent observations of the world are forcing us to reckon with the claim that we have no framework on which to make moral claims about different cultures. To look at cultures from a quantum standpoint allows us to move beyond the horrors that attend to cultural hegemony while simultaneously allowing us to make moral claims about different cultures. We accomplish this feat in the most interesting of ways.

Adopting a culturing standpoint reveals how the constant evolving and changing nature of cultures constantly undermines efforts to establish and sustain one truth, one meaning, one interpretation. Culturing highlights the quantum tensions and contradictions that are found in all cultures. The political, moral, and existential struggles, and the many contests over meanings, interpretations, and symbols, also become visible. We ultimately come to understand that claims of cultural uniformity and stability will always be illusory. There will always be spaces where hope resides.

Culturing reframes our understanding of cultures in a way that neither undermines hope nor the possibility of us forging new ways of being together with others who seem to be so culturally different and alien to us, even to the point of being seen as less human than us. Hope resides in the points of disruption, disequilibrium, and dissent that constantly destabilize the status quo. Hope also resides in the quantum tugging found in all organic systems. No culture can escape the quantum order of the world. Cultures that focus on ending ambiguity and diversity will eventually devolve. The quantum order of the world will tolerate only so much variability. In this way, though never certain, there is always the possibility for constructive and nonviolent ways of being together to emerge and make for new realities. Thus "for future generations to condemn themselves to prolonged war and suffering without so much as a critical pause, without looking at interdependent histories of injustice and oppression, without trying for common emancipation and mutual understanding seems far more willful than necessary" (Said, 2001).

CULTURES AS NARRATIVES

Increasingly, intercultural communication studies are turning to narrative theory to better understand our diversity, complexity, and potentiality (Cooper, Calloway-Thomas, & Simonds, 2007; Rodriguez, 2002). As A. G. Mojtabai once famously wrote, "We are all authors. Adding here, deleting here, we people the world with our needs: with friends, lovers, ciphers, enemies, villains—and heroes." In this authoring, as Jim Corder (1994) explained, we accumulate "what we know as evidence and insight, ignoring what does not look like evidence and insight to us, finding some pieces of life that become life for us, failing to find to find others, or choosing not to look, each of us creates the narrative that he or she is" (p. 413). Also,

> We tell our lives and live our tales, enjoying where we can, tolerating what we must, turning away to re-tell, or sinking into madness and disorder if we cannot make (or re-make) our tale into a narrative we can live in. Each of us forms conceptions of the world, its institutions, its public, private, wide, or local histories, and each of us is the narrative that shows our living in and through the conceptions that are always being formed as the tales of our lives take shape (p. 413).

In the authoring of our narratives, what is true and what is make-believe vanish into each other. In other words, there is no objective and subjective, no fiction and nonfiction. As Corder explained, "None of us lives without a history, each of us is a narrative. We're always standing some place in our lives, and there is always a tale of how we came to stand there, though few of us have marked carefully the dimensions of the place where we are or kept time with the tale of how we came to be there" (p. 413).

That each of us is a narrative means that intercultural communication is really about us engaging and negotiating each other's narrative. Many times, as Corder explained, "Our narratives can be congruent with other narratives, or untouched by other narratives. But sometimes another narrative impinges upon ours, or thunders around and down into our narratives. We can't build this other into our narratives without harm to the tales we have been telling. This other is a narrative in another world; it is disruptive, shocking, initially at least incomprehensible, and, as Carl Rogers has shown us, threatening" (p. 415). Currently, for most persons in the United States, this "shocking" and "threatening" narrative is Islam. But negotiating any narrative that seems contrary to our narrative or seems to threaten the integrity of our own narrative is always difficult. "Sometimes we turn away from other narratives. Sometimes we teach ourselves not to know that there are other narratives . . . Sometimes we go to war. Sometimes we sink into madness, totally unable to manage what our wit or judgment has shown us—a contending narrative that has force to it and charm and appeal and perhaps justice and beauty as well, a narrative compelling us to attention and toward belief that we cannot ultimately give, a contending narrative that shakes and cracks all foundations and promises to alter our identity, a narrative that would educate us to be wholly other than what we are" (p. 416). Thus, "we cannot without potential harm shift from the past and present of one narrative into the future of another, or from the future we are narrating into a past that is not readily ours . . . How can we expect another to change when we are ourselves that other's contending [and threatening] narrative?" (p. 416).

From the standpoint of narrative theory, what most of us view as cultures are really *narrative communities,* and intercultural communication is communication between peoples of different narrative communities. Specifically, intercultural communication is about peoples of different narrative communities embodying and sharing different narratives, contesting and challenging each other's narratives, and collectively creating and weaving new narratives. Our diversity resides in our different narratives and how peoples enact these narratives. Narratives are always plural. We are always of different narrative communities, and as such, our narratives are always converging and diverging. Our families, friends, neighbors, fellow book club members, teammates, fellow church members, classmates, and work colleagues are all different narrative communities. Thus our narratives are never stable. We are always being exposed to new narratives and exposing others to new narratives. Indeed, every new relationship brings a reservoir of new narratives. As such, our narratives are always changing, and as our narratives change, so do our identities and positionalities. From the standpoint of narrative theory, the challenge of intercultural communication is to appreciate our natural proclivity for narrative diversity, to facilitate the sharing and enacting of different narratives, and to promote the co-creation of new narratives.

The primary premise in narrative theory is that human beings are storytelling beings. We experience, organize, and make sense of the world in storytelling. For

Richardson (1990), "Narrative displays the goals and intentions of human actors; it makes individuals, cultures, societies, and historical epochs comprehensible as wholes; it humanizes time; it allows us to contemplate the effects of our actions, and to alter the directions of our lives" (p. 117). As Barbara Hardy noted, "We dream in narrative, daydream in narrative, remember, anticipate, hope, despair, believe, doubt, plan, revise, criticize, construct, gossip, learn, hate, and love by narrative" (quoted in Mink, 1970, p. 557). Bruner (1996) wrote, "Narrativized realities, I suspect are too ubiquitous, their construction too habitual or automatic to be accessible to easy inspection. We live in a sea of stories and like the fish who (according to the proverb) will be the last to discover water, we have our own difficulties grasping what it is like to swim in stories" (p. 147).

We find in most understandings of narratives the assumption that we construct and portray our understanding of self through our narratives (Atkinson, 1998; Czarniawska, 1997; McAdams, 1988, 1993; Riesman, 1993). Rodriguez claims that looking at narrative from the standpoint of *being in the world* challenges us to consider new questions. In addition to knowing how different narratives shape and constitute us, we also need to know how different discursive, communicative, and performative practices recursively promote or undercut the evolution of different narratives; how different narratives are resisted, contested, and co-opted; and how different narratives bear on the human condition and the condition of the world. That is, how compellingly do different narratives speak to the human condition and the condition of the world? That is, does the narrative give us new and different vistas of our potentiality and that of the world? Does the narrative give us new possibilities, that is, new and different ways of understanding and experiencing the world? Most important, what are the implications and consequences of different narratives on our humanity and the condition of the world?

Compelling narratives push us to act on the world. They challenge us to understand and reckon with the implications and consequences of our actions and lack thereof. Moreover, compelling narratives encourage us to risk life—to strive to understand and experience the world differently. Such narratives assume that no understanding of the world can be achieved outside of being. Compelling narratives push us to look holistically at the world by urging us to make connections and identify complex and nonlinear relationships. They also force us to understand how our ways of being bear on the condition of the world. In this way, compelling narratives end the divide between theory and politics.

Narrative as a way of being in the world assumes no separation between the world and us. We are as much in the world as the world is within us. Compelling narratives assume that we have no power to control and predict the rhythms and movements of the world. Such narratives also assume no distrust and suspicion of the world. There is no inherent conflict between the world and us that requires us to marshal our efforts and skills to supposedly order and control the malevolent forces of the world. Compelling narratives help us understand the beauty and harmony that come with the potentiality of the world. In this way, such narratives lessen the threat of our differences. Compelling narratives speak to the commonality and universality of being human. Such narratives draw us together by revealing our common humanness and humanity. Yet, on the other hand, such narratives foster the fullest articulation of the diversity that abounds in the human condition. Compelling narratives highlight both our commonality and diversity.

Compelling narratives are intensely interpretative. No narrative is ever transmitted. We are narrative beings because we are also interpretive, communicative, and performative beings. We change the world by merely being in the world. It is, however, through interpretation that narratives find life and prosperity. Interpretation makes for new and different meanings, experiences, and understandings. It allows different narratives to belong organically to different moments and spaces. The legitimacy of different narratives is derived through interpretation and negotiation. The interpretive nature of narrative pushes us to reckon with different interpretations and understandings of the world. That is, all narratives have tensions of order and chaos, stability and instability, continuity and discontinuity, meaning and ambiguity, and so forth. Compelling narratives celebrate the quantum rhythms that come from the rich interplay between and among these tensions. As such, no interpretation or meaning is ever complete. There is always a new and different interpretation. Instead of trying to preserve one meaning or interpretation, compelling narratives promote the evolution of many interpretations and meanings.

No compelling narrative legitimizes each and every meaning. Compelling narratives strive to promote only those interpretations that affirm life. On the other hand, there is no need for us to be afraid of new and different interpretations and meanings. Narratives that block the evolution of new interpretations and meanings will always be resisted and contested as evolution is the mission of every ecology. Moreover, no narrative can belong to only us or remain off limits to new interpretations. Such a narrative is a closed system, and from an ecological standpoint, such systems will always perish. Narratives prosper and flourish by being open to interpretation.

THE PROMISE OF GLOBALIZATION

There is a popular view in many circles that globalization is the solution to ending conflicts and wars between peoples of different cultures. Thomas Freidman, Pulitzer Prize–winning columnist for *The New York Times,* is arguably the most ardent proponent of this view. In *The Lexus and the Olive Tree: Understanding Globalization,* Freidman (1999) explains that "The driving idea behind globalization is free-market capitalism—the more you let market forces rule and the more you open your economy to free trade and competition, the more efficient and flourishing your economy will be. Globalization means the spread of free-market capitalism to virtually every corner in the world. Globalization also has its own set of economic rules—rules that revolve around opening, deregulating and privatizing your economy" (p. 8).

Freidman believes that globalization will bring forth the prosperity and resources that will turn us away from the feuds and tensions that presumably have origins in material deprivation. He offers "The Golden Arches Theory of Conflict Prevention"—which stipulates that when a country reaches the level of economic development where it has a middle class big enough to support a McDonald's network, it becomes a McDonald's country—"and people in McDonald countries prefer to wait in line than fight wars" (p. 196). According to Freidman, "today's globalization system significantly raises the costs of countries using war as a means to pursue honor, react to fears or advance their interests" (p. 197).

> The Golden Arches Theory highlights one way in which globalization affects geopolitics—by greatly raising the cost of warfare through economic integration. But globalization influences geopolitics in many other ways. For instance, it creates new sources of power, beyond the classic military measures of tanks, planes and missiles, and it creates new sources of pressure on countries to change how they organize themselves, pressures that come from classic military incursions of one state into another, but rather by more invisible invasions of Supermarkets and Super-empowered individuals. (p. 204)

Freidman also believes that globalization will bring order and civility to places that are corrupt and lawless as all participants in a global economy are bound by a common set of rules and regulations. Finally, globalization will foster a common set of values among different peoples that will mitigate against violent conflict and war. One such value is openness, which is necessary for markets to function. Without openness and transparency, the global economy collapses, and both buyers and producers suffer. So both buyers and producers have a vested interest in promoting open and transparent business practices. Freidman believes that this cultivation of open and transparent business practices will eventually make for open and transparent government practices.

But history strains any thesis about the promise of globalization as defined by Friedman. The 20th century, which is arguably the most violent ever, was all about the wars that occurred among the most prosperous nations in the world. Besides the material prosperity, all these nations had highly sophisticated educational systems. Moreover, these nations, most of whom currently have vast stockpiles of nuclear weapons, continue to pose the most risk to the world. In short, history lends no support to any relationship between material prosperity and harmony. In fact, many emerging nations are using the new spoils of globalization to buy larger and better weapons. Underlying Friedman's thesis is the belief that discord springs from deprivation. But this reduces all conflicts between different peoples to a psychological formulation and, accordingly, downplays the cultural, political, epistemological, and communication forces that help to construct these conflicts. It underestimates the complexity that comes with the human experience. We are by no means merely psychological beings who are mechanically driven by desires to end various material deprivations. Being human comes with enormous complexity. We are biological, emotional, cultural, relational, historical, sexual, spiritual, and sensual beings. How different human beings define, experience, and relate to deprivation is enormously complex.

That human behavior is enormously complex means that the reasons why people start violent conflicts are also complex, and the solutions no less so. But deprivation is by no means the only thing that concerns Friedman. He views culture and religion as obstacles to harmony and progress. He believes that globalization can loosen the grip these forces have on various peoples, especially indigenous and non-Western peoples. Globalization will make us rational, and through this rationality, prosperity and democracy will come forth. However, what of the supposed rationality that the most prosperous nations now supposedly possess? Is the stockpiling of nuclear weapons rational? Is our destruction of the planet rational? For Friedman, globalization will bring forth a secular and rational world, implying that our prosperity depends on us freeing ourselves from the vestiges of religion and culture, or at least marginalizing these forces.

But rationality will always be bound up with culture. It always reflects a vision of the world. On the other hand, nothing is wrong with religion and culture. Many of our great virtues come from the world's great religions, and cultures give us different visions of the world. In other words, there is nothing fundamentally wrong with the diversity that comes with our many different religions and cultures. Yet Friedman wants to lessen this diversity through globalization. He is suspicious of our dissimilarity. He believes that similarity is better, implying that prosperity and democracy ultimately depend on less diversity. There is nothing extraordinary about this view. Our dominant worldview in the Western world favors similarity. But what seems to have proponents of globalization most excited is the achievement of global similarity without a shot being fired or any system being imperialistically imposed on us. Presumably, globalization captures our natural yearnings for prosperity and democracy. It supposedly undermines the institutions and arrangements that deny the flourishing of such yearnings. Globalization is seen in terms of social evolution. It constitutes, as Francis Fukuyama famously claimed, the end of history—the highest moment in our evolution. Presumably, no other system will come after globalization. Within globalization resides the solution to all the problems that have long plagued us as a species. Globalization will finally bring peace, prosperity, and democracy to all peoples.

But such prospects show no signs of being on the horizon. In *World on Fire: How Exporting Free Markets Breeds Ethnic Hatred and Global Instability*, Amy Chua (2003) claims that globalization is only fueling strife and disintegration. She argues that, "far from making the world a better and safer place, democracy and capitalism—or at least in the raw, unrestrained form in which they are currently being exported—are intensifying ethnic resentment and global violence, with potentially catastrophic results." On the other hand, Philip Jenkins (2002), author of *The Next Christendom: The Coming of Global Christianity,* believes that "globalization creates the means, motive, and opportunity by which the deadliest enemies of the West can sustain an enduring campaign of the kind of violence we witnessed [on September 11]. Is there a better example of globalization and interdependence than the Al Qaeda network, which on every continent pursues its struggle against the continuation of human civilization? Globalization, it now appears, is a self-limiting and self-defeating process" (p. 17). Indeed, reality *seems* to be against the case for globalization that many proponents like Freidman and Fukuyama lay out.

There is a lot about the case for globalization that is appealing. History is laden with war, strife, and genocide. Globalization promises to end all these horrors. History is also laden with poverty, misery, and disease. Globalization also promises to end these conditions. History is also laden with tyrants, corrupt regimes, and all manner of zealots. Globalization promises a world of order and democracy. It also promises to give us all these things without asking much from us. We can keep our religions, our cultures, our traditions. We merely have to commit to promoting open markets. For proponents of globalization, nothing is fundamentally wrong with globalization. The problem is with its adoption, such as governments being unwilling to completely open all markets, or with corrupt governments who wish to keep the spoils of globalization, or with the incitement of violence by religious interests who fear the coming of globalization. Even Amy Chua believes that the problem is with adoption. Underlying globalization is the belief that our prosperity resides in the formation of new institutions that will bring order and control to the human condition. These institutions will presumably save us from ourselves. Globalization promises to exercise this restraint without the overt use of coercion.

But the problem with globalization exceeds adoption. It is about theory. In many ways, globalization is contrary to the world's natural rhythms. These rhythms favor diversity. Although globalization seems to have no overt hostility to diversity, by reducing us to objects of either consumption or production, globalization undermines diversity. In downplaying our complexity, globalization downplays our diversity. In short, understanding our humanity requires understanding our complexity. It is the quality of our communities rather than the quality of our markets that determines our health and well-being. The quality of our communities can be found in the density and richness of our relationships with others.

Through community, human beings become fully human. Through community, human beings avoid the ravages of isolation. Globalization promises that through open markets our prosperity will spring. But globalization offers no promise of community. It lacks any appreciation of the complexity that makes us human. Yes, human beings do have material needs, and open markets do help us best meet such needs. But human beings also have other needs, other yearnings, other ambitions. Moreover, human beings have a certain constitution that obligates us in various ways. Our humanity resides within each other. We can never separate our condition from the condition of others. Isolation is death. It implodes our humanity. Ultimately, our prosperity resides in community. When the quality of our communities increase, our fear, distrust, and suspicion of each other decrease. Forging community makes us less afraid of each other. It also enlarges our empathy and compassion for each other and enhances our willingness to share our resources and seek favorable outcomes for others. In making us human, community alters our view of the world, as well as ways of experiencing the world.

In many ways globalization undermines community. It undermines community by simply paying no attention to the demands of community. It propagates the view that our prosperity depends on our own doing. We can prosper as individuals. Globalization also undermines community by fostering competition and a spirit of survival of the fittest. The result is a world that seems to comprise a series of zero/sum games. Focus is on self-interest. But self-interest is always defined individually rather than collectively. Globalization also undermines community by making no room for community. This reality is seen in the steady erosion of social capital that Robert Putnam documented in *Bowling Alone*. Social capital constitutes our involvement and participation in voluntary organizations. We are increasingly isolated and less involved with each other. But as our isolation soars, so also do our levels of mental illness. As even Thomas Friedman acknowledged, globalization has no interest in our mental, emotional, or even spiritual condition. It views our prosperity in purely material terms. Globalization also undermines community by fostering inequality. When globalization arrives, the gap between rich and poor widens. In *World on Fire,* Amy Chua claims that this widening gap is what contributes to the animosity and violence against the minority groups that tend to benefit disproportionately from globalization. Indeed, inequality is consistently related to animosity, violent conflict, scapegoating, and strife. However, by undermining the flourishing of community, globalization places the world in peril by leaving in place the forces that put us at each other's throats. It is only though community that human beings develop the capacity to engage each other and hear each other's confusions, tribulations, and humiliations.

Community can neither be coerced nor manufactured. It must be forged. Community requires empathy and trust, patience and forbearance. It also requires suspension of our deepest prejudices and biases. But most of all, community requires vulnerability—the courage to understand and experience the world from the position of others. In other words, community is a communication practice. It is communication that distinguishes communities from markets. Markets merely demand rules and regulations. But communication is the lifeblood of communities. What helps make globalization appealing is the promise of getting us around communication and thereby the complexity that comes with the human condition. It views our complexity as a problem to be solved. In creating ambiguity, our complexity presumably makes order impossible. It also makes us messy and thereby makes everything messy. Thus globalization is always striving to limit communication. It does so by always striving to end ambiguity. Ambiguity is the catalyst of communication. But by limiting communication, globalization reduces communication to information—merely expressions of our thoughts and emotions. Yet when communication is gutted, so also is our humanity. We are reduced to merely objects of consumption and production. That is, objects that can be disposed as market conditions demand.

Every naturally occurring ecology promotes permeability to exchange resources and forge relationships with other ecologies. Without permeability, ecologies perish. This, of course, is also true of human ecologies. Through permeability, human ecologies—whether such ecologies are markets, cultures, or societies—flourish. However, by viewing permeability in terms of open markets, globalization operates on a narrow view of permeability. Besides cultural, political, and economic permeability, there is also sensual, spiritual, emotional, relational, and communicational permeability. Also, open markets in no way *naturally* lend for other kinds of permeability. In fact, using open markets as a measure of permeability requires much caution. There is nothing wrong with promoting open markets. However, achieving the kinds of permeability that are necessary for us to find any possibility of peace and prosperity in a global, multicultural, and plural world will only come by cultivating community. In fact, although globalization is decreasing the physical distances between different peoples, proponents of globalization make a serious error in assuming a correlation between physical distance and *social distance.*

Social distance deals with levels of intimacy, sympathy, or connectivity between members of different groups in a society. Intimacy is about influence. The fact that there is no correlation between physical distance and social distance means that members of various groups can live, work, and trade with each other and still have no relationship with each other. Indeed, whereas globalization is lessening our proximity to each other, many analysts also claim that globalization is increasing our social distance by cultivating and widening the gap between rich and poor. Donald Black (2004), of the University of Virginia, even believes that this trend—decreasing physical distance and increasing social distance—is responsible for the rise of modern terrorism. According to Black, "Although both the social and physical geometry of terrorism are necessary conditions for its occurrence . . . neither alone is a sufficient condition. Terrorism arises only when a grievance has a social geometry distant enough and a physical geometry close enough for mass violence against civilians" (p. 21).

No doubt, lessening social distance is important to ending strife and discord between different peoples. Yet we simply cannot assume that decreasing physical distance will decrease social distance. This is why the promise of globalization is yet to pan out. The forces that reduce social distance are fundamentally different from those that reduce physical distance. In fact, reducing physical distance without attending to social distance can heighten destructive conflict and strife.

When social distance persists in the face of declining physical distance, this means that members of different groups are relying on perception rather than on communication to understand each other. This, of course, is always dangerous, as perception is prone to distortion and error. Thus lessening social distance requires moving from perception to communication. It is about deliberately encouraging members of different groups to have contact with each other, but fundamentally about encouraging these persons to engage, deliberate, and negotiate with each other. Without such deliberate pushing and coaxing, most of us will remain within the physical and social confines of our groups, as such environs, by having the least ambiguity, bring us the least anxiety and discomfort. But remaining within the confines of our groups leaves us at the mercy of each other's perceptions, which in most cases are really distortions and misperceptions.

CONCLUSION

Verbing our understanding of culture assumes that human beings are fundamentally relational beings with a striving and potentiality for communion with the world and each other. We are culturing beings—always constructing and deconstructing cultures. Common understandings of culture mask the natural tensions that all cultures possess. This, again, is a world of chaos and order, ambiguity and meaning, homogeneity and diversity, stability and instability, and equilibrium and disequilibrium. Cultures are constantly negotiating these tensions. Yet these tensions are natural catalysts for life's evolution and expansion. We should, as a result, commit ourselves to promoting those practices that allow cultures to change, evolve, and strive. This involves promoting a communication sensibility that values ambiguity. The world's ambiguity will always exceed us. We will never have a language that will allow us to conquer this ambiguity. There will always be the possibility of a different meaning, a new narrative. Communication is about managing and encouraging the formation of new meanings and narratives.

No Laughing Matter in Denmark

INTRODUCTION

The origins of the Danish cartoon conflict are seemingly in-nocuous. The story began on September 17, 2005, when the Danish daily newspaper *Jyllands-Posten* published an article entitled, "A Profound Fear of Criticizing Islam," which de-tailed the difficulties encountered by Dutch writer Kare Bluitgen in finding an illustrator for his children's book on the life of the Prophet Mohammed. The author of the article pointed out that artists in Denmark were increasingly show-ing reluctance in providing images for such books for fear of being violently targeted by militant Islamists. Following this, the cultural editor of *Jyllands-Posten,* Flemming Rose, com-missioned 40 artists to draw Mohammed as they envisioned him. Rose received 25 entries and proceeded to publish 12 cartoons portraying Mohammed on September 30, 2005. Each cartoon depicted the Prophet Mohammed in distinct ways—one portrayed the Prophet wearing a turban with a bomb fuse attached to it; another portrayed him with a bushy gray beard holding a sword; a third showed Mohammed at the gates of Heaven, saying to men who seem to be suicide bombers, "Stop, stop, we have run out of virgins"; yet an-other had the devil's horns emerging from the turban. The re-sponse to the publication was wide ranging and unleashed an international controversy that eventually led to bloodshed and violence across various regions of both the Muslim and non-Muslim world. In this chapter, we discuss the conflict at length by focusing on three broad questions:

1. How is the conflict being constructed and by whom?
2. How are the forces of inclusion and exclusion being set up and by whom?
3. How are various factions avoiding seduction, intercourse, and ultimately impregnation?

EARLY RESPONSES

Early responses to the cartoon publications were mild, and it seemed like a small conflict that would mend itself with some dialogue. Denmark has about 250,000 Muslims who are immigrants from Pakistan, Turkey, Iraq, and Somalia; they make about 5% of the population. Muslim groups in Denmark protested the publication of the cartoons by organizing peaceful protests and asking for an apology from the newspaper. Two of the cartoonists received death threats and were advised to go into hiding. Some Muslim youth rioted in a suburb in Aarhus citing the cartoons as justification for their behavior. On October 17, the Egyptian paper *El Fagr* published six of the cartoons with the purpose of denouncing them. There were no protests from the public or religious leaders in Egypt. Upon receiving petitions from various Imams, on October 19, ambassadors from 11 Muslim countries requested a meeting with Danish Prime Minister Anders Fogh Rasmussen to ask that he distance himself from *Jyllands-Posten* and other anti-Muslim sentiments in the Danish media. A meeting was refused on the grounds that the prime minister would not interfere with the freedom of press and that publishing these cartoons was a constitutional right held by the paper. This refusal to meet the ambassadors was criticized by the Danish opposition. Following this, on October 27, a number of Danish Muslim organizations filed a complaint with the police claiming that the *Jyllands-Posten* had committed an offense under Section 140 and 266b of the Danish Criminal Code. Section 140 of the Danish code deems punishable publicly ridiculing or insulting dogmas of worship of any lawfully existing religious community in Denmark. Section 266b covers dissemination of statements or other information by which a group of people are threatened, insulted, or degraded on account of their religion. The case was eventually dismissed on grounds of insufficient evidence for a criminal offence.

The controversy rolled on, with a majority of the interest groups using diplomatic and by and large peaceful rhetorical channels to negotiate the standoff. The Danish Muslim community was interested in receiving an official statement from the Danish government that would underline the need for and the obligation of respecting all religions. Muslim groups and the Danish government seemed at an impasse, but there was no large-scale killing or rioting at this stage. In fact, the *Jyllands-Posten* eventually issued two open letters apologizing for hurting the sentiments of the Muslim community, but refrained from apologizing for the publication of the cartoons themselves. The Danish Muslim Association was satisfied with the apology and offered to help calm the situation, expressing regret that it had gotten out of hand. Little did they know that the controversy was about to explode on the world stage, aided and abetted by various parties. The conflict would lead to worldwide rioting and leave over 100 persons dead.

THE CARTOONS GO INTERNATIONAL

Between November 2005 and February 2006, a few significant events occurred that added fuel to the controversy and accelerated its spiral into an international crisis. Between this period, newspapers in Germany, France, Sweden, Greece, Chile, Jordan, Uruguay, Portugal, Switzerland, United States, Russia, Belgium, Hungary, Argentina, India, New Zealand, South Korea, Honduras, Costa Rica, and Australia, among others reprinted the cartoons, unleashing a series of violent responses from multiple groups about the decision to reprint such controversial material. The conflict began to be constructed more viciously and in earnest by various stakeholders. Or in other words, it was the reprinting that unleashed the wrath of various factions and groups, who insisted that the republication of the cartoons by various media was like adding salt to fresh wounds.

The following section lists the various positions taken by different groups and the diversity of opinion that came to the fore about the controversial Danish cartoons. These are not presented here in any particular order or timeline, as the goal is to illustrate the multiple viewpoints and strategies whereby the conflict came into being, rather than presenting a timeline. Therefore, in this portion of the chapter, we focus on how the conflict came to be rhetorically constructed by various members of the radical Muslim community, the Danish government, moderate Muslims, the European Union, the media, and the United States.

THE RADICAL MUSLIM RESPONSE IN DENMARK AND WORLDWIDE

The first responses to the cartoons came from the Danish Muslim community in the form of letters to the newspapers and peaceful protests demanding apologies from the media and the government. Muslims around the world were generally offended because Islam forbids the depiction of any prophet from the Quran. Mohammed is a momentous religious figure in Islam and is believed to be God's final prophet. Similar to other interest groups, the Danish Muslim community merely wanted to request *Jyllands-Posten* and the government to apologize. The slogans chanted across these protests were benign:

> God is great!
> Freedom of speech is like a plague. (BBC News, 2005)

Most of these protestors placed the blame on the Danish media asserting that the former was trying to stir controversy instead of helping to mend community relations. They generally felt that the Danish people were not to blame, and even though the Danes were not well informed about Islam, they were fair in their attitudes and tolerant toward the immigrant community. However, radical factions within the community, such as two significant Danish Imams—Raed Hlayhel and Ahmed Akkari—declared these protests inadequate and stated:

> Muslims will never accept this kind of humiliation. The article has insulted every Muslim in the world. We demand an apology. (*Jyllands-Posten,* 2005)

Imam Ahmed Abu Laban, considered to be the most powerful Imam in Denmark, teamed up with Hlayhel and created the Committee for the Defense of the Honor of the Prophet with the stated aim of obtaining an adequate apology for the cartoons:

> We are not threatening anybody, but when you see what happened in Holland and then print the cartoons, that's quite stupid. (*Jyllands-Posten,* 2005)

Laban also called on the Muslim world to "internationalize the issue so that the Danish government would realize that the cartoons were not only insulting to Muslims in Denmark, but worldwide" (*Qenawa,* 2005). The committee presented a 43-page document entitled *Dossier about Championing the Prophet Mohammed Peace Be upon Him,* which consisted of letters from several Muslim organizations that alleged the mistreatment of Danish Muslims, a statement detailing the persecution of Danish Muslims, the cartoons, and additional cartoons, some of which were unconnected with Islam (allegedly one of the cartoons depicted a pig contest in France) and the ongoing controversy. Rhetorically, this document framed the conflict as a clash between the West and Islam. It contained statements such as the following:

> The faithful in their religion (Muslims) suffer under a number of circumstances, first and foremost the lack of official recognition of the Islamic faith. This has led to a lot of problems, especially the lack of right to build mosques.
>
> This (Europe's) dictatorial way of using democracy is completely unacceptable.

A spokesperson for the Imams stated that additional and unconnected materials were added to the dossier to give insight into how hateful the atmosphere in Denmark was toward Muslims (Gudmundsson, 2006c). Sometime in the year 2006, Danish Imam Ahmed Abu-Laban, who was one of those responsible for spreading the cartoon row worldwide, said:

> Generally, we have seen a boom since the cartoons were published. Many Muslims are becoming stronger in their faith. They feel there is a need to practice the religion more. (BBC News, 2006)

In the West freedom of speech is sacred; to us, the Prophet is sacred (Rennie, Isherwood, & Barton, 2006).

The Danish imams received support from some of their radical Scandinavian counterparts. A radical imam from Norway, Mullah Krekar, was quoted as saying, "These drawings are a declaration of war" (Rennie et al., 2006, para 7). A member of the Muslim Brotherhood's office of Islamic Guidance also in Denmark, Sheikh Ahmed Abdullah Alkhateeb, wrote the following on the group's Arabic Web site:

> Overlooking such stabs is worse than the act itself, the Umma's duty, governors or governed, is to rise at once, and revolt in defense of their prophet, by ending relations with these countries from which these offenses come, expelling their representatives, and shutting down their embassies. (*The New York Sun,* 2006)

According to some media opinion, publication of the dossier, continued pursuit of the issue by the Imans, and the republication of the cartoons by major European and international papers is said to have escalated the controversy into an international issue. Demonstrators marched in Kenya, Iran, India, Pakistan, Afghanistan, Malaysia, Sri Lanka, Bangladesh, Indonesia, the Philippines, Israel, Egypt, and Jordan. There was also large-scale rioting in many areas.

Protests on a large scale took place in the Pakistani cities of Islamabad, Peshawar, and Karachi. Almost 50,000 people marched the streets of Islamabad shouting protests slogans such as:

> Hang those who insulted the prophet.
> Death to America.
> Death to Musharraf. (*China Daily,* 2006a)

In the Pakistani city of Peshawar, 5,000 demonstrators burned effigies and chanted:

> Hang the man who insulted the prophet. (*China Daily,* 2006a)

Peshawar, which is the capital of the Islamist-ruled North-west Frontier province, is a conservative bastion. Akran Durrani, the senior-most elected official in the city, stated,

> We demand that whoever made the cartoons should be punished like a terrorist. Nobody has the right to insult Islam and hurt the feelings of Muslims. (*The Guardian,* 2006)

A Pakistani cleric, Maulana Yousaf Quereshi, announced a bounty of one million dollars plus a car for killing the cartoonist who drew the Prophet Mohammed. Thousands of angry Indian Muslims across India kicked, spat on, and tore Danish flags and burned effigies in New Delhi, the Indian capital, and in the Indian-controlled parts of Kashmir. Minister Yaqood Querishi of the Uttar Pradesh government in India offered a reward of $11.5 million to anyone who could kill any of the cartoonists who drew the images of the Prophet Mohammed. Bangladesh saw protest marches of 5000 strength outside the Danish embassy in Dhaka with protestors shouting slogans such as:

> Death to those who degrade our beloved prophet. (*Washington Post,* 2006)

About 2,000 people marched around the dome of the rock shrine in Jerusalem imploring Bin Laden to strike again. Iran's supreme leader, the Ayatollah Ali Khamenei, claimed that the entire plot was an Israeli conspiracy motivated by Hamas's win in the Palestinian elections. He said that the cartoons were scandalous especially, because they came from those "who champion civilization and free expression . . . the West condemns any denial of the Jewish Holocaust, but it permits the insult of Islamic sanctities" (*Israel Insider,* 2006).

Mohsen Rezaie, a top Iranian government official, was among several Iranian leaders who blamed Israel for the cartoons, calling it a Zionist plot.

> Do you know of any place that does not have Zionists? We think this confrontation between Muslims and Christians is a premeditated attack by Zionists. (Stinson & Hampson, 2006)

In fact, a leading Iranian paper, the *Hamshahri Daily,* even launched a "faux" competition asking people to submit cartoons about the Holocaust saying it wanted to test the boundaries of free speech for Westerners.

The Osama Bin Laden and al-Qaeda response came in the form of an audio-recorded message attributed to them. The recorded voice on it suggested that the cartoon controversy was a part of the crusade involving Pope Benedict XVI and stated:

> If there is no check on the freedom of your words, then let your hearts open to the freedom of our actions. (BBC News, 2008c)

The Malaysian Prime Minister, Abdullah Ahmad Badawi, described the controversy in terms of "the huge chasm that has emerged between the West and Islam . . . Westerners think Osama Bin Laden speaks for the religion and its followers. Islam and Muslims are linked to all that is backward."

In Britain, members of the Muslim Council for Britain and the Muslim Association of Britain reinforced the radical Islamic agenda when they made the following statements:

> We say to the West that you are not allowed to dictate to us what we say . . . whatever our religion allows us to say we will say it. (Brandon, 2006, p. 4)

Demonstrations were organized outside the Danish embassy in London during which radical Islamists carried placards that read:

> Slay [also butcher/massacre/behead/exterminate] those who insult Islam.
> Free speech go to hell.
> Europe will pay, your 9/11 is on the way. (Pearce, 2006)

A London-based Arabic Web site *Al-Quds,* published the following message from the terrorist group *Abu Hafes al-Masri:*

> This is an open letter to the Danish government and all those who have considered insulting the most honorable prophet. We say to them: Your security is in danger and the coming days will mean a bloody war and series of attacks against you. (Gudmundsson, 2006a)

In the Middle East, the crisis was instrumentalized by Syria and Lebanon. In Damascus, demonstrations were organized outside the Swedish and Danish embassies, and the building that housed both was set on fire by the rioting mob. Syria and Saudi Arabia recalled their ambassadors to Denmark, and Libya closed its Danish embassy. The Danish embassy in Tehran was attacked by an angry mob. The Norwegian embassy was also burned. In Beirut, rioters set fire to the Danish embassy. In Gaza, a German cultural center was torched. Angry mobs stormed the Danish embassy in Jakarta. The Sudanese president, Omar al-Bashir, went on to state that he would ban Danes from Sudan and urged "all Muslims around the world to boycott Danish commodities, goods, companies, institutions, organizations and personalities" (*Arab News,* 2008). Al-Bashir also threatened to expel over two dozen Danes who worked in Sudan. Other Muslim countries such as Iran also boycotted Danish goods. The Danish–Swedish dairy giant Aria Foods saw their Middle East sales plummet to zero.

Moderate Muslim Response

The publication of the cartoons and the radical Muslim response to the publication caused a backlash, and moderate Muslims began to organize and rise up against what they saw as un-Islamic values. New and progressive Muslims groups formed across Europe to challenge the traditional and conservative Muslim response. A spokesperson for the Danish group Democratic Muslims, Fathi El-Abed, who is of Palestinian origin, stated:

> We want to use this group to tell ordinary Danes that we are also Danes first and foremost. We want to tell them, "We are democratic just like you—the only thing different is that we come from a Muslim background." (Brandon, 2006)

The new leader of the Democratic Muslims is Syrian-born social democrat Naser Khader, an MP who describes himself as a "cultural Muslim" and is famous for writing the "Ten Commandments of Democracy," which emphasize a strict separation of religion and politics, unreserved support of the freedom of expression, and a rejection of violence. Just in the initial months of its existence the organization grew to 700 members. Naser Khader made a statement criticizing the Imams (Brandon, 2006, March 6).

> If these imams think it is so terrible to live in Denmark, then why do they remain here? They can always move to one of the countries in the Middle East which are

based on the Muslim values they insist on living by. If they cannot be loyal to the values of this country they should leave and by that do the majority of Danish Muslims a big favor. (Gudmundsson, 2006b)

Other moderate voices in Denmark, such as those of Fatih Alev and Abdul Wahid Pedersen, defended Danish values and urged for the settlement of the cartoon controversy. They stressed that *Jyllands-Posten* had already apologized for offending Muslims and that the Danish press was not controlled by the government. They also pointed out that Muslims in Denmark were generally well treated and that any boycott of Danish goods in the Middle East also harmed Danish Muslims.

Moderate Muslims in Arhus, Denmark, announced that they intended to create a network of Muslims who did not want to be represented by fundamentalist Danish Imams or others who preach Sharia laws and the oppression of women. One of the organizers, Bunyamin Shimsek, also a city councilor, pointed out:

> There is a large group of Muslims in this city who want to live in a secular society and adhere to the principle that religion is an issue between them and God and not something that should involve society. (Malik, 2007)

Hadi Khan, chairman of the Organization of Pakistani Students in Denmark, pointed out that he did not feel that he was being represented by the radical Muslim groups and that when he went to Friday prayers the Imam did not say much that was useful to him. In fact he stated, "We have no need for Imams in Denmark. They do not do anything for us."

In Britain, a group called Progressive British Muslims came out to support rights of newspapers to publish controversial cartoons. The Pakistani President Pervez Musharraf declared himself a moderate but stated that he was nonetheless offended by the cartoons. He called for Muslims to restrain themselves. In Iraq, the country's top Shia cleric, Ayatollah Sistani, issued a statement against the cartoons, and at the same time pointed blame at the Muslim fundamentalists because, he said, "They projected a distorted and dark image of the faith of justice, love, and brotherhood. Many religious leaders across the world used the Friday prayers as an opportunity to tell people that the prophet himself withstood insults from the Meccans and told their fellow Muslims that they had "fallen into the trap of provocation" (Zuhur, 2006).

A Somali Muslim immigrant and Dutch Member of Parliament, Hirsi Ali, also a target of radical Islamists for her writing of the screenplay of the film *Submission* directed by Dutch filmmaker Theo Van Gogh (who was killed by a Muslim fundamentalist in 2004), made a statement on how radical Islam infringed the rights of citizens in Islamic nations and Muslims at large:

> A free discussion of Islam remains rare and dangerous, certainly in the Islamic world, and even in our politically correct times in the West . . . Apostasy is still punishable by long prison sentences and even death in many Islamic countries such as Pakistan and Iran . . . (Lifson, 2006)

An independent Jordanian tabloid, *al-Shihan,* reprinted three of the cartoons, saying people should know what they are protesting about. The editor, Jihad Momani, wrote,

> Muslims of the world be reasonable. What brings more prejudice against Islam, these caricatures or pictures of a hostage-taker slashing the throat of his victim in front of the cameras or a suicide bomber who blows himself up during a wedding ceremony in Amman? (BBC News, 2006a)

Having made the bold moderate statement, the editor found himself fired from his job after the publication of his editorial.

Jyllands-Posten and Other Danish Media Response

Jyallands-Posten's response to the Muslim indignation consisted of a series of statements issued by its culture editor, Flemming Rose, who initiated the drawing of the cartoons. The newspaper and the Danish media in general consistently invoked its right to free speech and freedom of expression under Danish law. These quotes have been drawn from Rose's statements and writings in various media outlets after the publication of the cartoons. In an early statement defending his decision to publish the cartoons, he said that he made the decision to elicit the material "in response to several incidents of self-censorship in Europe caused by widening fears and feelings of intimidation in dealing with issues related to Islam. It reminded me of what I had seen in the Soviet Union, where I saw a society where people were intimidated with the system" (*The New York Times,* 2006).

After receiving demands from Muslim groups to apologize, the paper put out two open letters, which contained the following statements:

> In our opinion, the 12 drawings are sober. They are not intended to be offensive, nor are they in variance with Danish law, but they have indisputably offended some Muslims for which we apologize.

The cartoonist who had drawn the most controversial "turban bomb" wrote:

> There are interpretations of it (the drawing) that are incorrect. The general impression among Muslims is that it is about Islam as a whole. It is not. It is about certain fundamental aspects that of course are not shared by everyone.

Upon the reprinting of the cartoons, an editorial in the conservative Danish paper, *Berlingske Tidende,* noted:

> We are doing this to document what is at stake in this case, and to unambiguously back and support the freedom of speech that we as a newspaper always will defend. Freedom of expression gives you the right to think, to speak and to draw what you like. (CNN, 2008)

In February and May 2006, Flemming Rose wrote two editorials in *The New York Times* and the *Washington Post,* where he again defended his decision to publish.

The Danish Government

A few weeks after the controversy exploded, ambassadors from 11 Muslim countries requested a meeting with the Danish prime minister. Prime Minister Rasmussen refused to meet them, stating,

> This is a matter of principle. I won't meet with them because it is so crystal clear what principles Danish democracy is built upon that there is no reason to do so. As Prime Minister, I have no power whatsoever to limit the press—nor do I want such a power. (Spencer, 2006)

Later he added many statements about the freedom of press and expression:

> The government has done what can be done. Neither the government nor the Danish people can be held responsible for what is published in an independent newspaper. And neither the government nor the Danish people have any intention whatsoever to insult Muslims or any other religious community. (*Washington Post*, 2006)
>
> Freedom of speech is the most valuable right of liberty—we must defend it to the very last. (BBC News, 2006c)

After the reprinting of the cartoons by various international papers and the international riots that followed, the prime minister told a news press conference in Copenhagen that

> We are now facing a global crisis over the cartoons . . . We need to resolve this issue through dialogue, not violence. The Danish people are not enemies of Islam . . . That picture is false. Extremists or radicals who seek clash of cultures and religions are spreading it . . . (BBC News, 2006b)

The Danish queen too joined the volley of criticisms targeted against radical Islam. In an authorized biography she called on Muslim immigrants in the country to improve their Danish language skills so that they do not feel excluded from society. She called for an opposition to radical Islam and said,

> We have let this issue float around for too long, because we are tolerant and rather lazy. We have to run the risk of being labeled in a rather unflattering way, because there are some things for which we should display no tolerance. (BBC News, 2005a)

Commenting on the radical Imams and their alleged conspiracy to hatch an anti-Danish campaign in the Middle East, the Danish Integration Minister asserted:

> I believe it has become obvious that the imams are not the people we should be listening to if we want integration in Denmark to work. (Gudmundsson, 2006c)

The United Nations

The then-secretary-general of the United Nations, Kofi Annan, criticized the affair and called for calm as riots broke out worldwide and in many parts of the Middle East:

I am distressed and concerned by this whole affair. I share the distress of the Muslim friends, who feel that the cartoon offends their religion. I also respect the right of freedom of speech. But of course freedom of speech is never absolute. It entails responsibility and judgment. (*The New York Times*, 2006)

The UN High Commissioner for Human Rights declared that the cartoons were "unacceptably disrespectful" to Muslims worldwide. Under pressure from Islamic countries, it launched an investigation into the cartoons' "racism."

The European Union Member Response

The European Union's response to the publication of the cartoons was mixed, and there were many disagreements among member nations about Denmark's demeanor during the entire conflict. The EU trade commissioner, Peter Mandelson, criticized the European papers that republished the cartoons, saying that "they were throwing petrol onto the flames of the original issue and the original offence that was taken" (*BBC News*, 2006a).

The Council of Europe attacked the Danish government's invocation of free speech as a defense of the cartoons. When many Islamic nations threatened and indeed carried through a boycott of Danish goods, the European Commission spokesperson, Johannes Laitenberger, stated,

A boycott of Danish goods is by definition a boycott of European goods. A boycott hurts the economic interests of all parties, also those who are boycotting, and can damage the trade links between the EU and the countries concerned. (Cooney, 2006)

The Italian prime minister, Silvio Berlusconi, said that the cartoons should not have been published and called for dialogue. Another Italian minister, Roberto Calderoli, on the other hand, said he was going to distribute T-shirts displaying the controversial cartoons. He wore the T-shirts in public saying, "I have had T-shirts made with the cartoons that have upset Islam and I will start wearing them today. We have to put an end to this story that we can talk to these people. They only want to humiliate people. Full stop. And what are we becoming? The civilization of melted butter?" (Balmer, 2006).

The British foreign secretary condemned the decision by European newspapers to republish the cartoons as "disrespectful" and that freedom of speech did not mean an "an open season" on religious taboos. Irish President, Mary McAleese condemned the drawings, saying that Muslims had every right to be angry.

Germany and some officials in France, on the other hand, took the stand for freedom of speech. German Interior Minister Wolfgang Schauble dismissed calls for the German government to reprimand the two German papers who republished the cartoons, stating, "Why should the government apologize for something that happens under the freedom of press?" France's then-Interior Minister Nikolai Sarkozy praised Danish Prime Minister Rasmussen for his firm stand on protecting freedom of expression, saying, "Freedom of expression is not an issue for negotiation and I see no reason to give one religion a special treatment." However, French President Jacques Chirac condemned the reprinting of the cartoons as "overt provocation," saying,

> Anything liable to offend the beliefs of others, particularly religious beliefs, must be avoided. (The Telegraph, 2006)

At the same time Chirac was also quoted saying, "France, a country of secularism, respects all religions and beliefs . . . but the principle of freedom of expression constitutes one of the foundations of the Republic" (*The Telegraph*, 2006).

The American Response

The United States sided with the protesting Muslims, and State Department spokesman Kurtis Coopers made the following remarks about the furor:

> These cartoons are indeed offensive to the belief of Muslims. We all respect the freedom of press and expression, but it must be coupled with press responsibility . . . I believe that the republication of these cartoons was unnecessary . . . it has been disrespectful and it has been wrong. (Rennie et al., 2006)

Another State Department spokesman, Sean McCormack, stated,

> Anti-Muslim images are as unacceptable as anti-Semitic images which are routinely published in the Arab press, as anti-Christian images, or any other religious belief. We vigorously defend the rights of individuals to express points of view. (*The New York Times*, 2006)

U.S. foreign secretary Jack Straw sided with the Muslim view when he stated,

> Freedom is a great virtue but it must be shared and it must not be unilateral. Freedom of satire that offends the feelings of others becomes an abuse and here we are talking about nothing less than the feelings of entire peoples who have seen their supreme symbols affected. (*The Telegraph*, 2006)

Former U.S. President, Bill Clinton, described the cartoons as "outrageous" and compared European Islamophobia with prewar anti-Semitism. He also pointed out that

> None of us are totally free of stereotypes about people of different races, different ethnic groups, and different religions . . . there was this appalling example in northern Europe, in Denmark . . . these totally outrageous cartoons against Islam. (*The Weekly Standard*, 2006)

Secretary of State Condoleeza Rice was even tougher and blamed the Syrians and Iranians for stoking the crisis:

> I don't have any doubt that given the control of the Syrian government in Syria, given the control of the Iranian government, which, by the way, hasn't even hid-

den its hand in this, that Iran and Syria have gone out of their way to inflame sentiments and to use this to their own purposes . . . (*The New York Sun,* 2006)

Senator John Kerry also addressed this criticism against the publications and said,

> These and other inflammatory messages deserve our scorn, just as the violence against embassies and military installations are unacceptable and intolerable forms of protest. (Lobe, 2006)

The U.S. response was mixed, but mostly opposed to the publication of the cartoons. Many U.S. officials were using the opportunity to make political statements against fundamentalist Muslims and against Syria and Iran, long held as foreign policy problems by the United States.

Media Response

Media pundits, academics, and editorial commentators in different papers provided very thorough analyses of the situation. The matter was debated for months and numerous essays and commentaries about the issues continue to be engaged in different media. Reuel Marc Gerecht (2006), writing in *The Weekly Standard,* made a point of acknowledging the diversity within Islam that many media accounts of the cartoon controversy were missing:

> The militant Muslims of Europe . . . helped fuel this controversy by emailing and faxing the offending cartoons to their spiritual allies in the Middle East. Most European Muslims . . . probably would not have cared about these caricatures . . .

On the other hand, another editorial in *The Weekly Standard* written by Paul Marshall (2006) contained the following:

> It is one thing to condemn *Jyllands-Posten* for offending millions of people. It is a very different thing to criticize the Danish or other governments, since the criticism itself . . . assumes that government should control the media.

Jim Lobe (2006) of the Inter Press Service wrote an article entitled, "Cartoon Crisis Echoes 'Why They Hate Us' Debate":

> . . . one side argues that radical Islam . . . represents an existential threat to Western ideals—in this case, freedom of speech and the press—and that any suggestion that European newspaper publishers should show greater sensitivity to Muslim sentiments constitutes weakness . . . the decline of Western civilization.

Papers in the Middle East published vigorous analyses of the controversy. According to Rami Khouri's (2006) editorial in *The Age,* it was too simple to think of the entire conflict in terms of the clash of civilizations:

> The cartoons, including one depicting the prophet's headdress as a bomb, are only the fuse that set off a combustible mixture of pressures and tensions anchored in a much wider array of problems . . .

An editorial opinion in *The Age* also pointed out:

> The Danish cartoons are . . . just stereotypical smears. Even given their curiosity value, such material carries a responsibility to consider whether the point of publication outweighs any likely offence. Having the freedom to publish does not mean we must publish to prove it.

Shakeel Sayed, the executive director of the Islamic Shura Council, a federation of more than 70 mosques in Southern California wrote a piece in the *Press Enterprise* (2006), "Callous Cartoons: Images Depict a Growing Islamophobia in the West":

> Why have Muslims pursued the matter? Islamophobia is a clear and growing trend throughout the West, and Muslim immigrants bear the brunt of this animosity and atmosphere of hatred and mistrust.

Reza Aslan, a commentator, wrote against the cartoons in *Slate.com* in February 2006, stating,

> . . . Muslims have objected so strongly because these cartoons promote stereotypes of Muslims that are prevalent throughout Europe: Mohammed dressed as a terrorist, his turban a bomb with a lit fuse . . . It is difficult to see how these drawings could have any purpose other than to offend.

So, while in Europe and the United States the row over the cartoons has been painted as a conflict between secular democratic freedoms and arcane religious dogma, the controversy is really about neither. Instead, it's another manifestation of the ongoing ethnic and religious tensions that have been simmering beneath the surface of European society for decades, like last year's Paris riots and the murder two years ago of Dutch filmmaker Theo van Gogh.

In the minds of many Muslims in Europe, the cartoons were intentionally inflammatory, published to further humiliate an ethnic and religious minority that has been socially and economically repressed for decades. Indeed, it seems as though the cartoons were deliberately meant to provoke precisely the reaction they did.

TACTICS AND RHETORICAL STRATEGIES BY FACTIONS

The storm over the publication and republication of the cartoons continued for well over a year and is indeed a subject of heated debate on many forums, print media, and blogs on the Internet. Various policy makers, governments, terrorist organizations, and diplomats gave their verdicts on the causes and consequences of the crisis, and in doing so employed a variety of rhetorical strategies with regard to the matters of inclusion and exclusion vis-à-vis Muslims in Europe. In this section, we offer a discussion of how the crisis was rhetorically framed and what kind of tactics were used by various parties to try to put a seeming end to the controversy that rages on to this day.

The radical Muslim response to the crisis was one that invoked the Samuel Huntington thesis about the clash of civilizations. The Hungtington thesis essentially holds that the West and the East are rooted in and originate from different worldviews, will always be in conflict, and can never be reconciled. In other words, these two civilizations can never reach a middle path of negotiation because they are diametrically opposed to each other. Even though the Huntington thesis was the main tactic utilized by radical Islam groups (it was never identified as the Huntington position), there were diverse responses to the cartoons within what would be a unitary group. For the Iranians, for instance, this was termed a Zionist conspiracy and something that Israel was instigating because of the Hamas's win in Palestine. The two Danish imams responsible for internationalizing the issue were most concerned about consolidating their own position within the Danish Muslim community within Denmark, and therefore their actions were power maneuvers that strengthened their own statuses rather than united a community. There is enough evidence to suggest that these two imams did not see eye to eye on various issues before the cartoon controversy came around. In fact, since the cartoon saga ended, the imams began much funding from foreign sources who were sympathetic to their cause and have even constructed a new mosque in Gellerup.

For other radical Muslims, the cartoons were another way of criticizing the "demonic" West, and the cartoon controversy came to be used to further reinforce the East versus West chasm. There were those who blamed all of Europe and referred to draconian immigration laws for the cause of the furor. In general, Muslim immigrant communities in Europe came to see the conflict as yet one more among a series of attacks on their religion. Some analysts suggest that the cartoon crisis further confirmed the immigrants' deeply marginalized stature in European society and proved the growing anti-immigrant sentiment in Europe, which has seen the rise of anti-immigration far-right parties all over the continent. Some of these include The Freedom Party in Austria, The Northern League in Italy, The People's Party in Switzerland, The National Front in France, The Flemish Block in Belgium, The People's Party in Denmark, and the Progress Party in Norway. Therefore, for many European Muslims, the issue became one that concerned their marginalized immigrant status and how they already felt like "others" in their adopted countries. A majority of Arab Muslims in many European countries live lives of struggle, residing in slums, and dealing with four to five times the unemployment rates of native Europeans. For many "White Europe" is not facing reality, and as Jah Jah, the head of the Arab European League, pointed out:

> It (Europe) does not want to adapt to the fact that their society is multicultural now. It still behaves and acts as if we were like 50 years ago, when everybody

here was white and Catholic and talking Dutch . . . We do not want to debate integration of assimilation because we don't believe in that kind of debate. We believe in a kind of debate about how a country should treat its own citizens because we are not foreigners. (Hurd, 2004)

Both the Danish government and *Jyllands-Posten* used similar rhetorical strategies in their initial responses to the cartoon uproar. They invoked the freedom of press and expression by insisting that the paper was within legal bounds in publishing the cartoons and that is how a democratic society worked. Yet, in reasserting their democratic ideals, they alienated the Muslims further by suggesting that Europeans stood for democracy whereas Islam seemed to stand against democracy. Most European nations within the EU, save a few nations such as England, sided with the Danish government on the issue. For Europe, which has seen a vast influx of Muslim refugees and immigrants from countries such as Algeria, Somalia, Afghanistan, Turkey, and so on, the issue came to be carved as an assimilation issue—many heads of state asserted that if the immigrants wanted to stay in Europe they had to live by European rules. This ethos was well captured by a statement made by Frank Vanhecke of the Flemish Block in Belgium, who said,

> This is the kind of people we are dealing with—people who do not come to our country to adapt, to make a new life, to start again, to make a living, to be thankful for the country that accepts them. We are talking about people, who want to become masters in our country. (Hurd, 2004)

Such statements further strengthened the creation of the us versus them stance, which consolidated the conflict further. Flemming Rose, the cultural editor of *Jyllands-Posten* and the man responsible for inciting the trouble, wrote two essays about why he published the cartoons. In the essay published in the *Washington Post,* Rose approached the issue with an interesting rhetorical strategy when he wrote,

> The cartoonists treated Islam the same way that they treat Christianity, Buddhism, Hinduism and other religions. And by treating Muslims in Denmark as equals they made a point: We are integrating you in the Danish tradition of the satire because you are a part of our society, not strangers. (Rose, 2006a).

Continuing this thread in *The New York Times,* Rose wrote,

> An act of inclusion. Equal treatment is the democratic way to overcome traditional barriers of blood and soil for newcomers. To me, that means treating immigrants just as I would any other Danes. And that's what I felt I was doing in publishing the 12 cartoons of Mohammed last year. (2006b)

Rose's response was balanced, at the same time he did not deny the existence of an us versus them mentality that was driving the conflict: "The Muslim face of Denmark has changed, and it is becoming clear that this is not a debate between 'them' and 'us,' but between those committed to democracy in Denmark and those who are not" (Rose, 2006c).

In emphasizing the primacy of democracy as a system of governance, it can be assumed that he was suggesting that it was "better" than what radical Islam believed in, or at least that is how these statements were perceived.

The moderate Muslim response, one that was most muted, was concerned with mostly differentiating itself from the radical Muslim response. In fact, progressive and moderate groups came into being as a response to the Danish Imams, as they did not want the radicals to "speak for them." Most of these groups addressed their concerns to the Danish government and were most interested in keeping with the mainstream ideas on democracy. Most radical Muslims attacked the moderates as people who were "selling out" to dominant values, thereby attacking Islam. The moderates fell on the side of the Danish government and *Jyllands-Posten* because they supported the right of the paper to publish what it wanted and supported the democratic ideals of Denmark. Naser Khader, a Syrian-born liberal politician in Denmark who heads a moderate group called Democratic Muslims, put forth the "Ten Commandments of Democracy" that all Muslims should follow. The first of these asks Muslims to separate politics and religion and never place religions above the laws of democracy. The sixth commandment asked fellow Muslims to respect freedom of expression, including of those with whom they disagreed most.

Ultimately, all these tactics used by the moderates were criticized by the radicals as stances that were too acquiescent to European governments. The moderates were referred to as "rats in a hole" and "cowards" responsible for the trouble of all Muslims in Europe. Even those Danish Muslims who supported the moderate view came to be afraid of the radicals because many who endorsed Khader's views received threats. For many Muslims who consider themselves moderate and secular, there was fear that they would be considered un-Islamic if they went against the imams and became supporters of *Jyllands-Posten.* Speaking to this, Omar Shah, an Afghan Danish commentator on Muslim affairs, said that "because of the racism on Muslim society, a lot of nonpracticing Muslims still identify themselves with Islam. A lot of them see Naser Khader as someone attacking Islam" (*San Francisco Chronicle,* 2006).

However, despite fears of being targeted, the most important outcome of the tactics employed by the moderates was their ability to create a binary between themselves and the radical imams across Europe.

The United States and the United Nations both condemned the publication of the cartoons and at the same time they upheld the freedom of press and expression as necessary ingredients of any functioning democracy. There seemed to be a split within the United Nations about how to handle the crisis because the Special Rapporteur on contemporary forms of racism, racial discrimination, xenophobia, and other related intolerance asked the Danish government to answer some questions regarding the cartoons. Despite receiving a substantial response from the government, the Special Rapporteur declared that the cartoon issues was a severe example of hatred against Islam and that the Danish government's handling of the matter could be considered a mechanism that trivialized Islamophobia at the political level.

Even though the UN and the United States condemned the actions, not very much was done by them to take any solid stance. The United States remained rhetorically sympathetic toward the Muslim community as well as the Middle East, but it has been suggested that this occurred due to its other interests vis-à-vis the wars in Iraq and Afghanistan. In other words, the United States could not afford to take a stronger stance "against" radical Muslims because it was suffering its worst losses in both wars in the Muslim world at the time that the conflict was at its peak. In fact, the crisis was used by Condoleeza Rice, the then-secretary of State to point fingers at Syria and Iran, the two countries that the United States blames for escalating the war in Iraq.

Each party used different means for different ends in the way that they approached the crisis. Ultimately, the most powerful way that it came to be framed was within the Samuel Hungtington thesis of the clash of civilizations or "us" versus "them." Having approached the crisis from various standpoints that show us how the crisis was rhetorically framed by the different parties involved, we will now examine how the crisis might have been resolved and whether or not a resolution of the crisis lay in the diverse voices involved in the conflict. We will do so by examining how the various factions involved in the conflict were unwilling to be wooed into dialogue by each other's perspectives and be changed by them. Ultimately, the conflict escalated not because different parties held different views, but because they were unable to open up and allow other views to permeate them.

RESISTING RESOLUTION AND NEGOTIATION

At first glance one can almost believe that the Danish cartoon controversy is intractable and could never be resolved. Nevertheless, a close look at the way the crisis was constructed tells us that there were clear lines opened for dialogue between the various factions that provided glimmers of hope in terms of a resolution. However, we will also see that lines of communication were often closed down because all parties refused to be wooed by each other's viewpoints.

Soon after the first publication of the cartoons and the mild outcry by Danish Muslims in the form of protest marches and editorials in newspapers, a group of ambassadors from 11 Muslim nations tried to meet with Danish Prime Minister Rasmussen to ask him to distance himself from the cartoons. Their response was moderate, and the group's intention was to initiate dialogue with the government in a peaceable, rational, and non-violent manner. Unfortunately, the group was rebuffed by the prime minister, who shut down all avenues for dialogue by refusing to meet them on the grounds that he could not infringe on the freedom of press. He refused the meeting two times in October of 2005. In other words, he took sides with *Jyllands-Posten* and refused to listen or be open to the point of view of the moderate Muslims who were merely asking him to condemn the publication of such material. What we have here is one group reaching out to another for a peaceful resolution and finding themselves shunned and sealed off from dialogue. It is possible that had the prime minister met the ambassadors and expressed his understanding for their concern and distanced himself and his government from any anti-Muslim and racist discourse, a lot of bloodshed and violence would have been avoided. This initial Danish response, which has been much criticized by the world stage, the Danish opposition, the UN, and other bodies, set the tone for the escalation of the crisis.

The second step taken by Muslim groups was to file a criminal complaint against *Jyllands-Posten* claiming that the paper had committed a criminal offence under sections 140 and 266b of the Danish Criminal Code. The case was dismissed on grounds of insufficient evidence. Further, the Danish prime minister took three months from the date of first publication of the cartoons to condemn any actions by anyone that demonize groups of people. He met with Muslim leaders for the first time in early February 2006, almost five months after the first publication of the cartoons.

The Danish prime minister had his own political agenda in shunning the Muslim community. Denmark has seen many years of a pervasive and populist anti-Muslim discourse and intense conflict between supporters and nonsupporters of this discourse. The Danish have also enacted various draconian anti-immigration laws that do not allow asylum to or are tough on people seeking asylum from various nationalities, are tough on spousal asylum seekers, and also do not provide governmental benefits for numerous years to immigrants who are then forced to live in extreme poverty, with low levels of education and substandard medical benefits. The prime minister came to power on the shoulders of the Danish People's Party, which was responsible for the enactment of such draconian immigration laws. His unwillingness to listen to the other side came from a need to protect his party position. He also refused the request to create a commission to look into the affair. His offices also denied public access to the documents that were relevant for the public and the media to analyze the development of the crisis and the government's handling of it. This was in direct contradiction to the principles on freedom of speech and expression espoused by the government. Ultimately, the prime minister met with the Democratic Muslims in February and spoke of dialogue and debate as the only solution to what had become a worldwide crisis. About the meeting, he said, "The objective of the meeting is to start a dialogue with Danes of Muslim faith about, among other things, integration and the current situation" (BBC News, 2006b). Although this statement was important, it came too late. Moreover, the meetings took place between the moderate Muslims and the government, and the so-called radical Muslims were still shunned from the talks. It was clear that the government was picking and choosing the Muslims that it would interact with, and these were Muslims who were already pro-Danish in their political views.

The cultural editor of a local daily, *Jyllands-Posten,* took it upon himself to rally for a dialogue between Islam and the media by provoking the cartoons that he ultimately published in the paper. Even though he was within his constitutional rights to do so, it might be a good time to note that this very daily had used its discretion in not publishing cartoons that insulted Christ. It had in the past few years contributed to dominant anti-Muslim discourse that prevailed in the country. Therefore, the very act of publishing these cartoons and choosing to do so at a political moment in world history may be considered an act of provocation. Having done so, the paper also refused initially to publish an apology. Eventually, when the apology came, the paper apologized for offending Muslims, but not for publishing the cartoons. Their claim was that they were protecting the freedom of press and to apologize for publishing would be tantamount to being open to censorship. They were unable to understand that even though censorship may not be good, some amount of self-censorship is a prerequisite for civilized dialogue, peaceful coexistence, and cooperation among groups of people. It has been pointed out that *Jyllands-Posten* launched the publication of the cartoons

> as an act of civil disobedience or freedom fighting . . . However . . . the "Face of Mohammed" can also be seen as . . . another example of how a reference to "freedom of expression" and "democratic values" can be an excuse for saying whatever you want . . . about what is considered a problem minority. (Jensen, 2006)

Flemming Rose, the editor of the paper, took a culture cop-out when he said that the publication of the cartoons was in keeping with the Danish culture of satire and the direct and informal form of debate in Denmark. However, as Jensen (2006) asserts, the editorial staff at the paper failed to explain why this resistance to self-censorship and defense of the freedom of press and expression was not launched a year before when a group of radical Christians forced a supermarket to stop selling sandals with pictures of Jesus. Additionally, the paper rejected unsolicited surrealist cartoons in 2003 that depicted Jesus. They also refused to publish holocaust denial cartoons offered by an Iranian newspaper. Three of these cartoons were later published in consultation with a rabbi in Copenhagen, a symbolic gesture that could have been carried out with Danish imams before the publication of the cartoons. It can only be concluded that by choosing to make Islam a scapegoat in their lobbying against media censorship, the paper was attacking Islam and reinforcing stereotypical images of Islam.

While the moderate Muslims were trying nonviolent and legal means of showing their discontent, radical imams in Denmark began inciting the crisis by attempting to garner international fundamentalist Islamic support for their cause. They traveled to Egypt and Lebanon to publicize the case and were able to incite violence against Danish and European embassies across the Muslim world through these actions. There were riots in virtually every nation with a Muslim majority and minority, Danish goods were boycotted, as were European goods in many countries. It is estimated that over 100 persons were killed in the year following the publication of the cartoons in related violence. Even though moderate Muslims were attempting to channel the crisis into one that could be negotiated through dialogue, the radical Islamists were slowly internationalizing and escalating the crisis and playing up the West versus Islam agenda. Perhaps what is most interesting is how the lines of communication and dialogue between the radical and moderate Islamists were shut down so much that the crisis gave rise to the creation of a moderate versus radical agenda, which has never formally existed.

The moderate voice could have provided a resolution to the crisis, but it was forced to remain mute vis-à-vis agenda's of other bodies. The moderate Muslim response called for dialogue with the Danish government and for a dialogue with the public about Islam. In fact, after receiving an apology from *Jyllands-Posten*, the Danish Muslim Association expressed satisfaction with the apology and promised to help with the integration situation in Denmark. They, in fact, apologized and expressed surprise for the crisis having gone out of hand. The radical imams, from the beginning remained against any reconciliation, and moreover the radical groups outside Denmark took a proviolence, provocative, and inflammatory approach to the entire crisis. They referred to the moderates as sellouts and labeled them bad Muslims.

It might be correct to say that both were at fault. The moderates can be faulted for wanting to distance themselves from the radicals instead of lobbying with them to reach a more moderate stance. The radicals could be faulted for their complete inability to listen to the moderate argument, which was in agreement with them over the condemnation of the cartoons, but wanted to use dialogic means to put an end to it. The radicals were unable to understand that creating a violent furor over the cartoons reinforced the "terror-based" image of Islam that is already prevalent in modern European society. Such a fact was stressed by the editor of a Jordanian daily, who published an editorial in his paper asking Muslims to think about how they were reinforcing the stereotype by becoming "militant" about the issue. Although the editorial was published, he was sacked from his job—another example of how lines of diplomacy, rationality, and dialogue were shut down on many levels. At one point moderate Islamic groups offered to provide the media with some education on Islam. This offer made by Muslim organizations in Norway was rebuffed by the Norwegian Press Association, who in turn asked that Muslims offer themselves up to be trained on the freedom of press and expression. In other words, they were telling Muslims that their values were incompatible with democracy and secularity.

The crisis might have actually come to an end by the early months of 2006, but many publications in Europe decided to republish the cartoons in solidarity with

Jyllands-Posten and the so-called freedom of press. This very act was not only provocative, but also offensive, given that the crisis was not past and there were clear tensions among the moderates, the radicals, the Danish government, and the Danish opposition. The media was not listening to the appeals of the UN, the violence in the Middle East, and the appeals of Western nations. The Council for Europe criticized the republication of the cartoons as did many other nations across the world. It can also be said that Europe's inability to take a firm stance proved deadly for the crisis. Europe was divided over the publication of the cartoons and never came to any agreement about what an EU stance needed to be. Moreover, in February, the European Parliament accepted a resolution that condemned all violence related to the cartoon crisis, but stated that it stood in solidarity with Denmark and all other countries that had been affected by the violence. This resolution also stated that even though Muslims may have been offended by the cartoons, they had the right to protest peacefully. At the same time the resolution stated that freedom of speech was absolute and could not be affected by any form of censorship. This was a mixed message to both the moderates and the radicals, as they would never really know the European stance on the issue. One can speculate that they were left feeling cheated by the European Union, which was technically also their own umbrella form of governance, as the Danish Muslims are also Danish citizens.

Eventually, the group that needed to be most heard, engaged, and associated with during the crisis—the moderate Muslims—were left on the margins. In the words of a moderate Muslim, Tabish Khair, an associate professor of English at the University of Aarhus in Denmark:

WE HAVE LOST OUR VOICE
Tabish Khair

When I first saw them, I was struck by their crudeness. Surely Jyllands-Posten could have hired better artists. And surely cartoonists and editors ought to be able to spot the difference between Indian turbans and Arab ones. In some ways, that was the essence of the problem to begin with. It is this patronising tendency—stronger in Denmark than in countries such as Britain or Canada—that decided the course of the controversy and coloured the Danish reaction.

One could see that the matter would take a turn for the worse when, late last year, the Danish prime minister refused to meet a group of Arab diplomats who wished to register their protest. In most other countries they would have been received, their protest accepted. The government would have expressed "regret" and told them it could not put pressure on any media outlet as a matter of law and policy. In their turn, having done their Muslim duty, these diplomats might have helped lessen the reaction in their respective countries. By not meeting them, the prime minister silenced all moderate Muslims just as effectively as they would be later silenced by militant Muslims around the world.

Like many other moderate Muslims, I too have been silent on these cartoons of the prophet Muhammad and the ensuing protests. Not because I do not have anything to say, but because there is no space left for me either in Denmark or in many Muslim countries.

This does not appear so to many Danes. Here the local controversy seems to be raging between two "Danish Muslim" public figures: Abu Laban, the Copenhagen-based imam who has coordinated much of the protest, and Nasser Khader, a member of the Danish parliament. Khader, liberal, clean-shaven, is posited against the bearded Abu Laban and seen as standing on the side of such "Danish" values as freedom of speech and democracy. He is supposed to represent sane and democratic Muslims. On the other hand, there is repeated talk of kicking Laban out of the country.

In actual fact, of course, both Khader and Laban make it even more difficult for moderate Muslims to be heard. Laban is not afraid of being kicked out of Denmark, because it is not his political territory. Similarly, Khader does not depend on Danish Muslim votes for his survival in politics; he depends on the votes of mainstream Danes, and his politics are geared towards that end. The prime minister's refusal to meet the diplomats was also partly the result of local political considerations: his government is supported by the xenophobic and anti-Islamic Danish People's party.

So much for Denmark, where complacency and smugness have reached extraordinary heights. In Muslim countries too we meet a similar string of local considerations. Surely the tensions between Hamas and Fatah played a role in the disturbances on the West Bank? Surely, some of the reactions—especially in Syria—were the working out of Islamic and pro-Iraqi frustrations on one of the allies of the US's invasion of Iraq?

One could, of course, follow the Qur'an's injunction against portraying Allah or Muhammad without forcing it on people who do not share one's faith. But then the question arises: why should people who do not share one's faith bother with images of one's prophet? For the sake of freedom of expression, said Jyllands-Posten. The only thing expressed by the cartoons, however, was contempt for Muslims.

But why, you might ask, should Islamic fundamentalists be worried about respect from a west that they mostly find unworthy of emulation? The answer to this lies in the histories of Islamic fundamentalism and European imperialism, aspects of which are horribly interlinked. As a reaction to European imperialism and, later, a political development of the west's fight against communism and socialism, Islamic fundamentalism is a quintessentially modern phenomenon. Hence, in their own way, Islamic fundamentalists are much more bothered about the opinion of "the west" than a person like me!

The Danish government should have apologised long before it did—but was right not to act against Jyllands-Posten. Freedom of expression is necessary not because it is a God-given virtue, but because if you let the authorities start hacking away at it you are liable to be left with nothing. But along with the right to express comes the duty to consider the rights of others. This applies as much to Jyllands-Posten as to the mobs in Beirut.

Between the Danish government and Islamist politicians, between Jyllands-Posten and the mobs in Beirut, between Laban and Khader, the moderate Muslim has again been effectively silenced. She has been forced to take this side or that; forced to stay home and let others crusade for a cause dear to her—freedom—and a cultural heritage essential to her: Islam. On TV she sees the bearded mobs rampage and the clean-shaven white men preach. In the clash of civilisations that is being rigorously manufactured, she is in between. And she can feel it getting tighter. She can feel the squeeze. But, of course, she cannot shout. She cannot scream. Come to think of it, can she really express herself at all now?

What was erroneously framed as a clash of civilizations came close to looking like one and created itself into one because the various factions remained closed from each other, protecting themselves from being wooed by each other's perspectives, experiences, and passions, thereby closing dialogue and channels of communication and ultimately disallowing the cross-fertilization of any ideas.

The Anglican Church and Gay Rights

INTRODUCTION

The controversy over homosexuality as a natural versus cultural process is age old. Within most dominant Christian churches, there are conflicting, even antagonistic, views over whether or not homosexuality should be allowed or is moral under the laws of the scripture. This very conflict came to the fore through the recent consecration of an openly gay bishop in America. In November 2003, Gene Robinson became the first noncelibate gay man to be ordained a bishop in the Episcopalian Church of the United States. His consecration continues to spearhead a split within the wider worldwide Anglican Church, of which the U.S. Episcopal Church is a part. In this chapter we discuss the controversy over gay and lesbian rights in the Anglican Church—a conflict that threatens to split the church into liberal versus conservative strains on a global scale, most specially within the United States and Canada.

Even though many incidents have triggered the gay and lesbian debate in the Anglican Church, in this chapter we focus on the controversy surrounding the consecration of Gene Robinson. Our goal is to discuss the Anglican Church conflict at length by focusing on three broad questions:

1. How is the conflict being constructed and by whom?

2. How are the forces of inclusion and exclusion being set up and by whom?
3. How are various factions avoiding seduction, intercourse, and ultimately impregnation?

Before proceeding to these questions, we discuss the lead-up to the conflict with brief background on the Anglican Church.

THE ANGLICAN CHURCH

Anglicanism is a denomination of Christianity that is either rooted in the beliefs, values, norms and practices of the Church of England or any denomination that maintains a liturgy that is complementary and parallel to the Church of England. The word *Anglican* has roots in the Latin phrase *ecclesia anglicana,* believed to be coined around 1246, and it literally means English Church. In the United States, the Anglican Church is referred to as the Episcopal Church. In general, the Anglicans or Episcopalians walk a middle ground between Roman Catholics and Protestants. Like all Anglican churches, "the Episcopal Church is both Protestant and Catholic, insists that people be able to worship in their first language, uses a Book of Common Prayer, and relies on Scripture, Tradition, and Reason to interpret God's Word" (http://www.episcopalchurch.org).

According to the official Web site of the Episcopal Church, during the Reformation in the 16th century, Henry VIII cut ties between the Church of England and the Roman Catholic Church and declared himself the head of the Church of England. Several political and theological factors gave rise to what we now call Anglicanism. The Episcopal Church in North America is a member of the worldwide Anglican Communion, the churches around the world that trace their roots to the Church of England and maintain a "communion" with it, hence the name "Anglican." Other members of the Communion include the Anglican Church of Canada and the Anglican Church of Nigeria. In fact, most Anglicans now live in Africa. Member Anglican churches are connected to each other by choice and hold no authority over each other. Further, the Archbishop of Canterbury, the head of the Church of England is considered the spiritual leader of the Anglican Communion. However, he does not have direct authority over any of the churches outside the Church of England.

About marriage, in general, conservative Anglicans believe that matrimony is a holy union and is a lifelong commitment between a man and a woman who make their vows before the church and God. The Episcopal Church in the United States has between two and three million worshippers in about 7,500 congregations across the country and related dioceses outside the United States. In total, there are believed to be 77 million Anglicans worldwide (*The New York Times,* 2006, 2007).

Even though many smaller conflicts led up to the eventual controversy about gay and lesbian inclusion, it was the consecration of Reverend Gene Johnson of

New Hampshire that has led to a worldwide schism in the Anglican Church. This consecration, coupled with another one in England (the consecration of celibate gay Bishop Jeffrey Johns, who later stepped down), has led to an ongoing debate about these matters in the Anglican Church (*The Daily Telegraph,* 2005). The controversy began in Concorde, New Hampshire, when on June 7, 2003, Gene Robinson was elected the first noncelibate gay bishop of the Episcopal Diocese of New Hampshire. There were celebrations in St. Paul Episcopal Church, over which Robinson presides, and he received standing ovations in the Sunday ceremonies following his consecration. His well-wishers were both the gay and the straight. His election was the first process in his step toward being a bishop, and it was generally expected that he would *not* win the majority to be confirmed as bishop in the General Convention of the Episcopal Church in July 2003. However, surprisingly, despite protests and strong opposition from the church, Gene Robinson was confirmed.

The gay and lesbian controversy in the Anglican Church rages on with no compromise in sight. Churches in Latin America, Africa, Asia, and some dioceses in England have threatened to split with the larger Church of England, unless it takes a stance against consecrating homosexuals and the blessing of gay and lesbian unions. In fact, some dioceses in the United States have already split with the liberal Anglicans and do not consider the head of the American Episcopal Church to be their presiding authority (*The New York Times,* 2004). In the following section, we take the reader back to the year 2003 and show how the Gene Robinson controversy came to be constructed by liberal and conservative Anglicans, laypeople, and so on.

THE CONSTRUCTION OF THE CONFLICT

The U.S. and global responses to Robinson's consecration and confirmation were wide ranging and in the following section we present how the conflict came to be constructed by the public, the Anglican establishment, and the laity at large. The section that follows is presented in a nonchronological manner and engages the different voices that gave rhetorical shape to the conflict. They are not listed in any particular order; rather, they show the diversity of opinion about the conflict itself. We begin with Gene Robinson's own stance on his election.

Gene Robinson, the man at the center of the controversy, came to represent the public face of the liberal Episcopal Church. A noncelibate gay man, Robinson was previously married to a woman and has two daughters; he has been living as a gay man for over 20 years. He was elected bishop by a majority of clergy and laity in his own diocese and later confirmed in the General Convention of the Episcopal Church. He has been dubbed by Evangelicals as the "the most dangerous man in the American Church" (*Sunday Telegraph,* 2003, p.17). Over the last seven years before and after his consecration and confirmation, he has made various statements about why the church must begin to acknowledge and accept the gay community. Speaking of closeted gay persons within the church in the *Sunday Telegraph,* he said,

> We all know that there are homosexuals in senior positions within the Church of England and the wider Anglican Communion . . . what sort of wholesome example is the dishonesty that we have fostered . . .? I personally can see a time when there is an openly active gay bishop in the Church of England . . . (Hastings & Day, 2003, p. 17)

Robinson pointed out that the Anglican Church's history of including minorities such as people of color and women into the communion proved his point. He was certain that his confirmation would not cause a split in the Church. Robinson pointed out that everyone was aware that there were gay priests and bishops and that the only thing different about him was that he had been openly honest about the matter.

In 2004, the Episcopal Church set up a committee to examine Robinson's election, and the committee released a report calling his episcopate "widely unacceptable" and suggested that the Anglican Church consider a moratorium on the ordination of other gays and lesbians as bishops. Broadly, the report rebuked the Episcopal Church of the United States for its confirmation of Robinson and also reprimanded the Anglican Church of Canada, where one diocese has been authorized to bless same-sex unions. To the report—widely referred to as the Windsor Report—Robinson responded,

> I think it's respectful of all the church's members, and I think it actually does provide us with a way to stay at the table with one another, to remain in communion.

Robinson also expressed anger that this issue was taking more attention than other political disasters in the world:

> How self-absorbed can we be, to be fighting over this when people are dying everywhere?
>
>   We have allowed the conservative religious right to take our Bible hostage, and I think it's time we took it back. (*The New York Times,* 2004, p.9).

Ultimately for Robinson, there was light at the end of the tunnel, but it would need to be directed judiciously:

> It seems to me the question before the Anglican Communion right now is: "Can we hold on to one another where we continue to disagree with one another?" I believe in the end God wins. In the end there is no one God does not love. I believe in the end we will see the incorporation of gay and lesbian people into the life and ministry of the Church. (*The Times* (London), 2005)

In 2008, Robinson was shunned by the once-a-decade summit of top Anglican clergy. In the last five years he has received many death threats and been called a "heretic." Robinson's response was moderate and tempered:

> I believe that God gave us the gift of sexuality so that we might express with our bodies the love that's in our hearts . . . In my relationship with my partner I experience just a little bit of the kind of never-ending, never-failing love that God has for me. (*Toronto Star,* p. A03)

Of his staunchest opponents, Archbishop of Nigeria, Peter Akinola, who is quoted as describing homosexuals as lower than dogs, Robinson questioned Akinola's tone in comparing lesbian and gay persons to dogs. He pointed out that it was unacceptable to compare his consecration to a satanic attack on the church. Robinson also said that Akinola and he would be in heaven together, and they would get along.

Liberal Anglicans

The voices of liberal Anglicans in support of gay and lesbian inclusion in the Church were loud and clear. One of the Anglican Church's most senior bishops, the Bishop of Oxford, Bishop Harries, had previously supported the consecration of a celibate gay bishop (Dr. Jeffrey John) in England. Ultimately there was such widespread opposition to the appointment that Dr. John voluntarily stepped down rather than cause a furor. Bishop Harries, who is a vocal supporter of gay and lesbian rights, said that it was necessary for the church to move with the times and become an "inclusive institution" and the "best pastoral provision for people who are gay and lesbian." He said that the church was misled and for most of Christian history, it was assumed that Jewish persons had no place in God's home. Similar to Robinson, Harries pointed out that just as slavery had been eventually abolished by the church and women had been ordained, one day gay persons would also be ordained. He said that there was no denying that there were gay and lesbian people out there who did not ask to be born that way and that the church needed to service them just as it did other laypersons. He commented on the forced resignation of another priest:

> I was very sad to see Jeffrey John step down and very sad to see the opposition there was to him. I feel he is gifted with the qualities of a good bishop and that he holds a position in line with the current teaching in the Church. (*Sunday Telegraph,* 2003, p. 01)

Another supporter of inclusion was Bishop Douglas E. Theuner, who was concerned that Gene Johnson would have trouble being confirmed by the General Convention.

A rector at St. Paul's, New Hampshire, David P. Jones pointed out that Episcopalians in his state were aware of the controversy that Robinson's confirmation would generate.

Other bishops, such as the Archbishop of Wales, Dr. Morgan, lent their support with statements such as these:

> There are people in the Anglican Church who are still arguing for a religion based on purity. Yet, if we are followers of Jesus, compassion not purity must be our hallmark. (*The Western Mail,* 2008, p.1)

The Archbishop of York, Dr. John Sentamu, pointed out that there needed to be a culture of "appreciative conversation" and "attentive listening" in the Anglican Church (*Sunday Mercury,* 2008, p. 17). There were others such as John Bryson Chane, Bishop of the Episcopal Diocese of Washington DC, who joined the debate for the inclusion of not only gay and lesbian diocese, but also gay and lesbian unions.

> The top official of the Episcopal Church in the United States, Presiding Bishop Katharine Jerrefts Schori, who was elected to the top position three years after Gene Robinson became bishop asserted that the gay rights struggle was not any different from the fight to abolish slavery or women's rights. Her own consecration came amid conflict, and she was narrowly elected from a field of several candidates after five ballots. Of gay inclusion in the church, she said (*The Boston Globe,* 2007, p. B3), "I don't believe that there is any will in this church to move backward." She also that it was necessary for the Episcopal Church to "keep questions of human sexuality in conversation, and before not just the rest of our own church, but the rest of the world."

Bishop Barbara C. Harris, the first woman to become bishop in the worldwide Anglican Communion, was on the side of the liberals. Harris is a black, divorced, and outspoken woman who was ordained despite not holding a traditional seminary degree. Retired and 77 years old, she lives in Massachusetts and is working on a memoir. She pointed out that the same persons who were condemning Gene Robinson had opposed the ordination of women, modernization of the traditional prayer book, and the consecration of a woman bishop (*The Boston Globe,* 2003, p. B1). She pointed out that here had always been a power struggle over who would run the church, and the "white boys" have always run it, and it was the latter who were resistant to any change in the church.

Harris had given some advice to Gene Robinson on how to withstand the assault. She was also an attendee at his consecration.

During the course of the controversy, Bishop Griswold was the presiding head of the Anglican Church of the United States. Many conservatives held him responsible for the schism and felt that he could have been more staunch in his opposition and critique of the liberals. On the eve of his retirement he said,

> Reconciliation won't come in trying to create one point of view but in common prayer. (*The New York Times,* 2006)

Bishop Griswold also pointed out that Biblical passages dealing with homosexuality refer to certain behaviors and not "patterns of affection." For instance, he pointed out that in the Gospels, Jesus said that he has more things to say to human beings, but they were not ready to hear them at that moment; this essentially indicated to us the organic nature of the God's truths in the book. Griswold asserted that if science was making us engage new truths, then why was it that when it came to sexuality, the church was unwilling to accept any new variations on the truth?

The general laity who supported the decision for Robinson to be confirmed said the following:

> I couldn't be more proud to be an Episcopalian. I'm so proud of my church that they had the courage to do this.

Gay members of Robinson's church were fully supportive and did not consider this much of an issue. They felt that it would make the church in New Hampshire a more inclusive one. Some other members said,

> The press has made more of this than we did locally . . . To us he was just a person who could make a great bishop.

A liberal group of bishops, priests, and laypeople from several countries called the Chicago Consultation, spoke of how the issues were being voted on and decided without any gay or lesbian representation on the decision-making committees; they blamed the head of the Anglican Church, Rowan Williams, for this:

> We are especially troubled by the absence of the openly gay members on the bodies that may ultimately resolve the issues at hand. The Archbishop's unwillingness to include gay and lesbians in the process perpetuates the bigotry he purports to deplore. (Davies, 2007)

Internationally, Robinson's case received scarce support. A staunch voice for gay rights and the inclusion of persons of different sexual orientations in African churches continues to be Reverend Desmond Tutu's:

> I'm deeply saddened at a time when we've got such huge problems . . . that we should invest so much time and energy in this issue. I think God is crying. (*African News*, 2005)

Back in the United States, there were two more openly gay priests who were consecrated into bishops immediately after the Robinson incident—in California and Newark. Liberal Anglicans responded consistently to the appointments. Reverend Sandye Wilson, who was the chairperson of the screening committee for the candidates in Newark, said,

> One of our core values is that there's a place at the table for everyone. (*The New York Times*, 2006, p. 1)

Reverend Susan Russell, who serves as the president of Integrity, a gay and lesbian advocacy group, said that the very fact that the Diocese of Newark came out so quickly with a gay man on its list of bishop candidates was proof enough that reason was prevailing in the church and the church was unwilling to be blackmailed by the conservatives.

The liberal Anglicans in the United States were the predominant supporters of Gene Robinson's consecration. Worldwide and even in England, the decision was seen as rebellious and blasphemous and as an act that would forever split the church. Bishops in Africa, Latin America, and Asia went so far as to announce that they would refrain from meeting with or worshipping with the leaders of American and Canadian churches (some churches in Canada have sanctioned gay unions). The bishops in the developing world joined forces with the conservative wing of the American, Canadian, and English Anglicans. They sent a letter to the Church of England asking them to discipline the church in New Hampshire and said, "If this request is ignored, then plainly we have reached the end of the Anglican Communion in its present form" (*Africa News,* 2004). Those who opposed gay and lesbian inclusion were following a more conservative interpretation of the Bible. In this section we present the opinions and words of the opposition and how its antagonistic stance continues to threaten a split in the global Anglican Communion.

The responses to Robinson's confirmation came from all parts of the world, in particular Nigeria, Kenya, many Latin American nations, and some parts of Asia. Most of the opposition came before and after Robinson's confirmation. We present them here in no particular order. The former Archbishop of Canterbury, Lord Carey of Clifton, said that there had been "incalculable" damage done to the Anglican Church by the Robinson confirmation and blamed the liberal element for the schism. His response was one of the milder responses:

> I can only add my voice to that of my successor in encouraging all those most deeply affected not to drift away from each other, but to strengthen the bonds of affection that remain at the heart of Anglicanism. (*Prophetic Times,* 2003)

Reverend David Phillips, who is the general secretary of the Evangelical group Church Society, said of the liberals:

> They are clearly not concerned about the unity of the Anglican Church. Our view is that the rest of the Anglican Church should now sever relationships with the whole of the North American Church. (*The Evening Standard,* 2003, p. 6)

Roseberry, a rector in Plano, stated,

> In two days, in two votes by less than 600 people, 4,000 years of Biblical teaching was overturned. (*The International Herald Tribune,* 2003, p. 5)

The responses from the African continent were full of animosity and antagonism. To protest the ordination of Johnson, many African bishops declared a ban on African congregations accepting funds from wealthy American churches. Kenya too joined in the ban. This was significant, as African bishops represent over half of the Anglicans in the world. Archbishop Peter Akinola, chairman of the Council of Anglican Provinces of Africa, was the most vehement in his denouncement of Robinson's ordination, calling it a "satanic attack on the church." Albeit he insisted that the African church would not split with the U.S. Anglicans over the issue. His focus was on cutting U.S. aid to African churches.

Archbishop Akinola was responsible for forwarding a letter on behalf of 14 primates in which he wrote,

> Unrepented sexual immorality, an offence so flagrant that Paul insisted that the sinner be expelled from the fellowship, and one of a type of sin which he said would cut the offender off from the kingdom of heaven. (Gledhill, 2005, p. 84)

Archbishop Nzeki, who is a Catholic archbishop, pointed out:

> The church action should be based on the faith in Jesus Christ and other influences should be shunned at any cost . . . Jesus is greater than the Western funding. (*Africa News*, 2004)

Bishop Akinola was the strongest denouncer of the ordination and said that the African Anglicans would take whatever steps seemed necessary if the U.S. Episcopalians did not within three months "repent" over the ordination of the gay Bishop Johnson. Later Akinola responded to the Windsor report stating that it "fails to confront the reality that a small, economically privileged group of people has sought to subvert the Christian faith and impose their new and false doctrine on the wider community of faithful believers."

Archbishop Njenga of Mombasa reiterated these points more sharply and said that the church would not accept any institution that used the Bible to confuse Christians, "The stand of the Catholic church is clear, we shall not associate ourselves with a church that supported evil." Another Bishop also said,

> We do not support gay marriage and anybody who supports the practice is not with us. What will this gay bishop teach his congregation about family life and the constitution of marriage? We know that we are poor as African faithful . . . we would rather be poor physically but be rich spiritually. (*Africa News*, 2004)

Bishop Thomas Kogo of Eldoret reinforced these points by stating that it was the poor who would see the kingdom of God; he entreated his followers not to accept any projects from the West that supported such indiscretions (*Africa News*, 2004).

Other bishops such as Tom Wright, the Bishop of Durham, asserted that liberals in the church has lost their mind in the 1960s, and they denounced Bishop Akinola as homophobic because they themselves felt racially superior to other Anglicans the world over:

> I hesitate to accuse anyone of racism, but there is an implicit sense that we in north-west Europe and America actually know how the world works and you poor people have to catch up . . . those who enshrine tolerance become extremely intolerant of anyone who disagrees. (*The Guardian*, 2003, p. 9)

In the midst of all this, a pro-gay bishop from Malawi, Nicholas Henderson, was denied ordination because he was the general secretary of a pro-gay Modern

Church People's Union. The leader of the Anglican church in Central Africa, Bishop Malango, said, "He (Bishop Henderson) has actively demonstrated that he was of no sound faith—that's what the court of Confirmation decided."

Of the Gene Robinson controversy, Malango asked, "How can you have a divorcee and, worse still, a man who sleeps with a fellow man, to head a communion?" (*Africa News,* 2005).

In Africa, the controversy was further heightened when the South African Constitutional Court ordered President Mbeki's government to amend the country's marriage laws within a year and begin to refer to marriage as a union between two persons rather than a man and a woman. As of December 6, 2006, it became lawful for same-sex marriages to take place. This occurred despite the government's refusal to act upon the court order.

There was further infighting within the African Anglican Church. Bishop Gladwin, a pro-gay bishop from Britain, was ostracized by the Kenyan Bishop Nzimbi while visiting Africa. He was, however, given a social welcome:

> When we differ with people in Africa, we still give them hospitality but this does not mean we agree with them. (*Africa News,* 2006)

During the height of the controversy, a convoy was sent to Kenya by the Bishop of Canterbury—the head of the Anglican Church worldwide—to diffuse the Bishop Gladwin situation. Reverend Kirker, general secretary of the Lesbian and Gay Christian Movement, spoke of this:

> Bishop Gladwin is sensitive to the fact that in the Church of England there are many hundreds of lesbian and gay clergy. (*Africa News,* 2006)

The Anglican Church in the Caribbean joined the protests and condemned the ordination of Gene Robinson. Bishop Sehon Goodridge of Windward Islands said,

> We cannot approve this if we agree that the church has to be a reference point for morals. So we have to work hard to see how we can guide and strengthen our people to get over this terrible onslaught. We do not want this in this part of the world. (BBC News, 2003)

Los Angeles Anglicans in the United States were caught in another row over homosexuality when there were rumors of the ordination of the first lesbian bishop. Three parishes announced that they were breaking away with the diocese and the Bishop of Los Angeles (who supported gay unions and Robinson). These parishes decided to put themselves under the governance of the primate of Uganda, Archbishop Orombi. The Los Angeles case was unique because there was a move to appoint a lesbian bishop despite a moratorium on gay and lesbian ordination recommend by the Anglican church in the Windsor report in 2004. The Archbishop of Canterbury, Rowan Williams, was deeply disturbed about the nominations and said,

There can be no doubt that these ordinations have not been encouraged or legitimized by the Communion over all . . . it opens the door to complex and unedifying legal wrangles in civil courts. (*The New York Times*, 2007, p. 15)

The Los Angeles case further confirmed the schism within the Anglican Church, especially between the Episcopalians of the United States and the rest of the Anglicans.

Eventually the Robinson case unleashed a series of other cases in the United States. Another gay ordination took place with the consecration of Bishop Michael Barlowe from Newark. There were various objections from the American Anglican Council:

We are shocked that just one week after the close of the General Convention and one day following the release of the Archbishop of Canterbury's statement on the Communion's future, the Diocese of Newark has sent a clear and defiant message nationally and internationally that there will be no turning back. (*The New York Times*, 2006, p.1)

Some bishops threatened to boycott the once-a-decade Anglican leaders meeting. The Bishop of Rochester Rt. Rev. Michael Nazie-Ali, who was a part of the Windsor Commission, suggested that those who had gone against the teaching of the church should not be allowed to attend these meetings:

I agree with the Windsor Report's recommendation those who have gone against Church teaching should not attend representative Anglican gatherings. We all need to repent for what we have done wrong . . . if those who have gone against the clear teachings of the Church . . . repent that would certainly change the situation. (*Birmingham Post*, 2008, p. 2)

Women bishops were split over the issue. Those who had lobbied for years for the ordination of women were on the side of the conservatives. Rev. Canon Mary Haggard Hays of Pittsburgh rejected the parallel between the role of women and that of homosexuals in the church. She pointed out that even if one was opposed to the ordination of women, it could not be disputed that there were moments in the scripture that were positive about women's roles as leaders. However, there was nothing positive in the scripture about homosexual behavior (*The Boston Globe*, 2003)

Conservative laypersons among the Anglicans supported their priests. John Albert a member of the Episcopal church in Savannah, Georgia, said,

This was the final step of the U.S. Church to put itself at odds with the larger Anglican community about this subject. So we face a time when there needs to be a greater discernment as to where we go individually and as a body. It is intolerable for us to be under a leadership that allows things that counter scripture to go on. (*The Boston Globe*, 2003, p. B1)

Archbishop of Canterbury—Head of the Anglican Church

Archbishop of Canterbury, Rowan Williams, took the middle path in the conflict. He criticized the American Episcopalians for departing from the Anglican Communion's consensus on scripture by ordaining Johnson and blessing same-sex unions in Canada. But, he was as critical of the primates in Africa, Latin America, and Asia for "annexing American parishes" and an entire California diocese that have recently left the Episcopal Church and for ordaining conservative Americans as bishops and priests. "There can be no doubt that these ordinations have not been encouraged or legitimized by the Communion over all. On the ground, it creates rivalry and confusion. It opens the door to complex and unedifying legal wrangles in civil courts" (*The New York Times,* 2007, p.15).

For Williams, the only solution was to keep talking. However, Williams came under pressure to not invite Gene Robinson as well as the newly ordained conservative Episcopalian bishops and priests (ordained by African prelates) to the once a decade conference of the Anglican Church.

> Sometime in 2003, after the consecration of Gene Robinson, the Archbishop of Canterbury set up a body known as Fulcrum, a movement for "open evangelicals" which aims to "renew the center of the Church of England by developing a form of Evangelicalism that is capable of moving beyond the present controversies over sex." (Gledhill, 2003, p. 10).

By July 2008, 1,300 English clergy were threatening to defect if gays or women were given equal rights (note: England still does not have any women who are ordained) in the Anglican Church. Moreover, 800 others were promising to form a "church within a church." In the interim, some states in the United States and some parts of Canada began legitimizing same-sex unions with the blessing of the Anglican church (10 of 110 Episcopalian dioceses in the United States bless same-sex unions). In February 2007, the Anglican Communion presented the Episcopal branch in the United States with an ultimatum—ban blessing of same-sex unions or risk a reduced role in the worldwide communion. By 2007 more than a third (and almost half) of the Anglican churches worldwide had moved back on any communiqué with the U.S. liberal branches.

A survey of the media coverage of the issue reveals that most policy makers and national governments stayed away from the issue, and their voice within the construction of the conflict is mute. In the following section we discuss the various rhetorical strategies utilized by the various parties. In effect, we show that a solution to the conflict lay within the different opinions about it, but no side was willing to be seduced by the viewpoint of the other.

DIFFERENTIAL TACTICS AND STRATEGIES

The controversial consecration of Gene Robinson, which threatened to split the Anglican Church, is now five years old, and there seems to be no end in sight.

From the preceding section on responses to the ordination and the construction of the conflict, it is clear that there were a wide variety of responses to the move. In fact, the repercussions of the consecration took most conservative Anglicans by surprise. Individuals, organizations, policy makers, the world community, and the media gave their verdicts on the issue by rhetorically constructing it and offering specific tactics to end it. In this section, we discuss those strategies and show how each was unsuccessful because the conflict over the gay and lesbian rights in the global Anglican Church rages on in the United States, Africa, the Caribbean islands, Asia, and Canada.

Liberal Anglicans have been quite straightforward about their stance. They are interested in inclusion of all persons and insist that the Church must practice what it preaches—that is, tolerance of all human beings and a belief that God is for everyone, not just the chosen few who are heterosexual. For them, inclusion of other nationalities, women, and blacks was no different from the inclusion of gay and lesbian persons into the Anglican diocese. They see the debate and the fight as no different and consider it an issue of civil and religious rights. They created parallels between the treatment of gay and lesbian priests with slavery and pointed out that the two forms of discrimination were equal and equally despicable. Their stance was the need for the church to move with the times and embrace an issue that had been festering in the Anglican Church. For them, the Bible needed to be revisited, so it could be reinterpreted in the light of contemporary issues.

The conservatives were also very clear about their position. They stayed close to the scripture and maintained a zero-tolerance approach to gay and lesbian ordinations as well as same-sex unions. They blamed the liberals for causing a schism in the church. It was the conservatives who had, in the past, opposed the entry of women clergy, modernization of the Biblical interpretation, and same-sex unions. All of their maneuvers to block gay and lesbian ordinations, same-sex marriage, and women's entry into the fold can be considered consistent with patriarchy and the hegemony of masculinity and heterosexuality.

It was the African bishops and primates who took a stronger stance against liberal American Episcopalians. For most African bishops, the moves by the American dioceses were consistent with a form of colonization. They attacked the liberals by suggesting that just because American churches had more money, they could not subvert the teachings of the Bible in any way they pleased. They condemned all the moves toward homosexual inclusion as well as same-sex unions, pointing out that all these issues were inconsistent with the scripture and that one could not pick and choose what to follow and what not to follow. Their main argument, however, was a West versus Africa argument or a developed versus developing world argument, whereby they asserted that this was just another case of the rich West exploiting the African population, in this case African Anglicans. For them, the issues became that of an arrogant privileged West trying to impose its values on other churches in the developing world.

LET A CHURCH SO FOND OF DIVISION TEST ITS WORTH IN THE MARKETPLACE OF BELIEF
Simon Jenkins

Those eager for small talk with Gordon Brown should try Scots Presbyterian schismatism, on which he is remarkably well informed. British rulers since the days of Trollope have found the politics of religion an absorbing relief from the trials of office. It usually means someone in even bigger trouble.

But the show has always stayed on the road through the remarkable tolerance of the Anglican community, "broad of church and broad of mind, broad before and broad behind". From Anglo-Catholics to happy-clappies, old codgers to gays and lesbians, the ever benign Church of England embraced them all, no questions asked.

Now those versed in these things tell us that the elastic has stretched too far. The church is on the brink of snapping apart. Need we care?

The scenario is near unbelievable. At a meeting last week in Jerusalem a dissident body called the Global Anglican Future Conference summoned 300 bishops and archbishops from round the world to set up a Fellowship of Confessing Anglicans, within or without the "70-million strong Anglican communion". So-called Gafcon and Foca might be from the satirical film Life of Brian. We read that Lagos is threatening to denounce Canterbury. Sydney is at loggerheads with Ottawa. America is threatening to create a "new province". All and sundry are castigating the saintly Archbishop of Canterbury, Rowan Williams, for failing to show "moral leadership"; if he did, they would certainly refuse to follow.

Meanwhile, 1,300 English clergy are about to defect if gays or women are given equal rights (or rites), while 800 more are forming "a church within a church". St Bartholomew the Great is told that it may "disagree but not disregard" Lambeth Palace in blessing gay unions. Journalists must pore over the Book of Common Prayer to see how a blessing relates to a marriage, or an ordination to an enthronement.

It might be simplest to conclude that these are the last twitches of the British empire. The mind and the body may be long dead, but the soul has taken some time to catch up. It must be absurd to expect 70 million worshippers worldwide to accept the "discipline and leadership" of an archbishop selected by just 1 million in distant England—especially when each of 38 archbishoprics are referred to as "self-governing".

Equally absurd is to expect the cultures and belief systems of Polynesians, Chinese, Africans and Americans to harmonise with the fast changing social mores of the white Anglo-Saxon Protestant diaspora. How can African bishops commune with gay American ones, whom they regard as in mortal sin?

People of whatever spiritual disposition are less inclined to take dictation on how to conduct their lives. Few Roman Catholics adhere to doctrine on sex and procreation. The day has long passed when religious edicts can be enforced at law—though the sword can still do it.

The last great schism in the Church of England came with John Wesley's Methodist defection in the 18th century. His was a protest against authority, not doctrine. Methodists, he wrote, should be "churchmen or dissenters, Presbyterians or Independents, it is no obstacle. None will contend with them. They think and let think." His tolerant message was crucial in turning early America against Anglicanism.

The Church of England, for all its prominence in national life, is a modest phenomenon. Church attendances in Britain are in steady decline. A report in May concluded that in 2033 there would be more worshippers in mosques than churches. Even now, only some 1.2 million people go to an Anglican church at least once a month, fewer than to a Roman Catholic one.

The church has become bureaucratised, multiplying over the past century into 42 English dioceses and 114 bishops, whose obsession with faction and controversy has always been the curse of Anglicanism. Like medieval barons they are a nuisance to the king and a burden on the people. This week's Church Times has feuding bishops dominating every one of seven news pages.

It would be better surely to detach this ecclesiastical conglomerate from its so-called establishment: from the monarchy, the bizarre 26 seats in parliament and the humiliating antics in Jerusalem. Repatriate it to Britain and allow it to find its own level in the marketplace of belief. The Church of England should be a church in England. If that means live and let die, which I doubt, so be it.

That said, critics rarely look beyond the doctrinal conflicts that so consume the headlines, and examine the church's true costs and benefits. The picture is mixed. British churches have a good record in short-term tolerance but a dreadful one in divisiveness.

Religious doctrine is a menace that has spattered the world with blood as it now spatters it with acrimony. Rival narratives are deeply embedded in every community's DNA. The shrill conflicts of Ulster, still enshrined in its politics and in public policy on schools and housing, show how fragile is the veneer of civilisation over the rock of religious bigotry.

I once attended a ceremony in Liverpool at which the then Anglican and Roman Catholic bishops, David Sheppard and Derek Warlock, staged one of their periodic reconciliations. Their personal bonding was impressive, as are all such top-down interfaith gatherings. But the led seldom follow the leaders.

When I suggested to the bishops that they could best practise what they preached by merging their offices, cathedrals, churches and schools and make religion a force uniting Liverpool, they looked appalled. Institutional division by faith remains the curse of urban Britain. The churches, now expanding their educational empires, are doing little beyond exhortation to heal it. Yet churches are community institutions and as such a fact on which reconciliation has to build. As in Ulster, so in the Muslim communities of England, also riven with doctrinal faction; grappling with religious discord probably holds the key to staving off ethnic conflict.

With the dismantling of local political responsibility by the Thatcher and Blair regimes, churches have stood increasingly alone in poor communities. Priests are often the only professionals still resident on inner-city estates. They are informal mayors, social workers, marriage counsellors, police and conciliators. They offer value beyond price—and beyond recompense.

Atheists should be realists. Churches, and for historical reasons especially Anglican ones, are among the nation's most visible public institutions, and thus natural bases for social action. That they should be tearing themselves apart in the imperial detritus of world Anglicanism is a tragedy.

The Church of England is confounded by an absurd argument over gender and sexual discrimination, albeit often as code for a growing challenge to the authority of what is seen abroad as a still imperial church. A looser confederation of churches, a commonwealth of faith, ought to be good news.

It should enable the English church to concentrate on its home base, serving parochial communities in ways that extend beyond religion. But that is unlikely to happen if, as seems likely, even the church in England cannot find peace within itself. In which case, who gets the nave and who the steeple?

The most interesting position was one taken by women bishops. Women were split in half over homosexual inclusion. Those who supported it were consistent in their approach about the idea of tolerance extending to everyone, no matter who they were. Some other female clergy, however, took the conservative stance arguing that scripture did not talk kindly about homosexual behaviors as it did of women leaders. These women remained on the side of the conservative Anglicans, ironically siding with persons who had probably in early days denounced women's inclusion in the church clergy.

The head of the Anglican Church, Archbishop Rowan Williams, took mostly a middle path. Given that he could not take one side or the other for fear of a permanent split within the Communion, he emphasized dialogue, discussion, and setting up commissions and groups to bring the conservatives and liberals to the table. Although it can be said that he was inclined to agree with the conservatives on most other issues.

RESISTING RESOLUTION AND NEGOTIATION

Controversy over homosexuality is not new to the Christian world or to the church. In fact, it is a debate that has been encountered in various religious communities. In this particular case, it is clear that the debate split the church along conservative and liberal lines. The conservatives want to stay with one interpretation of the Bible, whereas the liberals want to modernize it to the times, respond to and indeed mirror the needs of the contemporary lay. When one examines the rhetoric of all the parties in the conflict, it seems that there can be no solution to the controversy because how does one really change one's religious belief systems? However, a closer look at the debate, the actions, and the controversy show that there was indeed a solution to the conflict embedded in the voices that were heard.

First, as Simon Jenkins pointed out, the Church of England is a church that originated around a certain group of people and served the needs of those persons. Even when it was expanded worldwide, consistent with colonization, it failed to keep into account the local values, norms, and customs of the persons it was serving. As Jenkins suggests, how can one body know what someone in Polynesia or China needs versus the needs of the lay and clergy in the United States. The dioceses in the United States were responding to the needs of the persons they were serving. The original ethos of a worldwide Anglican communion was to allow the various dioceses to be self-governing, as each diocese took care of its own under the wide umbrella of the church. However, this ethos of each diocese as an autonomous entity was forgotten and indeed submerged in the vitriolic debates that ensued.

The Archbishop of Canterbury took many steps to reconcile both sides, but he was rebuffed in his endeavors. For instance, he agreed with the African primates to set up a commission, the Windsor Report, which recommended a moratorium on homosexual ordinations and unions. He was responsible for forcing the parties to sit together and talk by creating a group called the Fulcrum. He tried to placate the conservatives by asking Gene Robinson to absent himself from certain conventions and conferences. However, all his maneuvers came a little late in the controversy. They needed to have taken place years before the consecration of Gene Robinson to pave the way for a smooth transition toward inclusion.

Gene Robinson's gestures of goodwill toward the conservative and his desire to talk to them were rebuffed. At the peak of the conflict when the African Communion was attacking him, he remained open to dialogue. However, no one stepped in to engage with him, thereby further heightening the conflict.

In fact, it was the church lay who the church serves who remained completely out of the process. There was no real attempt for any civic engagement in the debate. Ultimately, the debate raged on in the upper bureaucracy of the church, and as a result many conservative and liberal lay were ignored and indeed sidelined. Their opinions and ideas were never circulated, except journalistically, and they were kept outside the debates.

The loudest voice in the debate was that of the African primates. Had there been an attempt to engage with these primates even before the Robinson consecration, the conflict might not have taken such antagonistic forms. For the African primates living in largely postcolonized nations and economies, the act was one of symbolic violence by the West. Indeed, it is surprising that their response was not anticipated by the liberal Episcopalians.

On July 29, 2008 the Anglicans had just completed the 20-day Lambeth conference—the 140-year-old annual meeting of the Anglican Communion, which occurs every 10 years. The Lambeth Conference is the only visible symbol of unity within the communion, but this year it was the epitome of disunity. A quarter of the bishops worldwide declined invitations from the Archbishop of Canterbury and refused to sit down with the liberal Anglicans, who they felt had committed sacrilege. They agreed to set up a new pastoral forum is to bring rebel provinces into line in the Anglican Communion. About 650 bishops attended the Conference and debated proposals that would halt any more consecrations of gay bishops or same-sex blessings. This proposed forum would "clamp down on 'cross-border interventions' such as those where conservative bishops from Africa have consecrated bishops to pastor congregations in the United States" (Gledhill, 2008). Further, the forum requested a further moratoria on gay consecrations, same-sex blessings, and cross-border interventions. Even as they did so, they acknowledged that moratoria would be difficult to enforce. They said,

> The failure to respond presents us with a situation where, if the three moratoria are not observed, the [Anglican] Communion is likely to fracture.
>
> We believe that the pastoral forum should be empowered to act in the Anglican Communion in a rapid manner to emerging threats to its life. (Gledhill, 2008)

The forum also warned that "a 'proliferation' of ad hoc episcopal ministries such as those put in place by conservatives could not be maintained. It calls for all existing ministries already set up to be placed 'in trust' to be reconciled back into their original provinces" (Gledhill, 2006, p. 11). Ultimately, their goal through the forum was to force a resignation from the openly gay Bishop of New Hampshire, Gene Robinson, suggesting that the Anglican church would not survive as one body until he was a part of it. There has been no end to the debate, and each week there are new reports on the status of the controversy. In August 2008 it was continuing unabated with no end in sight.

The Veil Conflict in France

KEY TERMS

Assimilation

Fundamentalism

Headscarf

Immigration

Nationalism

INTRODUCTION

In March 2004, French President Jacques Chirac signed into law a ban on all conspicuous religious symbols, including the Muslim *hijab* (head scarf), in French public schools, starting what is often referred to as the veil controversy. This is an issue that is, in fact, an ongoing intercultural and global conflict in many European countries, such as Holland, Britain, and Germany, and other countries, such as Iran and Turkey. The French ban came into effect under article 141–5–1 of Law No. 2004–228 of National Code d'Education, and it explicitly stated,

> In public elementary schools, middle schools, and high schools, it is forbidden to wear symbols or clothes through which students conspicuously display their religious affiliation. Internal rules require that a dialogue with the student precede the enforcement of any disciplinary procedure. (Commission de réflexion, 2003, p. 14)

No sooner had the law been declared than France was beset by widespread demonstrations, strikes, threats of lawsuits, international outrage, terrorist threats, and so on. The French head scarf conflict had begun.

In this chapter, we discuss the conflict at length by focusing on three broad questions:

1. How is the conflict being constructed and by whom?
2. How are the forces of inclusion and exclusion being set up and by whom?

3. How are various factions avoiding seduction, intercourse, and ultimately impregnation?

Before proceeding to these questions, we discuss the lead-up to the conflict with
more background on how the ban came to be law.

How the Head Scarf Ban Came to Be

The roots of the veil conflict in France are complex, but the first incident that made
clear that it was a contentious issue occurred in 1989 in a public school in the
small French town of Creil near Paris. The school headmaster at Creil refused access to the school to three girls who were unwilling to remove their head scarves.
Media coverage of this incident led to angry public debates about the issues and
copycat incidents in other parts of the country (Brems, 2006, p. 118). The Minister
of Education, Jospin, asked the Conseil d'Etat—the highest administrative court in
France as well a body advising the government—for advice on how to calm down
the situation. The question Jospin—the minister of education—posed was whether
wearing accessories that symbolize religion in public schools were compatible
with "la laïcité," or the French term for secularism. The court responded by stating
that the accessories were compatible with "la laïcité" as long as the signs:

> by their nature, by the circumstances in which they were worn either individually
> or collectively, or their ostentatious or claiming character are an act of pressure,
> provocation, proselytism or propaganda, or interfere with the dignity or the free-
> dom of the student . . . or threaten their health or security . . . disturb educational
> activities . . . (Brems, 2006)

The court concluded that the school had a right to include these restrictions in their
internal rules and use them.

Even though this particular incident triggered the head scarf controversy, it
can also be said that the conflict is as old as the emigration of Muslims—most of
whom are part of a postcolonial diaspora from former French colonies in North
Africa—into Europe in the last six decades or so. France has a Muslim population
estimated at over 5 million—the largest in any European country (Ibrahim, 1994).
Even though there is no universal prescription in Islam to wear the hijab, in some
interpretations of the religion, on reaching puberty women are required to cover
their heads in public life (Abu-Rabia, 2006). In modern usage the hijab is a head
scarf that fully covers the hair, neck, and ears of Muslim women. Originally, the
term meant "curtain," and even though women are supposed to wear it after puberty, in some more conservative Muslim communities, even prepubescent girls
can be seen wearing them. The terms *veil* and *hijab* are often used interchangeably

in the West; however, it has different connotations in various parts of the world, even within Islam. In France itself, there are persons of different Islamic traditions, not all of whom believe in wearing the hijab.

Given this background, in 1994, another minister of education from another party issued a new circular that asked schools to prohibit religious symbols that were so ostentatious that they segregate students from the common school life. This circular included a model clause that was to be inserted into school rules. Yet the Islamic head scarf was not qualified as a symbol in itself. Even so, this directive led to the suspension of 68 girls from schools. In November of 1994, the Conseil d'État responded to the September circular stating that the former/latter had no legal force and advised school directors to make their own decisions. In 1999, two Turkish schoolgirls in Fleurs started veiling, and the schoolteachers called a strike in protest. Despite their offer to compromise and wear knit hats over their hair instead of scarves, they were expelled from the school. In another incident in 2002, school officials banned a schoolgirl in the Tremblayan from wearing the head scarf to school. The student struck a deal with school officials and began wearing a loosely draped blue scarf instead of a tight black one. However, all 90 teachers in her school went on strike when she was readmitted. In 2003, the expulsion of two Muslim sisters, Alma and Lila Levy, from their school in a Parisian suburb was the case that inflamed the existing controversy. Even though the girls had followed the rules of the school and worn patterned and colored scarves (deemed less aggressive by schools, which consider white, black, brown, or navy blue to be religious symbols), they were sent home for disobeying the so-called ban on religious head scarves (Levy & Levy, 2004).

The conflict simmered throughout the 90s and early 2000s, and school authorities were often frustrated because they bore the responsibility of deciding whether head scarves were allowed or not. In essence the "problem" had been tossed back to the schools to be dealt with on a case-by-case basis. In the last decade or so, it is estimated that about 2,000 to 3,000 young women began wearing the head scarf to school. Thus the "problem" was seen as simmering and continuing.

In 2003, in light of these persisting issues, then French president Jacques Chirac set up a "commission of wise persons" to study the issue of "la laïcité," particularly in the area of public education (Brems, 2006). The French tradition of laïcité came into being against the influence and domination of the Catholic Church in public affairs. Chirac's stated goal was to "strengthen" French republican values of secularism and reinforcing the separation of church from state, an idea that was instituted by Jules Henry, the father of French secular education, in the 19th century. A crucial law passed in 1905 decreed the separation of church and state. The president's desire to rekindle and reignite these values was his way of responding to overt religious expression.

The French Secular Tradition

1789: The French Revolution

1789 and 1809: France marches on Rome to abduct recalcitrant popes

1905: Law on separation of church and state

1937: Schools instructed to keep religious signs out

1989: School ban on religious signs ruled illegal

1994: Minister says school can ban "ostentatious" signs

2004: MP's vote in support of ban in religious symbols in schools

This commission was given the goal to study the application of the principle of "la laïcité." It was headed by Bernard Stasi, a former cabinet minister and official ombudsman in matters involving French secularism, who put together a group of 19 members, including three Muslims, three Jews, and six women. Each member was loyal to the notion of separation between church and state, and the goal of the commission was to determine whether the laws on secularism were sufficiently easy to understand or whether they needed clarification. After five months of studying the different ways of reconciling public conduct and religious values and beliefs, the commission presented a 67-page report whose tenor indicated "that the state intends to reassert what it regards as its traditional right on how religion influences public life in France" (Sciolino, 2003a). Apart from the veil, the commission also investigated issues such as Muslim women refusing treatment by male doctors, students challenging teachers about the holocaust, and the "new anti-Semitism" among disaffected Muslim youth. The commission secretary Remy Schwartz said,

> This anti-Semitism is real in our country . . . we found children to leave public schools in some areas because they are not secure . . . this has profoundly shocked the commission. (CNN, 2003)

The report stated,

> In one century, because of immigration, French society has become diverse in terms of is spiritual and religious aspect. (Sciolino, 2003a)

Stasi, the commission head, announced that the members of the commission were astonished to see that

> The situation was more serious than we previously thought . . . and there are without any doubt forces in France that try to destabilize the republic, and it's time for the republic to react. (Sciolino, 2003b)

Eventually, the report made the recommendation to ban all conspicuous religious symbols, including large crosses, scarves, yarmulkes, and even the wearing of

Sikh turbans from public institutions. However, it showed some leniency in the use of small crosses, Stars of David, and hands-of-Fatima pendants. Additionally, the commission urged the establishment of a national school of Islamic studies and Muslim chaplains for prisons; it also urged making Yom Kippur and Id Al-Adha national holidays. The bill was passed into law by an overwhelming majority of 494–36, with 31 abstentions in the National Assembly, and the ban came into effect with the start of the school year in September 2004.

The process of creating and then passing the law was intensely contentious and unleashed a debate about the pros and cons of the head scarf ban not only in France, but also in Europe and the rest of the world. Even though the majority vote exhibited broad support for French secularism, it deepened resentment against native French within the French Muslim community and Muslim nations. In the following section, we discuss how the conflict was set up by different parties who were directly or indirectly involved in the process.

THE CONSTRUCTION OF THE VEIL CONFLICT

The veil controversy took substantial shape with the passing of the 2004 law. In the lead-up to the bill's introduction in the French Parliament, there were serious debates about who the law targeted and whether or not it was necessary to maintain "la laïcité" a core French value that separates church and state. Even though the commission headed by Stasi was set up to reengage secularism, it was often popularly believed that the law was specifically created to target Muslim head scarves and ultimately came to be seen as a French stance against Islam. In this section we engage with different voices that gave rhetorical shape to the conflict. They are not listed in any particular order; rather, they show the diversity of opinion about the conflict itself. We begin with the official French government's construction of the conflict.

Jacques Chirac and the French Government

Even though the Ministry of Education had passed small circulars in 1989 and 1994 addressing the idea of "la laïcité," the issue was taken up by Jacques Chirac, who spearheaded the movement to return secularism to French schools. Chirac used various tactics to support his decision to set up the commission and finally promote support for the bill that banned head scarves among other religious symbols in school. At different points during the debate, Chirac gave reasons for his support of the ban. For instance, talking to students from a French school in Tunis, President Chirac said he felt there was "something aggressive" in the wearing of veils and that his government would forbid "ostentatious signs of religious proselytism" (BBC News, 2003b). In initial speeches where he backed the ban, Chirac said that if France accommodated demands by all religious communities, it would sacrifice its heritage; it would compromise its future; it would lose its soul.

CHIRAC BACKS LAW TO KEEP SIGNS OF FAITH OUT OF SCHOOL
Elaine Sciolino

PARIS—Ignoring opposition from Muslim leaders within France and beyond, President Jacques Chirac on Wednesday called for a new law banning the wearing of head scarves for Muslim girls, large crosses for Christians and skullcaps for Jewish boys in public schools.

In a speech at Élysée Palace broadcast live on television, Mr. Chirac recalled centuries of history that, he said, defined France as a guarantor of individual liberty, and said the secular identity of the French state was at stake.

If France succumbs to the demands of its religious communities, Mr. Chirac said, "It would sacrifice its heritage; it would compromise its future; it would lose its soul."

Calling secularism a "pillar of our Constitution," he said that he would urge Parliament to pass the law in time for the start of the next school year, in September 2004.

"In all conscience, I believe that the wearing of dress or symbols that conspicuously show religious affiliation should be banned in schools," Mr. Chirac told an audience of 400 guests, including members of the cabinet and Parliament, representatives of the major political parties and religious, human rights and union leaders.

He added: "The Islamic veil—whatever name we give it—the yarmulke and a cross that is of plainly excessive dimensions: these have no place inside public schools. State schools will remain secular. For that a law is necessary."

Mr. Chirac was responding to an official report presented to him last week on the place of religion in French society and how best to preserve the French republican ideal separating church and state.

Among other proposals from the expert commission Mr. Chirac appointed in July was a recommendation that public schools add religious holidays, like Yom Kippur for Jews and Id al-Kebir for Muslims, a proposal that Mr. Chirac rejected in his speech on Wednesday. More holidays would burden working parents, he said, but he added that students should be able to take time off for their religious holidays, so important exams should not be given on such days.

But Mr. Chirac embraced the commission's recommendation to pass a law banning "conspicuous" religious symbols but allowing "discreet" ones. As the argumentative French news media have been pointing out, there is no indication of who will make that determination, or how.

Mr. Chirac also called for a law to prevent patients from refusing treatment by a doctor or health-care professional of the opposite sex; for the development of the teaching of basic religious facts in schools; for a "code of secularism" for civil servants to use as a guide in the workplace; and for the creation of a watchdog agency to monitor violations.

Although Mr. Chirac spoke about the general need to prevent religion from encroaching into the public sphere, it is the increasing demands of France's growing Muslim population and the wearing of the Islamic veil that has infused the issue with new urgency.

Many schools quietly allow girls to keep their heads covered. But there is a conviction, both within the government and among a large swath of society, that the veil is as much a defiant political challenge as it is a religious display.

At the same time, leaders of the country's Christian and Jewish communities have joined Muslim leaders in criticizing a ban.

The struggle to integrate France's estimated five million Muslims into French society is also a hot-button political issue, one that has been exploited by the far-right National Front, which has criticized the Chirac government for not being tough enough on crime and illegal immigration. Regional elections are scheduled for March, and with the country suffering high unemployment and a poor economy, Mr. Chirac's government has been losing popularity.

In his speech, Mr. Chirac acknowledged the alienation of France's Muslim youth.

"I share the feeling of incomprehension, of disarray and sometimes even of revolt by those young French people—immigrants by origin—whose job applications go into the garbage because of the sound of their names," he said, "and who are too often faced with discrimination when they want to find housing or even get into a place of recreation.

"All the children of France, whatever their background, whatever their origin, whatever their belief, are daughters and sons of the republic."

Mr. Chirac's announcement follows the recent unveiling of draft legislation by the German states of Bavaria and Baden-Württemberg to ban Muslim teachers from wearing head scarves in public schools.

In the *New Yorker,* Chirac was also quoted as saying,

> . . . laicity is a part of the social contract in France. The state does no put a foot in any belief. It is a very French conception and we hold on to it . . . Religion is not a subject we impose on French children. The law is because of that. (*The New Yorker,* 2004, p. 62)

Chirac's party deputy, Jerome Riviere, asserted that France was being challenged by a small minority of hard-line Islamists. He insisted that the law was not suppressing religious freedom and instead noted,

We have to give a political answer to what is a political problem. We don't have a problem with religion in France. We have a problem with the political use by a minority of religion. (*BBC News,* February 11, 2004)

A socialist MP, Martine David said,

This law is indispensible for us as teachers need a clear judicial framework. (Henley, 2004)

In introducing the bill to the National Assembly, the French Prime Minister, Jean-Pierre Raffarin, said,

Certain religious signs, among them the Islamic veil, are multiplying in our schools. They are taking on a political meaning . . . We are giving them a response today . . . Religion cannot be a political project . . . For the most recently arrived, I'm speaking here of Islam, secularism is a chance, the chance to be a religion of France. (Sciolino, 2004f, p. N10)

The ruling party's general secretary, Philippe Douste-Blazy, said in support of the ban that it would

. . . help all those millions of Muslims in France who are genuine republicans, who believe in an Islam in France rather than an Islamic France . . . (otherwise) 10 or 20 years down the line we could have some very serious republican problems indeed. (*The Guardian*, November, 2003).

The house speaker, Jean-Louis Debré, stated that the law was a

. . . clear affirmation that public school is a place for learning, not for militant activity or proselytism. (Henley, 2004)

The head of the law commission of the National Assembly, Pascal Clement, called the measure:

. . . the flag of France whose colors we want to raise today, once again, above the schools. (Sciolino, 2004e, p. A3)

The French education minister, in an interview to *Le Point,* stated,

We must respect the culture and faith of the Muslims, but the history and the will of our people was to build a united, secular society . . . My instructions to school heads will be very clear. We will continue to accept discrete religious signs . . . But we cannot accept ostentatious signs that divide or youth. (Ibrahim, 1994)

The French anticipated protests from the Muslim world and therefore as soon as the ban was imposed, they sent ambassadors to various Muslim nations to convince them that it was not an attack on Islam, but rather a domestic French issue. For instance, then-interior minister and present French president, Nicolas Sarkozy, went to Cairo, where he managed to secure a declaration from a prominent Sunni religious figure, Mohammed Sayyed Tantawi, that women in non-Muslim states should obey local laws. Sarkozy, a supporter of the ban stated,

You shouldn't see in it a humiliation for anyone . . . You shouldn't see in it a lack
of respect for your religion. You must understand that secularism is our tradition,
our choice . . . I thank the grand imam of Al Azhar for indicating that in a secular
and non-Muslim state, it is the duty of everyone to respect the law . . . There are
no rights without duties, and if the Muslims of France have the same rights as
other believers, they have the same duties. (Sciolino, 2003b)

Sarkozy's statements reinforced the ruling party's agenda, which emphasized the
ban as a universal ban on "all" religious symbols and asserted that no one religion/
Islam was being singled out. However, ironically, Sarkozy had initially spoken
against the ban, calling such a move "secular fundamentalism." When Sarkozy
was elected president of France in 2007, he reinforced his support for the ban in
2008, stating,

In France, there is no place for veils in schools. There is no place in France for
polygamy, no place for ablations, no place for forced marriages, for veils in
school nor for hatred in France. Because behind this is the law of the tribe. And,
to live in France, you must respect France. (Barillas, 2008)

French Muslims

The ban received a mixed response from French Muslims as there was no single
stance taken by the Muslim community in France. Rather, there were differing
viewpoints and arguments both for and against it. In this section we present
Muslim voices of organizations, individuals, feminists, students, and teachers who
were either for or against the ban. In showing these diverse responses, our goal is
to illustrate how the issue is not one that can be discussed along neatly opposing
lines and is instead much more complex and problematic. Although 69% of French
citizens backed the ban, French Muslim women were divided over the issue (49%
in favor and 43% against). Some of the first protests against the ban began in
December 2003, when thousands of protestors included young women in hijab.
The predominantly Muslim demonstrators carried their French identity cards or
carried national flags and walked in the rain carrying banners that read:

My veil, my voice.
Veil, cross, kippa, leave us the choice.
Beloved France, where is my liberty?
Proud to be French Muslims. I vote!
(Leicester, 2003).

Organizers of the protests were quoted saying:

Liberty, equality, fraternity—apart from women who wear the veil.
    We are being undressed . . . We feel that we are considered second-class citi-
zens. (Leicester, 2003)

Some French Muslims said the law was discriminatory and would create more problems than it solved. Most Muslims were concerned that it would radicalize the moderates. Khalil Merroun, who is the Imam of the every mosque, pointed out that

> The government stresses that the new law refers to all religions, but nobody is fooled. How many school children turn up to class wearing crucifixes of a manifestly excessive dimension? It is not the crucifix or the kippa that is targeted. (Carle, 2004, p. 65)

Farhad Khosrokhavar, a sociologist, asserted that only 20% of France's 5 million Muslims were "religiously minded," but even the moderates would take offense to this ban because

> Even those who do not wear the headscarf are likely to feel offended because it is a denial of personal rights. Instead of fighting against Islamic radicalism it might encourage it, precisely because of this feeling of stigmatization. (*Sydney Morning Herald,* 2004)

Lhaj-Thami Breze, head of the fundamentalist Union of French Islamic Organizations, noted that a large number of devout French Muslims

> . . . want to practice their religion in peace and in total respect of the law. But when you persecute, when you make fun of, when you refuse, when you don't respect beliefs, what is the consequence? The consequence is radicalization. (Henley, 2004)

Fouad Alaoui, the vice-chairman of the Union of French Islamic Organizations, felt that his organization could not tell people not to protest the ban because

> Given their growing anger, we cannot tell Muslims who feel their fundamental liberties are being violated that they shouldn't demonstrate. (*Aljazerra,* 2004)

In a separate interview to the *New Yorker,* he said,

> The French have always had a problem with religion—it's a reflexive action. And they have a huge problem with women. They think that their model of emancipation is the emancipation. But girls who want to stay in school, girls who want to be doctors—that's not the only model. (2004, p. 68)

Kamal Nawash, president of the Free Muslim Coalition Against Terrorism, said,

> . . . you can be a Muslim even if you don't wear the veil. For example, my group, we come from a version of Islam where we don't even believe the veil is required. The Koran never said you have to cover your hair. All it says is you need to cover your bosoms. And the rest of it was just evolved through the years. I think it's partly cultural and a whole bunch of other things. But, one thing I supported—the reason I as a Muslim cannot criticize France, or at least I don't put any weight on Muslim leaders who criticize France, because, if you're going to criticize France, the only way I'm going to listen to you: I want to see you criticize Saudi Arabia

and Iran that force women to wear the veil. So either we have an international standard, where there is freedom of religion and so on, or then we leave it up to each individual country to make its own rules. And in that case, since we're not criticizing Saudi Arabia, we're not criticizing Iran, we're not criticizing a whole bunch of Muslim countries that force women or put enormous pressure on a woman to wear it, I don't think we have any obligation or any credence in criticizing France. And I think the French, when they hear criticism, I think they should use this argument. "Why would you ask us that we can't do this. All right, we'll stop doing this, then why don't you ask Saudi Arabia and Iran to give the women a choice." So it's good for us, I think it's good for Muslims, secular Muslims such as us, and by the way, we think Islam is secular, or there is a secular argument within the Koran: we think this is important. I would like to see this argument go one step forward. I haven't heard that from the French, those who support the ban, making this argument, challenge the Muslim clergy saying just the argument that I said, which I'd like to see. (Voice of America, 2004)

Yet there were other Muslims who supported the ban. For instance, Iranian-born writer Venus Kavoussian wrote that she valued and respected France's traditions and so supported the ban:

It's important that school stays non politic, non religious—personally I am in France because it is a secular space. (BBC News, 2004f)

Dalil Boubakeur, considered to be a moderate Muslim and president of the French Council for the Muslim faith, favored the ban, saying the following at different points in the debate:

As responsible Muslims it is our duty to explain the position of the president. The law of the state is our law . . . I warn my fellow Muslims, brothers and sisters, in the current climate of tense relations between Muslims and society in Europe in general and France in particular, we must play the democratic game. (*Middle-east Online,* 2003)

Elisabeth Badinter, a French intellectual gave an interview about the veil to the *Le Nouvel Obervateur* and explained,

The veil, is a symbol of oppression of a sex. Putting on jeans, wearing yellow, green, or blue hair, this is an act of freedom with regard to the social conventions. Putting on a veil is an act of submission. It burden's a woman's whole life. (As quoted in Carle, 2004, p. 67)

Other intellectuals, such as Dounia Bouzar, an anthropologist and member of the French Council of the Muslim Faith, said that wearing the veil was a way for women to remain close to their families alongside challenging other traditions such as arranged marriages. Fawzia Zouari, a French-Tunisian writer took a different approach and called the veil an emblem of feminism and not a sign of religious submission.

Feminists were clearly divided over the ban. Although a majority supported it by arguing that the head scarf is often imposed on girls by their fathers and brothers and the Koranic verse discussing veiling is open to interpretation, many feminists spoke against it. French feminist and Muslim activist Siham Andalousi spoke against the ban by talking of students who wear veils:

> Most girls who wear headscarves are excellent students. They get A's and become model members of society. Yet now they are *the* French problem. With the new law, they are deprived of an education and left to the mercy of their men. (Carle, 2004, p. 65)

French Muslim students were fairly nonviolent in their protest against the ban. A group of 200 protestors gathered outside the National Assembly to oppose the new law. Most were young Muslim women, all wearing head scarves. As expected, they were upset by the ban:

> It is unjust and I am very angry, angry yes, it's not just, it's a law, a segregation. (Wyatt, 2004)

As classes opened, one Muslim girl in the working-class Paris suburb of Aubervilliers left her head scarf at home because:

> I was always treated badly and I felt uncomfortable, so I decided to take it off. (BBC News, 2004d)

A young 15-year-old Turkish-Muslim girl, Cennet, was banned from wearing the head scarf in school after the 2004 ban. Her mother told reporters that Cennet tried everything—a beret, a bandana—but kept being refused into class. She said that her daughter just wanted to go to school like everyone else, but had been needlessly traumatized. Eventually, Cennet shaved her head and began coming to school and was allowed entry. Cennet was quoted saying,

> I will respect both French and Muslim law by taking off what I have on my head and not showing my hair. (BBC News, 2004e)

She also told journalists:

> I respect the law, but the law doesn't respect me. (BBC News, 2004e)

Some students opposed the ban, but had compromised by wearing bandanas to school to remain enrolled. For many, the ban reinforced and strengthened their belief in the hijab. As a Muslim student, Touria, explained,

> What does this veil mean to me? It's part of who I am. It's not just some bit of fabric on my head. It's everything. Looking back on it, I can't imagine taking it off. What I'm wearing today I consider the minimum. (Jones, 2005)

Khouloud, a model student who wanted to be a doctor, was expelled from school in Mulhouse:

They have just destroyed my life. My classmates liked me just the way I was. They didn't ask me to show my hair before electing me class delegate last year. (BBC News, 2004c)

Other ordinary French Muslim citizens were disturbed by the ban, but were not involved in violent demonstrations. Abdelkarim, a resident of Marseille asserted,

It's a total trap this law. Have you ever seen Christians wearing an immense cross? Of course not. It's meant to discriminate against Muslims 200 percent. Most girls who wear the veil will end up not going to school. But it doesn't matter. The real school is the Koran. (*Middle-east Online,* 2003)

Muslim World

There was fierce opposition to the veil ban in most of the Muslim world. Veiled women demonstrated in the streets of Cairo, Tehran, Gaza, and Amman. About 5,000 people protested in Beirut. However, there were no official protests from governments in the Muslim world. The former Iranian president, Ali Akbar Rafsanjani, stated,

The French authorities will not succeed in banning the Islamic veil in schools. But if they succeed, millions of Muslims will curse them. (*The Economist,* 2004, p. 25)

For many Muslim extremists, the ban was another manifestation of the West's war on Islam. Ayman Al-Zawahiri, who is considered the second-most-important person in Al-Qa'ida, stated the following in an Al-Arabiyah television broadcast:

Banning the hijab in France is consistent with the burning of villages along with their people in Afghanistan . . . It is consistent with torturing prisoners in the cages of Guantanamo . . . It shows the scope of the Zionist-Crusade's moral and doctrinal hypocrisy and the extent of its savagery in it was against Islam and Muslims. (Why-War.com, 2004)

Muslim clerics all over the world urged other Muslims to use their political and economic influence over France to fight the ban. Syria's top cleric, Mufti Ahmad Keftarou, called on Chirac to reconsider the law. In a letter to the French president, he requested of Chirac:

To reconsider backing this decision to be in harmony with the great history of France and its moderate tradition in allowing coexistence between religions, races, and various nationalities. (*Aljazeera,* 2003)

Even so, there were diverse voices within the Muslim world, some that supported the ban. One of the most influential Sunni clerics in the world, the Egyptian grand sheikh of Al Azhar, Muhammad Sayed Tantawi, issued statements that indirectly supported the French ban, saying that non-Muslim countries were free to impose bans as:

> Just as I do not allow non-Muslims to interfere in my affairs as a Muslim, at the same time I do not permit myself to interfere in the affairs of non-Muslims. (*The New York Times,* 2003, p. A5)

The cleric's opinions were not shared by the Muslim Brotherhood, which is considered the world's largest and most deeply influential Islamist group who opposed the French ban:

> The secular philosophy on which the French president based his decision to support this proposal, considering the hijab a religious symbol, is not correct . . . The Islamic hijab is a religious duty. (*The New York Times,* 2003, p. A5)

Even though there were some violent skirmishes over the conflict, the most significant "violent" incident inspired by the ban occurred outside France in Iraq in late August 2004, some weeks before the ban was to be executed in the new school year. Two French journalists were kidnapped by a militant Islamic group, the Islamic Army of Iraq, which demanded that the French ban be revoked within 48 hours and called the law unjust and an attack on Islam and individual freedom.

The French government refused to cow down to the demands of the terrorists. In fact a majority of French Muslim organizations cautioned the hostage takers that they ought to stay out of French interior affairs.

French Educators

France's teachers were more or less supportive of the ban and had, indeed, lobbied for it for many years. Raymond Scieux, headmaster of Lycee Eugene Delacroix in Drancy, a suburb northeast of Paris, explained his ideas on the ban to the BBC News in March 2005. Scieux said that there was a lot of tension about the matter among the Muslims in France, but that the law was indeed applicable to all religions.

A history teacher in Delacroix, Eric Finot, who strongly supported the ban, said the following at a public meeting, which was also attended by veiled girls:

> We are only asking you to abide by the principle of secularism . . . This law is here to protect those girls who are compelled to do things they don't want to do—not to be forced into marriage, not to wear the veil. (Jones, 2005)

Ghislaine Hudson, head teacher of another school, and a teacher who sat on the Stasi Commission and voted for the ban, said,

> It's a law for their well-being, they shouldn't take it as something aggressive, they shouldn't take it as a negation of what they are. (Wyatt, 2004)

A Paris secondary school teacher, Herve Ricard, supported the ban saying,

Schools are not just public spaces, they must be autonomous places progressive proselytism, intolerance, and polemic. Every religion must be treated the same, none must be singled out for favoritism or punishment. That is the intransigent condition of true neutrality; that is genuine secularity. (Henley, 2003)

A professor of political science in the University of Picardie in Amiens, France, Abderranhim Lamchichi felt that the Muslim world did not understand the law:

The Muslim world simply doesn't understand the law. It is deplorable that even liberal Muslims think that the law is against Islam. That is absurd. (Sciolino, 2004a)

French Opposition

In general, members of France's opposition parties opposed the law and believed that it was against integration and would hamper a multicultural society. For many, the legalization of the ban was unethical, as there was no Muslim representation in the National Assembly. Conservative politician and civil rights activist Zaïr Kedadouche lamented,

There isn't a single Muslim in Parliament to vote on this law and not a single Arab among all the country's mayors. France is broken. (Crumley, 2004)

Many of them pointed to a lack of logic in how the law might preserve French republican values. Green party leader Noel Mamer also opposed the new law:

I think it's a very bad law, a law which takes the risk to make worse the rift between two parts of the French population. (Protect Hijab, 2005)

Domoniqie de Villepin, the then-foreign minister, was of the opinion that the law would be seen as an act against the veil rather than one that protected secular values.

European Union

France received a strong level of support from most of the European Union on its ban on the head scarf. Indeed, some nations promised to follow suit. Belgian senator Alain Destexhe, inspired by the French ban, proposed a similar bill in Belgium.

The German response to France was supportive. The then-German Chancellor Gerhard Schroeder stated that head scarves had "no place" among public school-teachers, but unlike France, Germany would not be able to prevent Muslim school-girls from covering their heads in the classroom. The Dutch government declared its intent to seek the veil ban in public places for "reasons of public order, security and protection of citizens." The Vatican declared that veiling as a practice was disrespectful to local customs and cultures. In 2007, Canada, too, began its own debate about whether or not women should be allowed to wear the veil in public spaces.

In Britain, a veil controversy of its own kind began in 2006, when its foreign minister, Jack Straw, suggested that the full veil (in which only the eyes of the women can be seen) separates people and hinders integration and that he would ask women at his constituency surgery to remove their veils before talking to them. Straw's comments unleashed a huge furor in Britain and fueled the debate in different sections of society much like France. Eventually, a new uniform code was drawn up by the Ministry of Education whereby schools began to be allowed to ban pupils from wearing the full-face veil on grounds of security and safety. Similar to France, there were divided responses from the two-million-strong British Muslim community, with some in support and some vehemently opposed to the ban.

Media, Feminists, and Academics

The issue was debated with much zeal among academics, commentators, feminists, and media analysts. Presented here are a variety of voices from this segment of the population. Each faction presented the crisis in a different way. Fareena Alam, the editor of *Q-News,* Europe's leading Muslim magazine noted,

> Modesty is only one of many reasons why a woman wears a scarf. It can be a very political choice too. (BBC News, 2004f)

Vivienne Walt, correspondent for *Time* magazine, USA, compared French and American values when she said,

> Well, it's something that Americans find extremely difficult to understand. . . . I mean, France is extremely committed to the principle of secularism in government institutions. (Voice of America, 2004)

Amir Taheri, an Iranian author and journalist based partly in Paris, considered it a wrongful ban:

> The headscarf ban is a political move. (BBC News, 2004f)

Rachida Ziouche, a journalist and daughter of an Algerian imam has been living in exile in France since fleeing her homeland. She was in support of the ban, especially in how she felt it would empower women.

Alice Schwarzer a prominent German feminist wrote,

> This issue is about the constitution, and the division between state and religion— a hard fought for achievement of the enlightenment.

Speaking about the veil controversy that shook Britain a few years after it did France, Sir Salman Rushdie, Indian-born British novelist and a Muslim, said about the veil:

> . . . as somebody with a very large female Muslim family, there is not a single woman I know who would have accepted wearing a veil. The battle against the

veil has been a long battle against the limitation of women. I think the veil is a way for taking power away from women. (Western Resistance, 2006)

Juliette Minces, a sociologist and author of the book, *Veiled: Women in Islam,* discussed the issue as one of identity:

> It has become an important issue in France because France is, as said before, a very strongly secularized country. Which means, not to consider that the main identity should be religious. You are a person and whatever your religion is, first of all, at school, you are a pupil. (Voice of America, 2004)

A French commentator, Guy Sorman, writing in the *Wall Street Journal* Europe, wrote,

> What this shows is that the present debate, and the legislation that will come out of it, have less to do with an actual Islamist threat than with perceptions and symbols. . . . But French politics is more comfortable dealing with symbols than with reality.

Binnaz Toprak, a political science professor at Bosphorous University in Istanbul, Turkey, agreed with the French ban:

> Civil servants and schoolgirls should not wear the veil.
>
> In the case of civil servants, I think that when people refer to someone in government office, they should be able to feel that they will not be discriminated against because they do not share the same beliefs as that civil servant. A headscarf could be seen as a symbol of those beliefs.
>
> The issue in Turkey at the moment is whether university students should be allowed to wear the hijab. Many students wear it for political reasons but others wear it for religious reasons and I think that choice should be respected. (BBC News, 2004)

Tariq Ramadan, a professor of Islamic Studies and Philosophy at Switzerland's Ecole de Geneve and University of Freibourg, stated,

> Muslims in France believe they are being targeted. Muslim population, and many Europeans are afraid of losing their identity. The debate in France and other countries over the headscarf appears to be a manifestation of this, and it doesn't help.
>
> Muslims should see the ban in France as a sign that the road ahead is not going to be easy but it is not the end of the road. It is just the beginning of the dialogue. (BBC News, 2004)

Other Religious Groups

There were also mixed reactions to the ban from other religious groups. Although some supported the ban, others were against it. Fanny Dethloff, a pastor at a Hamburg church who is responsible for refugee issues in the community, spoke against the ban:

> It makes absolutely no sense at all to bar Muslim women from public places because they wear the scarf. (BBC News, 2004)

Dethloff was clear that Muslims wanted to condemn and pointed out that this could not be done are the cost of punishing women who are hardly involved in popularizing an intolerant form of Islam. He felt that the crackdown would just lead to more victimization.

Many French Christian, Jewish, and Muslim leaders alike were opposed to the conflict. Catholic, Protestant, and Orthodox leaders issued a statement before the government warning that the ban would be perceived as discriminatory and would be more harmful than beneficial.

The president of the Protestant Federation of France, Jean-Arnold Clermont, criticized the ban as "anti-Islamic" and stated and asserted that everyone knew that people no longer wore large crosses, so it was indeed hypocritical to say that this law was for all and not just the Muslims and the Jews in France.

The bishop of Angouleme, Claude Dagens, stated,

A law would reawaken old conflicts, confrontation and exclusion. (Henley, 2003)

The bishop of Evry, Michel Dubost echoed this sentiment:

Legislation would target the surface of things. The root problem is far bigger than that of headscarves in schools—it is the whole question of how to successfully integrate third-generation Muslim immigrants in France. (Henley, 2003)

Greville Janner, vice-president of the World Jewish Congress, said that French legislators had "disgracefully punished the entire Muslim population and other religious communities."

Grand Rabbi Joseph Sitruk pointed out that French persons of all faith should be encouraged to show tolerance for each other rather than issuing bans on any single religion or symbol. He said,

The right way is not to pass a law, which I fear would end up banning all religious symbols. What an aberration it is to muzzle religion in the name of secularism. (*Haartez*, 2003)

The Sikhs, a religious minority in France, which was not included in the ban, came to be a part of the conflict because Sikh men wear turbans over uncut hair. For Sikhs, the hair is sacred, and both men and women are not allowed to put shears to it. Even though Sikh turbans are not religious symbols, the French Sikh community was concerned that they would be construed as such. This community, which comprises only a few thousand in France, were overlooked in the Chirac report that supported the ban. Speaking to a reporter from the *The New York Times,* a Sikh student stated,

I'm 100 percent French, I speak French, I was born here. But it's impossible for me to take off my turban. (Sciolino, 2004g, p. A4)

Some Sikh leaders sent a letter to the president asking for an exemption of the Sikhs. In it, a Sikh temple leader, Chain Singh, wrote,

This will not only be a failure of our freedom to practice our religion here in France but also of the attitude of the French toward the Sikh community. (Sciolino, 2004g, p. A4)

United States

The ban was criticized by the United States, which issued an official statement against the ban. For this, it was chided by the French government for interfering in an internal French matter. In an official public statement made by John W. Hanford, the Bush administration's top official on issues related to religious freedom, the U.S. government criticized the ban:

> A fundamental principle of religious freedom that we work for in many countries of the world, including on this very issue of the headscarf, is that all persons should be able to practice their religion and their beliefs peacefully, without government interference. (Aslan, 2003)

United Nations

The UN response was to send its special rapporteur on freedom of religion or belief, Asma Jahangir, on an 11-day fact-finding mission to France. She concluded that the ban was put in place without a full appreciation of all possible consequences. Jahangir pointed out that the ban was being rigidly employed at "the expense of the right to freedom of religion or belief." Jahangir, who is also a human rights lawyer in Pakistan, asserted that the ban had

> . . . in a number of cases, led to abuses that provoked feelings of humiliation, in particular among young Muslim women. The issue is one of principle and not a number game. (It denied) the rights of those teenagers who have freely chosen to wear a religious symbol in school. (GG2. Net News, 2005)

Human rights watch considered the law a violation of the freedom of religion and expression, as well as being discriminatory against Muslim girls. They officially stated,

> The impact of a ban on visible religious symbols, even though phrased in neutral terms will fall disproportionately on Muslim girls. (Human Rights Watch, 2005)

DIFFERENTIAL TACTICS AND RHETORICAL STRATEGIES

The controversial French ban on religious symbols has spanned over 20 years from the expulsion of the three Muslim girls from their school in Creil to the enactment of the 2004 law that banned "all" religious markers. From the preceding section on responses to the ban and the construction of the veil conflict, it is clear that there were a wide variety of responses to the controversial ban; in fact, the repercussions of the ban seem to have taken the French by surprise. Individuals, organizations, policy makers, the world community, and the media all gave their verdicts on the ban by rhetorically constructing it and offering specific tactics to end it. In this section, we discuss those strategies and show how each was unsuccessful because the conflict over the veil rages on in most of Europe, many countries in Asia, and some North African nations such as Algeria, with a return in Turkey where it has been banned from public institutions for many decades.

Chirac and the French government stance on the conflict were clear and unrelenting. They used the secularism agenda to target the banning of religious symbols, but it is clear from the voices presented in the previous section that their particular focus seemed to be on the head scarf worn by Muslim girls (Hamdan, 2007). According to Chirac, "Secularity is one of the Republic's great triumphs. It is a crucial component of social peace and national cohesion. We cannot let it weaken" (quoted in Ziegler, 2007, p. 106). The French position was simply that it was safeguarding French republican values of "la laïcité," which were recently elaborated on by Windle (2004, p. 97):

> The French stakes its claim to legitimacy on the identification of citizens who share the "universal values" of equality, secularism, and freedom offered by the Republic. Cultural and religious differences must be managed in order to preserve a space ordered by the common good alone, and open to all.

The French Assembly passed the law by suggesting that any symbol that seemed ostentatious and proselytizing would come under the ban, and the hijab was the only symbol that had been under contention for the past 20 years. The official government stance on it suggested that it was an "equal" law that was equally applicable to all persons and that persons who were living in France would follow French law—"la laïcité." Summarizing an interview with President Chirac, Kramer (2004) reported in *the New Yorker:*

> . . . now the veil has come to be what he (Chirac) calls "the siege of a politics of Islamization," it has no place in a French public classroom. (p. 64)

For defenders of the ban, the main argument used was that France has historically had a strict separation of the church and state, and the ban was necessary to uphold that value of the French Republic. The official French discourse on neutrality focused on the exclusion of symbols (particularly the hijab), all the while imposing "one" discourse or the French way of life in the schools, thereby decreasing diversity. In other words, it took a position of secular neutrality based on exclusion (it is the opposite to the United States, which (in theory) supports the inclusion of all symbols in support of neutrality). As the French government coerced neutrality through exclusion and a nonnegotiable stance, it ended up creating divided lines between the five million strong French Muslims and the so-called native French community and as predicted further radicalized some of the Muslim community. It was sacrificing diversity over neutrality and the imposition of one French national voice on its citizens, or what was referred to as secular fundamentalism by those who opposed the ban.

Non-Muslims who were broadly against the ban argued that France's draconian civic secular tradition creates a default nonneutrality of secularism (Gereluk, 2005). Gereluk (2005) pointed out that this secularism favors French Christians who can practice their faith without seriously compromising their beliefs because the French "neutral" education system falls alongside Christian calendar practices. Thus non-Christians were often placed in noncompromising positions that forced them to break rules of faith and practice. For instance, even though "all" visible religious symbols are now banned from public schools, the bans on crucifixes and *yarmulkes* are inconsistently enforced. For those who have been opposed to the ban, it is clear that Islam is being unnecessarily targeted. Or as Thomas (2006) pointed out:

> . . . many derided that the new law was an attack on Muslims thinly disguised as an even-handed prohibition of religious signs in general . . . One might therefore be tempted to argue that the French were really just seeking a way to permit only typical symbols of Christian faith . . . (p. 245)

The stance taken by the antiban factions was that a moratorium on all religious symbols is in reality a ban that targets Muslim girls who are a part of the French Muslim community that has never been allowed to or graciously invited to fully assimilate into France. An imposition of a "neutral" secular policy has been seen as persecution and as an imposition of one way of life over another. Even though the French might be given the benefit of the doubt in not being solely focused on eliminating the hijab, their tactics, strategies, and statements throughout the course of the conflict suggested otherwise. They were inadvertently sculpting the controversy into an embodiment of the Huntington thesis by suggesting that French values were secular values and Islamic values were fundamentalist and that somehow Islam was not consistent with secularism.

Other non-Muslims who were against the ban were resisting it for different political ends, and their focus was immigration and integration policies. For instance, the far right party, the National Front (FN), was against the ban because it wanted to see overt support for a French Christian culture and an end to massive Muslim immigration. In an editorial published in the FN weekly *National Hebdo,* it was argued,

> The solution to the problem rests in assimilating those who accept being assimilated and returning to their countries of origin those who do not. Legislating on the veil in school is legislating on the accessory. (Thomas, 2006, p. 246)

The right left was propounding the Huntington thesis in its anti-immigration pro-Christianity stance. The EU's relative support for the French ban echoed this position, and initiatives to propose similar bans in Germany, the Netherlands, Belgium, and England are evidence of such support. The lack of support for the ban from Human Rights Watch and the UN was to be expected, as these are more or less neutral organizations when it comes to freedom of speech and expression. The United States' criticism of the law was not unexpected because the United States is already targeted as an anti-Muslim state and has been trying hard to convert this image ever since its army offenses in Iraq and Afghanistan.

Yet other opponents of ban were those non-Muslims who said that the ban on the veil would hardly help to integrate a marginalized Muslim minority that has been ignored for almost five decades. In fact, they considered the veil as a minor skirmish in the battle between Muslim practice and French law. For instance, Contenta (2004) argued that the hijab ban was one of the first measures to discourage Muslim immigration into France (in Hamdan, 2007). After September 11, 2001, the right-wing French government headed by Chirac began various initiatives to curtail the migrations of Arab Muslims into France (similar to many other European nations). For instance, you could not get a French ID if you covered your head or could not speak French, and so on. Thus, many saw this as just one more anti-immigration measure. They felt that the veil was being used as a political weapon to force integration through exclusion, when what was needed were sustained policies and programs for Muslim integration and participation in French society.

The extreme Muslim response was not very different in strategy from the Western response in the sense that they, too, invoked versions of the Huntington thesis and correlated the ban with the war on Islam, the war on terror in Afghanistan and Iraq, and the post–September 11 climate against Muslims the world over. For many (not all) Muslim fundamentalists in France as well as across the world, the hijab ban was seen as a West versus Islam conflict. Some fundamentalist interpretations of Islam consider the hijab not as a form of oppression against women, but as a vital component to being a Muslim woman. The conservative Muslim position was straightforward and intractable. The conservatives were unwilling to think in terms of the ban from the point of view of French nationalists. For them, rather than being oppressive, the hijab protects women from being seen as sexual objects and allows them to be treated as human beings. As Gereluk (2005) stated,

> Muslims argue that they recognize the importance of established differences in the roles of boys and girls . . . These roles are not seen as hierarchical between men and women, but rather are advocated as complementary to the relationship between the husband and wife in Muslim society . . . (p. 268)

The fundamentalist response was an anti-West response, and the hijab happened to be the symbol that was under discussion. It can be said that the symbol under attack could have been polygamy, female genital mutilation, evolution, holocaust denial, and so on. In fact, all these issues were cited in the Stasi report, but the hijab seemed to take center stage in public debates, as it seemed to its opponents to be a visible symbol of female oppression.

The moderate Muslim response asked for dialogue, supported the ban, reinforced a "French-first" identity, but cautioned that these very measures often caused radicalization among moderate populations. For instance, only 2,000 women were said to have been regular wearers of head scarves among a population of five million Muslims, so this issue itself was overtly magnified by the French government as well as extremist groups.

The groups most divided over the issue were French feminists, who included members of the media, academe, and teachers. The official French stance on the ban was pro-feminist in orientation because it purported to ban the scarf to protect the rights of young Muslim girls who were often forced to wear it. For those feminists who supported the ban and therefore the French official line, many arguments were used. These arguments were well analyzed in various periodicals over the last four years since the implementation of the ban. Even before the controversy resurfaced in 2003, the veil had been under intense debate in French feminist circles, and two opposing books had been published about it. One of these, coauthored by prominent feminist scholar Françoise Gaspard, currently French government delegate to the United Nations on the Elimination of Discrimination Against Women (CEDAW), and Farhad Khosrokhavar, called for a tolerant approach to head scarf wearing in schools and suggested that it was perhaps a passing phase. However, the other book, authored by Elizabeth Altschull, a schoolteacher, argued for a firm approach supporting secularism. She also discussed the difficulties encountered by teachers when confronted with students who refused to take off the hijab and also follow parts of the curriculum, to attend interviews or vivas (oral examinations) with male teachers, and so on.

Thus, many feminists who opposed the ban did so because they considered it a symbol of oppression. Others considered banning it as an act of oppression and wanted it to be treated as a small nuisance. Indeed, French Muslim feminists, French feminists, and other feminists were completely divided over the ban. For instance, Segolene Royale, a presidential nominee in 2007 and Socialist deputy, had reservations about the law and said she was more worried about the effect of pornography on children than she was about scarves. Despite this, she voted for the ban:

> Yes, I would say that the veil is a symbol of oppression and segregation of women, but how do you resolve the problem of Muslim women in a society like this, where all the bus kiosks have advertising posters with naked women on them? (*New Yorker*, 2004, p. 68)

Another French feminist who has, in fact, worked toward integrating Muslim women in the community is Ann Hidalgo, a French Spanish immigrant, the deputy mayor of Paris, whose portfolio includes women's rights. For Hidalgo, the law was necessary:

> We've been very perturbed about the veil. To see those very young girls veiled . . . The "evolution" of the veil here isn't about choice, or religion. Perhaps, the veil once said something religious, but now it's a sign of oppression. It isn't God, it's men who want it. (*New Yorker*, 2004, p. 68)

Another Muslim feminist, Tamzali, wrote on the feminist Web site *Sisyphe:*

> I object to the idea that one must wear the veil to be a good Muslim. I object to the idea that it enables one to be freer and better respected—this is a trap. I denounce the instrumentalization of these women . . . (Winter, 2006, p. 283)

The French feminist philosopher Sylviane Agacinski said the law was necessary:

> The law was made to protect the bodies of girls, of minors. It is easy to be against it in retrospect, and to say that now those girls will be "twice victims"—victims of Islam, victims of French exclusion. But the veil here isn't Islam, it's politics . . . All fundamentalisms pretend that religion is ahistoric, but religions evolve. (*New Yorker*, 2004, p. 69)

Those feminists who were opposed to the ban interpreted the observance of hijab differently. For instance, Françoise Gaspard, who coauthored one of the first books on the veil law, asserted that it would keep young girls from Islamist families from getting to school at all and they would be forced to become "martyrs" to the Islamist cause through no fault of their own. Hamdan, another feminist, who in fact wears the hijab, wrote against the law by explaining not only "why" women wear it, but how and why it has been constructed as a symbol the represents the so-called backwardness of the Middle East as compared to the so-called developed West:

> . . . For many Muslim women adhering to the *hijab,* it is a symbol of chastity and modesty; for some, it is a purely religious symbol and a form of worship. In recent years the *hijab* has become a form of resistance to Western imperialism. (2007, p. 3)

Hamdan (2007) further pointed out that the ban was a curtailment of individual freedom and would eventually curtail multiculturalism.

Therefore, feminists who were against the ban also said they resisted the law as a part of a strategy against past French colonization, the government's lack of willingness to integrate the French Muslim community, racism, and the general lack of attention to social welfare. They were accused by the pro-ban feminists of adopting extreme cultural relativism and supporting an Islamist propaganda that was oppressive toward women. Pro-ban feminists also accused them of leaping to an uncritical defense of conservative Islamic politics and Islamic extremism in the name of antiracism and multiculturalism. As Abu-Rabia pointed out, such well

meaning and uncritical solidarity with the Islamists would not help the really oppressed Muslim women or the discourse and process of multiculturalism.

There was a third groups of feminists who were interested in other alternatives
such as correspondence courses, monitored home schooling, and even parochial
Muslim schools (and in fact, there was a mushrooming of Muslim religious
schools after the ban, a rise that one can only argue would lead to the further mar-
ginalization of a minority community). This group was a minority faction within
the feminist voices.

Finally, it is quite clear that each and every faction in the veil controversy used
different rules of logic and differing rhetorical strategies to argue their case, making it a very complex issue that seems beyond negotiation. However, in the next
section, we provide a discussion of how each party was resisting the other and refusing any opportunities to be wooed by another/other perspectives. And if there
was to be a resolution via dialogue in the conflict, it can be found in the diversity
of responses to it.

RESISTING RESOLUTION AND NEGOTIATION

The veil controversy is not new to the non-Muslim world. As pointed out in the
previous section, it has been around since the 18th century. From the 18th to mid
20th centuries, the hijab had been targeted as a symbol of oppression by colonial
powers in the colonies. Now with the return of the postcolonized to former colonial countries, the debate has taken different, yet similar, political dimensions. At
the heart of the debate is the acceptance and, indeed, flaunting of the Huntington
thesis, which has us believe that the West and the rest are incompatible, are in opposition, and will remain divided. However, it is possible that this conflict could
have been negotiated had each faction given in to the other's viewpoint even mini-
mally. I begin first with some facts that were muted before, during, and even after
the entire debate—facts that I have presented in the previous sections of this chapter. After this I discuss the Stasi Commission and the feminists' inability to work
more intellectually and rigorously with the issues and the Muslim community, and
that had they done so such a long conflict might not have come to pass.

First, it might be pointed out that 81% of French Muslims were in support of
the ban. Of these, 50% were French Muslim women. This was a very striking sta-
tistic that continued to be underplayed by Chirac's right-wing party that had taken
up secularism via an exclusion agenda. The support for the ban from moderate
Muslims and indeed women was neither emphasized nor highlighted by the government or the media. In fact, it was Muslim organizations who categorically told
the kidnappers of the two French journalists to not meddle in France's internal affairs. Had all these facts been kept in view, it is possible that the conflict would not
have escalated, but died a natural death.

Second, before the ban only about 2,000 Muslim schoolgirls in public high schools all over France wore a head scarf of any kind. This is so also because most French Muslims come from communities where the hijab is not necessarily worn by women (Abu-Rabia). In earlier years (from 1989–2003), if there was a certain problem, the cases were dealt internally through dialogue within the specific school. After the ban, about 600 girls still continued to come to school with the head scarf. Only 250 girls defied the veil ban, and among these were a handful of Sikh boys. But in October after schools began dialogues with about 700 students (following recommendations by the Stasi Commission), only about 80 girls were still arriving to schools in head scarves. Only nine were formally expelled from their schools. So, in a sense, the situation was magnified by the French government and Muslim fundamentalist groups alike. The government was vehement about the ban, and the fundamentalists were vehement about keeping the conflict alive, and the figures actually show that it was a very negotiable situation. The government's overzealous imposition of the ban and its particular focus on the hijab made Muslims more wont to hold on to the veil.

Additionally, had the ban not been imposed so blindly, matters would have naturally resolved. For instance, a French Muslim girl offered to wear a bandanna instead of a head scarf, but was told to go home. She was willing to take off the veil and compromise, but the school authorities were determined and disallowed any variation to the scarf. The girl in question, Cennet, ended up tonsuring her hair because she felt there was no other solution. This is an example of a lack of any "openness" to dialogue, compromise, or negotiation on part of the French government. And in fact, it highlights their bias because there were almost negligible reports of students being returned home for wearing Christian or Jewish symbols. It was clear that this further inflamed an already angered and marginalized Muslim community, who viewed these gestures as evidence of their continuing subaltern status in France.

Another group that was responsible for keeping the conflict fueled included teachers and educators. For many years, the French government had asked schools to deal with persons carrying or wearing visible religious symbols on a case-by-case basis. It is obvious that not all Muslim girls wear the hijab for the same reason, thus there needed to be a flexible negotiating space for each person to be dialogued with on an individual basis. Given that only 2,000 girls in "all" French schools were actually wearing the hijab when the ban went into place, the case-by-case strategy was still the most viable solution. But schools were unwilling to face the responsibility, seemed to target Muslim girls, and to a large extent spurred the creation of the Stasi Commission.

The constitution of the Stasi Commission was controversial from the start. Many French intellectuals who were strong proponents of la laïcité stayed away from the commission and the ban. In fact, Jean Bauberot, a leading member of the Stasi Commission, abstained from endorsing the recommendations of the reports.

The groups did not include a single Arab Muslim, a community that was going to be most influenced by the ban. There was also no representation from the moderate or conservative Muslim community. The media and the government failed to highlight the fact that members of the Stasi Commission complained that the 26 proposals dealing with social reform focused on the social and economic inequities faced by the French Muslims were ignored, but ultimately for political reasons the hijab ban was made into a central focus. Moreover, it was reported that the decisions were made in a hurry and there was a rush to implement the ban. For this reason, another religious minority, the Sikhs, were unmentioned in the report and unrepresented in the commission. Already a minority community in France, lack of acknowledgment of their mere existence further marginalized them.

The lessons from this fiasco are quite clear—had the government given the Muslim community, the pro- and antiban non-Muslim organizations, schoolgirls, and even some extremist groups a say in the negotiations, the outcome might have been different. The commission went on to disregard the guidance of other religious groups' leaders who were also against the ban. The constitution of the commission was imperialist and arrogant, and it seemed as if it knew the outcome on its creation. It showed great disdain for the will of the Muslim community or the will of other French minorities.

In fact, it might even be said that instead of creating the Stasi Commission, the government might have tested the waters and initiated interfaith dialogue and public discussion about the hijab in particular. These dialogues should have been consistent and ongoing for a few years, and then the government could have made the recommendation to create a commission choosing persons from the community to be a part of the decision-making process. Unfortunately, the Stasi Commission came to represent an elite imperial voice and disregarded the lived reality of the persons about whom they were creating a law. They exhibited an inability to focus on the everyday stories of the marginalized Muslim communities and focused instead on official "educator" accounts of persons who saw the hijab as a nuisance.

Feminists went to war with each other over the issue and were to blame for overaccelerating the conflict further. On the one hand there were those who took the pro-Western stance that suggested the veil was an oppressive symbol for Muslim women. Their position merely reinforced the predominant conception about Muslim women that exists in the West. Those feminists who were against the ban were by default supporting the fundamentalists, who often use the hijab deliberatively as a symbol of female oppression. Yet, there was indeed a middle ground, and feminists were in a powerful position to negotiate with the government using other strategies. But their internal agendas dominated the discussions, and they failed the women they were supposed to be supporting. The middle-ground approach was already in place and could have been modeled more broadly across the country. In many parts of France, many female politicians had already been working to integrate Muslim women and the Muslim people at large in the community using various strategies such as the opening of storefront prayer rooms in immigrant neighborhoods where people had nowhere to pray but the sidewalks; sponsoring Friday lunches in high school neighborhoods so girls and teachers could talk openly; throwing a big party at city hall to celebrate the end of Ramadan each year; and closing municipal schools to men for several hours a week so that Muslim women could bathe alone. All these were dialogic and benign middle-ground approaches that remained unstated and unheard during the entire controversy.

It is clear from the preceding discussion that a solution or rather a negotiation of the conflict was present in the voices of the various factions. But their inability to stay open to the perspectives of others shut down any channels of communication between and betwixt parties. Ultimately, the ban and the subsequent conflict unleashed a public dialogue about the role, history, and symbolism of the hijab, "allowing Muslim scholars to dispel some of the myths about the hijab of Muslim women by keeping the discussion alive. The discussion allows a continuous negotiation and analysis, not only of the hijab, but also of Muslim women's status in Western and Eastern contexts" (Hamadan, 2007, p. 4). We agree that this is a healthy outcome of the conflict, but it is a process that should have begun before any official dictum was placed on French citizens.

CHAPTER 10

Contemporary Hindu Arranged Marriages in Urban India

INTRODUCTION

Arranged marriages continue to be a norm in many Asian cultures such as India, China, Japan, and Korea (Applbaum, 1995). Premised on similarity of social standing, which often includes the caste, class, religion, and education of the prospective couple, the arranged marriage is the most popular form of organizing a marital relationship among Hindus in India (Mullatti, 1995). Despite forces of modernization and urbanization, the number of arranged marriages in India far outnumbers "love" or "self-arranged" marriages. In fact, an estimated 95% of all Hindu marriages in India are still arranged marriages (Bumiller, 1990; Kapadia, 1958; Kapur, 1970; Mullatti, 1995). In this chapter, we begin by exploring the evolution of the Hindu marriage by telling the story of its historical and religious evolution. Further, we review some recent social-scientific literature on the arranged marriage and discuss contemporary media portrayals of this marital system. Following this, accessing narratives from an ethnographic life history study, *Arranged Selves: Role, Identity, and Social Transformations among Indian Women in Hindu*

Arranged Marriages (Chawla, 2004), we present the stories of four contemporary Indian women's experiences in Hindu arranged marriages. The stories embody the diversity of the arranged marriage system and show us that it might be erroneous to harbor a monolithic and essentialist image of Indian women who choose this form of conjugal arrangement.

THE ARRANGED MARRIAGE IN HINDU RELIGION AND HISTORY

There are competing explanations about the origination of Hindu texts that refer to marriage. Writing about the Hindu marriage dates back to 4000 BC (Kapadia, 1958). However, some historians have proposed that it may date back to the origin of agriculture in the Indus Valley, where Hindus are said to have settled in 7000 to 6000 BC (Shattuck, 1999). Nevertheless, it is easy to speculate that the history of the Hindu marriage is about 5,000 years old. There are vast bodies of literature available on the Hindu rituals, norms, and marriages, and original writings and descriptions about the structure of the Hindu marriage can be found in Hindu religious texts (Sastri, 1972). Social scientific literature, on the other hand, is fairly recent; the oldest and most comprehensive sociological study, relevant to this study, was conducted in India and is now almost a half century old (Kapadia, 1958). Literary writing in the vernacular on the arranged marriage dates as far back as 600 BC and before (Tharu & Lalitha, 1993). Indian English fiction writing has always explored issues of marriage, family, and religion (Tharu & Lalitha, 1993). Contemporary Indian English writing in the last 25 to 30 years has explored this form of marriage—overtly and covertly (Chawla, 2004). In the following sections, we offer a review of these secondary historical and religious literatures with the hope of providing an understanding of how the system evolved into what it is today.

A HISTORICAL AND RELIGIOUS UNDERSTANDING OF HINDU MARRIAGE

The Hindu marriage is said to be derived from laws interpreted in the *Dharmashastras,* which in turn have their roots in the 3,000-year-old hymns called *Vedas* and *Smritis.* The *Vedas* and the *Smritis* are considered the oldest surviving documents from the Vedic and Epic age (what are considered the first recorded periods of Indian civilization from 4000 BC to 1200 AD; Kapadia, 1958). Through these texts it has been speculated that the Hindu marriage dates as far back as 4000 BC. These texts are said to have been written by male Aryan sages who inhabited the areas across the Indus River, long before the word *Hindu* came to be associated with religion. *Hindu* was simply an evolved Persian word for the people who lived across the river Indus or Indu (Shattuck, 1999; Lipner, 1994; Zysk,

1989). Written by holy men of the time period, these scriptures are a collection of rules and conducts for society at the time (Zysk, 1989).

A general theme across these scriptures was that marriage was a duty and a religious sacrament that was required of all human beings for the well-being of the community. Through different periods of Indian history, these texts were interpreted by different holy men. One of the most influential interpreters and creators of these texts was the sage Manu (This is documented in the *Manu Smriti,* said to have been written in 200 BC; Shattuck, 1999). He is said to have benn instrumental in laying out marital laws that are followed even in comtemporary times (Kapadia, 1958; Kapur, 1970).

All the texts outline four main aims of life for Hindus. These were *dharma, artha, kama,* and *moksha* (Kapadia, 1958; Lipner, 1994). The four aims were specifically meant for men, and women were more or less written out of the documents. *Kama* represented the instinctive, the primal, and the sexual. It was connected with the satisfaction of emotional, sexual, and aesthetic urges of man. *Artha* referred to the acquisitive instinct and signified man's acquisition and enjoyment of wealth. *Dharma* was of primary concern because it aimed to balance the instinctive and acquisitive in man. *Dharma* was achieved by gaining the knowledge that *artha* and *kama* were means, not ends. *Dharma* represented the harmony between "temporal interests and spiritual freedom" (Kapadia, 1958, p. 27). *Dharma* is so crucial that the two Hindu epics, *Mahabharata* and *Ramayana* (written during the Epic period 400 BC–1200 AD), are centered on the achievement of *Dharma* (see Shattuck, 1999, for a closer understanding of this concept). *Moksha* represented the end of life and the realization of an inner spirituality in man. Once achieved, these four aims represented the righteous life.

The four aims of life were to be accomplished by dividing life into four stages and following them. These stags were: *bhramacharya, grahastha, vanaspratha,* and *samnyasa.* The first stage, *Bhramacharya,* was the stage of learning and giving oneself over to one's teachers or *gurus.* The achievement of studentship was the path to an ethical life (Kapadia, 1958). The second stage, *grahastha,* included the goals of *dharma,* progeny, and sex. *Vanaspratha* was a stage within marriage when a man readied himself to sacrifice all worldly possessions and achieve self-determination. This was a process that was accomplished by detaching oneself from family, social relations, and material possessions. *Samnyasa* represented the last stage, when man entered the life of an ascetic to attain *moksha* or freedom from the material world.

It is evident from the preceding discussion that marriage was a duty and obligation of every "man." There is no reference in the literature reviewed that any of these life stages and aims were structured toward women. Therefore, although marriage was required for all Hindus, its advantages were only enjoyed by men, who benefited from both the spiritual and economic understandings of the Hindu marriage (Mukherjee, 1978). Spiritually, men benefited because they married to beget sons who would light their funeral pyre. This activity ensured these men a place in heaven, rebirth in the next life as a human being, and the liberation of future generations of the family (*moksha*). The need for a male heir was also an economic necessity—a male heir was desired because he alone could continue the family line and inherit ancestral property. Therefore, historically, the Hindu arranged marriage was "male-emphasized" (this is a term used by Mukherjee, 1978, in her book *Hindu Women*). It has even been suggested the word *wife* was often used interchangeably with *household* (Mukherjee, 1978; Shastri, 1972). In fact, the Sanskrit word for marriage, *vivaha*, translates into procuring and carrying away of a maiden from the house of her father to the house of her husband. In other words, a woman's role in her own home as well as her marital home was largely objectified.

THE EVOLUTION OF THE HINDU ARRANGED MARRIAGE

This objectified and prescribed role can also be understood by looking at the forms of marriage that were considered "righteous" and those that were considered "nonrighteous." Mukherjee (1978) in her study, *Hindu Women*, asserts that the notion of *vivaha*, or procurement, led to the formation of eight forms of acceptable and unacceptable marriages. As already mentioned, what is significant here is that in each form a bride was either "procured" or given as an object.

The first four forms of marriage, considered righteous forms, were *Brahma*, *Prajapatya*, *Arsa*, and *Daiva*. These forms of marriage were organized by the bride's and the groom's fathers and paid for by the bride's family. The bride's family received a negotiated "bride-price" from the groom's parents, but her personal wealth, or *stridhana* (a bridal gift from her parents), was inherited by the groom's family. So, in the end, the "bride-price" would be kept by her parents and the *stridhana* by her husband's family—leaving the wife economically impoverished.

In the *Brahma* form of marriage, the girl was given away as a gift to her husband. In *Prajapatya*, the girl was given away after honoring the bridegroom. In the *Arsa* form, the bride was procured by giving a gift of two cows to the father of the bride. In *Daiva*, the girl was given as a sacrifice to the officiating priest at an altar. According to Mukherjee (1978), these forms of marriages were "male-emphasized" and/or beneficial to men for various reasons. First, the bride contributed to the economic prosperity of her husband's family by bringing in her *stridhana*. Second, each of these marriages aimed at begetting sons who would inherit the family wealth and liberate future generations by ensuring that they were all born human in the next life. The number of generations that were supposed to be liberated decreased from the *Brahma* to the *Daiva* form of marriage. Third, ritualistic family duties were only conducted by men because women were considered too "impure" to carry them out. This impurity was attributed to menstruation and childbirth (see Sharma, 1997, *Social Stratification in India: Themes and Issues*). Overall, each of these four forms that were beneficial to the male line and were organized by kin began to be referred to as "arranged marriages" in contemporary times (Mukherjee, 1978).

Contemporary arranged marriages are generally organized by parents and elderly kin (Sur, 1973). In earlier times, intermediaries called *sambhalas,* or traditional matchmakers, were employed to keep the genealogical history of each family and make sure that the bride and groom were not related from five to seven generations (Sur, 1973). In more recent times, these criteria have stretched to include other characteristics. Mullatti (1995) outlined seven criteria that are currently followed (not necessarily in this order) by matchmakers, kin, parents, and relatives. These are caste, social structure, moral value compatibility, academic compatibility, occupational compatibility, the family's moral history, and horoscope compatibility. In the past two decades, parents have begun looking for matches for their children through matrimonial columns in newspapers, magazines, and now the Internet, which hosts various region and caste specific Web sites (Mullatti, 1995).

However, when kin and family arrangements were not followed, and marriages were self-arranged, they were considered nonrighteous (*adharma*). The forms of marriage considered nonrighteous were *Gandharva, Asura, Rakshasa,* and *Paisaca.* These forms of marriage were "female-emphasized." This has been attributed to social and economic reasons (Mukherjee, 1978). First, at the level of status, the marriage was not arranged by the bride or the groom's fathers. Second, on the economic end, the bride and her family benefited from the union. For instance, the bride kept her *stridhana,* her parents were not expected to bear the economic burden of the marriage, and she was independently rich because it was she, not her parents, who received the bride-price (paid to her parents by the groom's family).

In the *Gandharva* form, the bride and groom culminated their union in secret (an elopement). In the *Asura* form, the bride was procured by giving as much wealth as possible to her family, and she was given to him voluntarily. In the *Rakshasa* form, the bride was abducted from her home. In the *Paisaca* form, the bride was seduced while intoxicated, asleep, or in a weakened intellectual state. It has been speculated that these forms of marriages, which were not arranged by kin involved outright "buying" of the bride and were often self-arranged, came to be later called "love marriages" (I used the term love-marriage and self-arranged marriage to mean the same thing). Although the first four righteous forms of marriage (also male emphasized) were supposed to liberate future generations of the groom's family, the next four did not do so (Mukherjee, 1978).

Structurally, these eight forms of marriages have numerous implications. First, they clearly show that marriage was organized around inheritance and there was a need to protect sons. Second, because marriage forms were righteous and non-righteous, women within each form began to be treated accordingly. As a result, women in the righteous forms of marriage were treated with more respect than women in the nonrighteous forms (Mukherjee, 1978). Finally, the Hindu woman who had never been attributed much status and authority in the *Vedas* and the *Smritis,* eventually experienced a more devaluated status in the nonrighteous form of marriage. Men, on the other hand, had not only written the holy texts, but were also the clear beneficiaries spiritually as well as economically. These structural implications can perhaps be better understood by looking at the internal workings of a traditional Hindu family, which, despite urbanization, exists both in urban and rural settings (Gore, 1968).

The Hindu Joint Family

In his study, *Urbanization and Family Change,* Gore (1968; see also Sharma, 1997) points out that an ideal Hindu joint family in contemporary India consists of a man and wife, their adult sons, their wives and children, and younger children of the parental couple. A joint family can often be looked on as a multiplicity of genealogically related nuclear families living under the same roof and sharing in worship, food, and property. On the other hand, a semijoint family could mean one in which one son and his family live together with his parents while the other siblings live elsewhere. Very often, a joint family has been described as a group of adult male coparceners and their dependents—the dependents being wives and children (Gore, 1968). A coparcener is a joint heir. For instance, if a father has two sons and one daughter, the sons would be considered joint heirs, but a daughter would not inherit property. According to Hindu law, an adult male and his sons were coparceners in ancestral property (Gore, 1968).

In the joint family described by Gore (1968), women in the joint family were given an overall subordinate status from the men who were supposed to maintain them as well as the children. Formal authority was always centered on the oldest male and thereby hierarchically bound by age. This hierarchy occurred on many levels. Women were married and brought into the family, which consisted of men who were all related by blood. The women were not only biologically on the outside, but they were also treated as symbolic outsiders until they gave birth to a son. Daughters-in-law would be completely included in the family only once they begot a son. And if they did not beget a son, then a new wife could be brought in (although this changed with the Hindu Divorce Bill in 1952; Kapadia, 1958). A wife from the same caste, class, and economic status was intrinsic to maintain the religious purity of the family. Once married, the "conjugal relationship" between couples was discouraged from becoming romanticized and too strong because the emphasis was on the socioeconomic welfare of the family. This, according to Gore (1968), was a major cause of the degradation of women's status in the family, which in turn was supported by denial of property rights to women and their inability to achieve economic independence. In fact, role and authority segregation of men and women was essential to the well-being of a joint Hindu family. The goal was the economic well-being of the family and the discouragement of individualism. In fact, in her recent study, *Marriage, A History: From Obedience to Intimacy Or How Love Conquered Marriage,* Stephanie Coontz (2005) argued—using anthropological, historical, and archival research—that even in the Western world marriage was a deeply economic institution and was separate from love and intimacy, which was expected to be provided from individual/s outside of the marriage. Within the context of the Hindu arranged marriage, although women remained necessary to the family, they also remained powerless, propertyless, and dependent within the "household," which they symbolized.

What we have here is robust asymmetry. If one were to look at this social field in terms of power distribution and power relations, we can see that there are two concentric circles of power in the household, distributed relationally. The outer, more powerful circle is the circle of male relatives, who are biologically and economically bound, and so obligated to each other. The second circle of power is the inner circle, which consists of women who are not biologically related, have negligible economic rights, and thus have few obligations to each other. They find themselves thrown into the inner circle with little or no say in the goings-on of the outer circle. They are aware that they are largely an instrument of procreation in the Hindu marriage system. By being relegated to the "inside," their only connection to the outside is their husband on whom they have little influence. As a result, power and resistance as they experience it is bound within a structural framework, specifically the inner circle. However, the stories that are presented later in this chapter show that contemporary urban women who "choose" to have these marriages navigate these arrangements quite adeptly and seem more empowered than historical understandings of this system would let us believe.

Historically, everything about an arranged marriage favored, and to some extent still favors, the patriarchal system. For instance, Hindu women were not entitled to any property rights until 1956[1] and therefore were economically dependent on their fathers, husbands, and later on their sons if they were lucky to have male progeny (Gore, 1968; Kapur, 1970). With the amendment of Hindu property

---

[1] Some of this history was transformed with the passing of the Hindu Marriage Act by the Government of India in 1955, which allowed for dissolution of marriage via divorce and annulment and property for women, widows, and daughters-in-law. Under this act (amended in 1964 and 1976) a marriage is considered "Hindu" if the following requirements are fulfilled: (i) both parties are Hindu, (ii) both parties were separated from each other by seven generations, and (iii) the marriage is conducted according to Hindu rites (Derrett, 1976; Uberoi, 1996, p. 327). These were legal attempts at shifting the understanding of the Hindu marriage from sacrament to contract. However, in a study of recent judicial decisions, Uberoi (1996) found that Indian judges still tend to make decisions about dissolution/consent/custody using the precolonial understanding of "sacrament."

laws in 1956 allowing for female inheritance and given increased levels of women entering the workforce "by choice" in the latter half of the 20th century, there has been tremendous change in gendered roles within families (Gore, 1968; Indian National Commission Report for Women, 2001; Kapadia, 1958; Kapur, 1970). Further, in the 1980s and 1990s, the liberalization of developing world economies created new jobs for women throughout the world, including India (Indian National Commission Report for Women, 2001). In particular, the last two decades saw an upsurge of women in the both the urban and rural work-forces. Of the 314 million Indians currently in the workforce, 89 million are women (Indian National Commission Report for Women, 2001). Despite the promise and arrival of economic independence and change in property and di-vorce laws, many urban Hindu women continue to accept and choose arranged marriages. It would seem that the breakdown of economic disparities would lead to an increase in self-arranged or love marriages, yet that has not been the case (Bumiller, 1990). Speculatively, this can be attributed to the structural continuity of Hindu family life and tells us that the system is perhaps more culturally than economically embedded in Hindu family life. Historical accounts of the arranged marriage, such as the one presented here, show a system that seems to be op-pressive and disadvantageous to women; however, historical accounts are often inorganic and do not take into account the dynamic nature of communities and societies. The stories that make a major portion of this chapter show the arranged marriage in a different light from essentialist accounts that position the arranged marriage as a representation of Third World "backwardness."

Before moving to the stories, we review social scientific and media accounts of the arranged marriage to provide how it has been perceived and interrogated in the past five to six decades. Given its popularity and continuing prevalence, there has been consistent research on the arranged marriage in the social sciences in the Indian as well as the Western academy. In the following section, I briefly review this specific line of research to explore what it tells us about how social researchers approach the arranged marriage.

BRIEF REVIEW OF SOCIAL SCIENTIFIC LITERATURE

Research on the arranged marriage in the social sciences has been limited to com-parative sociological analyses. Historical literature has generally emphasized the structure of the family, Hindu norms, traditions, caste, and so on. Social-scientific work on the arranged marriage in the last five decades includes sociopsychological surveys that focus on comparisons between arranged and self-arranged marriages in India (see Chandak & Sprecher, 1992; Dhyani & Kumar, 1996; Kapadia, 1958; Kapur, 1970; Rao & Rao, 1975; Ross, 1961). More recently, sociologists and his-torians at the University of Delhi have explored issues surrounding kinship, sexu-ality, same-sex marriages, marital laws, and the state (Uberoi, 1993, 1996).

One of the oldest longitudinal social scientific studies of the Hindu arranged marriage dates back to the late fifties. In his study, *Marriage and the Family in India,* a University of Bombay sociologist, Kapadia (1958), traced the history of the marriage up to the early 1950s (the study was first published in 1955) and concluded that although there were changes in marital trends with industrialization and urbanization, marriage among Hindus remained a holy sacrament, an obligation, and a duty that went beyond industrial progress. In other words, the Hindu cosmology seemed to extend beyond economic changes or changes in property laws.

This seminal study that explored, explained, and tried to show the workings of Hindu marriage was followed by a spurt of studies about Hindu marriages in the ensuing decades. In 1968 Gore's study on urbanization and family change, similar to Kapadia, found that Hindu traditions won over forces of urbanization and industrialization in both rural and urban areas. Another study, within the decade span of 1958 to 1968, by Ross (1961) also pointed to family and traditions taking precedence over modernization and urbanization. A 1970 study by sociologist Promilla Kapur studied urban working women in Indian marriages and concluded that women's roles remained more static within the home and the joint family system, and that marital satisfaction was not significantly related to type of marriage. These studies are all sociological and used survey data from large samples. Chawla's (2004) study of contemporary women's experiences in arranged marriages exhibited common experiences across three groups of married women in different demographics. At the same time, Chawla's interpretive analysis also found significant thematic differences in stories across the groups (divided by age and decade), which seems to be a testimony to growing social change within this form of marital system.

In the past four decades or so, social scientific research on arranged marriage across India, Japan, China, and America has dealt with marital satisfaction, adjustment, attitude change of college students about the arranged marriage, and comparisons between love and arranged marriages. The results over the past few decades, often based on urban samples, although valid, seem somewhat contradictory. In a study about attitudes toward the arranged marriage, Rao and Rao (1975) found that 91% of the college student sample ($n = 182$, evenly distributed by gender) did not approve of the traditional form of "arranged" marriage. Only 9% of the sample expressed approval for the traditional setup. The high disapproval rate was attributed to factors such as modernization, industrialization, education, and the breakdown of the joint family system. However, there is no descriptive data that tells us why the 91% disapprove of the system. Although this is not a shortcoming of the study, it is evident that questions addressing lived experience were not asked.

A similar study conducted almost two decades later by Chandak and Sprecher (1992) found that in a survey sample of 66 respondents ($n = 66$, 48 women and

18 men), over half the sample still favored the traditional system. This study, conducted two decades after the Rao and Rao (1975) study, suggested somewhat of a reversal in the modernization trend. At the same time, the sample size used by Chandak and Sprecher is interesting in that it includes more women. This study also does not explore why the approval for the arranged marriage is a trend that holds.

Historically, studies on marital adjustment and satisfaction displayed some consistent results. As already mentioned, Kapur's (1970) sociopsychological survey, entitled *Marriage and the Working Woman in India,* focused on marital adjustment and Indian urban working women ($n = 300$; 100 schoolteachers, 100 doctors, and 100 office workers). Kapur found that women in self-arranged marriages did not adjust better or worse than those in arranged marriages. In other words, there was no significant relationship between type of marriage and marital adjustment. Kapur's study was by far the most descriptive study because she used a combination of qualitative and quantitative data in presenting her conclusions. However, given the large size of the sample ($n = 300$), detailed descriptive research was not presented. Moreover, the study, though seminal, is now over three decades old.

In a similar more recent study, Dhyani and Kumar (1996) examined the relationship between type of marriage, marital duration, sexual satisfaction, and adjustment. The sample consisted of 240 urban-based women who had been married for at least one year. They found that the type of marriage and marital duration did not produce any significant relationship with marital adjustment. However, a study conducted by Yelsma and Athappilly (1988) in America, which compared Indian arranged marriages, Indian "love" marriages, and American "love" marriages, found that satisfaction was rated higher by couples in Indian arranged marriages.

Similar studies conducted in China and Japan revealed some inconsistent results. In a study that compared Japanese arranged marriages to love marriages, Walsh and Taylor (1982) found that the type of marriage had no significant relation to marital understanding. Xiaohe and Whyte (1990) conducted a similar comparative survey in China and found that couples in arranged marriages were more satisfied than those in love marriages. Although structurally China, Japan, and India are distinct and may not be comparable to a Hindu community, the arranged marriage remains a common theme among the three nations. In all three countries these marriages are organized around membership in kin groups, which may be religious, caste, community, ethnicity, or class based.

Most of the social-scientific studies do not focus on the lived experiences of women in this form of marital arrangement. Albeit, they do offer us valuable understandings of some of the processes that constitute the arranged marriage relationship. In these studies identity, gender, and marriage are used as variables, and their goal is not to probe the arranged marriage as a social context where identities are negotiated and co-constructed, and how this context itself is dynamic over time. Second, research on the arranged marriage has been driven by the need to compare it to love marriages in almost all regions where such research has been undertaken—India, other parts of South and East Asia, as well as America. The contextual intricacies of identity negotiations within role expectations in both forms of marriage are often overlooked. Third, the arranged marriage has been studied as an isolated relationship and not as a negotiation that is informed by multiple social identity and role relationships in which family and kin are as much involved. (Some discussion about these matters is available in Kapadia, 1958, and Kapur, 1970, but both these studies are now five and three decades old, respectively.)

Both these lines of research—the historical and the social scientific—provide us with rich structural and variable-analytical understanding of what goes into the sociological process that is the arranged marriage. Another line of research/inquiry has contributed to framing the arranged marriages in an essentialist way for persons from the Western world, particularly North America and Europe. In the following section, we present media portrayals of the arranged marriage to see how it is rhetorically constructed for the audience.

MEDIA PORTRAYALS OF ARRANGED MARRIAGE

In the United States, the general public's knowledge about the arranged marriage is shaped by the information available in media outlets. It is commonly known now that most coverage of arranged marriages in the West have been consistently conflated with the tradition of forced marriages in certain societies. An arranged marriage usually makes news in the West if there are instances of martial abuse, violence, and so on. Although this type of stereotypical coverage continues, there are some other themes in media coverage of such relationships. A cursory review of the contemporary media coverage of arranged marriages shows that this form of marital relationship consistently comes under discussion along three themes that are related to yet distinct from the predominant discussion of forced marriages. In this section, we discuss briefly the three ways in which this relationship seems to be framed by those writing in the media.

First, media portrayals largely focus on descriptive accounts of this form of relationship and how different it is compared to so-called love or self-arranged marriages. They tend to create a binary between an arranged and a self-arranged marriage. These descriptive accounts treat the arranged marriage as a curiosity, a custom from other worlds that are not a part of the mainstream. They tend to reinforce a backward image of the East, suggesting that even in these modern times, some archaic customs persist. Consider the following descriptions from media outlets written and published within the last decade:

> Marriage is a sacramental union in the Hindu faith. "One is incomplete and considered unholy if they do not marry" (Parakasa 14). Most females are married

before puberty, with almost all girls being married before 16, while most boys are married before the age of 22 (Gupta 146). (Flanigan, 2000)

Other portrayals also reinforce stereotypes of the arranged marriage as a medieval custom and mostly present totalizing images of the institution:

> Age, caste and dowry play important roles in arrangement of marriages in India today (year 2005). A type of arranged marriage where the maternal cousins and sometimes maternal nephews married was/is also common in India. This was known as rightful marriage alliance in some communities . . . (Kamat, n.d.)
>
> Arranged marriages have always been a debatable subject. It is in the major outlook on relationships that Indians are vastly different, in the way they perceive the institution of marriage, to those beliefs of other countries especially in the west. (Noreen, 2009)

The second theme in portrayals is the telling of anecdotal stories about the form of marriage and how these can be surprisingly successful. Such portrayals display a sort of indulgence for the arranged marriage in the Western media. By this we mean that the relationship is covered as a form of trivia about the East. Treating it as trivia with the use of abbreviated stories and anecdotes relegates such a marriage to a curiosity, thereby keeping the West and the East tidily apart. These media stories help to maintain binaries such as the East and West, developing and developed, and archaic versus modern. Because of such portrayals, the East is created as a place that is stymied and stuck to traditions, and as a result arranged marriages tend to inherit an unchanging and stable quality—as marriages that remain untouched by contemporary social transformations. In other words, such portrayals tend to privilege a view of the East that is inorganic and unchanging. Consider the way the following stories are presented:

> He was from India, but made his home in the United States. She was Indian to the core, and dead set against leaving her native country. So what brought Anil and Navita Batra together in marriage six years ago? Her aunt's brother-in-law was his dad's childhood friend . . . Aunt Seema . . . (Caffazo, 2004)
>
> As a young girl growing up in India, Meenakshi Jayaraman never dated. She came from a conservative Hindu family, and even though her friends went on dates, Jayaraman always knew she would meet her husband through the ancient practice of arranged marriage. Years later, she's still surprised it worked as well as it did. (Lalwani, 2005)
>
> The set up was typical for the early stages of an arranged marriage when the prospective bride and groom meet each other for the first time. KJ and Deep's parents had made sure of social, cultural and economic similarities when they introduced their children to each other. (Easley, 2005)

Recent trends in the coverage of the arrange marriage show that much of the discussion is relegated to how the process has become web-based and high tech. Most of this coverage details how new technologies are being used in the service of ar-ranging marriages. This coverage also focuses on trivia—descriptions of new Web sites, online matchmakers, cell phone providers who provide services to parents of potential brides and grooms, and so on.

All the aforementioned coverage neglects and indeed bypasses the reality of the relationship as a marriage between individuals. In the next section we present four life histories of women in arranged marriages taken from a larger research study that looked at Hindu women's experiences in arranged marriages from the 80s through the early 2000s.

Four Women, Four Stories

In this section we present stories of four urban North Indian women in their early thirties who chose to have arranged marriages in the early 2000s. These stories were part of an ethnographic life history study of contemporary north Indian women's experiences in arranged marriages entitled *Arranged Selves: Role, Iden-tity, and Social Transformations among Indian Women in Hindu Arranged Mar-riages* (Chawla, 2004). The intent is to present the stories to the readers as diverse experiences of the arranged marriage system, thereby showing that historical ac-counts, social science research, or media portrayals are unable to capture the complexity of these marital arrangements. Our goal here is merely to show that women make choices within such nuptials, and these are often disparate from how the system is represented in research, history, or by the media. The stories also show that the experience of the Hindu arranged marriage is also a product of its time.

GEETA'S STORY

Geeta grew up in a small city in a North Eastern state and had moved to Delhi upon her marriage at the age of 24. In her own telling of it, Geeta's story became divided into two self-defined moments of "Before 17" and "After 17." In her own words, her mother's death became a punctuated moment in her life that forced her to grow up. She referred to her mother's death and "After 17" as the "bitter side of the story."

Before 17

In Geeta's narrative, the "Before 17" period was the childhood idyllic period during which she described herself as stubborn, playful, and pampered. Geeta was the only daughter of somewhat unconventional middle-class Indian parents, both of whom had been married once before. Her mother had been widowed, and her fa-ther was divorced. They had met at work, fallen in love, and married after years of being single. Geeta had two half-brothers from her mother's first marriage, and she was the only child from her parents' current marriage.

Not only was her parents' marriage in her own words, "unconventional," work at home was not gendered. Her parents shared equally in household work. This had clearly influenced Geeta, who was not the primary "householder" in her own marital life. When she spoke of a "regular" childhood evening, Geeta described this unconventional division of labor in her maiden home:

> They (parents) were in tune with each other's needs. So, if my mom was careless about a lot of things, my dad was very careful in how to fill in the gap. And if my mom was the one who used to come back from the office and cook, then my dad wasn't the one who would sit and watch the television or go out with friends. He would sit there and peel off the vegetables and cut them for my mom. So, if you were not doing half of your share, then she is not going to do the other half. So, all that was very well laid out between them, which was unlike a lot of marriages that I know of now.

Geeta's model of work and marriage had been an egalitarian one and this became clear in her "After 17" story when she spoke of her own marriage and the division of labor within it.

Literally and figuratively, "Before 17" became the girlhood period of Geeta's life. While speaking of that time, Geeta told stories about knowing that marriage was compulsory, inevitable, and something that she would certainly undertake as a grown-up. She described some early conflicts at home about learning how to cook. Having observed her parents sharing in cooking duties, she had failed to understand why her mother would want her to learn how to cook. This "requirement" contradicted what she had observed, and Geeta recalled rebelling against it. When asked to cook, she would talk back making statements such as: "I hate the bloody kitchen." This, according to Geeta, had in her parents' eyes set her apart from other girls. Describing this perceived distinctive quality in herself, she said,

> I do remember my mom and at times others referring to me as: "God only knows what your mother-in law is going to end up with."
> Researcher: What made them say these things?
> Because I wasn't according to them, you know, I hardly was like a girl. I don't know what they meant by it. There was a wall just below our house and I would never ever go out of the gate, walk on the road and come out of the gate. I would just jump across the wall, like in seconds; I would lift heavy things (like furniture); I would shift everything on my own. I never asked for help. So they always thought that I was unlike conventional girls and they said, "God alone knows what your mom-in-law is going to end up with." (My mother) She would say, "Well, you're supposed to cook, you know, being a woman you are supposed to cook."

Geeta rebelled against the contradictory messages that she was experiencing. She was being raised by parents who were egalitarian about housework, yet these very parents were telling her to learn how to cook because of her biological gender. This rebellion had set Geeta apart as a "different" girl.

Additionally, in her "Before 17" story, Geeta was feisty, unconventional, naughty, and essentially still childlike. She referred to herself as bright, talkative, and curious in school. Although a marriage had been inevitable in the future, it had not been an immediate reality. And because marital inevitability had been reinforced, she was not pressured to choose any serious career options. Explaining this further, Geeta said, "They thought that the girl is going to get a bachelor's degree, marry, sit at home, and have kids, and that is that." Her brothers, on the other hand, had been mentored into career paths by her father. All this changed and was changed by Geeta herself in her "After 17" story.

AFTER 17

Geeta's brothers had protected her from her mother's illness and subsequent death because she was the youngest. However, once her mother died, various new roles were immediately attributed to her. In "After 17," Geeta became the person who "took over" and became "responsible." She explored this in a descriptive manner when she said,

> I took over and I was still very busy. But now things were that, rather than being busy with my own things, I was busy with the responsibilities. I would say because 'til then I did not have the "responsibility." Actually after my mom, which is after 17, I would go to the college, come back, make sure that things are cooked. At times I had to cook and I had to clean the house. I mean I had to clean the house regularly because I am a cleanliness freak as well (pause).
>
> There were other things that you have to take care of. As in, you know, you have to keep a certain distance from people or you have to keep a certain relationship with people; I had to maintain that, with relatives and friends of my mom's and dad's.
>
> And then, being a girl also was a little bit problematic. Because you know you go through a period when you have your "periods," and you have your depressions, and you have to learn how to deal with men outside the house as well as inside the house, all those little things . . .
>
> I've now lost complete touch with them since my dad is also not there anymore. My mom was the one—you know—who used to kind of keep forcing dad to go back to his relatives which he was not very keen on, probably they were not very friendly with each other; those things had to be taken care of. Then you have people being nasty to you because they know that you are alone.
>
> Or simple things that like my younger brother, (the elder one was married) the second one had to get married. And I had to take care of each and every thing—right from calling up a tent-wallah; to put the tent to the caterers, to what is going to be on the menu and all that . . .
>
> So much so that I wore her (my mom's) sari to my brother's marriage. My brother told me, "You should wear this sari which belongs to mom, don't buy another one." I mean I had already bought another one, but I had to wear this one.

Her mother's death seemed to move Geeta's story into a "good girl" story. In fact, Geeta described a "good girl" as "herself." From the preceding exchanges it is quite clear that, in her mind, the "good girl" was someone who took over her mother's role, who was "responsible," and who "maintained relationships" for the family. Geeta reinforced the meanings of these roles in the following exchange:

> It probably means me, actually. Good girl—as in what I call a good girl—is you know being responsible, I mean you can enjoy your life, but there is a certain responsibility of probably (pause) maintaining relationships, and of course making sure that things are not going haywire in the family.
>
> I don't put myself anywhere outside the family. Somehow I can't think beyond my own family. I'm not the kind of person who would interact with a whole lot of people. I mean I would interact, but my relationships are limited in that sense. (They include) everybody in the family and very close friends who I have known after several years of being with them; so (good girls) probably maintaining those relationships and just taking care of people.

Therefore, the transformation from "girl" to "woman," which would have occurred gradually, was accelerated by her mother's death. This role had again shifted when both her brothers got married. Now there were sisters-in-law in the home to share in the "responsibilities." During this time, much to her family's surprise, the 22-year-old Geeta had begun to get serious about getting a master's degree in Women's Studies at the university in her town (incidentally, this is one of the first Women's Studies programs in the country). She had enrolled in a master's program and had also begun working in a battered women's shelter. Geeta's maternal role had gradually begun to fade away, and her story "transitioned" into a "young single woman's professional story."

Despite the obvious emphasis that Geeta had begun to place on her career, during these years her family consistently pressured her to get married. Geeta's father had commenced trying to arrange her marriage when she was 21 to 22, but he had passed away. Geeta had carried on with her job and her master's program, but the pressure to get married had remained. Now the pressure was coming from her brothers, who had taken over as her guardians. They became actively involved in searching for a match for Geeta.

During the next few years, Geeta was introduced to many men. At first she vehemently resisted the idea of marriage for many reasons. One of these was an overexposure to violence in her work with the battered women's shelter. She was afraid to get married. Recalling those moments, Geeta said,

> For me marriage was not important at this age. I mean when I used to think about marriage—it was like all violence—because I had started work already. I was working in the social sector; I was meeting women; and I was looking at marriages which were not fairy tale weddings at all. So, I had this thing—I don't think you should get involved with men at all. And I was also, at the same time, very clear

that I am not attracted to women. Well I thought okay, it is not working anyway, so I will just be alone for a while.

My brothers were very supportive, especially the younger one who I had lived with most of my life. He had shifted in with me, and he said, "You continue your studies, don't get into this bullshit." So, I finished my post-graduation, started working, then this whole thing of—probably people saying things or whatever it is might have begun. My brothers only told me, "Look now you are 24, if we start looking for people now you would be like married in another year and a half or is it you are interested in someone else?" I said, "No." "You're not interested in marriage?" they asked. I said, "No." So they said, "Well, that is not a choice—the choice that you will get is that as and when you want to marry you will, but you will get married." That was the baseline.

So, although Geeta had resisted marriage for some time, she had also known that it was inevitable. After a while she became actively involved in the search process. She "accepted" that she "had" to get married, she outlined clear criteria about her requirements in a groom. She wanted a well-educated, well-settled person who had a close-knit family. Geeta was also clear that she wanted her own house, her own room, and a husband who shared in the housework. One of her conditions was to marry someone who was comfortable with a working spouse. Another significant requirement for Geeta was the need for freedom in terms of decision making and being monitored and asked questions all the time:

Questions as in, "Why are you doing this? I don't think you should do this." Those things—I didn't want. I wanted to be free to decide what I want to do, and I also wanted/expected people to understand why I have taken a certain decision and to go with it.

However, her main emphases in marital criteria, which is significant for her "narrative bridging" of her "Before 17" and "After 17" story, was the need for a family. Exploring this, Geeta stated,

See the thing was that (pause) since I didn't have a "family family," and I am the kind of person who would want to be with a family. I am a tough person to be with, but I really wanted to marry someone with a family. Also, somehow my experiences told me that to have a support at the back, to have a backing sort of things, you know, somebody is there to help you out. Like there (natal home) you have two brothers and the sister-in-laws; and there you would have something else. That is the kind of relationship I wanted.

So, I used to meet the parents first, and if I liked them I would go ahead with it. There were many parents who did not want to go ahead with me for whatever reasons; maybe not so pretty, maybe no dowry coming in or too headstrong. And I didn't like most of them, so I kept meeting people.

After a year of searching, Geeta finally met a man (her husband) who seemed to fit all her criteria. There was a courtship period of nine months, after which they were married, and Geeta moved to Delhi into her in-law's home. During the engagement, Geeta and her husband met often and consciously tried to get to know each other. There were a few difficulties during her first year of marriage because she and her husband were getting to know each other. These seemed in my hearing less to do with Geeta's marital life and more connected with a change in place, jobs, and so on.

A major transition for Geeta had been her move from her somewhat small hometown to a larger city. She had quit her job when she got married and moved to Delhi, a much larger city and the nation's capital. In the initial months she felt underconfident about getting a job in Delhi and had lost some confidence in her professional abilities. Economically, too, Geeta felt unequal in her marital relationship. Speaking to economic power differences, Geeta explained,

> I am not used to it and I was not used to it. Being lower, being on a lower platform than anyone. I start feeling uncomfortable, I start cribbing and then (after getting a job in Delhi) I think that now my level of confidence has increased and that's how it affects my relationship. I mean I have just realized this. That has affected our relationship. My relationship with the family, husband and of course the individual (reinforces husband's status as an "individual")—I just realized this.

Geeta reached this realization about her rising self-confidence during the course of our interview, and it was an illuminating event for her. She seemed to have been surprised that she articulated it while we conversed. The epiphany was important in allowing me to interpret Geeta's self-transformation at that moment in our conversation and time in her life.

It became clear that having a distinct identity, in her case, work, was essential to Geeta's happiness in her relationship. The troubles in the initial months of her marriage had originated from her low self-esteem in not holding a job. Her marital identity was intricately connected with her professional identity. Not having a work identity for a few months made her feel inferior to her husband and influenced their relationship. Now when she described her relationship, it was about relational and professional equals:

> I think my husband is my best (emphasis) friend. Best friend, I think. I think I mean I have the best of friends that I could have. These are my husband, my own brothers, and my husband's sister. And I can go and speak to him about anything and everything.

Geeta's story moved back and forth (between "Before 17" and "After 17")—between wanting to be a child, to being pushed into the role of mother, to becoming a professional yet wanting to be a daughter/daughter-in-law. Her "selves" were focused on the "'self within family." Family was central to her way of being in the world, yet she had carved spaces for her individual selves within this unit. However, there was no question that Geeta had a sense of self outside the family.

JHUMPA'S STORY

When Jhumpa was in elementary and high school, she had lived in four different cities (in four different states), and her descriptions of her emotional selves emerged amid the telling about these moves. A conarrative that ran through her self-story was her identification with "school institutions" in these places. Articulating these spatial and institutional juxtapositions, Jhumpa said,

> I don't remember Delhi at all. I begin my childhood from Assam. I started my schooling in the first standard (grade) itself in Central school (in Assam) and then I shifted to Bombay after half of the first standard. So, that shift was slightly tough, in the sense, that Assam was a very friendly/familiar place and suddenly we had come to a totally new place. It was difficult to adjust in the beginning because I used to speak only Assamese and Hindi; so, I had to start picking up English and I used to just imitate things from the board (the letters) without really understanding. I was in Bombay at that time from the 1st to the 5th (grade). So that was about five years '81–'86, and then we shifted to Calcutta. So, that's about 12 years old. Okay.
>
> Now the shift to Calcutta was another tough thing because by that time I had gotten used to Bombay and we stayed in this lovely place. It was a colony with 100 odd families, swimming pool, badminton courts and stuff like that. So we used to be really busy—come home from school and go for swimming and badminton classes and things like that. And suddenly I went to Calcutta in this one building, and here were only two other kids (in that building), and it was so cramped. And, there were these power (electric) failures in Calcutta which used to take the life out of us. Also, I was in a Maharashtra board school in Bombay, and in Calcutta I joined a Central Board School. So that was another like—shock—educational shock. So, I did very badly in my 6th standard. Got a 3/25 in Hindi, and all that stuff.
>
> So, Calcutta was again tough. I don't think I ever got over that shift in '86 from Bombay to Calcutta. 'Til that time I was doing so much as a child—taking part in plays and annual functions; and basically a very involved extracurricular type of a person. And, suddenly I went to Calcutta (where I took part in school functions), but never again with that much confidence. If no one picked me, I would never say, "I'll do it."
>
> So that's where the change started, I think. Maybe it is also that age when you are 12, 13, 14 years old. So when we came back to Bombay in '88 I was really happy. I was really happy to be leaving Calcutta, but I really enjoyed my school in Calcutta because I had made a lot of very good friends; they are still very good friends, and whenever I go to Calcutta or they come here, we try and meet up.

Although these were memories of early years of her life, the association of self with space was emergent in Jhumpa's self-story. For instance, when she spoke of her marriage later on, Jhumpa recalled wanting a "winter wedding in Bombay." In other moments of discussing her marriage, Jhumpa mentioned "liking Chennai," shifting to Delhi, "disliking the Delhi winter" and so on. Although she never directly articulated these emotional connections, Jhumpa was enacting and naming her emotional experiences in "space and place."

Jhumpa had grown up in a nuclear family and was the older of two daughters. She described childhood moments in terms of the consecutive spaces in which she had lived. Within these "locations," Jhumpa described herself as a naughty child who was a responsible "older" sibling, yet one who bullied and "bossed" over her sister. Jhumpa proudly related incidents from playschool that she thought had set her apart from her classmates. Explaining this difference in herself, she said,

> I had a lot of friends and some of the memories are so clear that sometimes I am amazed that I actually "thought" at that age. Like maybe school. I started my schooling in a prep-school—tiny tots. I mean tiny-tots is supposed to be really tiny and stuff, and kids are not supposed to be thinking so much. But, I remember myself thinking about; I remember all my friends' names and how we used to decide who's going to sit next to whom (laughs). And then other things like when the seniors had a play or whatever, we used to spy on them. You know things like that which you wouldn't even imagine.

Jhumpa's most intricate and intimate memories were of her times in school. When she spoke of home, she made some observations, but her descriptions seemed less detailed. Nevertheless, within descriptions about life at home she described her parents' relationship with humor. Jhumpa's parents had a substantial age gap; her mother was six years younger than her father. In Jhumpa's observations, their relationship had been that of a parent–child. Her father had always treated her mother like a little girl. This observation, told with humor, assumed significance later on in Jhumpa's life-story because she chose to marry a man who was much closer in age to her.

In her own constructions, Jhumpa's home-life and growing years were smooth. She had fared well in school, but experienced her first academic conflict with her parents when she had chosen to get a degree in economics instead of engineering or medicine. This was somewhat different from a few other younger participants who had not been directly encouraged to have "primary" full-time careers. On a speculative note, this pressure might have been unique to Jhumpa because she did not have a male sibling, and so occupational expectations befitting a male child had been projected on her. In some ways, this lack of work/occupational gendering was reflected in her marital relationship in which she seemed to be more in charge and on an equal footing with her husband—at least behaviorally. Nevertheless, Jhumpa had chosen to study within her own interests, and soon after completing her education she had begun working as a print journalist with a weekly magazine.

During her initial working years, when she was in her early 20s, proposals of marriage by eligible grooms and families had begun pouring in. Although she never acknowledged it, Jhumpa spoke of these with pride. These were also described in terms of "places." The first one was in Calcutta, the second one was in Bombay, and a few others took place in a club in Bombay. Jhumpa had resisted most of these meetings, yet she had gone along with them. Speaking to this contradiction, Jhumpa said,

> After this, say about a year later, my parents spoke to me. They said, "We'd like you to get married, and so we are looking for proposals." No, actually they didn't have to start looking; the point is that the proposals had started coming. The second one also just came on its own.
>
> I had begun working at that time. And I didn't like the entire idea because people came over to meet me and stuff. Because I was not ready for it. And I thought that "If I liked the guy when I talk to him then maybe I'll think about it." But, at a point of time when I am not ready to settle down, maybe I shouldn't waste their time. But, another part of my mind was saying—What if I like him? What if I miss this opportunity of meeting a person who I might like later?

Jhumpa had been quite sure that she wanted to marry someone closer to her in age because she wanted a "friend-like" relationship with her husband. She was determined that she would not be treated like a child as her mother had been. She explained this very well when she said, "And I thought it would be a more friendly relationship rather than up and down and I could speak my mind. This is important. That I should be able to speak my mind to the person who I am going to spent my entire life with." Jhumpa was also determined to marry someone who was professionally qualified and earning more than she did. As all the other younger group participants, she was aware of the inevitability of her marriage, but was trying to make sure that she would be materially and emotionally comfortable within it. Her marriage was ultimately arranged according to the criteria that she had outlined.

Jhumpa's description of her marriage and her relationship with her husband was spatially described in terms of Chennai (a Southern Indian city), where they had lived as a nuclear unit, and Delhi, where they were currently residing with Jhumpa's in-laws in an extended family unit. Jhumpa had been a working spouse from the very start of her marriage. When she spoke of her marital life in Chennai, there was a day-by-day quality to her descriptions that centered on what they used to "do." Within the "Chennai" descriptions, she was sketching for me a sense of camaraderie between her husband and herself. For instance she described a regular workday in the following manner:

> My office was really close to my husband's office. So, he used to drop me and go to work. Or he used to go to work and I used to just walk it from there or take a

rickshaw or whatever. It was very commutable—the distance. And, we used to meet sometimes for lunch. For my first assignment I had to go to British High Council, and I didn't know where it was. It was closer to his office than to mine. Then we met up on the road, we had a dosa (South Indian pan-cake style tortilla) and stuff, then he showed me the way and all that stuff. So, I had a good time basically.

The move to Delhi had brought with it many changes. In terms of family dynamics, they had moved from a nuclear family to a joint family. Jhumpa spoke of this as the "shift to Delhi" which had encroached upon her space. Explaining this loss of autonomy, Jhumpa said,

> So, Chennai was good. When I shifted to Delhi, the set-up got changed a bit because there were (other) people there. Out there we were just the two of us. And here—there was the family. So there was compromise in that end. In the sense that suddenly from a two bedroom flat you are down to one room. In terms of space, I mean, I don't know.
>
> In terms of my own space, it had shrunk. And the fact that—if I don't feel like talking I still have to talk. Not because they expect me to talk, but because I feel like I should not be ignoring the other person in the room. I mean it is not the right thing to do. So, maybe that is a pressure—to be responsible for two other people. Not in the terms of anything else, but to maintain and have a good relationship with them.

Jhumpa's relationship with her husband in Delhi had become more "shared," with other people and space, and they had learned how to communicate with each other via telephones when they were at work or they would fix a time and place to talk. Jhumpa emphasized that there were a few things that they preferred not to talk about at home. When I asked her to describe her current relationship with her husband, Jhumpa referred to it as a companionship that involved give and take; and she often found herself on the "advising end" of their relationship. Speaking to this, she said,

> So I have to be very patient while talking to him like trying to (pause) to work it out. In the sense, he is really bothered about his relationship with his superiors (at work), with this senior. I mean the botheration is actually nothing, but for him it is like staring at a wall as if there is no way to go beyond it. But there is a way to go beyond it. So, I advise a lot (laughs). I have got into this counseling mode and I do a lot of advising, which now suddenly, I've started to enjoy.

Jhumpa eventually began to urge her husband to accept a job offer in Chennai where they had initially lived. It had been a happy space for her, and she was determined to return to it.

MEENA'S STORY

Meena had experienced a nurturing and loving childhood home. She grew up in a nuclear family and had lived in Bombay and Delhi. She was the older of two children and had been very close to her younger brother. When Meena spoke about her family, she spoke of them as always being there for each other as strongholds of support. Although she did not speak of being spoiled or pampered, her explorations of life at home placed her as an important part of the family unit. She was sketching a unit in which everyone was equal and important. This was clear from Meena's own words when she described growing up:

> It was good. I have a younger brother; he's three years younger to me and we two are really close, still very close. He always shared his things and I always shared with him. My mother is also a very good friend of mine, you can say. I always share my problems with her and my father. So, I mean we had this thing in our house that at night everyone sat together for dinner, and we always discussed things. My father used to take suggestions from us like, "What do you think I should do in this situation?" So I think we were always very close. We never felt lonely. During my exam time, my parents used to, you know, sit with me if I wanted, and they would help me out with all the problems. I mean I always felt that they were really a support for me for everything.

Therefore, the relational narrative at home had been one in which everyone was intrinsic and equal. Meena related that her parents treated each other with respect, and in her view they were the "perfect couple." She said that they rarely fought, and when they did quarrel they would "patch up" quickly by talking with each other rather than allowing a conflict to fester. Meena had taken this quality as a relational lesson and was practicing it in her own married life.

This supportive and democratic environment at home had empowered Meena with the freedom to choose her own intellectual path in school. She had never felt pressured to take up any specific area of study. Rather, her parents had wanted her to choose whatever she found suitable. Speaking to this, Meena said,

> I always wanted to be a doctor, since childhood. But (my parents never said anything in particular) that, "You have to be this or that." I was much interested in surgery and all, but I couldn't get into these other medical exams, so I opted for homeopathy. My father was always a support for me. He never forced me to do anything. He said, "Whatever you want I'll help you there."

Having chosen to study medicine, Meena had made it clear to her parents that although she was keen on eventually getting married, she would do so only after completing her degree, which would take about five years. There had been no conflict about this decision. This respect for personhood in her maiden (natal) home had deeply influenced Meena. She valued this quality in her ongoing relational life, and it became clearer in her story as Meena's self-story proceeded.

After completing her undergraduate degree and starting a job at the age of 24, Meena was ready to get married. The process of searching for a groom, as most filial events in her home, had been collaborative, and Meena's opinions were crucial to the matchmaking. Meena was clear about wanting to marry an educated, well-to-do person because she wanted to lead a "luxurious life," or at least one similar to the one she was used to. She had rejected many men who she thought were not making enough money to support a family. She had also rejected some men who she thought would not pay as much attention to her and her family. Describing some such incidents, Meena said,

> I met some other guys who were intolerable. You know there was one guy—he didn't even—I mean I felt that he was insulting my parents.
>
> I mean he just came in alone, first of all. Okay, that is okay. And then, (pause) he was not even talking well with them (my parents). And you know like showing them that, "I can only talk to her." He was showing that he is like a rich boy and, you know, he is "best." He was showing that, "You guys (her parents) will be sidelined and we are just taking your girl." So I said, "What bullshit! My parents are 'something.' If you give respect to them then I will give respect to you."
>
> Then there was one more guy. He had a mother and he says, "She is my main responsibility and you will be second for everything." So, I said, "Leave it. I mean I am giving my whole life to you, and of course you have to respect your mom, even I would, but that doesn't mean that you leave me aside and do all that." So I said, "No."

Eventually, Meena met an "appropriate person" (her husband) and married him when she was 24 years old. Meena had been satisfied with her parents' and her own collaborative choice for a groom, except for one glitch. She would be getting married into a joint family and was going to live with her parents-in-law. This made her somewhat uncomfortable because she had wanted to live in a nuclear family similar to her maiden family unit. Yet, Meena decided to marry Ravi (her husband) because he had made it quite clear to her that their marriage would be a priority, and that if Meena and his parents did not get along then "they" (Meena and her husband) would move out and get their own place. Having been assured that her "center" would remain intact, Meena had agreed.

So, after her marriage Meena moved to her in-law's home. Her new family comprised her husband, his parents and her unmarried sister-in-law. At first, things had been smooth, but in a few months her parents-in-law had begun encroaching on Meena and her husband's time. They had been involved in searching for a groom for their daughter. They would often require Meena and her husband to be present at each meeting. Meena felt that it was "their" family matter, and wanted to stay outside the decision-making process. Further, Meena had conceived in the first few months of her marriage. During her pregnancy, Meena felt neglected and not taken care of by her husband's family. Talking about this in depth, Meena said,

I used to cry for the whole year. I was pregnant; I immediately got pregnant after marriage, so somewhere after 2–3 months I got pregnant. One thing was good that they (her in-laws), like on Sundays, they gave us time to be alone. You know otherwise there are a few in-laws (whom I know)—they will go roaming around with you. They never interfered in all that. My father-in-law was in Bareilley at that time, and only my mom-in-law was there.

And one more irritating thing was that my sister-in-law was to get married. So we were looking out for boys for her. So, it was only the weekend which we used to get. And at that time we had to go out to look at the boys or they used to just come home, so I mean most of the weekends were wasted (doing this). I used to get frustrated and feel, "I just recently got married and I am pregnant. Next year I'll have a baby and I won't be able to move out." I used to say, "Why can't they do it on their own." They always gave preference to my sister-in-law's holidays. She was in NIIT (a computer training school); she was teaching there. They never asked us, "Are you free, should we call anyone?" It was just an order for us: "This fellow is coming and you have to be there." I mean I always got irritated on this point and felt that, "We are two people; we also have some life." They could at least ask us if we are free and if we are going out somewhere. This was really irritating during that whole year.

And then there was one more thing. Like my father is very much a health freak, you know? He likes eating fruits, taking care of his health, doing walks and all. Even I have always done all that. I always eat fruits, drink milk and go for walks. I am not much into fast-food. My sister-in-law was the opposite. So, my mother-in-law always felt that, "This girl (Meena) can take care of herself." You need pampering sometimes, as a person, right? But she always said that, "Too tho apane aap khaa legi" (you will eat on your own). So, she never got fruits for me. It was my parents who used to send them, you know.

I remember the milk thing. I mean these small small things are irritating. She would never ask me, "Do you want milk, should I give you milk?" During your pregnancy you should have these things. She would give it to her daughter and she would get jealous if I ate something. You know like if I am eating a mango, she'll keep saying to her daughter, "You eat one too." I told my husband one day; I really cried and I said, "I don't want to stay here, I want to go back to my place so that I can eat properly and I can take care of myself. I always feel that I am just staying here and I have to do everything on my own. There's no one to pamper me, she's always doing it for your sister." You know you need some pampering which was not present. So he said, "It's okay we will surely shift out."

He was with me. That was a very good point in Ravi: he is always with me, and even if he doesn't say anything to them (his parents), at least he sympathizes with me. That is more important, you know. You can't expect him to be against his parents. So, that was a very good thing in Ravi; I got support from him always for this.

Eventually, finding herself continuously sidelined, Meena convinced her husband to break away from the family and moved into her own apartment. In some ways, her marital life really began after the first year when they had moved out of her husband's parents' home. Now they were busy with their marriage and their daughter, and Meena explained how this "unit" was the center of everything:

> We shouldn't give much importance to other people. It should be just between husband and wife, our relationship. We should understand each other and not ruin our relationship because of our parents. Maybe my husband doesn't like few things about my parents and even I don't like thing about his. So, I think now I've understood this—you can't fight over these things. I mean we have to live together. They are just sidey people who, once in a while, you have to meet. So you can compromise on all this.
>
> I think once you have a kid—it's a major responsibility. I always tell my husband, "She is the first priority. Even if we feel like sometimes not liking each other or something, we should give first priority to her. She will feel neglected if we two are not together." That is why I have started ignoring my in-laws because I think that (situation) can't be changed. We are three members in our family who have to live together. The in-laws will come over, do something in a day or two; we need to forget that, you know.

Meena's struggles were those of any person trying to find a center for herself in all her relational stories. Even in describing her marital relationship, Meena was concerned about the role that each of them played in the relationship and was concerned about any one of them being neglected:

> I tell him everything like, in the sense, if I want something. He is very bad at giving gifts, so, I always tell him about that. Although he has done it twice: he has given me surprise gifts twice. But for Valentine, I did a surprise dinner for him, just both of us, and I left my daughter at my parents' place. So he was shocked and he forgot about it. Then (he said) he was planning to buy flowers in the evening when he remembered that it was Valentine's. So he said, "Now it has been four years, why do you want to do all this, we're getting old." I said, "What rubbish, if now you'll think you're old that what will we do when we are 50?" So I told him that all men went out somewhere, took their wives and all, then he felt bad (pause).
>
> If I am angry with him, I tell him. I try to sort out the problem within a day or that day itself, you know. One or two days, maximum. I speak out. Or, you know, previously I had the habit of writing a letter and telling him. If I didn't want to speak out, I would write the whole thing, "This this this this is the reason why I'm angry and this is what is happening and all that." And he used to read it.
>
> He responded very well. He liked it because you know when two people are arguing or something, if I just say one sentence which you don't like, you may answer back, which will create a bigger scene. So, after reading the whole thing calmly you can at least come to some conclusion about what is wrong. So, whenever I went to my clinic and I had time, I used to write, "This this this has happened, please do something about it." So, he would then give me an answer (not in writ-

ing); he would then talk to me, hug me, kiss me and say, "Okay, fine, I am sorry for this and that." So, I always found writing as a very good solution, instead of fighting.

Once or twice we did have a fight. It is basically always about the in-laws, always related to them. And my daughter got scared because she is sleeping with us and if you are talking at night. So, I've decided that even if we are to have an argument we do it early in the morning or when she has slept off; never in front of her because she really gets scared and thinks, "What is happening between my parents?"

Now we rarely argue, and one thing is good that he really understands me and gives importance to my parents. My in-laws, whenever they came over or my parents invited them for dinner, (if you are going to someone's house for dinner or something you would usually take something, especially when it's your in-law's side) never bothered to bring anything; they must've gone hundreds of times. My husband agreed to gifts, so whenever we go out we are buying gifts. If am buying for his parents, he will give importance to my parents and tell me that, "Yes we will buy for them (her parents) or my brother." When my brother went to Germany he got many of things for my daughter. So, when we went to Singapore we got a watch for him (her brother), a nice watch and all that. I mean, I am happy in that at least he is giving importance to my family, even if his parents are not. So, I really have started ignoring his parents.

Meena's story was about respect for personhood within relationships. She carried with her the socialization that she had encountered as a child in her parents' home. The "center," and "importance" were crucial to her narrative identity in every aspect of her life, be it with her parents, her in-laws, her daughter, or her relationship with her husband.

RADHIKA'S STORY

Radhika had been married for five years and lived in an extended family with her husband and his parents. She had a two-year-old son. She had been working as an anesthesiologist for seven years and had been married when she was 25. Radhika grew up in a nuclear family in a small north Indian hill town. She was the youngest of four siblings. Medicine was her family legacy; every person in the family except her mother was a doctor.

Radhika's first recollections of herself were that of a child who spent a lot of time on her own—dreaming and wasting time in the back yard. Laughing through descriptions of the "queenly dreamer," Radhika said that as a child she had been least interested in studying:

I am the youngest of four brothers and sisters. My father is a doctor and my mother is a housewife. We had this huge house in Nainital. There was a nice big backyard and a front lawn. It was a very interesting backyard with a pond and ducks, and there were chicks, and there was a cock, and there were three hens. They were all our pets. It was a nice, very comfortable childhood. I was more of a— not exactly a loner—but I was very happy with myself. I used to go and explore that particular backyard and just go out. And there were orchards there, and I used to play there, and be on my own. Often, I'd just be sitting in a corner and pretending that I am some queen or something, you know, with a cloak. In fact, that's what my sisters tell me that I was generally always talking to myself. I was not interested in reading and in studying—ever.

In fact, conspiring with her father, Radhika often skipped school. She was enrolled in a Catholic school and was barely managing to pass her classes. Her father always managed to convince the nuns to pass his daughter into the next grade:

I used to flunk miserably, you know. My father had to go and speak to those nuns and he knew them very well. He's a very charming man, my father. He could always, you know, make sure that I was passed. (Laughs). And whenever it would rain I would tell my father I don't want to go to school, so he used to say, "Okay, it's a day off, it's a day off." He'd call up (my school) and say, "My daughter is not feeling well."

Continuing the "royal" self-narrative, Radhika even described herself and her siblings as little "prince-lings" of the town. She attributed this to her father's status as a doctor and said, ". . . being a doctor in those days was a very big thing. He had a very good practice. We were financially very well off . . . not proud, we were never allowed to be rude to anyone, but generally we were very happy." In other words, Radhika and her siblings had not lacked for anything during those years.

Academically, Radhika had grown up in the shadows of her female siblings, who had been achievers, while she had barely made average grades in school. She had been interested in arts and crafts and had, at one point, evinced an interest in fashion design. Of course, she went on to get a degree in medicine, but from her story it seemed clear that the decision not to go into fashion design had been steered by her family. Fashion design as a profession was connected with her "dreamer" status. Very perceptively, Radhika explored an incident that led to a shift in the dreamer status:

Actually they never pushed me, not directly. But, to be very frank, that emotional blackmail was, I think, always there. Like "Beta (child) you can do anything you want, you are very good at it, but you know what, like pick up, it's your wish, but we feel that you'll be much happier you know doing this or doing that; if you want my advice."

Those days fashion designing was not really "in" and even now, very frankly, my father would just tremble at the thought of anybody in the family becoming a fashion designer. He's quite conventional and orthodox. He said, "No it's a very good line, I agree with you, but the kind of security and respect a woman has in society when she's in a professional field like medicine and engineering is alto-gether different, but it is up to you beta. We will not force you to do anything." I think—now I feel that deep down at that time—I just wanted to do something that would make my parents happy. You know when you are young you think your parents are the smartest and the best.

Radhika remembered another incident that had shifted her into her "radical" self, as she self-defined it. This second incident was related with marriage and oc-curred when Radhika was 16 years old. It was a family conversation about the pros and cons of the love and arranged marriage. Describing it, Radhika said,

Actually my father properly sat down with us—I think I was just 15–16—and he said, "Let us talk about marriage" (tongue in cheek tone). So, he said, "Okay, let's talk about marriage." And, you know he wanted to talk about love marriages and arranged marriages. And he said, "We have no problem, if you want to, then you girls go ahead for the love marriages (and for my brother also), but whatever you do let us sit and discuss what are the pros and cons of what kind of a marriage and all that ..."

I think he was really scared deep down that we may go ahead and get some wrong guy and he was just trying to get a feeler. You know one of those things.

We have this tradition at home that after dinner we always sit down and talk, and sometimes the conversations would go on until even 12 in the night. We used to have an early dinner, around eight, and then we used to sit together, either in the lawn or the dining table itself. Always there ...

I responded, like at 16, as every girl does. Like a mature, very intelligent indi-vidual. When you think you are really smart.

I said, "In love marriages you understand the other person." I said all those things that you say at 16. And then my father said, "In an arranged marriage you can eliminate difference because you are marrying into the same social strata, you're marrying into the same sort of a community background and everything." So we just sat and had a discussion over it. There was no conclusion drawn or any-thing. But everybody was free to voice their opinions. I think it must have given my father quite a bit of heartburn after that because I was pretty radical, my sister is very radical in her outlook, and my brother would just refuse to answer anything. That was even more scary for them (laughs).

Radhika was in the top five in her class in medical school and her career was on an upswing. After Radhika had completed her education and was well settled professionally, her parents began asking her if there was any person in her work-place that she was interested in. Ironically, a proposal had arrived from her work-place. The potential groom was a resident in her department at the hospital. They became engaged. The engagement did not last long, but it was an event that still seemed to shock Radhika:

I'm a very different person. I'm not the routine person. I don't know, I think I am re-ally weird. I have a lot of weird friends also. I would've never probably settled for a conventional marriage. It so happened that when I was doing my post graduation there was a colleague who was quite interested in me. And his family approached us—nice very good looking guy and everything and a very attentive fellow; his family approached my parents for the match and actually everything was done. And I was supposed to get married.

You'll be amazed actually. A lot of people cannot even relate to that situation. We had a wedding date fixed. We called it off a week before the wedding.

I was just not comfortable with that fellow.

I knew him from before. It was not exactly an affair, but we were working together, so we knew each other and everything. But, I felt that his attitude became different, once we got engaged. After that, I was not supposed to talk too much with that person, or I was not supposed to do this. You know, I've always been very active in my college (I've never been wild), but there are some things I feel very strongly about and I really go ahead full steam with them. So, around that time we had the case of a doctor who was facing some sexual harassment by her senior doctor. So we had gone on a strike and all. When you go ahead and strike, I'm very "go ahead and strike." I feel very strongly about certain things. He was quite embarrassed by it. And as it was getting closer and closer to the wedding, I was getting more and more uncomfortable.

Actually, I was better than him. I was slightly better qualified than him. But, somehow it was that the comfort level was decreasing, you know. So then I called it off. I spoke with my father, I spoke to him, and then my father spoke to both of us. We spent a lot of time together. Then I called it off. So, it's weird.

I don't know. My father was very supportive of it. My mother, father and my family were very supportive of it. And I am really glad I did it.

In breaking the engagement, Radhika underwent transformations of her marital criteria. From then on, she had to think carefully of the kind of person that she wanted to marry. She was now certain that she wanted to marry a doctor. Because she was financially independent, economics were not an issue, but she did admit that only a doctor would understand her life and lifestyle. Moreover, when she met her husband and agreed to marry him, she had placed conditions that were meant as a test. He had passed them with flying colors. Describing these negotiations, Radhika said,

Actually, I really wanted somebody I'd be really comfortable with.

Somebody I could speak to and talk to. Somebody who would actually listen when I am speaking, you know listen in the sense of actually listen. Somebody who would respect me for just what I am and who could take me as I am and like me for it.

I just liked him (her husband) very much. He was so comfortable and we had similar views on things. He wasn't hassled by my views. I told him that I didn't want to settle abroad. And most doctors do go abroad, you know. I told him from the very beginning that, "Look I am not going to go abroad, are you interested in going abroad?" He said, "No I am not interested in going abroad." I said, "Down the years you might just want to go and I may not want to go." And he said, "Okay I will respect your decision and we will not go because we have to make decisions together."

I liked this about him—that he was very cool about everything, even when I made inflammatory statements about things that I feel strongly about. (I used to say things like) "Don't expect me to bring any dowry or anything and I hate all these things about marriage, and I'm not going to do this and do that." He was pretty okay about it. He would just smile and say, "Okay" (laughs). He told me, "I don't have any expectations from you. I'll take you as you are. We'll grow together, and we'll get to know about each other."

When Radhika married her husband, she moved into the new house with these "bargained for" identities. Her relationship with her husband was an equal negotiation, something that she had set up in the premarital phase. Having had a baby a few years ago somewhat shifted their relationship, with Radhika having chosen to take on regular daytime hours in her work. Yet she did not seem to resent it. She had an in-house baby-sitter, but wanted to spend time with her son in the early years.

In her relationship with her extended family, Radhika was unchanged. She was as much a champion of independence and autonomy as she had always been. Radhika felt that her in-laws had a very conventional understanding of a daughter-in-law, and they expected her to serve them and be around whenever they desired. She said, "Probably, they were not expecting such a radical daughter-in-law. And I never warned them about me." She had resisted and did not partake in social activities that they expected her to attend. Exploring this via instances, Radhika said,

Instances like, there will be a festival and since I am the daughter-in-law and the bhabhi (sister-in-law), I am supposed to be sitting with them and I am supposed to be entertaining them the whole day. And why should I do that? You come, you be here, you enjoy yourself and let me also be on my own. I'll sit with you for a half hour, an hour and I'll serve you, I'll do that whatever it is. If it is rakhee (a festival that celebrates the brother–sister bond) you (sister-in-law) do whatever with your brother and that's it. I am going to my parents' now because I also need to spend good time there. I can't spend time with you the whole day; I can't do it like that. It's not that I don't like you or something; it's just that I mean I can't sit and keep discussing jewelry all the time. I can't discuss clothes all the time. I don't have much jewelry and clothes as it is, so I don't have much to discuss about too.

I am so much happier with my own little nice good book. And please don't come and keep disturbing me after some time. It irritates me like anything. So, it's like, you know, I'm actually much happier on the weekend with my good book or a nice movie or just spending time with my son or husband or just going with my husband you know doing anything going to a nice art gallery or something like that. I'm not a very social person, so I just can't go meet every maasiji and mausaji and chachaji and chachaji (different uncles and aunts) and keep saying, "Namasteji and how are you ji? And I am missing you so much ji."

I can't do that.

Radhika's present sense of her selves was deeply protective of her autonomy within the extended family. Her relationship with her husband was egalitarian, and standing her own and "speaking out" were intrinsic to her identities. In many ways the radical transformations seem to be radical "negotiations," which had become one of her permanent garbs. They were central to her way of being in that time and space.

Conclusion

The four stories presented here are certainly contemporary experiences of women in Hindu arranged marriages, yet the differences within the stories illustrate how disparate the experience of the arranged marriage is for every woman. Further, each of these stories is different from the way that arranged marriages are explored in the mainstream media. The experiences of these four women in their arranged marriages show that the arranged marriage is shaped by the distinct personalities and identities of the women who experience them. In short, this chapter illustrates that there is no "single" story of an urban Hindu arranged marriages, and like all cultural realities it is dynamically shaped by the time, place, and persons who co-produce those realities.

CHAPTER 11

Landscape Troubles as Intercultural Conflict

INTRODUCTION

Northwestern Avenue in West Lafayette, Indiana, the town that houses Purdue University, looks like most suburban neighborhoods in Middle America. Its homes are neatly placed against each other, its turf lawns are immaculately kept, and the sidewalks are pristine, showing no trace or evidence of overgrown grass on any side. Every weekend homeowners, mostly men, can be seen patiently mowing their lawns as they chat with their neighbors. The women of the homes are generally busy weeding flower beds, planting seasonal bushes or bulbs around the lawn, or planting vegetables in the side lots and backyards. In short, the scene is an ideal picture of modern American suburban life in which the lawn has cultural and symbolic meaning for a community. As you inch toward house number 1807, which is right across the now "out-of-business" local grocery store called Smitty's, you find it hard to peer into the lot because it is shaded by trees and greenery. When you enter the gravel driveway (or what might be a driveway in conventional terms), you feel as if you are being enclosed inside a serene green forest. The house is certainly present. At a mere 50 feet from the main road, it is built in the center of the lot and looks much like a log cabin. Walking around it is literally like taking a walk in the woods.

This woodlot, an anomaly among its neighborhood companions, is home to anthropologist Myrdene Anderson, a professor at Purdue University, who, starting in 1988, found herself in the midst of an arduous battle with her neighbors and the city over her unmowed yard and naturalized garden. Her yard came to be referred to as a "public nuisance" in a seven-year-long legal battle, during which time Myrdene was asked to pay the city fines totaling to about $216,000. The case, though never officially closed, was finally resolved in 1995 with the help of a third-party arbitrator, who suggested a health inspector monitor the house for rodents and "noxious" weed every few years, for a fee paid by Myrdene.

This chapter is an exploration of one specific yard controversy in Indiana as a case among cases of an urban and suburban debate about the viability of lawns in urban and suburban America life. It can be referred to as an intercultural conflict with violent underpinnings because in this case the violence, in the form of legal harassment, was meted out against Anderson by her neighbors, who demanded that she conform to a certain worldview and habits of being that are actually ecologically destructive. The attacks against Myrdene are also interesting from the standpoint that she has devoted most of her scholarly career over the last four decades to studying violence and peace in non-Western worlds. Her most recent book on violence is entitled *Cultural Shaping of Violence.* In this chapter, we start by looking specifically at the controversy over Myrdene Anderson's Indiana yard, by showing how the conflict was given shape by the involved parties. The yard case differs only in degree to the previous cases presented in our book. In this exploration, we had access to the person involved in the controversy and therefore much of the text is constructed in her own words via many interviews with her. Then we look at the rhetorical stances taken by the different parties in the Indiana town to see how the conflict was shaped. We believe this case study nicely captures our point in this book that intercultural conflict is fundamentally about our unwillingness to understand the humanity of others rather than merely the differences of others. Finally, we show how a resolution to the conflict could be found in the conversations that existed in the local community about the conflict. Before turning to the conflict, we first explore Myrdene's childhood and life as an ordinary person who grew up at one with nature.

THE YARD IN/AND THE PERSON

Myrdene Anderson was born and spent most of my life on the west coast of the United States. She joined the faculty in the anthropology department at Purdue University in the late seventies. In the last 40 years or so, her anthropological research has been conducted in a variety of settings, and technically she is an ethbobotanist in the field of anthropology. Myrdene's early work focuses on the language and study of plant classification, plant use, and plant belief. In the United

States she has studied community gardening associations and the artificial life movement, but she is best known in the discipline of anthropology for her 30-plus years of fieldwork with reindeer breeders in Norwegian Lapland, where altogether she lived for over seven years. Her doctoral work with the Saami of the Norwegian Lapland region explored ecological systems including landscape, animals, plants, and how these are embodied and articulated within this community. Through her ethnographic work with the Saami, she was responsible for coining the term, "ethno-ecology." Some of her larger edited and coedited volumes bear titles such as, "Human-Alloanimal Social and Symbolic Relations" (1986), "Self and Society, Stereotype and Ethnicity" (1991), "Refiguring Debris—Becoming Unbecoming, Unbecoming Becoming" (1994), and more recently her 2004 book, *Cultural Shaping of Violence.* At Purdue University, Myrdene teaches undergraduate and graduate courses in linguistic anthropology, ethnography, semiotics, and anthropological theory.

Even though ecology and culture are Myrdene's formal professional domains, her interest in and passion for nature, culture, and the environment can be traced back to her childhood in which she was raised with an "appreciation and knowledge of plants" (Iszler, 1995). Born on August 13, 1934, Anderson often refers to herself as a Depression-era baby who learned to value economy and finds worth in the smallest things, be they plastic containers, cardboard cartons, or scrap metal or as she says, "everything must and can be reused and recycled." A nomadic childhood and eventual life of travel further reinforced these life principles. Before and after she went to kindergarten, her family moved back and forth between different states, cities, and countrysides. She points out that her earliest memories are of living in a small clearing in a forest. In some private papers detailing her passion for green and greenery, Myrdene explores her childhood:

> Everything was green, even in the winter, given the prevalence of conifer trees. The house had no curtains and no shades; nature outdoors provided both, and they were green. To this day, I have neither curtains nor shades where I live, and no lock on my door, either. Outdoors in the garden clearing in the middle of the forest, under some apple trees, I had a sandbox. The clearing permitted me to gain some speed in running and playing, which was not an option in the very thick virtual rainforest extending in all directions. Going back and forth between the forest and the sandbox was a creature, my friend, named Dennis. It was a garter snake, and the only person I knew named Dennis, and virtually my only playmate, as the region was sparsely settled. Where I found the name Dennis remains a mystery. When I had to go inside the house to eat, I would pack Dennis in the sand, and instruct him to wait for me. He never did, and I never discovered that he must have been many snakes, many serially frightened snakes.

Myrdene's love for trees and a longing to be surrounded by them is a continuous refrain in the story she narrates of her childhood. The specificity of the memories displays a keen awareness of her understanding that nature and humans are en-twined and must sustain each other:

> Climbing trees was a favorite pastime, both in the clearing and in the forest. I fell a few times but only got temporarily dizzy. Humans are, after all, primates, and naturally inclined to arboreality. To this day, I cannot look at a tree without judg-ing its climbability, although I stopped climbing some years back. And I can't see a dead branch, attached or fallen, without thinking: firewood! Growing up in the Great Depression, even old toothpicks find other later uses: kindling! Venturing only a meter or two into the forest, one would be hidden from view, but nothing could be seen at a distance from these secret places either. So little eyes would fo-cus on little things close at hand. Berries and bugs, for instance. There was also furniture in the forest, or so I thought. Stumps and fallen logs, and anthills, for ex-ample. More than once I could not resist sitting on an anthill, shaped like a perfect little cushion, and had to leap up and thrash out of the forest, seeking medical at-tention for the ant bites. I never learned fear, although the ants and the Dennises may have. To this day, for me, the distinction between inside and outside is mini-mal, as well as that between the cultural and the natural. I have no fear of heights or of animals, despite being attacked by a couple of animals in recent years. I chalk up these accidents to statistics, my being around so many animals, and as to the offending creatures, I volunteer excuses.

Even while living in the city, she found woods and greens:

> Then there were the city scenes of my youth. Sometimes there were woods in the neighborhood of our house, across the street, or at least a park nearby. Cities also afforded different kinds of attractions such as museums and zoos. The natural his-tory museum in San Francisco captured my attention even more than the zoo, al-though when a tiger, or was it a lion, escaped the zoo, my father and I went out looking for it. Fortunately, the venture was not successful.
>
> By age 8 I was living in back in Seattle and had taken up rock collecting, es-pecially on family outings. In between outings, I would comb through the pile of gravel my father kept by the back alley for his own construction purposes. Sure enough, I found the most marvelous of stones in this pile of rocks. Often enough the stones had been cut with flat surfaces, and sometimes these surfaces would be polished. I even found geodes. One piece of petrified wood had been cut and pol-ished into a small cube; I have still have that one and the others, somewhere, be-cause while I may give things away, I throw nothing out.
>
> Growing up in so many different places, I observed my family judging past, present, and potential future properties and landscapes. What was desirable or un-desirable? Any kind of trees, especially fruit trees, were good; rocky soil was not good. Three-hundred-sixty degrees of green, or blue, if sky and water were in-volved, was desirable; any interruption of that view by a human-made structure was not good, no matter how distant it was. And the land had to have "running water." Of course, by this time most houses did have modern plumbing and run-ning water, but the idiom from my father suggested that the land had to have it

too. Translated, this meant that there should be fresh surface water suitable for drinking should one wish, and otherwise for irrigation or, especially, just for enjoyment and looking at. No doubt the running water also indexed the water table and how successful any well might be. Salt water was a plus, to be sure, but would not trump fresh "running water."

In my family it was my father who tended both yard and garden. In cities, my father might put the productive vegetable garden in the front yard, and the flowers in the more private back yard, to the consternation of my mother, and me. I had to weed his vegetables and berries in full view of the neighborhood. He was not so interested in lawn unless for the playing of croquet, but if he had lawn, it was the best, flattest, and greenest in the neighborhood. I got a lot of my exercise in helping at every stage, from removing rocks to mowing.

While her father, on occasion, nurtured lawns in some of their homes, Myrdene is vehemently opposed to them:

I am willing to emulate my father in other respects, but I do not "do" lawns. This turns out to be a major character flaw, given the Lawn Culture that has since overgrown the U.S. Paradoxically, my aversion to lawns, as much stubborn deviance as an innate character flaw, is sustained by strengths of character developed at the same time—my having no choice about weeding in public or being responsible for chores, when my far-flung peers might be unencumbered, or so I imagined. At least for everyone this was before television; my generation should be thankful.

In the countryside, my family could have various kinds of livestock along with food plants and flowers, always flowers and berries, sometimes for sale, along with eggs. We also harvested for sale many things from nature: many kinds of berries (for the market); sallal greenery, ferns, and huckleberry bushes (for florists); and cascara bark (for druggists). My impression was that my father taught me how to do these things as a part of my education, not for the income. For instance, one never took bark from the whole circumference of the cascara tree, or it could not grow back and the tree would die; one always left a strip of bark.

My father would also selectively log the timber from segments of his property, hiring professionals to do the work. He would interview prospective loggers carefully, making sure they would cut *only* the trees he had marked, and would *only* traverse the land along certain trails, and also that they would hire his teenage daughter, me, to be firewatch for four hours at the end of each workday, as prescribed by law. I spent a lot of time in the woods anyway, when not engaged in what I viewed as conscript labor in and around the home. I never did bond with housework, but the forest and everything in it were my friends. When a firewatch, I would take some ridiculously obtuse text in Latin or perhaps Shakespeare into the woods at 4 p.m., while it was still light. Then I would become distracted by the animals, whom I imitated, and when it was quite dark I would get conscientious about the possibility of seeing a fire. Again fortunate, there were no calamities. Nor was there any danger from the animals, although some were larger than a human—very occasionally bear, cougar, wolverine, although more often read through their signs than greeted face-to-face.

As an adult, I had to live in cities again, because of school and jobs. And even when I might have the choice of commuting from the countryside, I value more the flexibility in being able to walk within the city rather than being dependent on a car or public transportation. I did not own a single car until the age of 55, when I inherited by father's old car. It still runs, a 77 Buick. I never wanted this or any other car, but since it belonged to him, I've incorporated it into my life and lifestyle, like a stray animal, for better and for worse.

But what about living indoors and outdoors in a city—could I sculpt spaces suitable to my habits, as spoiled as I had been by the good fortunes of my early life? Without question, I knew I could not live in an apartment. My own first homes were just rented houses, which limited what I might modify inside or out. But I always found structures where there were no intrusive views from the outside in, and yet unobstructed views from the inside out. This means that only a very deliberate person could get close enough to a window to peek in, and I trusted the surroundings to neutralize all evil . . .

I preferred houses with many windows and with windows of many panes, and with doors leading in many directions so that I could step directly into the garden, with the garden in each direction being very distinctive, according to shade and cardinal direction. The gardens built on whatever plants were already there. Even if there were ugly or nonnative plants, I would protect them in the absence of any immediate alternatives, because I figured they were important to hold the soil. Anyway, they were there before I was. Trees would be even more sacred, whether fruit-bearing or cone-bearing.

. . . I have never tilled the land, which would be a very muscular, "developmental," and "cultural" way of forcing a relationship with the land. Instead, I take what is given as an invitation to a conversation with those and future plants and landforms . . .

. . . My gardens seldom provide vegetables anymore, because of my traveling schedule, but some herbs can be harvested as can perennial wild plants such as nettles and berries. I live in a thicket, which not only shields me visually from the street traffic and vice versa, but also absorbs noise, smells, and weather. Even more importantly, my garden isolates me from neighbors on all sides, in every way. Now I even have a fence, that I call my Fibonacci fence . . . The story explaining why I have a fence, in a part of the U.S. where fences are considered antisocial if not downright suspicious, may or may not fully fit into our conversation of the moment.

This fence in Myrdene's house came into being as a result of the seven-year-long battle with the City of West Lafayette, Indiana. Upon arriving in Indiana in the late 1970s Myrdene co-bought a house with a then partner in 1981 and decided to create a natural yard (she is now the sole owner of the home). That is, she did what she had been used to doing, legally, all her life—she consciously surrounded herself with a protected growth of flora and fauna, which provided her with privacy, fragrance, beauty, food, and sometimes medicine (Iszler, 1995). Myrdene describes her yard as, "a forest that offers her sensory escape from the urban landscape, a place of meditation and contemplation and a constant source of surprise and delight." Her thicket or forest, as she refers to it, is well taken care of and remains a mixture of what she calls volunteered plants, and deliberately planted grasses, flowers, and trees. Trees line the front of the yard to screen the house from traffic fumes alongside blocking the line of vision to the main road. The yard offers a variety of trees and grasses that are mostly indigenous to Indiana, including maple, elm, ash, sycamore, mulberry, redbud, plum, yew, and hemlock among others. It also harnesses flowering plants such as daylilies, hollyhocks, poppies, and flowering alum, among others. She says she encourages tall prairie grasses to grow between the tress and smaller grasses (not turf) to intersperse with the strawberries. She keenly encourages black raspberries to spread across the property line. Eventually all living creatures around the house contribute to its ecological balance. The naturalness of the yard attracts all kinds of birds and animals, a development that she is immensely proud of.

For Myrdene and most other nature enthusiasts, the creation of the forest around her home was an attempt at ecological sanity because she was nurturing a healthy micro ecological system. She does not mow grasses and composts dead plants out of a landfill. She refuses to grow anything that needs fertilizer, pesticides, or herbicides. She believes her yard offers itself up as a model for an ecologically sound alternative to turf grass. It encourages birds and other animals to become inhabitant and attracts insects that are native to Indiana and should be a part of all green areas in the region. Not only trees, but cats and dogs populate her home. There are times when a dozen cats and dogs have lived with her in the home and the yard, at peace with one other. As she explains,

> Privileging the "forests" of my Pacific Northwest and Scandinavian ancestry, I protected any and all woody volunteers, and planted many more myself. This leaves little sunlight but for the strip by the street receiving brief morning sunlight. That's where I planted and transplanted exotic spring bulbs and native wildflowers. Bamboo species were experimental nonnatives. Because they don't drop foliage until spring, they afford a very nice screen against neighbors and the street.

THE YARD BATTLE BEGINS

Ironically it was this ecologically sound idyllic space that became the scene of a seven-year court battle in the city of West Lafayette. More ironically, Myrdene's scholarship as an anthropologist has focused largely on a self-sustaining and largely nonviolent fourth world community, the Saami of Lapland in Norway. In her chapter, "The Saami at Loose Ends," Anderson discusses how overt violence is largely outside the Saami, and most of the violence that can be evidenced in the community is meted out by regional, local, national, and occupational bureaucracies. In fact, there is only one recorded incidence of a Saami killing someone deliberately, and that occurred in 1854. In this chapter, Myrdene points out that had she observed a much more violent community during her early months in fieldwork, she might have changed her anthropological field—a testimony to how averse she is to any form of violence. Her choice of subject, region, and population was therefore entwined with her own ideas about nonviolent and peaceful living among all living and nonliving creatures.

In the years between 1981 and 1988, Myrdene received occasional complaints from the city over the riotous nature of her yard. She would handle those complaints by mail response by contesting the veracity of the complaint or its justification. She says that she remembers defending a great crop of ragweed, an allergenic for some, because it is a native "weed" that is also used in plant-dyeing, and when the moon was appropriate, she would harvest the whole batch of ragweed and boil it down. So, she was sure that the city had not found ragweed in any inspections that occurred. There were occasional complaints about the lack of a sidewalk in front of her house, a matter she would resolve periodically by traversing the front of the yard on foot a few times (after 1995, she built a sidewalk around the front as part of the settlement agreement with the city). Of these initial encounters with her neighbors, Myrdene notes,

> Between 1988–1989 and 1994–1995 I had occasional complaints forwarded by the city, and hardly any contact with any neighbors, which is very usual. Occasionally the wife to the south would find me gardening by the street, and say, as though my friend, that "neighbors" had been "complaining" about this or that. Usually this and that had to do with exactly what I was tending . . . neighbors could not see up or down the street and had difficulty getting out of a nearby street or their driveways. I always wrote back to the city, defending whatever practices they complained about.
>
> Until recently, no neighbor had any blooming thing in their yards. My yard, btw, never had a lawn, only groundcover tolerating shade, such as vinca and ivy and mostly pachysandra. Their yards were totally lawn, some professionally "poisoned" on a regular basis. In the past five years or so, one neighbor started planting perennials and another placed potted geranium annuals under a tree. But everything is lawn.

In August 1988, around the time that the daylilies were in full bloom, Myrdene's yard battle began in earnest. She remembers that the first formal citation from the city arrived at the end of the summer and beginning of the fall season. This time the complaint came in the form of a legal summons and a court date. The yard was cited as having "noxious" weeds and junk in the yard (which was bicycles), and untidy wood piles. The West Lafayette Department of Housing and Community Development ordered Myrdene to cut the grass, trim the trees, pull up the "weeds" and bring the yard into line with the city code (Smith, 1995a).

Myrdene appeared in court without an attorney. She barely remembers the day, but she remembers noticing seven to eight persons huddled together in the court, who she assumed were her neighbors. The judge, apparently, did not play a part in the process, but was present. The city inspector, the city development officer, and the city attorney tried to talk Myrdene into signing a consent decree. When I interviewed her about her response, she said,

> I had never heard of a consent decree, but it was perfectly clear it amounted to "promising to stop beating your wife." In other words, it was an admission of guilt. No way. I later discovered that there had been an inspection of my back yard, or entire yard, earlier in the summer, specifically in late June while I was visiting my father just before he died. I was away briefly in early July for the funeral, and then during the week before the semester started to bring back his car and my stepmother. I think the summons must have come later than that. Another, the third, summons in 1994 coincided with the year my stepmother died. I mention this because in my research with other case histories, persons were frequently legally attacked at a time of their great grief. In my case, though, I do not believe my neighbors had any idea of my family situation. In fact, I'm sure they thought I was not even born into the species.

Once this date was through, a stalemate of sorts existed for one year. In 1989, the city sent another summons and another court date. In her conversations with me, the case seemed to take a real significance for Myrdene this time around. So much so that she decided to get an attorney. But she firmly refused to cow down to the city's bullying and instead pledged renewed loyalty to her naturalized and ecological yard and continued to reject signing a consent decree. Speaking about the second summons, she explained:

> In this mail was a summons, the second, to a court date in early October as I recall . . . anyway, a date when I would be out of town. I was flustered. I caught the airport limo for my trip to Texas and from the airport wrote a hasty note to the only attorney whose name I knew, Speelman. I had no envelope, but folded up my note such that a stamp would hold it together. I explained that the year before I had a summons and no attorney, and that this year I would resort to getting an attorney, but that the first need was a "continuance." Another legal term new to me, meaning a postponement of the court date.

Myrdene describes the day of the second summons, the court, and her attorney's desertion of her:

> The 1989 court date resembled that in 1988, except now I had an attorney who quite literally took the city's side. I steadfastly refused to sign a consent decree, once more. In fact, I pointed out that I had refused the year before, without an attorney, so how could I consider signing anything this year, when I had an attorney.
> I remember what I was wearing that ?mid/late? October 1989, a balmy day. Wrap-around pants made of African cotton. Hours after arriving at the courthouse, without any resolution, the meeting disbanded. Again, the judge was there but not involved; we were in a back room only this time sometimes I met with just

my attorney and others with the whole battery of city minions, and my attorney on their side. Clearly, they wanted the "problem" to go away, they wanted to deal with this, with me, so they could report back. And maybe they were thinking of longer-term consequences; in 1994 I had to conclude just that that. I had no private or public understanding with the attorney. We and they just ambled off in separate directions, and I found myself on the street outside the courthouse in a daze. It had been hours, very confusing hours, a test of my stubbornness but also theirs. Some weeks or even months later, I received an envelope from my attorney. I never opened that for full inspection, until 1994, but put it in a drawer with bills I couldn't afford to pay at the time. I assumed he had the nerve to bill me for more than the $500 retainer, and I was incensed, especially as he never took my side. I received no further bills and put that envelope out of my mind. Except I did open it at one point and saw it was a consent decree. Again, how stupid can he be that I would sign it! Back into the drawer.

It was not a consent decree but a copy of the decree that that the attorney, Speelman, had taken on himself to sign. It stated that Myrdene would bring her yard up to code in one month. Things continued in this quiet vein for five years with both the city and Myrdene not doing anything. Myrdene was, in fact, unaware that Speelman had signed on her behalf. Eventually on August 23, 1994, the West Lafayette city housing inspector issues Myrdene a notice of violation. The letter cited her for, "failing to trim her grass and shrubs, keep trees free from dead or dying limbs, and keep her lawn free from weeds or plant growth that are noxious or detrimental to the public health" (Smith, 1995a). Myrdene was surprised by the turn of events, but was able to uncover why the notice of violation came five years after the second summons:

> The reason I now believe every bit of timing was premeditated, is that five years later, in 1994, I received summons number three. And it turns out that I found that envelope to enclose not just a consent decree, but a SIGNED consent decree. Yes, the attorney had put HIS signature on it, even though he did NOT have power of attorney. The first legal contest was mine to "contest" the consent decree. I lost, because I hadn't complained before five years were up.

The third summons was preceded by a petition against Myrdene's yard by her neighbors. Her neighbors managed to garner 68 signatures from other persons in the surrounding area. They continued to cite "conditions at 1807 Northwestern Avenue" in their written statements asserting that the yard was fostering mosquitoes, raccoons, possums and even rats. They blamed the yard for attracting feral cats and accused Myrdene of allowing her plants to grow into other people's yards. They even went as far as to say that the property values were declining in the area all because of the one yard. A neighbor, Mary Gatt, quoted in the *Lafayette Journal & Courier* said,

> It's just sad that Myrdene doesn't want to be a part of the community and abide by the rules. It seems that we have been fighting her forever over this.

As a result of the third summons and notice of violation, a fine totaling $216,000 was issued. The fine was calculated based on a daily rate of violation of $200 to 500 over a period of five years. Myrdene appealed this notice; it was heard on October 12, 1994, by members of the West Lafayette Board of Housing and Property Maintenance Code Appeals. By this time, Myrdene too had hired new lawyers (her attorney Speelman died in early 1994). Alongside, there were now two cases pending in court. One was a case filed by the city for code violations against Myrdene. The other was a case filed by Myrdene asking for a release from the 1989 consent decree signed without permission by her now deceased lawyer. This time around Myrdene was better prepared. She relates the last leg of the seven year war:

> There was a succession of "inspections" intended to intimidate me. I never changed a twig, and still haven't. This week Frederique (a former student) claimed that I had thinned the backyard because he remembers when it was thicker and shielded the area from street noise. He simply wouldn't accept my explanation: the trees and bushes have all matured and the greenery is much higher up now.
>
> Newspaper coverage tended to emphasize the cost to the city-cum-taxpayers (even though always underestimated) and the unreasonable fine assessed me (ditto, even though under-calculated). About the latter anomaly, the city code assesses a maximum fine of $500 per day from date of first inspection, that being late June 1988. That would be $182,500 annually, and over a million dollars by the time the case matured in 1995. This was too embarrassing for the city to admit, for a property valued at the time around $50,000. So they told the press the fine was $200,000 or $250,000. When given the opportunity, I would correct the number, by a million dollars.
>
> I had arranged for four experts to address various accusations: botanist, rat/bat ethologist, entymologist, and copse-professional. These people came from different states, the last one from Ohio with a business name of "urban thickets" (which he would install for a price); his license plate was URTH.
>
> As the final court date neared, long months after I had lost the contest about the consent decree, these individuals had made their travel plans. The judge became more and more anxious to settle out of court because of the negative press and cost. So they tried for the $200M, and this was my last chance to correct the calculation of the fine! Then they tried to get fractions of this.
>
> Somewhere in this process one of the city attorneys asked WHAT I would DO to possibly placate the situation (inspectors-cum-code-cum-neighbors). I always said, not a thing. My attorneys pointed out that I could/should venture SOME offer, just to keep the juices moving because an offer didn't mean I would actually have to do it. So finally I gave them (via my attorney) a longish reply, that I would CONSIDER building a fence, and that the thought had occurred to me back in 1987 and 1988. The reason, besides cost, that I didn't move in that direction reflected my awareness that urban fences are not part of Midwestern culture. The reply delivered to me by my attorney was a rant from the city—Anderson had better not even think of building a fence, who does she think she is, she will just continuing violating all those imaginary codes behind the fence: no way.

Here you can pick up my piece on the Fibonacci fence, which I managed to build in 1996, largely in defiance of the city. Of course, fences are perfectly legal, within certain strictures in various neighborhoods. But this is an aside.

Eventually, Myrdene agreed to some conditions:

On the last business day before the Monday trial, the judge actually locked us all inside his chambers, all day. There would be no trial unless it was over his dead body. Every hour or so he would stride through, giving encouragement to resolution. With evening upon the 40-hour-week city employees, they were getting desperate. They had come down to $10,000 fine. That's when my senior attorney, who's a specialist in arbitration and does this for the International Red Cross, pulled a proposition out of his pocket of tricks. I am too stubborn and inexperienced to contrive any alternatives to a digital solution. His was analogue: okay, the $10,000, but something like $2,000 would be excused roughly every year for five years—nothing was even, more like an amortization schedule.

Biannually, to get the credit, my property was to be inspected by a "neutral third-party arbiter." Forget about the words—no one is neutral and all the arbitration had been accomplished. If there were a failed inspection, all remaining fines would be charged.

The yard dispute was finally settled in August 1995 under the following key settlement agreements, which are summarized here:

- Myrdene Anderson drops her appeal of the city's enforcement action, and the city drops its petition to enforce a $216,000 fine.
- Both parties agree to select a third-party by August 28. If they can't agree on an arbiter, the court will appoint one.
- By March 1, 1996, the arbiter in consultation with both sides will submit a detailed landscaping plan including types of plants allowed and maintenance requirements. The arbiter's decision is final.
- Myrdene Anderson will bring her yard into compliance with the plan on or before May 15, 1996.
- Anderson will owe the city $10,000 for enforcement costs. However, if she complies with the landscaping plan for five years, all but the $1,500 will be forgiven.
- Anderson will be responsible for all costs of hiring and retaining the arbiter.

However, there were roadblocks when it came to choosing the arbiter. Telling that story, Myrdene says,

I was not concerned because I never conceded that there ever were any code violations. But I doubted we could get a neutral person. Each side submitted names. I didn't know enough candidates personally, so many of my names were just hunches. Each side would then reject summarily all the names submitted by the other side. The last desperate contest was between two persons named 'mike'. I actually knew THEIR 'mike', but not my own, and I trusted their 'mike' to be fair, but rejected him anyway.

After some months, the judge became impatient and pulled a name out of another hat, and both sides were told, this is IT, period. Meanwhile I pointed out that the judge wasn't all that clever, because what if that individual said NO. But he agreed. He's a retired forester from the department of transportation, had planted wildflowers along train tracks, and had a business selling native plants. Hardly neutral! What I didn't realize in all this flurry was that I had to pay this person, and he comes from Crawfordsville. It runs a little more than $100 every spring and fall. The above arrangement was to be for five years, remember? Well, my attorney must think this is cheap insurance; I do, anyway. So the arbiter comes twice a year, usually with some free native wildflowers in tow, and we have a nice chat before he goes home to print out another positive note to the judge, copying me and attorney.

In the meanwhile, Myrdene's own attorney hired a landscape consultant from New York. He inspected the home on July 7, 8, 9 of 1995 and wrote the following in the form of a personal report:

I am a bit perplexed that so much has been said and written about 1807 Northwestern Avenue which, in my opinion, is basically a private woodlot in which your house is located. Indeed, I see little difference between your property and other woodlots in the neighborhood with the exception of the presence of your neighborhood structure . . .

In my inspection of your property in the morning, afternoon, and early evening hours, I found no active presence of any rodents nor any passive signs (droppings, burrows, runs) of same. In an urban/suburban area in Indiana, commensal rodents such as the Norway rat (*Rattus norvegicus*) would be the most likely public-generated concern for health risks. This commensal species certainly does not appear to be present at 1807 Northwestern Avenue. Such commensal rodents can be a threat to public health, though in the United States most commensal rodent control work is not geared toward disease suppression per se . . . if any rodents are present, I can assume that their numbers are extremely limited, and they are not significant regarding any alleged health hazard.

Eventually the yard-dispute was "legally" settled, but Myrdene continues to be harassed by her neighbors. In fact, in summer 2008, she received three more indicators that her yard was still under fire from the community.

(There were) no legal summons per se, but in the few weeks after returning of Europe end of June this year there were three incidents. (1) face to face with neighbor immediately to south, telling me I had been "garaging" my car in front of his house . . . spoiling the view of his wife's plants (all new since 1994, when they only had grass). I pointed out it was a public street, and also that I scarcely ever had the car in the neighborhood (it was after all an entire month at Purdue), and that when I did park in the neighborhood the placement depended on many factors (closer to corner when I have things to lug; evidently that was okay by him . . .) (2) days later an enveloped card in the mail from the neighbor immediately to north, telling me that my mulberry tree had dropped fruit in her yard and that she meant business and I had better cut down that tree. I put a note into her mailbox saying not much of anything. (3) then days later a phone call from a city inspector (the one mentioned in the article), who said he had received a complaint from someone in a wheelchair or something who had difficulty using my sidewalk. I said I found that difficult to believe but would look into it. I then realized the timing was PERFECTLY THE SAME AS IN MANY EARLIER YEARS AND DECADES . . . just when the last color of the year, from daylilies, fades . . . evidently even evil neighbors can't get it up to complain when someone might think the frontage is attractive. I went out and pulled the dying daylily stems, and within a week Marcy was digging up some bamboo for transplanting anyway.

Do I think these three incidents are related? Yes. I immediately informed my attorney and my "arbiter." The fact that THREE issues have occurred in fewer than that many weeks after I returned from Europe, has me a little concerned. But I have documented these events (one face-to-face(!), one in a posted card-in-envelope, and one processed by the city by phone) for both arbiter and attorney. Also, I've not received a bill in a dozen years from the attorney, as I collect Red-Cross pins for his souvenir collection.

THE PUBLIC CONSTRUCTION OF THE LAWN BATTLE

While the preceding is mostly Myrdene Anderson's construction of her own yard story, the city and its inhabitants robustly took part in the process. The battle over the yard was at its peak between 1994 and 1995 because this time the violation citation came with the enormous fine. As the city waged a war against Myrdene's naturalized yard, the controversy moved into the public sphere with the community voicing its opinions about the issue in town meetings, editorials, petitions, and counterpetitions. Each side admonished the other, petitions and counterpetitions flew left and right, consultants gave their advice and opinions, and so on. The first petition against Myrdene contained the following statements:

"We, residents of the neighborhood on the east and west sides of Northwestern Avenue, are very concerned about the following conditions in 1807 Northwestern Avenue:

• the physical condition of the house is deteriorating, while other owners in the home are improving their homes and properties
• the front yard is not compatible with other yards in the neighborhood; it appears to be a jungle and obviously violates West Lafayette codes for proper yard maintenance
• the possibility of fire and the difficulty the fire department would have getting to the fire given the property surrounding the house; such difficulty presents a direct threat to lives and other properties in the neighborhood

- the existence of rats and rodents, which have increased in the neighborhood as conditions in 1807 have deteriorated; such animals are a potential health hazard
- the safety of neighborhood residents who have fallen on the property as a result of conditions in the front yard (a public right of way) and who now carry flashlights at night to protect themselves from rats and other rodents near the property
- the animal excrement which is a breeding ground for flies, mosquitoes, and other insects which adversely affect other properties in the area
- the harmful effects this property has on the value of all other homes in the area

At the same time, a large section of the West Lafayette community was enraged at how Myrdene had been unfairly targeted. Just after her neighbors filed a petition against her in 1994, a counterpetition was floated by Rebecca Rouch, a West Lafayette lawyer. This petition was signed by 654 people (of which 377 were residents of West Lafayette), and it was formally presented to the city on July 19, two days before the case was to be heard. It contained the following statements:

We, the undersigned, support Myrdene Anderson's right to utilize natural landscaping techniques on her property at 1807 Northwestern Avenue, West Lafayette, Indiana. We urge the City of West Lafayette to withdraw its objections to Ms. Anderson's approach to landscaping . . . We feel the city must reconsider the priorities which have prompted it to spend lavishly from scarce fiscal resources in the harassment of a single well-meaning individual. To date, attorney's fees submitted to the city are in the vicinity of $20,000 and are reputedly being reimbursed from federal Community development funds, surely not the best use of these resources.

Unlike the high-chemical-input manicured turf lawns the city seems to be encouraging, Dr. Anderson's landscaping practices harm nobody. Indeed, such landscaping reduces storm water runoff and erosion, moderates temperature extremes, and promotes cleaner air through the oxygen exchange activities of foliage. Sustainable residential landscaping of this sort is actively encouraged in many forward-thinking communities. A number of certification programs, including that of the National Wildlife Foundation, have been in place for over a decade to encourage homeowners to move toward this landscaping approach. The motives of Dr. Anderson's opponents are unclear, and their charges against her seem to spring from fantasy and fear. Nationally-respected experts have recently conducted extensive surveys of her property and have found absolutely no indications of the presence of rats or other rodents or of standing water which encourages the breeding of mosquitoes. Accusations that Dr. Anderson's approach to gardening is one of neglect are most unjust; her inputs of both time and money over the years have been consistently high, and her yard contains a carefully-selected and well-nurtured selection of plants. Many passersby have been particularly delighted by her springtime display of flowering bulbs and her midsummer show of daylilies and true lilies.

On the grounds of community health and safety, no reasonable complaint may be made against her. It would therefore appear that we are witnessing a simple difference in taste and aesthetics, issues which cannot be a matter of legal fiat. Certainly, the rights of the individual must always be judiciously balanced with the good of the community. In this case, there appears to be no harm, and indeed much good, which is presented to the community by Dr. Anderson's landscaping practices. Therefore, there are no justifiable grounds for constraining her landscaping practices as conducted upon her own property.

We therefore call upon the City of West Lafayette to withdraw is opposition to Dr. Anderson's approach to landscaping. In addition, this controversy has highlighted the need for a thorough reexamination of the current landscape ordinance. The wording of this ordinance is highly ambiguous and can be used to selectively persecute innocent individuals. Violations of specific provisions of this ordinance are commonplace, and a new policy of uniform enforcement would place an impossible burden on the city's resources. Furthermore, it appears to encourage an approach to landscaping which has long since been abandoned by mainstream practitioners of landscape architecture and which is inconsistent with our city's growing environmental consciousness. Let us treat this unfortunate episode as an opportunity to redirect the city's legal power toward the encouragement of a more sustainable and environmentally friendly approach to landscaping and planting design.

In addition to the petition, editorials and cartoons supporting Myrdene and chiding the city of West Lafayette periodically spurted in the local papers. They were targeted against the city and the city ordinance and in general supported natural landscaping.

Carol J. Widule, a West Lafayette resident, wrote an editorial entitled, "Let Owner Manage Own Yard:"

Unless there is some restriction written in the abstract for the property and/or she is violating a written law of the city, Myrdene Anderson should be permitted to deal with her property as she wishes.

Another entitled, "Get a Life, West Lafayette," in the *Community Times* stated,

The harassment of professor Myrdene Anderson by her neighbors and by the city of West Lafayette is shameful. They have spent outrageous sums of taxpayers' money attempting to coerce Anderson's obedience to narrow-minded and short-sighted rules which the city itself violates every day, as do many residents and corporate entities all over town.

Another resident who also was against the city's decision wrote,

I am appalled by the legal action taken against Dr. Myrdene Anderson by the city of West Lafayette. Natural landscaping is nothing new. Some of the most valued homes in West Lafayette are located on wooded ravines or have natural yards instead of traditional lawns.

Another person wrote a small piece on how weeds were no menace:

In response to those who are complaining about it, I would like to ask them they would rather live next doors to some of the folks near me. In one yard there are old vehicles piled with trash. In some places there are uninhabited trailer homes, some with overgrown lawns that are fire hazards. Compared to this, Professor Anderson's yard is hardly the menace . . .

Many other supporters pointed out that Anderson's yard was less of a public threat than well-groomed turf lawns:

Myrdene Anderson's property does not pose a danger to human health, but chemicals that are necessary to maintain the type of yard that the city apparently finds acceptable do pose such a danger.

Experts and landscape specialists also provided their opinions:

In the case of Myrdene Anderson's yard, her opponents have expressed an unfounded opinion that urban natural landscapes serves as a source of mosquitoes . . . The latter point may be true, but the sources of adult mosquitoes are suitable bodies of water in which the mosquito larvae develop, not the foliage with which adults are associated.

There were those who remained neutral about the matter. Joe Salmons, a resident of the adjacent town, Lafayette, wrote,

Long ago, I heard a disillusioned graduate student quip about his department, "You should be really worried about a place where so many faculty are more interested in lawn care than any intellectual exercise." What a shame that a similar obsession with grass mowing infects the West Lafayette City Hall.

There were more criticisms leveled at the West Lafayette City Council. In a letter to the editor, Keith Brown, a Lafayette resident, wrote,

Government's officials puzzled why they "don't get no respect" should ponder the persecution of Myrdene Anderson. We had such a mountain of laws and regulations that none can know all which might affect her, much less abide by all of them. Government has the resources to rigorously enforce only a tiny fraction.

Some residents took the middle ground, and felt it was time for both the city, Myrdene Anderson, and the neighbors to compromise:

Anderson refuses to change her "landscaping" techniques to a form more acceptable by her neighbors. She can't or won't pay her fine. The city apparently would rather let the matter drag through the courts. Enough! Settle this thing. It is time for both sides to get rational.

What is clear from all the viewpoints expressed is that each party really believed that they were in the right and as can be seen every person, organization, group, and even the city were unwilling to reason with each other. Even though there was a so-called end to the conflict, there was no real resolution to the impasse, apart from a third-party arbiter. Even so, both sides never really believed the other was right or that the opponents could have something useful to say.

THE RHETORICAL CONSTRUCTION OF THE YARD BATTLE

Each party and person involved in the lawn battle came to the table with a different set of ideas and assumptions about what constitutes a yard and a lawn. Each viewpoint was diametrically opposed to the other, and eventually even though there was a perceived end to the crisis, the resolution was conditional, and Myrdene continues to pay for an inspector to come to the house as per the agreement. Even though Myrdene resisted, she was held hostage to certain maneuvers by her neighbors and the city. In this section, we will try to understand how the conflict was rhetorically constructed by proponents of manicured lawns (the city, the neighbors, some public persons) versus Myrdene and her supporters, those who espouse a naturalized and therefore non-violent and peaceful yard care philosophy. We will intersperse the two viewpoints with larger viewpoints by pro- and antilawn lobbies in the United States and thereby show how this controversy is part of a larger environmental and cultural debate.

For Myrdene Anderson, the issue was one of civil rights and environmental consciousness. According to her own research as well as her attorneys, she had been following the rule of the law (and the fact that she was not fined and the battle ended in her favor with her being allowed to keep her space intact is a testimony to city's flawed battle). That is, the code ordinance is general and does not in any way require people to mow lawns, plant only certain bushes and trees, and consider tree growth around a house illegal. Her position was one that has been taken by most proponents of naturalized landscaping. Those who are in favor of such processes point to numerous reasons why lawns are unhealthy and unneeded in any setting. They argue that instead of the received view that lawns provide extra oxygen around a home, lawnmower fumes, pesticides, and other lawn-care procedures make a lawn a destroyer of oxygen. In fact, lawns in the suburbs require extra care and feeding because they are forced to grow in spaces that they were not supposed to. A leading environmentalist and researcher, Michael Pollan (author of the 2007 book *The Omnivore's Dilemma*), who has written at length about the pitfalls of lawns in urban and suburban life, points out that lawns are soaked with four times the amount of pesticides of farmland and because turf absorbs as little water as concrete, these chemicals are easily washed away into rivers and streams, thus poisoning our water and the environment in general. In addition, the nature of the turf grass itself is alien to the American landscape.

Anderson's own observations about the toxicity of lawns match those of the experts:

> Any monoculture (and a lawn is a monoculture, ecologically or ideologically) tilts toward pathology via over-determination plus instability. Lawns are neotenic

monocultures, seeded artificially, kept juvenile through mowing using fossil fuels and heavy equipment, nurtured through petroleum-based fertilizer, de-loused through herbicides and pesticides . . . you name it! I wish you could hear Bateson's lecture about what went before . . . no one, no one, even historically, can justify lawns. And now they have whole industries and lobbying groups behind them.

Myrdene's explanation of the lawn as created commodity is well supported by others.

A lawn may be pleasing to look at, or provide the children with a place to play, or offer the dog room to relieve himself, but it has no productive value. The only work it does is cultural. In Downing's day, the servant-mowed lawn stood, eloquently, for the power structure that made it possible: who but the very rich could afford such a pointless luxury? As mechanical mowers enabled middle-class suburbanites to cut their own grass, this meaning was lost and a different one took hold. A lawn came to signal its owner's commitment to a communitarian project: the upkeep of the greensward that linked one yard to the next.

"A fine carpet of green grass stamps the inhabitants as good neighbors, as desirable citizens," Abraham Levitt wrote. (By covenant, the original Levittowners agreed to mow their lawns once a week between April 15th and November 15th.) "The appearance of a lawn bespeaks the personal values of the resident," a group called the Lawn Institute declared. "Some feel that a person who keeps the lawn perfectly clipped is a person who can be trusted."

Over time, the fact that anyone could keep up a lawn was successfully, though not altogether logically, translated into the notion that everyone *ought* to. Many communities around the country adopted "weed laws" mandating that all yards be maintained to a certain uniform standard. Such laws are, for the most part, still on the books. Homeowners who, for one reason or another, don't toe the line have found themselves receiving citations and fines and, in some (admittedly unusual) cases, wrangling with the police. Just last summer, a seventy-year-old widow from Orem, Utah, was led in handcuffs to a holding cell, after letting her grass go brown. She became a celebrity in the blogosphere, where she was known as the Lawn Lady.

Pretty much by definition, a lawn is unnatural. (Anderson, 2003, p. 5)

Antilawn proponents argue that lawns are created to discipline a neighborhood, to keep the peace, and to maintain a tame environment. In a paper entitled, "Yards, Gardens, and Gender Urban America," Myrdene wrote:

In contrast, in urban and suburban areas, the areas surrounding dwellings are domesticated, but valued aesthetically rather than economically. Fewer and fewer persons grow vegetables, fruits, or even flowers in their gardens, in deference to the maintenance of that institution called The Lawn, a monocot monoculture dominating front yards and also back yards around many homes.

Such a lawn, covering the yard, mediates that space between private house and public street; it belongs to the domain of the male, who sows, fertilizes, applies pesticides to, waters, and mows the grass, often riding on impressive tools (or toys) driven on fossil fuels. The lawn mower nowadays is a major investment, and cannot be managed by children. If there is, besides lawn, a kitchen garden, fruit trees, or flower patches, these typically nestle alongside or behind the house, and are in the care of the female, whose technologies may be limited to kneepads and a watering can. But the female outfits herself with other traditional items as well: a smock, perhaps, or an apron with pockets for tools, a bonnet, various gloves, which contrasts with the quite contemporary garb of the male, which if special at all might just be more worn than his usual clothing worn for comfort.

Over time, cultural habits of yard and garden have been codified. Municipalities have codes which prescribe, proscribe, and otherwise regulate how privately owned space should appear. The aesthetic favoring the monoculture lawn of monocot grass is amplified such that an entire neighborhood—or town or city— becomes a monoculture of identical lawns in identical yards surrounding houses of increasingly identical architecture. I leave aside the fact that the lawn culture supports a massive commercial industry. (2003, p. 7)

In her paper, Myrdene asks some questions about the cultural construction of lawns: "What happens when a trace of the wild enters the urban and suburban landscape? Specifically, what happens should the lawn not be properly manicured, or, a worse transgression, when instead of lawn one has a garden or a thicket, or, even more egregiously, when the space insulating the private from the public happens to be naturalistically landscaped with plants indigenous to the region? Such deviations from lawn culture are regarded as wild, but unlike primeval wild landscapes, are not aesthetically appreciated. Quite the contrary." (2003, p. 8). She proceeds to answer these questions with the following speculations:

The simplest transgressions are easy to correct; an unmowed lawn may exceed the maximum height by some inches, and the property owner who fails to mow will have to pay a fine to the city if reported by neighbors—and city personnel will have done the mowing long before the fine has been paid. Although the yard is a male domain, when threatened by a fine, other members of the family may pitch in to do the mowing, and neighborly pressure may be mild or solicitous. The prevailing attitude is to train the family, not to oust it from the neighborhood.

Such a generous attitude does not prevail when the neighbor deviates from either conventional family structure or from the lawn culture. Obviously, single-parent families are at a disadvantage, particularly if there is no official yard tender who is male. Even though women and children may care for the lawn adequately, this is done in public gaze, in male space. Single unmarried individuals are also potentially deviant. Unlike in some countries in Europe, there is no government lobby attending to the concerns of non-married citizens, although there are protections for the homosexually-paired. Apropos yards and gardens, what better place to spy on such private relations than in public space.

So far the examples focus on normative yards and possibly nonnormative persons. When the garden is considered "overgrown" or wild, it is evident, both the causes and the solutions are much more complicated. First of all, much gardening is done by women, and virtually all "wild" gardening is done by women.

Not only that, but these gardeners have invested much time over many years to create their luxuriant space, whether naturalistic or not, and no simple solution suggests itself.

Not every wild garden will arouse the indignity of neighbors. Women gardeners who are otherwise ordinary, let's say buffered by conventional families, are ignored or excused by neighbors. Anomalous women, though, who are unusual for any reason, find themselves at risk of attracting neighborly hate and wider public controversy. The case studies reviewed from this research project include women who have been professional horticulturalists as well as just dabblers, women who have been both persecuted and prosecuted, and women who have resisted as well as those who tried to appease public pressures. Some have survived with their gardens, but some have not . . .

I refer to the project as being about Wild Women, which I will explain. One of my first subjects besides myself had the surname of Wildman . . . The case histories are so unique, that it is amazing that there can be found any threads of similarity, but they are there . . .

First, only women turn up in my data set, although I have hopes of making contact with some men too. Second, these women are considered anomalous because they do not fit the normative profile for an adult woman, who should have a family, whether still married or not. Third, these women tend to be quite motivated about their gardening practices, and sometimes are recognized experts in horticulture or pollinating insects. But fourth, not all women victimized by neighbors on the excuse of their gardening practices come through unscathed.

What is clear is that the charges against these wild women, about their gardens, is a ruse. The problem is their existence in the community, *not* their gardens. This is particularly clear in following the cases of some women who made an effort, in good faith, to please and appease the neighbors. This only fans the flames of antagonism.

And it's appropriate to refer to flames here. It happens that the cultural narrative which matches these situations is none other than witchcraft accusation. Witchcraft is a belief system quite universal though culturally distinct. In Western societies, it is often women who are accused of being witches; in other societies, it varies . . . But not every woman is at risk of being accused of witchcraft: rather, only those singled out for being anomalous—too fat, too thin; too many children, not enough; hair too long, too short; too rich, too poor; and on and on, just different, depending on culture and situation. The dynamic is simply that women-at-risk-of-accusation are scapegoats and take the brunt when other things are not going well in the social order. Sometimes accusations coincide with some tragedy in the personal life of the accused, too. Several in my small sample had just lost an elderly parent, one to suicide. Witches do not DO anything to become witches, they are anointed by being accused. There is no "craft" to witchcraft other than in the accusation. And, most importantly, there is no method of defense or way to defuse the situation when it comes to neighborly hate in the ascendance.

So what is amiss in the society that scapegoats must be sacrificed? One could inventory many local and global crises, and no doubt they could all contribute to the collective sense of societal disease. Closer to the situation, though, are threats to Lawn Culture from many angles: depending on the region, the issue might be water; or accumulations of chemical pollutants; or diesel exhaust. Lawn care companies must flag lawns having just had treatments of fertilizers or other chemicals, as children and pets have become ill and even died. Some good citizens don't know how to address their own mounting concerns other than by subtly decreasing the size of their lawn each season.

All these responses will take time, but already the Lawn Culture suffers from a rigor mortis that strikes back at its more active detractors.

Myrdene's antilawn standpoint is rooted in a sound ecological argument. Proponents of naturalized landscaping, such as her, use both a nature and a culture argument to respond to being disciplined by the lawn-culture. Those who brought the charges against Myrdene Anderson were using a tactic of "neighborhood disciplining" and were persons that Galant in the *New York Times* refers to as the "Lawn Police" (Galant, 2001). They wanted her to conform to their standards and aesthetics of what constitutes a yard and used legal means to attempt to enforce their values and aesthetics on her—a different kind of violence. Additionally, they used an economic argument in their petition suggesting that Myrdene's lawn was driving down the property values in the neighborhood, something that proved to be quite strong. In fact those who are proponents of lawns are usually unaware that they are living surrounded by toxins and that the lawn is merely a set of cultural values that they have imposed on themselves, or one that has been imposed on them.

RESOLUTIONS

Myrdene was targeted for reasons that were nonecological, even though the petitions filed against her made it seem otherwise. In fact, her "thicket" is the most environmentally friendly piece of land in the neighborhood. In a recent interview, Myrdene once again reinforced her position on the entire issue.

> So the situation we've discussed is emphatically *not* about the yard/lawn at all. And by extension I could say it's *not* about *me*, either; it's about *them*. Because the accused victim has not "earned" the accusation through "craft" or "doing" something. The only "craft" or "action" comes by the action of the accusers, who unwittingly follow the (Robert Rosen) anticipatory system called culture. Victims might here and there be cross-eyed or red-haired or too fat or too thin or too fecund or "childless" (note *markedness*). I have to recall a Thai graduate student in communication studies who heard about my predicament from someone and became genuinely concerned. I calmed him down when he came to me all agitated, what could he do? Anyway he found a classmate with a car to drive by my yard, and he reported back: "I don't understand the problem; you have long hair, your yard has long grasses; you wear long dresses, your trees wear long skirts."

CHAPTER 12

Beyond Multiculturalism: Emerging Approaches in Intercultural Communication

KEY TERMS

Cognitivism

Cosmopolitanism

Deep Pluralism

Postmulticulturalism

Pluralism

Universalism

There is increasing recognition that multiculturalism (identity politics) undermines our understanding of diversity. It is deficient in regard to helping us deal constructively with the challenges that now threaten to push the world to the brink of violence and strife. Although multiculturalism remains the dominant framework in shaping public policy, guiding the development of curriculums, and defining popular intercultural communication discourses, new frameworks are beginning to appear. All these frameworks promise to escape the problems that plague multiculturalism. This chapter overviews these frameworks: *Cognitivism, Postmulticulturalism, Pluralism, Cosmopolitanism, Universalism,* and *Deep Pluralism.* We look carefully at the promise of these emerging frameworks to present a new vision of intercultural relations.

COGNITIVISM

In *Ethnicity without Groups,* Rogers Brubaker (2004) claims that constructivist theorizing—which forms the foundation of much of the identity politics in the social sciences and humanities—continues to use race, ethnicity, and nationality as reliable ways of categorizing human beings. In so doing, Brubaker argues, constructivist theorizing continues mistakenly to frame accounts of ethnic violence as conflicts between internally homogenous and externally bounded ethnic groups. Brubaker contends that through this practice, that is, using race, ethnicity, and nationality as reliable ways of categorizing human beings, sociologists, historians, journalists, and policy makers unwittingly become participants in perpetuating and even intensifying these conflicts by promoting aggregation and thereby masking the heterogeneity and other tensions found within supposedly stable and homogenous racial and cultural groups. In other words, constructivist theorizing, by reifying race, ethnicity, and nationality, promotes homogeneity and downplays diversity. This makes constructivism, "once an insurgent undertaking, a bracing challenge to entrenched ways of seeing," incapable of generating "the friction, force, and freshness needed to push arguments further and generate new insights" (2004, p. 3).

Brubaker showcases many examples of how the language of race, ethnicity, and nationality misrepresents what is supposedly ethnic conflict. He believes that "ethnicity, race, and nation should be conceptualized not as substances or things or entities or organisms or collective individuals—as the imagery of discrete, concrete, tangible, bounded, and enduring 'groups' encourage us to do—but rather in relational, processual, dynamic, eventful, and disaggregated terms" (p. 11). This would mean "thinking of ethnicity, race, and nation not in terms of substantial groups or entities but in terms of practical categories, situated actions, cultural idioms, cognitive schemas, discursive frames, organizational routines, institutional forms, political projects, and contingent events" (p. 11). In short, this is the project of cognitivism. Cognitivism focuses on how cognitive structures influence and shape how we classify and categorize stimuli and experiences. It assumes that all human beings classify and categorize. As such, rather than trying to end race, ethnicity, nationality, sexuality, and other such ways of organizing human beings, cognitivism focuses on sensitizing us to the cognitive structures and processes that make for certain ways of classifying and categorizing others. For Brubaker, the primary implication of cognitivism is the recognition that "ethnicity is fundamentally not a thing in the world, but a perspective on the world" (2004, p. 65).

Brubaker contends that cognitivism allows us to understand that categorizing, classifying, and even stereotyping are natural and vital cognitive processes. It "focuses our analytical lens on how people see the world, parse their experience, and interpret events. This raises a different and broader set of questions about racial, ethnic, and national categorization" (2004, p. 77). So instead of "conceptualizing the social world in substantialist terms as a composite of racial, ethnic, and national movements—cognitive perspectives address the social and mental processes that sustain the vision and division of the social world in racial, ethnic, and national terms" (p. 79). Moreover, rather "than take 'groups' as basic units of analysis, cognitive perspectives shift analytical attention to 'group-making' and 'grouping' activities such as classification, categorization, and identification" (p. 79). In other words, "Race, ethnicity, and nationality exist only in and through our perceptions, interpretations, representations, classifications, categorizations, and identifications. They are not things in the world, but perspectives on the world—not ontological but epistemological realities" (2004, p. 79).

Brubaker also believes that the study of violence should be emancipated from the study of conflict because violence is qualitatively rather than merely quantitatively different from other kinds of conflict. It also has its own dynamics. Violence therefore requires a different kind of theoretical attention, beginning with paying sustained attention to the forms and dynamics of ethnicization and the many subtle ways in which violence takes on ethnic hues. Brubaker claims that what we commonly describe as ethnic violence differs fundamentally from one context to the next, and the ethnic component only tends to emerge as the result of after-the-fact analysis and theorizing. In the end, however, Brubaker's call for assimilation reflects a deep suspicion of diversity. Diversity is still something that must be carefully and strategically managed so as to avoid the supposed threat of chaos, disharmony, and disunity. In this way, Brubaker's cognitivism sustains the belief that without homogeneity, or a focus on promoting similarity, our differences will intensify and produce disharmony, disunity, and anarchy.

POSTMULTICULTURALISM

Brubaker is by no means the only person criticizing identity politics and calling for a new diversity politics that exceeds commonly held notions of race, ethnicity, and nationality. David Hollinger (2005) contends that classifying peoples by traditional categories of race and ethnicity makes no sense in the face of emerging realties in which increasing numbers of people are unwilling to abide by such categories. "Multiculturalism breeds an enthusiasm for specific, traditional cultures that can sometimes mask a provinciality from which individuals are eager to escape through new, out-group affiliations" (p. 107). Hollinger favors a postethnic perspective that "prefers voluntary to prescribed affiliations, appreciates multiple identities, pushes for communities of wider scope, recognizes the constructed character of ethno-racial groups, and accepts the formation of new groups as a part of the normal life of a democratic society" (p. 116). In short, a "postethnic perspective challenges the right of one's grandfather or grandmother to determine primary identity" (2005, p. 116). Hollinger believes that the promotion of a postethnic perspective will eventually make for the demise of many descent-communities and the creation of new identity-communities that stress voluntary participation. The latter will challenge the common prejudice that "affiliations based on choice are somehow artificial and lacking in depth, while those based on the ordinance of blood and history are more substantive and authentic" (2005, p. 119). In fact, Hollinger believes that undermining the rigid boundaries of descent-communities is vital to end many questionable cultural practices, such as clitoridectomy, that many descent-communities often claim that outsiders have no moral or cultural authority to condemn. For Hollinger, the enclosures that descent-communities often construct should no longer function as a kind of birthright, especially when such enclosures are used as a cover to defend practices and taboos that harm and threaten others.

Hollinger believes that postethnicity will bring new communities and societies built on intersubjective reason, immanent critique, a democratic-egalitarian ethnos, and the "expansion of a human rights culture" (2005, p. 115). On the other hand, however, Hollinger cautions that the success of this emergent postethnic project depends on the addressing of various social and economic inequalities that continue to impede upward and social mobility. "The more inflexible the class structure, the longer will the ethno-racial groups caught in its lower segments remain there. The members of these groups will find it harder to hope for a middle-class existence and will have more and more reason to interpret as structural or institutional racism those policies that . . . have a disproportionately negative impact on them" (pp. 167–168). Therefore in "the absence of a more ambitious national program for enabling poor people to find their way out of poverty and attendant suffering," Hollinger fears that "ethno-racial particularism will flourish" (p. 168).

Hollinger's postethnicity appeals to the reality that increasing numbers of persons are forming unions with persons of different races, ethnicities, sexualities, nationalities, and spiritualities. In most cases, such postethnicity unions are producing persons who prefer voluntary associations. However, this emerging reality is happening in the face of another emerging reality—the exploding gap between rich and poor. Hollinger acknowledges that these realities are inseparable and that something needs to be done to alleviate the latter. He supports expanding economic and educational opportunities so that "members of historically disadvantaged ethno-racial groups [can] attain the standard of living associated with the middle class" (p. 167). He believes that these opportunities will "provide the crucial occasions for members of such groups to test the social and cultural barriers that have traditionally disadvantaged them" (p. 167).

Interestingly, neither Brubaker's cognitivism nor Hollinger's postmulticulturalism challenges our commonly held definitions of diversity. Both assume that our supposed diversity problem is about how best to manage our differences. Hollinger believes our diversity problem is fundamentally conceptual. By embracing postethnicity and alleviating poverty, our diversity problem will supposedly be resolved. On the other hand, for Brubaker, our diversity problem is fundamentally methodological. We merely have to find new ways of organizing our experiences with others. In this way, neither Brubaker nor Hollinger gives us an understanding of diversity that is different than that found in multiculturalism. We still get an understanding of diversity that is deserving of suspicion. There is no consideration of new definitions of diversity. In other words, both perspectives downplay the role of communication in forming and negotiating expressions of diversity that genuinely defy our commonly held ways of organizing our differences.

Pluralism

Pluralism is another new perspective emerging in intercultural communication discourses. Pluralism stridently opposes any ideology that seeks to organize and categorize human experience. It believes that any ideology that aims to do so is dangerous for the following reasons:

- The process of categorizing and organizing human experience is unnatural. Human beings are profoundly complex beings and our diversity is always unfolding.
- The process of categorizing and organizing human experience is arbitrary. That is, the categories that are commonly used to categorize and organize— such as race, ethnicity, religion, and so forth—are arbitrary.
- The process of categorizing and organizing human experience is unnecessary.
- The process of categorizing and organizing human experience is unhealthy. It forces us into unnatural groups.
- The process of categorizing and organizing human experience diminishes our diversity by sorting us into a limited set of categories. So whereas our understanding of sexual diversity goes from heterosexuality, homosexuality, to bisexuality, the natural world is laden with hundreds of different models of sexuality.

Pluralism is premised on the notion of sovereignty, as found in the First Amendment to the Constitution: "Congress shall make no law respecting an establishment of religion, or prohibiting the free exercise thereof; or abridging the freedom of speech, or of the press; or the right of the people peaceably to assemble, and to petition the government for a redress of grievances." In this way, pluralism believes that no government or institution has the moral and legal authority to restrict how we choose to experience the world and organize ourselves, as long as how we do so never infringe on the sovereignty of others. Pluralism therefore requires tolerance for different faiths and creeds.

However, what happens when a group is determined to use every available means, including violence, to violate our sovereignty? According to Connolly (2005), "It may well be necessary to take military or police action against them to forestall the return of violence. However, once you acknowledge the potential for evil within every faith, including your own, you will also attend to the insistence by some proponents of your own faith to exaggerate and over generalize this danger. You now take another look around at the public representations of alternative faiths by your allies. And you explore how to reengage those who, while not directly making violent attacks against you, provide the attackers with material and spiritual conditions of support. You explore how to reduce the passive tolerance of violence. Here, war is not the answer" (p. 35).

Pluralism aims to show persons of different faiths and creeds that the promotion of sovereignty ultimately serves the interest of all faiths and creeds. As such, pluralism in no way believes in tolerance for purely the sake of tolerance. It believes in restraint, as in the restraint necessary to maintain the sovereignty of all faiths and creeds. As Connolly noted, "Pluralists think it is extremely important, for instance, how people of diverse faiths hold and express their faiths in public space. And we seek to limit the power of those who would invest their own creed with unquestioned territorial hegemony. We think that in a world marked by the coexistence of multiple faiths on most politically organized territories, the horizontal relations between faiths require as much attention as the vertical dimension of each. Expansive pluralism supports the dissemination of general virtues across diverse faiths. The key, again, is the relational sensibility with which individuals and communities express their faiths and the general ethos through which relations between alternative faiths are negotiated. (2005, p. 49)

Just as well, pluralism believes time will eventually change everything. No faith or creed can avoid the changes that come with time. Eventually, all faiths and creeds will change. So time is a destabilizing force. It is always working against the order of things. This reality is nicely seen in what is currently happening to the religious landscape in the United States.

AMERICANS CHANGE FAITHS AT RISING RATE, REPORT FINDS
Neela Banerjee

WASHINGTON—More than a quarter of adult Americans have left the faith of their childhood to join another religion or no religion, according to a new survey of religious affiliation by the Pew Forum on Religion and Public Life.

The report, titled "U.S. Religious Landscape Survey," depicts a highly fluid and diverse national religious life. If shifts among Protestant denominations are included, then it appears that 44 percent of Americans have switched religious affiliations.

For at least a generation, scholars have noted that more Americans are moving among faiths, as denominational loyalty erodes. But the survey, based on interviews with more than 35,000 Americans, offers one of the clearest views yet of that trend, scholars said. The United States Census does not track religious affiliation.

The report shows, for example, that every religion is losing and gaining members, but that the Roman Catholic Church "has experienced the greatest net losses as a result of affiliation changes. The survey also indicates that the group that had the greatest net gain was the unaffiliated. More than 16 percent of American adults say they are not part of any organized faith, which makes the unaffiliated the country's fourth largest "religious group."

Detailing the nature of religious affiliation—who has the numbers, the education, the money—signals who could hold sway over the country's political and cultural life, said John Green, an author of the report who is a senior fellow on religion and American politics at Pew.

Michael Lindsay, assistant director of the Center on Race, Religion and Urban Life at Rice University, echoed that view. "Religion is the single most important factor that drives American belief attitudes and will end up on politics, culture, family life. If you want to understand America, you have to understand religion in America."

In the 1980s, the General Social Survey by the National Opinion Research Center indicated that from 5 percent to 8 percent of the population described itself as unaffiliated with a particular religion.

In the Pew survey 7.3 percent of the adult population said they were unaffiliated with a faith as children. That segment increases to 16.1 percent of the population in adulthood, the survey found. The unaffiliated are largely under 50 and male. "Nearly one-in-five men say they have no formal religious affiliation, compared with roughly 13 percent of women," the survey said.

The rise of the unaffiliated does not mean that Americans are becoming less religious, however. Contrary to assumptions that most of the unaffiliated are atheists or agnostics, most described their religion "as nothing in particular." Pew researchers said that later projects would delve more deeply into the beliefs and practices of the unaffiliated and would try to determine if they remain so as they age.

While the unaffiliated have been growing, Protestantism has been declining, the survey found. In the 1970s, Protestants accounted for about two-thirds of the population. The Pew survey found they now make up about 51 percent. Evangelical Christians account for a slim majority of Protestants, and those who leave one evangelical denomination usually move to another, rather than to mainline churches.

To Prof. Stephen Prothero, large numbers of Americans leaving organized religion and large numbers still embracing the fervor of evangelical Christianity point to the same desires.

"The trend is toward more personal religion, and evangelicals offer that," said Mr. Prothero, chairman of the religion department at Boston University, who explained that evangelical churches tailor many of their activities for youth. "Those losing out are offering impersonal religion and those winning are offering a smaller scale: mega-churches succeed not because they are mega but because they have smaller ministries inside."

The percentage of Catholics in the American population has held steady for decades at about 25 percent. But that masks a precipitous decline in native-born Catholics. The proportion ahs been bolstered by the large influx of Catholic immigrants, mostly from Latin America, the survey found.

The Catholic Church has lost more adherents than any other group: about one-third of respondents raised Catholic said they no longer identified as such. Based on the data, the survey showed, "this means that roughly 10 percent of all Americans are former Catholics."

Immigration continues to influence American religion greatly, the survey found. The majority of immigrants are Christian, and almost half are Catholic. Muslims rival Mormons for having the largest families. And Hindus are the best-educated and among the richest religious groups, the survey found.

"I think politicians will be looking at this survey to see what groups they ought to target," Professor Prothero said. "If the Hindu population is negligible, they won't have to worry about it. But if it is wealthy, then they may have to pay attention."

Experts said the wide-ranging variety of religious affiliation could set the stage for further conflicts over morality or politics, or new alliances on certain issues, as religious people have done on climate change or Jews and Hindus have done over relations between the Unites States, Israel and India.

"It sets up the potential for big arguments," Mr. Green said, "but also for the possibility of all sorts of creative synthesis. Diversity cuts both ways."

COSMOPOLITISM

Our notions of citizenship are changing. Many of us increasingly own multiple passports. We are unwilling to claim citizenship to just one country. We want our different heritages to be recognized. We wish to make plain that no one country can claim our identity or take full responsibility for shaping our humanity. Our humanity belongs to the world. We are citizens of the world and thereby have an obligation to all that share this world with us. We are cosmopolitan.

In *The Ethics of Identity*, Kwane Anthony Appiah (2005) makes a compelling case for cosmopolitanism. For Appiah, cosmopolitism begins with the premise of liberty, specifically John Stuart Mill's definition of liberty. Appiah is attracted to Mill's notion that liberty is vital to creating the individuality that uniquely makes us human. In *On Liberty*, Mill writes,

He who lets the world, or his own portion of it, choose his plan of life for him, has no need for any other faculty than the ape-like one of imitation. He who chooses his plan for himself, employs all his faculties. He must use observation to see, reasoning and judgment to foresee, activity to gather materials for decisions, discrimination to decide, and when he has decided, firmness and self-control to hold to his deliberate decision. And these qualities he requires and exercises exactly in proportion as the part of his conduct which he determines according to his own judgment and feelings is a large one. It is possible that he might be guided in some good path, and kept out of harm's way, without any of these things. But what will be his comparative worth as a human being? It really is of importance, not only what men do, but also what manner of men they are that do it. (p. 34)

Cosmopolitanism promotes a dialogical conception of identity. We form ourselves from the resources our communities and societies make available to us. As Appiah explains, "We make up selves from a tool kit of options made available by our culture and society. We do make choices, but we don't individually determine the options among which we choose. To neglect this fact is . . . to fail to recognize the dialogical construction of the self, and thus to commit what [Charles] Taylor calls the 'monological' fallacy" (p. 106). Thus "to create a life . . . is to create a life out of the materials that history has given you. An identity is always articulated through concepts (and practices) made available to you by religion, society, school, and state, mediated by family, peers, friends" (p. 231). Appiah believes that many versions of multiculturalism commit this monological fallacy by viewing our identities as purely products of our race, ethnicity, nationality, religion, sexual orientation, and culture. "It would be too large a claim that the identities that cry out for recognition in the multicultural chorus must be monological. But it seems to me that one reasonable ground for suspicion of much contemporary multicultural talk is that the conceptions of collective identity they presuppose are indeed remarkably unsubtle in their understandings of the processes by which identities, both individual and collective, develop" (Appiah, 2005, p. 107). Moreover,

> The politics of recognition [as found with multiculturalism] . . . can seem to require that one's skin color, one's sexual body, should be politically acknowledged in ways that make it harder for those who want to treat their skin and their sexual body as personal dimensions of self. And personal, here, does not mean secret or . . . wholly unscripted or innocent of social meanings; it means, rather, something that is not too tightly scripted, not too resistant to our individual vagaries. Even though my race and sexuality may be elements of my individuality, someone who demands that I organize my life around these things is not an ally of individuality. Because identities are constituted in part by social conceptions and by treatment as, in the realm of identity there is no bright line between recognition and imposition. (p. 110)

Identity needs both liberty and resources, which means that the lack of liberty and resources compromises our ability to form ourselves fully and completely. It also means that liberty cannot be separated from our resources. How much liberty a person can potentially exercise is influenced by how much resources are available to a person. As such, Appiah believes that a primary function of government is to help us gain access to the resources that are vital for the full exercising of liberty. Such resources include education, health care, and food.

So whereas pluralism believes that government gets in the way of liberty, cosmopolitanism believes that government is necessary for the flourishing of liberty. Thus, although both believe that liberty is necessary for diversity, both are looking at liberty and diversity differently. With regard to pluralism, liberty begins and ends with sovereignty. The focus is on stopping government and other institutions from interfering with and violating our sovereignty. However, cosmopolitism believes that liberty without the resources to exercise liberty is really no liberty. So whereas pluralism believes in a freedom from, cosmopolitism believes in a freedom to. For pluralists, government meddling, even for supposedly benevolent reasons, ultimately undermines diversity by limiting liberty. In other words, no government action is ever morally neutral. By relying on government to help promote liberty, liberty must eventually conform to the moral bent of government, and this moral bent will always be a threat to diversity. Of course pluralists would contend that the situation becomes much more dangerous when one believes—as Appiah believes—that governments are morally obligated to provide all the resources human beings need to have liberty. Appiah recognizes this matter and acknowledges the need to look at each situation on case-by-case basis. However, Appiah still believes that without resources, diversity, rather than merely liberty, is impossible. In this way, Appiah and other proponents of cosmopolitism claim that the promotion of diversity involves a redistribution of resources so all persons can fully exercise liberty. But for pluralists such redistribution is a violation of sovereignty and, ultimately, diversity. So whereas for pluralists there can be no diversity without sovereignty, for cosmopolitans there can be no diversity without equity.

Resources figure prominently in cosmopolitism. That we shape our identity and humanity through the resources that are available to us means that quantity and quality of resources matter. Our ability to shape our best humanity and identity is related to what resources are available to us. As Appiah explains, "Cosmopolitism imagines a world in which people and novels and music and films and philosophies travel between places where they are understood differently and welcome to their difference. Cosmopolitism can work because there can be common conversations about these shared ideas and objects" (2005, p. 258). In this way, cosmopolitanism believes there is a moral obligation to make available to us all the resources that the world can potentially make available to us. In turn, drawing on these resources to make our humanity and identity make us global citizens. Thus cosmopolitanism opposes borders, walls, passports, and other such mechanisms that impede our access to all the resources that the world can potentially make available to us. It believes that by limiting our access to those resources, such mechanisms undercut the making of our best humanity and identity. That is, such mechanisms ultimately undercut diversity and liberty.

Thus many persons view cosmopolitanism as a threat to the integrity of nation states and even any institutions that view us in terms of race, ethnicity, nationality, sexuality, and religion. Indeed, cosmopolitanism is suspicious of all heritages and traditions that keep us bound to the past and undercut our dialogical impulses. It believes in contamination. It also believes that diversity belongs to the future and resides in the resources that are yet to be made fully available to us, which also means that diversity resides in the liberty that is yet to be achieved. That cosmopolitism opposes borders and the sanctifying of cultures means that cosmopolitism also opposes the institutions that maintain these practices. It believes these institutions are also guilty of impeding the coming of our best humanity and identity by keeping tribal rather than global. For cosmopolitanism, tribalism—regardless of whether our tribes come in the form of race, ethnicity, sexuality, and religion—is a primitive and morally regressive condition. It reflects a humanity and identity that is shaped by access to limited resources. Thus tribalism promotes a limited (and distorted) view of the world. Cosmopolitism believes that this limited view of the world is at the heart of most intercultural conflicts. In this regard, cosmopolitanism claims that access to all the world's resources make us fundamentally global and thereby gives us an expansive and inclusive view of the world, or, to use Appiah's father's words, "a great love for mankind and an abiding desire to see mankind, under God, fulfill its highest destiny." From a cosmopolitism perspective, the case against all forms of nationalism, fundamentalisms, and tribalisms is moral. These movements undercut our moral evolution, as in the coming of the global citizen, or what Pico Iyer refers to as the global soul—the ones who will love all the peoples in the world because of being of a humanity that is shaped by all of the peoples of the world.

UNIVERSALISM

In *The Claims of Culture: Equality and Diversity in the Global Era,* Seyla Benhabib (2002) argues for a universalist perspective that positions democracy as the path to diversity and improving intercultural relations. Like Appiah, Brubaker, Connolly, and others, Benhabib criticizes many proponents of multiculturalism for viewing cultures as seamless, coherent wholes that seem to be devoid of diversity, tension, dissent, conflict, and even contradiction. "I think of cultures as complex human practices of signification and representation, or organization and attribution, which are internally riven by conflicting narratives. Cultures are formed through complex dialogues with other cultures" (p. ix). Moreover, "any view of cultures as clearly delineable wholes is a view from the outside that generates coherence for the purposes of understanding and control. Participants in the culture, by contrast, experience their traditions, stories, rituals and symbols, tools, and material living conditions through shared, albeit contested and contestable, narrative accounts. From within, a culture need not appear as a whole; rather, it forms a horizon that recedes each time one approaches it" (p. 5).

Benhabib believes that viewing cultures as seamless, coherent wholes suppresses the democracy that is vital to protect persons who wish to break from the will and the wishes of the majority. She believes that people are always exercising autonomy, thereby always making for diversity, dissent, and conflict with all cultures. So without democracy, which is vital to defend our exercising of autonomy, diversity is impossible. Thus the goal of democracy is to protect the exercise of individual autonomy from the will of the majority. Benhabib's universalism rests on a model of democracy that involves a national component and a federal component. The federal component involves principles of egalitarian democracy (all members of cultural, racial, national, tribal, and religious groups must be entitled to equal degrees of civil, political, and cultural rights), voluntary self-ascription (the right to choose our membership and obligation to any group), and freedom of exit of association (the freedom to exit any group must be unrestrained).

The federal level supports the robust involvement of various groups and associations representing and advocating for different peoples, like the National Organization of Women (NOW), the National Association of Colored People (NAACP), the Latino Action League (LAL), the American Italian Association (AIA), and so forth. But such groups must comply with national principles. This is necessary so that members of all groups can exercise autonomy and thereby control over the making of one's life. According to Benhabib,

> If the right of culture derives from the right of autonomous individuals to have access to a meaningful range of choices in their lives, then no differentiations can be allowed between different cultures' value or worth except as expressed through the activities, the value of such cultural allegiances. So the goal of any public policy for the preservation of cultures must be the empowerment of the members of cultural groups to appropriate, enrich, and even subvert the terms of their own cultures as they may decide. Therefore, the right to cultural membership entails the right to say no to the various cultural offers made by one's upbringing, one's nation, one's religious or familial community. Members of cultural groups cannot be autonomous if they are unable to participate in the cultural reproduction and cultural struggle, including the transformation of some cultural traditions. (p. 66)

Benhabib claims that universalism is especially relevant to women and minority groups within various cultures that are given less autonomy by others and, as a result, usually suffer all kinds of discrimination and subjugation from persons who are privileged in those cultures. Case in point, many men in Jordan defend honor killings—the killing of a sister who is accused of disgracing a family—on the claim that "our culture accepts this practice as appropriate behavior." Benhabib believes this practice must be stopped. It violates the autonomy of women and, in doing so, undermines the making of a vibrant democracy. On the other hand, however, Benhabib warns us against falling back into the habit of viewing cultures as seamless wholes. Benhabib supports a deliberative model of democracy. Such a model emphasizes communication, negotiation, deliberation, rather than legislation, regulations, and institutions. For Benhabib, the latter lacks the flexibility and agility to deal with the new models of diversity that are increasingly on us as the world shrinks. She uses the head scarf controversy in France as a case study. Instead of passing legislation prohibiting the wearing of this scarf by women in public schools, a deliberative approach would try to understand what is the meaning of the women's action as regards wanting to wear this scarf.

DEEP PLURALISM

Religion will continue to play an integral role in shaping our identity and our view of the world as this century unfolds. In fact, for many peoples, culture is religion, and intercultural communication is really about communication between peoples of different religious persuasions. Thus problems of communication are seen as arising from the differences between our religious persuasions. Of course many peoples continue to believe that our religious differences are irreconcilable and therefore the possibility of communication between peoples of different religious persuasions is impossible. However, to view our religious differences as intractable is to miss the diversity within all religions, especially those denominations within all the world's great religions that challenge us to nurture, care, and provide for each other, especially those of different religious persuasions. This reality is the foundation of deep religious pluralism.

In *Deep Religious Pluralism,* David Ray Griffin (2005) and other contributors to this volume discuss the various denominations within the world's great religions that challenge us to engage, nurture, and fertilize other denominations by recognizing that all religions contain different truths, that our town truths are fertilized by other truths, and that religious pluralism is better for the world than religious absolutism (the promotion and devotion to one truth). For example, within Christianity there are those denominations that focus on our resolve to love those who are most different from us, even those of different religious persuasions. These denominations have no interest in conversion. Instead, the focus is on extending "well-being to those whom we neither require nor expect to become like ourselves" (Griffin, 2005, p. 12). This involves living "a reign of God that reaches not toward an imperialism of one religion—our own!—sweeping the planet, but that reaches toward a new form of community: a community made up of diverse religious communities, existing together in friendship" (p. 12). These Christian denominations stress compassion rather than retribution, community rather than religion, humility rather than rigidity, and grace rather than doctrine. Ultimately, these deep pluralists Christian denominations believe that our redemption will be found through action rather than submission.

Within Judaism there are denominations that begin on the deep pluralist notion "that the primary responsibility of all people is to honor and promote the value of every life." Irving Greenberg, an Orthodox rabbi, believes that religious pluralism promotes self-restraint and self-criticism. In this way, pluralism saves from the ravages that history shows again and again that come with the promotion of absolutism. So pluralism promotes democracy, whereas absolutism promotes autocracy. For Greenberg, "The practice of pluralism is essential to the exercise of power . . . Pluralism divides power; this guards against excesses. Pluralism distributes power so more interests are accommodated and fewer feel left out" (p. 116). As to why "should people instructed by God (as they understand it) grant serious weight to other views which are merely human (as they understand it)? . . . Pluralism answers that there are real truths and ultimate claims. But humans of good will differ on which of the conflicting views are real and ultimate. Therefore we are left with genuine disagreements. Out of the unity of a common goal, then, people pledge not to delegitimate. This self-restraint will contain conflict and not let it tear society and community apart—lest everything be destroyed" (p. 116). Greenberg therefore believes that different religions do point to different truths. However, based on the limited nature of human understanding, and the great and infinite nature of God, no religion can claim to possess all the truths and thereby a complete understanding of God. Similarly, David Hartman, an Orthodox rabbi, believes that religious pluralism is "spiritually redemptive" and can lead to "a new level of spiritual dignity." For Hartman, according to Sandra Lubarsky in *Deep Religious Pluralism,* religious pluralism "preserves the understanding that God is greater than any single faith community; it frees humans from the mistaken belief that any revelation is universal; and it reasserts the sacredness of all human life, regardless of different truth claims" (Griffin, 2005, p. 122). Hartman also believes that religious pluralism can make for a new spiritual consciousness that promotes novelty. Novelty is about being unbound and always flirting with the limits of our comprehension.

Within Hinduism there are those denominations that view Hinduism as the womb of deep religious pluralism, as Hinduism did give birth to many of the world's great religions, including Jainism, Buddhism, and Sikhism. Pluralism is found explicitly in many Hindu scriptures. "Reality is one, though the wise speak of it variously." "Truth is one, paths are many." "As humans approach me, so I receive them. All paths, Partha, lead to me." There is also the Hindu creed that includes the line, "I believe that no particular religion teaches the only way to salvation above all others, but that all genuine religious paths are facets of God's Pure Love and Light, deserving tolerance and understanding." Pluralism is also found in two of the seven points in the definition of Hinduism used by the Indian Supreme Court: "[a] spirit of tolerance, and willingness to understand and appreciate others' points of view, recognizing that truth has many sides," and the "[r]ecognition that paths to truth and salvation are many." Moreover, Mahatma Gandhi, wrote, "Religions are different roads converging upon the same point." Indeed, many claim that the term *Hinduism* masks the great spiritual diversity found among Indians. It is really a conglomeration of diverse spiritual and philosophical traditions.

Within Islam there are those denominations that view Prophet Mohammed's declaration that there shall be no compulsion in religion as the foundation of religious pluralism. The Qur'an also contains other lines that affirm pluralism. "If it had been the Lord's will, they would all have believed—all who are on earth! Wilt thou then compel mankind, against their will, to believe!" "Say, 'the truth is from your Lord': Let him who will, believe, and let him who will, reject (it)." Mustafa Ruzgar points out in *Deep Religious Pluralism* that Islam also provided persons of different religious persuasions with considerable economic, cultural, and administrative rights.

Islamic support for religious pluralism is also found in the notion that Allah has sent a messenger for every community and nation, which means that every community and nation has received a message from God. Ruzgar writes that all Muslims are required to believe in the prophets and their various messages. On the other hand, Ruzgar acknowledges that there are many verses in the Qu'ran that seem hostile to religious pluralism. "If anyone desires a religion other than Islam (submission to Allah), never will it be accepted of him: and in the Hereafter he will be in the ranks of those who have lost (all spiritual good)." But Ruzgar advises us to note other verses in the Qu'ran. "Those who believe (in the Qu'ran), and those who follow the Jewish (scriptures), and the Christians and Sabians—any who believe in Allah and the last day, and work righteousness, shall have their reward with their Lord; on them shall be no fear, nor shall they grieve." "Whoever works righteousness, man or woman, and has faith, verily, to him will we give a new life, and that life that is good and pure, and we will bestow on such their reward according to the best of their actions." Ruzgar believes that these verses show that the Qu'ran ultimately puts much more emphasis on "being just and righteous than on doctrinal correctness" (Griffin, 2005, p. 164).

The primary thesis in *Deep Religious Pluralism* is that no religion is a seamless, coherent monolith. There are many denominations and persuasions that reflect different interpretations of the various scriptures. Yet this diversity is both irreversible and inescapable. Religious pluralism constitutes the natural order of the world. It reminds us that God is too great to be captured by just one religion. Yet this reality in no way means that all religions are morally and scripturally equal. It merely means that there is an onus on us to treat other religions with respect, to exercise self-restraint, and to dialogue with other religions so that our different truths can fertilize each other. Our religious diversity is in no way an impediment to communication. It is, actually, a catalyst. Whereas many would have us focus on either limiting or ending our religious diversity, or would have us believe this diversity makes communication impossible, deep religious pluralism gives us a different story of communication. It is the lack of communication between peoples of different religions that threaten us most rather than our religious diversity.

CONCLUSION

It is difficult for most worldviews to tolerate and encourage diversity. Diversity challenges the authority and rule of any worldview by pointing to the possibility of other legitimate—even superior—ways of understanding the world. In the face of such a possibility, no worldview can claim the authority to possess complete and absolute truths. On the other hand, to acknowledge the possibility of other world-views is to recognize the need to encourage ourselves to look at the world in fundamentally new ways, including ways that are disconcerting, threatening, and even disorienting. This is what distinguishes diversity from plurality. Diversity genuinely pushes us to look at the world anew. It rattles our ordinary and comfortable ways of being in the world.

Yet to look at the world anew is difficult. This requires courage, and courage is always difficult to muster. But being unwilling to explore other possible ways of viewing the world robs us of the opportunity to change and evolve and, ultimately, the opportunity to acquire new ways of understanding the world. Diversity is mentally, emotionally, cognitively, and relationally demanding. It is about embracing the possibility of more expansive and constructive ways of understanding and experiencing the world. It is also about embracing the notion that this is a world of infinite possibilities. No worldview will ever possess absolute and complete understandings of anything. Diversity requires a stance of possibility and humility. In other words, diversity is moral, meaning that diversity is developmental. We have to develop the mental, emotional, sensual, relational, communicational, and spiritual constitution to imagine and forge new ways of understanding and experiencing the world. Diversity is about the possibility to imagine and forge other ways of being in the world that invite the world to change and evolve.

But we cannot reimagine the world if we are afraid of the world. Neither can we reimagine the world if we believe that the world possesses a finite diversity. Just as well, we cannot reimagine the world if we believe there is no compelling and even moral need to do so. The pursuit of possibility requires that we care deeply about this world. It also requires that we believe the world possesses an infinite potentiality. We must also be open to the possibility that we have a unique relation to the world. Ultimately, to believe in possibility requires that we be ready to embrace this world, including all peoples and sentient beings who share this world with us. For what this embrace constitutes is courage, such as the courage to share, to give, to nurture, to reconcile, to forgive, to love, and most important, to believe. Without courage, possibility is dead.

References

Africa News. (2004, April 17). Kenya: Anglican bishops back gay ban. *Africa News.*

Africa News. (2006, June 3). Kenya: Fresh row over gay rights bishop. *Africa News.*

Africa News. (2006, May 26). Kenya: Envoy sent to resolve gay row. *Africa News.*

Alam, F. (2006, November 27). Beyond the veil: Few controversies divide Europe more deeply than the question of the veil. Newsweek. Retrieved March 3, 2008, from http://newsweek.com/id 45503

Alexander, B. (1978). Male and female restroom graffiti. *The International Journal of Verbal Aggression, 2,* 42–59.

Aljazeera. (2003, December, 3). Thousands protest in Paris against the Muslim veil. Retrieved March 4, 2008, from http://www.aljazeerah.info/News%20archives/2003%20News%20archives/December/21

Aljazeera. (2004, January 8). French Muslims split over hijab ban. *Aljazeera.* Retrieved on March 3, 2008, from http://aljazeera.net/europe

Allport, G. W. (1954). *The nature of prejudice.* Reading, MA: Addison-Wesley.

Ammitzbøll, P., & Vidino, L. (2007). After the Danish cartoon controversy. *Middle Eastern Quarterly.* Retrieved February 26, 2008, from http://www.meforum.org

Anderson, M. (1999). *Wild women cultivating lawn alternatives in late 20th century U.S.* Paper for Women's Worlds '99: The 7th International Interdisciplinary Congress on Women. Tromso, Norway.

Anderson, M. (2003, April 28). *Gardens: Naturalized, culturized, personalized; OR Ontogeny of a careful natural historian, a careless gardener, and a carefree muse; being a reflexive conversation between a participant, an observer, and many memories.* Paper for the public seminar series, Personal Natures, at the Naturalists' Society, Tartu, Estonia.

Anderson, M. (2003) *Yards, gardening, and gender in urban America.* Paper for: A Transcultural View, the Sixth International Tartu Conference on North-American Studies, and 10th Anniversary of the Baltic Center for North-American Studies at the University of Tartu; Tartu, Estonia.

Anderson, M. (Ed.). (2004). *The cultural shaping of violence.* West Lafayette, IN: Purdue University Press.

Aoki, K. (1991). Some theoretical aspects of the origin of cultural transmission. In S. Osawa & T. Honjo (Eds.), *Evolution of life: Fossils, molecules, and culture* (pp. 439–452). New York: Springer-Verlag.

Appiah, K. A. (2005). *The ethics of identity.* Princeton, NJ: Princeton University Press.

Appiah, K. A. (2006). *Cosmopolitanism: Ethics in a world of strangers.* New York: Norton.

Appleton, J. (2003, December 17). Veiled concerns. The French state's proposed ban on schoolgirls headwear seems to make Muslims feel more French. *Spiked.* Retrieved March 2, 2008, from http://www.spiked-online.com

Arab News. (2008, February 28). Thousands in Sudan back Danish boycott. *Arab News.* Retrieved February 12, 2009, from http://www.arabnews.com/

Arana, M. (2008, November 30). He's not Black. *Washington Post*, p. B 01.

Aref, A. (2006). The veil and Muslim women in France: Religious and political aspects. *Anthropology of the Middle East, 1*, 89–107.

Aron, A., & Aron, E. N. (1986). *Love as the expansion of self: Understanding attraction and satisfaction*. New York: Hemisphere.

Aron, A., Mashek, D., & Aron, E. (2004). Closeness as including other in the self. In D. Mashek & A. Aron (Eds.), *Handbook of closeness and intimacy* (pp. 27–41). Mahwah, NJ: Erlbaum.

Arrogance not appreciated by the public. (1995, August 20). *Journal & Courier*, p. A 12.

Arthos, J. (2000). Who are we and who am I? Gadamer's communal ontology as palimpsest. *Communication Studies, 51*, 15–34.

Asante, M. K., Miike, Y., & Yin, J. (Eds.). (2008). The global intercultural communication reader. In M. K. Asante, Y. Miike, & J. Yin (Eds.), *Introduction: Issues and challenges in intercultural communication scholarship* (pp. 1–8). New York: Routledge.

Aslan, H. A. (2003, December 11). U.S. advocates religious freedom and criticizes secularism in France. *Today's Zaman*. Retrieved February 5, 2009, from http://www.todayszaman.com/tz-web/yazarDetay.do?haberno=4563

Aslan, R. (2006, February 9). Depicting Mohammed why I am offended by the Danish cartoons of the prophet. *Slate.com*. Retrieved February 12, 2009, from http://www.greatertalent.com/GTNnews.php?articleId=48

Astier, H. (2004, September 1). The deep roots of French secularism. *BBC News*. Retrieved May 12, 2008, from http://newsvote.bbc.co.uk

Atkinson, R. (1998). *The life story interview*. Thousand Oaks, CA: Sage.

Bailey, L. (2006, October 17). Britain's Islamic veil controversy senior politician's comments encourage rising discrimination against Muslims. Retrieved May 10, 2008, from http://english.ohmynews.com

Bandura A., & Wood R. (1989). Effect of perceived controllability and performance standards on self-regulation of complex decision-making. *Journal of Personality and Social Psychology, 56*, 805–814.

Banerjee, N. (2006, June 11). Episcopal leader resigns amid divisive debate on sexuality of bishops. *The New York Times*, p. 28.

Banerjee, N. (2007, May 5). Anglican Church intercedes as an Episcopal rift widens. *The New York Times*, p. 14.

Barillas, M. (2008, February 8). French president comes out against Muslim veil, French president Nicolas Sarkozy said there is no place in French schools for the Muslim veil. The veil in Spanish schools is at issue in the upcoming general elections. *Spero*. Retrieved February 2, 2008, from http://www.speroforum.com

Bates, S. (2003, July 12). Synod puts off bishop debate: Claims of racism fuel controversy over gay canon. *The Guardian, London*, p. 9.

Bateson, M. C. (1994). *Peripheral visions: Learning along the way*. New York: HarperCollins.

BBC News. (2003a, August 11). Denmark banks on new visas. *BBC News*. Retrieved March 4, 2008, from http://newsvote.bbc.co.uk

BBC News. (2003b, December 11). France awaits headscarves report. *BBC News*. Retrieved http://newsvote.bbc.co.uk

BBC News. (2003c, October 11). French school ban headscarf girls. *BBC News*. Retrieved http://newsvote.bbc.co.uk

BBC News. (2004f, February 10). Viewpoints: Europe and the headscarf. *BBC News*. Retrieved March 4, 2008, from http://newsvote.bbc.co.uk

BBC News. (2004, February 11). French headscarf ban opens rifts. *BBC News*, Retrieved on March 3, 2008, from http://news.bbc.co.uk

BBC News. (2004a, February 18). Denmark to restrict radical imams. *BBC News*. Retrieved March 4, 2008, from http://newsvote.bbc.co.uk

BBC News. (2004b, January 28). French cabinet backs scarf ban. *BBC News.* Retrieved March 3, 2008, from http://newsvote.bbc.co.uk

BBC News. (2004c, October 20). French girls expelled over veils. *BBC News.* Retrieved February 26, 2008, from http://newsvote.bbc.co.uk

BBC News. (2004d, September 2). French scarf ban comes into force. *BBC News.* Retrieved May 12, 2008, from http://newsvote.bbc.co.uk

BBC News. (2004e, October 1). Muslim girl shaves head over ban. *BBC News.* Retrieved May 12, 2008, from http://newsvote.bbc.co.uk

BBC News. (2004d, September 2). French scarf ban comes into force. *BBC News.* Retrieved May 12, 2008, from http://newsvote.bbc.co.uk

BBC News. (2005a, April 14). Danish queen raps radical Islam. *BBC News.* Retrieved March 4, 2008, http://newsvote.bbc.co.uk

BBC News. (2005b, January 21). Denmark rejects headscarf plea. *BBC News.* Retrieved March 4, 2008, http://newsvote.bbc.co.uk

BBC News. (2006a, February 2). Anger grows over Muhammad cartoon. *BBC News.* Retrieved February 26, 2008, from http://newsvote.bbc.co.uk

BBC News. (2006b, February 13). Danish PM talks to Muslim group. *BBC News.* Retrieved May 6, 2008, from http://newsvote.bbc.co.uk

BBC News. (2006c, October 3). Denmark row: The power of cartoons. *BBC News.* Retrieved February 26, 2008, from http://newsvote.bbc.co.uk

BBC News. (2006d, February 7). Mohammed cartoons' global crisis. *BBC News.* Retrieved March 4, 2008, from http://newsvote.bbc.co.uk

BBC News. (2006e, February 19). Muslim cartoon row timeline. *BBC News.* Retrieved February 26, 2008, from http://newsvote.bbc.co.uk

BBC News. (2006f, October 5). Straw's veil comments spark anger. *BBC News.* Retrieved May 7, 2008, from http://newsvote.bbc.co.uk

BBC News. (2006g, November 29). Survey finds support for veil ban. BBC News. Retrieved July 5, 2008, from http://newsvote.bbc.co.uk

BBC News. (2007, March 20). Schools allowed to ban face veils. *BBC News.* Retrieved May 7, 2008, from http://newsvote.bbc.co.uk

BBC News. (2008a, February 12). Danish cartoons "plotters" held. *BBC News.* Retrieved May 7, 2008, from http://newsvote.bbc.co.uk

BBC News. (2008b, February 18). Danish Muslims despair at portrayal. *BBC News.* Retrieved May 7, 2008, from http://newsvote.bbc.co.uk

BBC News. (2008c, March 20). New "Bin Laden tape" threatens EU. *BBC News.* Retrieved May 5, 2008, from http://newsvote.bbc.co.uk

BBC News. (2008d, May 2). Setback for Danish Koran translator. *BBC News.* Retrieved May 7, 2008, from http://newsvote.bbc.co.uk

BBC World Monitoring Media. (2008, February 26). Egypt furious at Danish cartoons reprints. *BBC World Monitoring Media.*

BBC Worldwide Monitoring. (2003, October 24). Caribbean bishops condemn planned ordination of gay bishop in USA. *Caribbean Media Cooperation News Agency.*

BBC Worldwide Monitoring. (2005, December 2). African Anglicans overturn election of "pro-gay" Malawi bishop. *BBC Worldwide Monitoring.*

Bearak, B. (2008, May 19). Anti-immigrant violence in Johannesburg. *The New York Times.* http://www.nytimes.com/2008/05/19/world/africa/19safrica.html?_r=1&partner=rssnyt&emc=rss&oref=slogin

Belay, G. (1993). Toward a paradigm shift for intercultural and international communication: New research directions. *Communication Yearbook, 16,* 437–457.

Benhabib, S. (2002). *The claims of culture: Equality and diversity in the global era.* Princeton, NJ: Princeton University Press.

Bhabha, H. (1994). *The location of culture.* London: Routledge.

Bickerton, D. (1995). *Language and human behavior.* Seattle: University of Washington Press.

Birmingham Post. (2008, June 24). Bishop of Rochester will boycott over gay ordination. *Birmingham Post,* p. 2.

Bishop, B. (2008). *The big sort: Why the clustering of like-minded America is tearing us apart.* New York: Houghton Mifflin

Black, C. F. (1995, November/December). An open letter to the community, 14 November 1995. *Community Times,* p. A 3.

Black, D. (2004). The geometry of terrorism. *Sociological Theory, 22,* 14–25.

Bohm, D. (1980). *Wholeness and the implicate order.* New York: Routledge.

Borger, J. (2006, March 13). California weighs up cost of electing first lesbian bishop: Bishop increases fears of schism over sex and faith: Appointment would defy Anglican moratorium. *The Guardian, London,* p. 23.

Brandon, J. (2006a, March 8). European Muslims rise up in defense of democratic values. *SFGate.* Retrieved May 8, 2008, from http://www.sfgate.com

Brandon, J. (2006b, March 6). Europe's Muslims divided in wake of cartoon furor. *Christian Science Monitor,* p. 4.

Brems, E. (2006). Diversity in the classroom: The headscarf controversy in European schools. *Peace and Change, 31,* 117–131.

Brinkley, J., & Fisher, I. (2006, February 4). U.S says it also finds cartoons of Mohammed offensive. *The New York Times.* Retrieved May 7, 2008, from http://www.nytimes.com

Broad, W. J. (2005, January 11). Deadly and yet necessary, quakes renew the planet. *New York Times.*

Brody, S., Wright, S., Aron, A., & McLaughlin-Volpe, T. (in press). Compassionate love for individuals outside one's social group. In L. Underwood, S. Sprecher, & B. Fehr (Eds.), *The science of compassionate love: Research, theory, and practice.* Malden, MA: Blackwell.

Broster, P. (2006, October 14). Straw insists: I was right to raise the veil. *The Express,* p. 12.

Brown, K. C. (1995, July 24). Bad choice made by WL officials. [Letter to the editor]. *Journal & Courier,* p. A 4.

Brubaker, R. (2004). *Ethnicity without groups.* Cambridge, MA: Harvard University Press.

Bruner, E. M., & Kelso, J. P. (1980). Gender differences in graffiti: A semiotic perspective. *Women's Studies International Quarterly, 3,* 239–252.

Bruner, J. (1996). *The culture of education.* Cambridge, MA: Harvard University Press.

Bryson, B. J. (2008, June 26). Comment & debate: The framing of mutual joy: Our church's evolving attitude has led us to the point where we must consider gay marriage. *The Guardian, London,* p. 32.

Buchanan, P. J. (2007). *Day of reckoning.* New York: St. Martin's Press.

Buch-Andersen, T. (2005, June 8). Arson highlights Danish tensions. *BBC News.* Retrieved March 8, 2008, from http://newsvote.bbc.co.uk

Buch-Andersen, T. (2006, October 6). Denmark row: the power of cartoons. *BBC News.* Retrieved May 7, 2008, from http://newsvote.bbc.co.uk

Bumiller, E. (1990). *May you be the mother of 100 sons: A journey among the women of India.* New York: Fawcett Columbine.

Burke, D. (2008, August 3). US Anglican churches stand on same-sex issues draws "ridicule," bishops say. *The Post-Standard,* p. A18.

Burke, K. (1969). *A rhetoric of motives.* Berkeley: University of California Press.

Burt, R. S. (1992). *Structural holes: The social structure of competition.* Cambridge, MA: Harvard University Press.

Bushnell, J. (1990). *Moscow graffiti.* London: Unwin Hyman.

Butt, R. (2008, June 21). National: Conservatives rule out Anglican reconciliation on gay clergy. *The Guardian, London,* p. 8.

Butt, R. (2008, June, 17). National: London controversy: Priests in civil partnership blessing were reckless, says bishop. *The Guardian, London,* p. 11.

Caffazo, D. (2004, June 22). Arranging has own set of benefits. *Tacoma News Tribune.* Retrieved July 22, 2008, from http://infoweb.newsban.com

Caldwell, C. (2003, December 21). In Europe, secular doesn't quite translate. *The New York Times.*

Capra, F. (1983). *The turning point: Science, society and the rising culture.* New York: Bantam Books.

Carle, R. (2004). Hijab and the limits of French secular republicanism. *Society,* 63–68

Casmir, F. L. (1993). Third-culture building: A paradigm shift for international and intercultural communication. *Communication Yearbook, 16,* 407–428.

Chaffee, L. G. (1989). Political graffiti and wall painting in Greater Buenos Aires: An alternative communication system. *Studies in Latin American Popular Culture, 8,* 37–60.

Chandak, R., & Sprecher, S. (1992). Attitudes about arranged marriage and dating among men and women from India. *Free Inquiry in Creative Psychology, 20,* 59–69.

Chane, B. J. (2008, June 26). Comment & debate. The framing of mutual joy: Our church's evolving attitude has led us to the point where we must consider gay marriage. *The Guardian London,* p. 32.

Chawla, D. (2004). *Arranged selves: Role, identity, and social transformations among Indian women in Hindu arranged marriages.* Unpublished doctoral dissertation, Purdue University, West Lafayette, IN.

Chawla, D. (2007). I will speak out: Narratives of resistance in contemporary Indian Women's discourses in Hindu arranged marriages. *Women and Language, 30*(1), 5–19.

China Daily. (2006a, March 6). More cartoon protests as embassy opens. *China Daily.* Retrieved February, 12, 2009, from http://www.chinadaily.com.cn

China Daily. (2006b, June 20). US Episcopal church names 1st woman leader. Retrieved from http://www.chinadaily.com.cn

Chomsky, N. (1968). *Language and mind.* New York: Harcourt.

Chomsky, N. (1988). *Language and politics.* Montreal: Black Rose Books.

Chong-Yeong, L. (2003). Language and human rights. *Journal of Intergroup Relations, 29*(3), 57–65.

Chua, A. (2003). *World on fire: How exporting free market democracy breeds Ethnic hatred and global instability.* New York: Doubleday.

CNN. (2002, May 31). Denmark passes tough migrant laws. *CNN.* Retrieved May 7, 2008, from http://cnn.worldnews.printthis.clickability.com

CNN. (2003, December 11). French report backs veil ban. *CNN.* Retrieved May 26, 2008, from http://cnn.com/worldnews/

CNN. (2008, February, 13). Newspapers reprint Mohammed cartoons. Retrieved February 12, 2009, from http://edition.cnn.com/2008/WORLD/europe/02/13/denmark.cartoon/index.html

Cocker, M. (2008, May 10). The sex life of plants. *The Guardian.* Retrieved August 11, 2008, from http://www.theguardian.co.uk

Cole, C. M. (1991). "Oh wise women of the stalls . . ." *Discourse & Society, 2,* 401–411.

Cole, E. (2008, February 13). Newspaper reprint Mohammed cartoon. *Christian Post Reporter.* Retrieved May 7, 2008, from http://www.christianpost.com

Conquergood, D. (2002). Performance studies: Interventions and radical research. *The Drama Review, 42*(2), 145–156.

Cooney, D. (2006, February 7). Widespread cartoon protests underway. Retrieved from http://spamusement.com/forums/viewtopic.

php?p=11178&sid=7b4c22193858c653f04
73414e6779171

Coontz, S. (2005). *Marriage, a history: From obedience to intimacy or how love conquered marriage.* New York: Viking.

Cooper, P. J., Calloway-Thomas, C., & Simonds, C. J. (2007). *Intercultural communication: A text with readings.* Boston: Allyn & Bacon.

Corder, J. W. (1994). Argument as emergence, rhetoric as love. In T. Enos & S. C. Brown (Eds.), *Professing the new rhetorics* (pp. 413–428). Englewood Cliffs, NJ: Blair Press.

Crumley, B. (2004, February 22). After the headscarf ban. *Time.* Retrieved March 3, 2008 from http://www.time.com.

Currie, C. M. (2002). Should we negotiate with terrorists? *Mediate.com.* Retrieved from http://www.mediate.com/articles/currie4.cfm

Czarniawska, B. (1997). *A narrative approach to organization studies.* Thousand Oaks, CA: Sage.

Czubaroff, J., & Friedman, M. (2000). A conversation with Maurice Friedman. *Southern Communication Journal, 65,* 243–254.

D'Angelo, F. J. (1976). Fools' names and fools' faces are always seen in public places: A study of graffiti. *Journal of Popular Culture, 10,* 102–109.

Daily Excelsior. (2004, January, 8). French Muslims split over pro-veil protest plans. Retrieved January 26, 2008, from http://www.dailyexcelsior.com

Davies, M. (2007, December 17). Communion is 'gift of God' Canterbury tells primates in advent letter, Episcopalife online, Retrieved May 2, 2010, from www.episcopalchurch.org/

Day, E. (2003, September 28). Bishop compares opponents of gay tradition to anti-Semites and supporters of slavery. *Sunday Telegraph,* p. 1.

Debusmann, B. (2000, April 30). *Around globe, walls spring up to divide neighbors.* Reuters.

Deetz, S. (1992). *Democracy in an age of corporate colonization.* Albany: SUNY.

Deetz, S. (1995). *Transforming communication transforming business.* Cresskill, NJ: Hampton.

Dennett, D. C. (1995). *Darwin's dangerous idea.* New York: Touchstone.

Derrett, J. D. M. (1976). Society and family law in India: The problem of Hindu marriage. In G. Gupta (Ed.), *Family and social change in modern India* (pp. 47–61). New Delhi, India: Vikas Publications.

Dervin, B. (1991). Comparative theory reconceptualized: From entities and states to processes and dynamics. *Communication Theory, 1,* 59–69.

Dhimmi Watch. (2003, December 6). Chirac: There's something about the veil. *Dhimmi Watch.* Retrieved February 26, 2008, from http//www.jihadwatch.org

Dhyani, J., & Kumar, P. (1996). Marital adjustment: A study of some related factors. *Indian Journal of Clinical Psychology, 2,* 112–116.

Dougherty, H. (2003, October 31). Gay bishops row makes split with US Anglicans "inevitable." *The Evening Standard, London,* p. 6.

Doughty, S. (2003, June 25). Bishop urges church to be gay friendly. *Daily Mail, London,* p. 2.

DW-World. (2006, February 2). Mohammed cartoon conflict gets even hotter. *DW-World.* Retrieved May 7, 2008, from http://www.dw-world.de

Dyson, F. (2000, May 16). Progress in religion. *Edge.* http://www.edge.org/documents/archive/edge68.html

Easley, H. (2005). A family affair. *The Journal News.* Retrieved July 22, 2008, from http://infoweb.newsban.com

East African Standard. (2007, February 22). Africa; Anglican bishops issue ultimatum over homosexuality. *Africa News.*

Economist, The. (2004). The war of the headscarves. *The Economist, 370,* 24–26.

Elbaum, R. (2006, May 25). Abuse and Germany's Muslim women. *MSNBC* http://www.msnbc.msn.com/id/12812607/

El-Nadi, S. (n.d.). A cross cultural analysis of the Danish prophet Mohammed cartoonist. *Kwintessential Cross Cultural Solutions.* Retrieved February 26, 2008, from http://www.kwintessential.co.uk

Evans, I. (2007, March 20). Heads to get powers to ban veils in class. *The Times, London,* p. 8.

Feynman, R. (1998). *The meaning of it all: Thoughts of a citizen-scientist.* New York: Perseus Books.

Fish, S. (1997). Boutique multiculturalism, or why liberals are incapable of thinking about hate speech. *Critical Inquiry, 23,* 378–395.

Fisher, I. (2006, February 3). Tens of thousands protest cartoons in Gaza. *The New York Times.* Retrieved February 12, 2009, from http://www.nytimes.com

Fixsen, A. (2007). Veil of isolation Britain tackles the Niqua debate. *Harvard International Review,* p.10.

Flanigan, S. (2000). Arranged marriages, matchmakers, and dowries in India. Retrieved July 25, 2008, from http://www.english.emory.edu/Bahri/Arr.html

Flint, A. (1992, December 18). Hate graffiti are reported in Wellesley College dorm. *Boston Globe,* p. A12.

Fogel, A. (1993). *Developing through relationships.* Chicago: University of Chicago Press.

Fong, M. (2003). The nexus of language, communication, and culture. In L. A. Samovar & R. Porter (Eds.), *Intercultural communication: A reader* (pp. 198–204). Belmont, CA: Wadsworth/Thomson.

Fontes, D. (1995, August 8). Weeds are no menace. [Letter to the editor]. *Journal & Courier,* p. A 10.

Fotion, N., & Elfstrom, G. (1992). *Toleration.* Tuscaloosa: University of Alabama Press.

Fox News. (2008, February 27). Sudanese president urges Muslim boycott of Denmark over reprinted Muhammad cartoon. *Fox News.* Retrieved May 7, 2008, from http://www.foxnews.com

Fraser, B. (1980). *Meta-graffiti. Maledicta: The International Journal of Verbal Aggression, 4,* 258–260.

Friedman, T. L. (1999). *The Lexus and the olive tree: Understanding globalization.* New York: Farrar, Straus, Giroux.

Gadamer, H. G. (2005). Heidegger as rhetor: Hans-Georg Gadamer Interviewed by Ansgsar Kemmann (L. K. Schmidt, Trans.). In D. M. Gross & A. Kemmann (Eds.), *Heidegger and rhetoric.* Albany: SUNY Press.

Galant, D. (2001, June 17). Watching grass grow, a suburban pursuit. *The New York Times.* Retrieved August 8, 2008, from www.newyorktimes.com

Gaunt, J. (2007, March 6). Veil needs to be banned in all schools. *The Sun, England.*

Geiger, E. (2005, December 4). Muslim girls in Austria fighting forced marriages. *Chronicle Foreign Service.* http://www.sfgate.com/cgibin/article.cgi?f=/c/a/2005/12/04/MNGH0G1B7L1.DTL

Gentleman, A. (2003, September 25). French school bars girls for wearing headscarves. *The Guardian,* p. 19.

Gerecht, R. M. (2006, February 20). Selling out moderate Islam. *The Weekly Standard.* Retrieved February 12, 2009, from http://www.weeklystandard.com/Content/Public/Articles/000%5C000%5C006%5C700hlpwn.asp

Gereluk, D. (2005). Should Muslim headscarves be banned in French schools? *Theory and Research in Education, 3*(3), 259–271.

Get a life, West Lafayette. (1995, June/July). *Community Times,* p. A 2.

GG2.Net News. (2005, September 30). UN religious freedom watchdog raps French. Retrieved February 26, 2008, from http://www.prohijab.net

Giannangeli, M. (2007, March 20). 2,500 pupils to face safety ban on Muslim veil. *The Express,* p. 2

Glendhill, R. (2003, November 6). Consecration of gay bishop harms church, says Carey. *The Times London.*

Glendhill, R. (2005, November 19). In the end, there is no one God does not love. *The Times, London,* p. 84.

Glendhill, R. (2006a, January 9). Church wants woman bishops by 2012. *The Times London,* p. 11.

Glendhill, R. (2006b, October 10). Muslim veils suck, Rushdie says. *The Times, London,* p. 13.

Glendhill, R. (2008, July 29). Anglicans halt gay bishop consecrations and same-sex blessings. *The Times London.* Retrieved February 3, 2008, from http://www.timesonline.co.uk/tol/comment/faith/article4417984.ece

Glossic, J. L. (1995, July 24). Natural yards have support. [Letter to the editor]. *Journal & Courier,* p. A 4.

Goldenberg, J., & Mazursky, D. (2002). *Creativity in product innovation.* Cambridge, UK: Cambridge University Press.

Goodstein, L. (2007, December 17). Anglican Archbishop faults factions. *The New York Times,* p. 15

Gonzalez Echevarria, R. (1997, March 29). Is "Spanglish" a language? *New York Times,* p. A29.

Gooddard, J. (2008, May 4). A moderate Muslims longs for a more moderate spiritual faith. *The Star.* Retrieved May 6, 2008, from http://thestar.com

Goodstein, L. (2004, September 11). Bishop says conflict on homosexuality distracts from vital political issues. *The New York Times,* p. 9.

Goodstein, L. (2007, December 15). Anglican Archbishop faults faction. *The New York Times,* p. 15.

Gordon, R. D. (2000). Karl Jaspers: Existential philosopher of dialogical communication. *Southern Communication Journal, 65,* 105–117.

Gore, M. S. (1968). *Urbanization and family change.* New York: Humanities Press.

Government of India. (2001). *National Commission for Women Report.* New Delhi, India: Ministry of Education and Social Welfare.

Granovetter M. S. (1974). *Getting a job: A study of contacts and careers.* Cambridge, MA: Harvard University Press.

Gray, J. (2007, September 10). Countries around the world are wrestling with religious rights. *The Globe and Mail, Canada,* p. A10.

Gribbin, J. (1984). *In search of Schroedinger's cat: Quantum physics and reality.* New York: Bantam Books.

Griffin, D. R. (Ed.). (2005). *Deep religious pluralism.* Louisville, KY: Westminister John Knox Press.

Grimes, D. S. (2002). Challenging the status quo? Whiteness in the diversity management literature. *Management Communication Quarterly, 15,* 381–409.

Guardian, The. (2003, November, 13). MPs urge on ban on religious symbols. *Guardian News & Media.* Retrieved January 20, 2008, from http://www.buzzle.com/editorials

Guardian, The. (2006, February 7). Cartoons "part of Zionist plot." *Guardian.* Retrieved February 26, 2008, from http://www.guardian.co.uk

Gudmundsson, H. (2006a, April 2). British appease while moderate Muslim speaks out. Retrieved September 9, 2008, from http://www.brusselsjournal.com

Gudmundsson, H. (2006b, February 5). Danish Muslims rebel against Imams. Retrieved May 6, 2008, from http://www.brusselsjournal.com

Gudmundsson, H. (2006c, January 19). Denmark: Moderate Muslims oppose Imams. Retrieved May 6, 2008, from http://www.brusselsjournal.com

Gudmundsson, H. (2006d, February 13). More and more moderate Muslims speak out in Denmark. Retrieved May 6, 2008, from http://www.brusselsjournal.com

Gudykunst, W. B., & Kim, Y. Y. (2003). *Communication with strangers: An approach to inter-*

cultural communication. Boston: McGraw-Hill.

Haartez. (2003, December 10). French chief rabbi urges no ban on Muslim veil. *Haaretz.* Retrieved February 26, 2008, from http://haaretz.com/hasen

Hall, S. (1991). Ethnicity: Identity and difference. *Radical America, 23,* 9–20.

Hamdan, A. (2007). The issue of Hijab in France: Reflections and analysis. *Muslim World Journal of Human Rights, 4,* 2–27

Hansen, R. (2006). The Danish cartoon controversy: A defense of liberal freedom. Retrieved February 26, 2008, from http://www.bris.ac.uk/sociology/ethnicitycitizenship

Hastings, C., & Day, E. (2003, July 20). God wants openly gay priests in C of E church has a tradition of promoting minorities, says homosexual who will be confirmed as a bishop today. *Sunday Telegraph,* p. 17.

Haywood, B. (2006, February 13). How free should the media be? VCE express-issues in the news: Cartoon controversy. *The Age,* p. 10.

Hedetoft, U. (2006, November). Denmark: Integrating immigrants into homogenous welfare state. Migration Information Source. Fresh thought, Authoritative data, global reach. Retrieved May 7, 2008, from http://www.migrationinformation.org

Henley, J. (2003, November 14). MPs urge French ban on religious symbols. *The Guardian.* Retrieved February 2, 2008, from http://guardian.co.uk

Henley, J. (2004, February 11). French MPs vote for veil ban in state schools. *The Guardian.* Retrieved from http://guardian.co.uk

Hentschel, E. (1987). Women's graffiti. *Multilingua: Journal of Cross-Cultural and Interlanguage Communication, 6–3,* 287–308.

Herald, The. (2005, December 9). South Africa: Tutu's gay campaign illogical. *Africa News.*

Herbert, N. (1987). *Quantum reality: Beyond the new physics.* New York: Anchor Books.

Higgins, R. (1989, February 26). BC investigates painting of racial phrase in dorm. *Boston Globe,* p. A28.

Hollinger, D. A. (2005). *Postethnic America.* New York: Basic Books.

Human Rights Watch. (2005, February 24). France: Headscarf ban infringes on religious freedom. Human Rights Watch. Retrieved February 5 2009, from http://www.hrw.org/en/news/2004/02/26/france-headscarf-ban-violates-religious-freedom?print

Huntington, S. P. (2004). *Who we are: The challenges to America's national identity.* New York: Simon & Schuster.

Hurd, D. (2004, July 9). Putting Islam to the test: The rise of Islam in Europe. *Islam Review.* Retrieved on May 5, 2008, from http://islamreview.com/articles/puttingtoleranceprint.htm

Ibrahim, M. Y. (1994, September 11). Face bans Muslim scarf in its schools. *The New York Times,* p. 4.

Imhoff, G. (1987). Partisans of language. *English Today, 11,* 37–40.

International Herald Tribune. (2006, October 8). Controversy over the veil swirls on in the U.K. Retrieved February 12, 2008, from http://www.iht.com

Israel Insider. (2006, February 7). Iranian MP calls for contest of holocaust cartoons. Retrieved February 12, 2009, from http://isrealinsider.ning.com

Iyer, P. (2000). *The global soul: Jet lag, shopping malls, and the search for home.* New York: Knopf.

Iszler, B. K. (1995, June/July). Windows with curtains of greenery outside: Myrdene Anderson's battle with *Community Times.* pp. A1, A6.

Jackson, S. (2006, February 15). Turban-bomb tragedy-dominant response to the Muhammad cartoon only underlines the original barb. *Jerusalem Post.*

Jantsch, E. (1980). *The self-organizing universe.* Oxford: Pergamon Press.

Jenkins, P. 2002). Nor shall my sword rest in my hand. *Chronicles,* p. 17.

Jenkins, S. (2008, July 4). Comment & debate: Let a church so fond of division test its worth in the marketplace of belief: Anglicanism is often the last servant of the poor, that it can tear itself apart in an absurd imperial argument is a tragedy. *The Guardian, London,* p. 35.

Jensen, T. (2006, February 6). The cartoon crisis revisited: A Danish perspective. *Análysis del real Instituto.* Retrieved February 26, 2008, from http://www.realinstitutoelcano.org

Jones, C. E. (2005, March 28). Muslim girls unveil their fears. *BBC News.* Retrieved May 12, 2008, from http://newsvote.bbc.co.uk

Jones, P. E. (1991). The impact of economic, political, and social factors on recent overt Black\White racial conflict in higher education in the United States. *Journal of Negro Education, 60,* 524–537.

Jussawalla, F. (1996). Rushdie's Dastan-e-Dilruba: The Satanic Verses as Rushdie's love letter to Islam. *Diacritics, 26,* 50–73.

Kamat, V. (n.d.). *Indian culture: India's arranged marriages.* Retrieved July, 25, 2008, from http://www.kamat.com/indica/culture/subcultures/arranged_marriage.htm

Kapadia, K. M. (1958). *Marriage and family in India.* Calcutta, India: Oxford University Press.

Kapur, P. (1970). *Marriage and the working woman in India.* Delhi, India: Vikas Publications.

Kelley, T. (2006, June 26). Gay Episcopal priest named as possible network bishop. *The New York Times,* p. 1.

Khair, T. (2006, February 7). Comment & debate: We have lost our voices: Moderate Muslims from Denmark to Middle East, are caught in the vice of a manufactured conflict. *The Guardian, London,* p. 30.

Khalid, A. (2007, April 28). Why I am not a moderate Muslim. *Alter Net.* Retrieved May 6, 2008, from http://www.alternet.org

Khan, M. (n.d.). Who are the moderate Muslims? Retrieved May 6, 2008, from http://www.islamfortoday.com

Khouri, R. (2006, February 9). The real truth behind the cartoons fury. *The Age.*

Kim, Y. Y. (2003). Intercultural personhood: An integration of eastern and western perspectives in L. A. Samovar & R. Porter (Eds.), *Intercultural communication: A reader* (10th ed., pp. 436–448). Belmont, CA: Wadsworth.

Kirk, J. (1990, May 5). Racial graffiti found on walls at Wesleyan U. *New York Times,* p. A 29.

Klopf, D. W., & McCroskey, J. C. (2007). *Intercultural communication encounters.* Boston: Pearson.

Knox, N. (2004, February 2). Effort to ban head scarves in France sets off culture clash. *USA Today.* Retrieved February 26, 2008, from http://usatoday.printthis.clickability.com

Kolbert, E. (2008, July 21). Turf war. *The New Yorker.* Retrieved August 18, 2008, from http://www.newyorker.com

Kostka, R. (1974). Aspects of graffiti. *Visible Language, 8,* 369–371.

Kramer, J. (2004, November 22). Taking the veil. How France's public schools became the battleground in a culture war. *New Yorker,* pp. 59–79.

Kraus, C. (2003, July 5). The Saturday profile: In blessing gay unions, Bishop courts a schism. *The New York Times,* p. 4.

LaFraniere, S., & Goodstein, L. (2007, February 20). Anglicans rebuke U.S. branch on blessing same-sex unions. *The New York Times,* p. 1.

Lake, E. (2006, February 6). Rice is faulting Syria, Iran for stoking riots. *New York Sun.* Retrieved February 12 2009, from http://www.nysun.com

Lalwani, S. B. (2005, April 5). Arranged quite nicely. *The Milwaukee Journal Sentinel.* Retrieved July 22, 2008, from http://infoweb.newsban.com

Leckrone, J. (2006, June 16). Gays embrace first Anglican woman head. *The Courier Mail,* p. 20.

Lee, D. (1987). *Freedom and culture.* Prospects Heights, IL: Waveland Press.

Lee, W. S., Wang, J., Chung, J., & Hertel, E. (1995). A sociohistorical approach to intercultural communication. *Howard Journal of Communications, 6,* 262–291.

Leicester, J. (2003, December 22). The veil, my choice say French Muslims. Associated Press. Retrieved January 26, 2008, from http://findarticles.com

Levy, A., & Levy, L. (2004). Cover up. *Index on Censorship,* pp. 117–125.

Lewis, D. (1986). *On the plurality of worlds.* Oxford, UK: Basil Blackwell.

Lifson, T. (February 6, 2006). The cartoon crisis: Conspiracy and moderate Muslims. *Americanthinker.com.* Retrieved May 2, 2010, from http://americanthinker.com/2006/02

Lifson, T. (2006, February 7). The cartoon conspiracy and moderate Muslims. *Real Clear Politics.* Retrieved May 6, 2008, from http://www.realclearpolitics.com

Lightfoot, D. (1999). *The development of language.* Malden, MA: Blackwell.

Lingis, A. (1994). *The community of those who have nothing in common.* Bloomington: Indiana University Press.

Lipner, J. J. (1994). *Hindus: Their religious beliefs and practices.* New York: Routledge.

Lippi-Green, R. (1997). *English with an accent: Language, ideology, and discrimination in the United States.* New York: Routledge.

Lobe, J. (2006, February 17). Cartoon crises echoes "Why they hate us" debate. Retrieved February 12, 2008, from http://ipsnews.net/news.asp?idnews=32213

Lochhead, D. (1989). *The dialogical imperative: A Christian reflection on interfaith encounter.* New York: Orbis.

Lowndes V., & Skelcher C. (1998). The dynamics of multi-organizational partnerships: An analysis of changing modes of governance. *Public Administration, 76,* 313–333.

Luft, A. (2007, October 20). Montreal Anglicans vote to bless same-sex unions; Controversy within church? Hey, why not? Bishop says. *The Gazette,* p. A 47.

Malik, K. (2007, February 5). Free speech in a plural society. eurotopics. Retrieved February 12, 2009, from http://www.eurotopics.net/en/magazin/

Marder, M. (1945, September 19). Navajo code talk kept foe guessing. *The New York Times,* p. 9.

Marquis, C. (2003, December 19). U.S Chides France on effort to bar religious garb in schools. *The New York Times,* p. A8.

Marshall, P. (2006, February 9). The Mohammed cartoons. Western governments have nothing to apologize for. *The Weekly Standard.* Retrieved February 12, 2009, from http://www.freedomhouse.org/template.cfm?page=72&release=328

Martin, J. N., & Nakayama, T. K. (1999). Thinking dialectically about culture and communication. *Communication Theory, 9,* 1–25.

Martin, J. N., & Nakayama, T. K. (2007). *Intercultural communication in contexts.* Boston: McGraw-Hill.

McAdams, D. P. (1988). *Power, intimacy, and the life story: Personological inquiries into identity.* New York: Guilford Press.

McAdams, D. P. (1993). *The stories we live by: Personal myths and the making of the self.* New York: Morrow.

McClain, DaCosta, K. (2008, November 18). Viewpoint: Is Barack Obama black? *BBC News.* Retrieved from http://news.bbc.co.uk/go/pr/fr/-/2/hi/americas/us_elections

McDaniel, E. R., Samovar, L. A., & Porter, R. E. (2006). *Intercultural communication.* Belmont, CA: Thomson Wadsworth.

McNamee, S., & Gergen, K. (1999). *Relational responsibility: Resources for sustainable dialogue.* Thousand Oaks, CA: Sage.

McPhail, M. L. (1996). *Zen in the art of rhetoric.* New York: State University of New York Press.

Michaels, W. B. (2006). *The trouble with diversity: How we learned to love identity and ignore inequality.* New York: Metropolitan Books.

Middle-east Online (2003, December 18). Chirac's veil ban gets mixed reaction in France. *Middle-east Online.* Retrieved December 5, 2008, from http://middle-east-online.com/english

Mill, J. S. (1956). *On liberty.* London: Longman.

Milliken, F. J., & Martins, L. L. (1996). Searching for common threads: Understanding the multiple effects of diversity in organizational groups. *Academy of Management Review, 21,* 402–423.

Mink, L. O. (1970). History and fiction as modes of comprehension. *New Literary History, 1,* 541–558.

Modood, T. (2006, January 6). The liberal dilemma: Integration or vilification? *The Cartoon Affair.* Retrieved February 26, 2008, from http://www.bris.ac.uk

Moon, D. G. (1996). Concepts of culture: Implications for intercultural communication research. *Communication Quarterly, 44,* 70–84.

Morales, E. (2002). *Living in Spanglish: The search for Latino identity in America.* New York: St. Martin's.

Mortensen, C. D. (1991). Communication, conflict, and culture. *Communication Theory, 4,* 273–293.

Mukherjee, P. (1978). *Hindu women.* New Delhi, India: Orient Longman.

Mullatti, L. (1995). Families in India: Beliefs and realities. *Journal of Comparative Family Studies, 26,* 11–25.

Muslim American Society. (2003, December 22). Thousand protest against headscarf ban in France. Retrieved May 12, 2008, from http://www.masnet.org/new.asp

Myers, B. R. (2008, April). Keeping a civil tongue. *Atlantic Monthly.* Retrieved from http://www.theatlantic.com/doc/200804/myers-robinson

Neuliep, J. W. (2000). *Intercultural communication: A contextual approach.* Boston: Houghton Mifflin.

New York Times. (2003, December 31). Muslim leader says France has right to prohibit head scarves. *The New York Times,* p. A5.

Newall, V. (1986–1987). The moving spray can: A collection of some contemporary English graffiti. *The International Journal of Verbal Aggression, 9,* 39–47.

Noreen. (2009). The culture of arranged marriages in India. Retrieved February 17, 2009, from http://www.indiamarks.com/guide/The-Culture-of-Arranged-Marriages-in-India/961

Norfolk, A. (2006, October 20). I won't be treated as an outcast, says Muslim teacher in veil row. *The Times, London,* p. 4.

Norval, M. (2002, March). Pandora's box. *Chronicles,* p. 22.

Ong, W. J. (1988). *Orality and literacy.* New York: Routledge.

Onishi, N. (2004, March 17). Letter from Asia: Japan and China: National Character Writ Large. *New York Times.* Retrieved from http://query.nytimes.com/gst/fullpage.html?res=9A07EEDE1431F934A25750C0A9629C8B63

Onishi, N. (2008, June 8). For English studies, Koreans say goodbye to dad. *New York Times* http://www.nytimes.com/2008/06/08/world/asia/08geese.html?r=1&ei=5087&em=&en=b15766e40c698da6&ex=1213070400&pagewanted=print

Pagden, A. (2008). *Worlds at war: The 2,500-year struggle between east and west.* New York: Random House.

Paulson, M. (2003a, November 1). Episcopal pioneer reflects on debate. *The Boston Globe,* p. B 1.

Paulson, M. (2003b, August 2). Panel black gay bishop Episcopal conservatives prepare to fight N.H. nomination. *The Boston Globe,* p. A1.

Passel, J., & Cohn, D. (February 11, 2008). Immigration to play lead role in future U.S. growth:

U.S. population projections: 2005–2050. Pew Research Center. Retrieved May 4, 2010 from http://pewresearch.org/pubs/729/united-states-population-projections

Paulson, M. (2004, October 21). Gay bishop speaks out on report. *The Boston Globe*, p. B1.

Paulson, M. (2007, April 25). Episcopal leader holds firm on gay rights says N.H. bishop's election a blessing. *The Boston Globe*, p. B3.

Pearce, J. (2006, August 11). Islam as a religion of peace. *The Journal of Religion Culture and Public Life*. Retrieved February 12, 2008, from http://www.firstthings.com/

Pearce, W. B., & Littlejohn, S. W. (1997). *Moral conflict: When social worlds collide*. Thousands Oak, CA: Sage.

Perlez, J. (2007, June 22). Head-to-toe Muslim veil test tolerance of stridently secular Britain. *The International Herald Tribune*, p. 3.

Petre, J. (2005, July 26). "Marriage" but no sex for gay clergy. *The Daily Telegraph*, p. 2.

Petre, J. (2006, November 30). 33 pc back Muslim veil ban, survey says. Retrieved July 7, 2008, from http://www.telegraph.co.uk

Pettigrew, T. F., & Tropp, L. R. (2006). A meta-analytic test of intergroup contact theory. *Journal of Personality and Social Psychology, 90,* 751–783.

Pettigrew, T. F., & Tropp, L. R. (2008). How does intergroup contact reduce prejudice? Meta-analytic tests of three mediators. *European Journal of Social Psychology, 38,* 922–934.

Pinker, S. (1994). *The language instinct*. New York: HarperPerennial.

Polakov-Suransky, S. (2002, August). Denmark: Rebuffing immigrants. *World Press*. Retrieved May 7, 2008, from http://www.worldpress.org

Pew Research Center (2008, February 11). U.S. population projections: 2005-2050. http://pewhispanic.org/reports/report.php?ReportID=85

Polgreen, L. (2003, August 12). Anglicans in U.S. grapple with choice of gay bishop; Decision called "intolerable" and "courageous." *International Herald Tribune*, p. 5.

Pollan, M. (1991). Why mow? In M. Pollan, *Second nature: A gardener's education* (pp. 65–78). New York: Dell.

Potter, M. (2008, July 14). "I think God wants us to be bold"; Gay bishop Gene Robinson calls for end to the Anglican rift in the first sermon to UK worshippers. *The Toronto Star,* p. A03.

Powers, S., & Arsenault, A. (2006). *The Danish cartoon crisis: The impact of public diplomacy*. A partnership of the USC Annenberg School of Communication and the USC College of Letters, Arts & Sciences School of International Relations.

Prigogine, I., & Stengers, I. (1984). *Order out of chaos*. New York: Bantam Books.

Protect Hijab. (2005, October 30). UN religious freedom watchdog raps French veil ban. *Protect Hijab*. Retrieved February 26, 208, from http://prohijab.net/english/france-hijab-news25.htm

Prophetic Times. (2003, November 8). Former Arch Bishop says gay Bishop harms Anglicans. *Prophetic Times*. Retrieved February 3, 2009, from http://treybig.org/PropheticTimes/2003–1108-PT.pdf

Pyle, G. (2004). *Testimony of Chief Gregory Pyle given on behalf of The Choctaw Nation of Oklahoma before The Committee on Indian Affairs of The Senate of the United States: September 22, 2004*. http://web.lexisnexis.com.libezproxy2.syr.edu/congcomp/attachment/a.pdf?_m=d5f81bc2b1c446c1fbe28459a8d1bb11&wchp=dGLbVzWzSkSA&_md5=6c6b1ed95045bed90baf11db3782c631&ie=a.pdf

Qenawi, A. (2005, November 18). Danish Muslims internationalize anti-prophet cartoons. *Islam Online*. Retrieved February 12, 2009, from http://www.islamonline.net

Ranalli, R. (2003, June 9). Ovations greet gay N. H. bishop-elect. *The Boston Globe*, p. B4.

Rao, V. V., & Rao, N. (1975). Arranged marriages: An assessment of the attitudes of college students. *Journal of Comparative Family Studies, 7,* 433–453.

Recorder Report. (2008, March 2). Business recorder: Blasphemous caricatures: Students, traders stage protest demonstrations. *Financial Times Information Limited.* Retrieved March 3, 2008, from http:///www.infoweb.newsbank.com

Reich, W., Buss, R., Fein, E., & Kurtz, T. (1977). Notes on women's graffiti. *Journal of American Folklore, 90,* 188–191.

Rennie D., Isherwood, J., & Barton, J. (2006, February 4). America backs Muslims over cartoons as thousands of voices anger worldwide. *The Telegraph, London,* p. 4.

Reuters. (2003, October 12). French chief rabbi urges no ban Muslim veil. Haaretz. Retrieved February 2, 2008, from http://www.haaretz.com

Reuters. (2004, October 20). France: First students expelled over head scarves. *The New York Times,*. p. A14.

Reuters. (n.d.). French Muslims split over Hijab ban. *Aljeezeera.net.* Retrieved March 4, 2008, from http://english.aljazeera.net/news

Richardson, L. (1990). Narrative and sociology. *Journal of Contemporary Ethnography, 19,* 116–135.

Riesman, C. K. (1993). *Narrative analysis.* Thousand Oaks, CA: Sage.

Rodriguez, A. (2002). The heuristic promise of the narrative paradigm for intergroup relations. *Journal of Intergroup Relations, 29,* 52–69.

Rodriguez, A. (2003). *Diversity as liberation (II): Introducing a new understanding of diversity.* Cresskill, NJ: Hampton.

Rodriguez, A. (2006). A story from somewhere: Cathedrals, Communication, and the search for possibility. *International and Intercultural Communication Annual, 29,* 4–21.

Rodriguez, R. (2002). *Brown: The last discovery of America.* New York: Penguin.

Rogers, E. M., & Steinfatt, R. M. (1999). Intercultural communication. Prospect Heights, IL: Waveland.

Rose, F. (2006a, February 19). Why I published cartoons. *The Washington Post.* Retrieved May 6, 2008, from http://www.washingtonpost.com

Rose, F. (2006b, May 31). Why I published cartoons. *The New York Times.* Retrieved May 6, 2008, from http://www.nytimes.com

Rose, F. (2006c, February 21). Why I published the Muhammad cartoons. Retrieved March 4, 2008, from http://www.nytimes.com

Ross, A. D. (1961). *The Hindu family in the urban setting.* Bombay: Oxford University Press.

Ryan, N. (2006, October 4). NASCAR betting Hispanic flavor flows into cup with Montoya's arrival. *USA Today.*

Sacks, J. (2003). *The dignity of difference: How to avoid the clash of civilizations.* London: Continuum.

Said, E. (2000). *Reflections on exile and other essays.* Cambridge, MA: Harvard University Press.

Said, E. (2001, September 16). Islam and the West are inadequate banners. *The Observer* http://www.observer.co.uk/comment/story/0,6903,552764,00.html

Salam, A. (2002, January 28). Rising voices of moderate Muslims. Retrieved May 6, 2008, from http://www.state.gov

Salins, P. D. (1997). *Assimilation American style.* New York: Basic Books.

Salmons, J. (1995, July 21). Lawns unimportant. [Letter to the editor]. *Journal & Courier,* p. A 4.

Samovar, L. A., Porter, R. E., & McDaniel, E. R. (2007). *Communication between cultures.* Belmont, CA: Thomson Wadsworth.

Santana, F. (2000). *Arranged marriages, matchmakers, and dowries in India.* Retrieved July 25, 2008, from www.english.emory.edu/Bahri/Arr.html

Sastri, H. C. (1972). *The social background of the forms of marriage in ancient India* (Vol. I). Calcutta: Sanskrit Pustak Bhandar.

Sastri, H. C. (1974). *The social background of the forms of marriage in ancient India* (Vol. II). Calcutta: Sanskrit Pustak Bhandar.

Sayed, S. (2006, February 7). Callous cartoons: Images depict a growing Islamophobia in the West. *The Press-Enterprise.* Retrieved February 12, 2009, from http://www.pe.com/localnews/opinion/localviews/stories/PE_OpEd_Opinion_D_op_08_syed_loc.628d7e0.html

Scanlon, T. M. (1996). The difficulty of tolerance. In D. Heyd (Ed.), *Toleration* (pp. 226–240). Princeton, NJ: Princeton University Press.

Scheibel, D. (1994). Graffiti and "film school" culture: Displaying alienation. *Communication Monographs, 61,* 1–18.

Schmidt, A. J. (1997). *The menace of multiculturalism: Trojan horse in America.* Westport, CT: Praeger.

Schofield, H. (2003a, December 18). Chirac's veil ban gets mixed reaction in France. Some hail reassertion of France's secular principles, others call proposed law counterproductive, discriminatory. *Middle East Online.* Retrieved May 12, 2008, from http://www.middle-east-online.com

Schofield, H. (2003b, October 1). Jewish dad backs headscarf daughters. *BBC News.* Retrieved February 26, 2008, from http://newsvote.bbc.co.uk

Sciolino, E. (2003a, December 12). Ban religious attire in schools, French panel says. *The New York Times,* p. A1.

Sciolino, E. (2003b, December 18). Chirac backs law to keep signs of faith out of school. *The New York Times,* p. A17.

Sciolino, E. (2004a, September 3). Ban on head scarves takes effect in France. *The New York Times,* p. A8.

Sciolino, E. (2004b, February 4). Debates begin in France on religion in the schools. *New York Times,* p. A8.

Sciolino, E. (2004c, April 5). France's new dress code: A ban on religious symbols in schools shows how differently France and the U.S.

think about religion and pluralism. *The New York Times.* Retrieved March 4, 2008, http://www.newyorktimes.com

Sciolino, E. (2004d, August 30). France won't meet demand to stop ban on head scarves. *The New York Times,* p. A7.

Sciolino, E. (2004e, February 11). French assembly votes to ban religious symbols in schools. *The New York Times,* p. A3.

Sciolino, E. (2004f, Jan 18). French Muslims protest rule against scarves. *The New York Times,* p. N10.

Sciolino, E. (2004g, January 12). French Sikhs defend their turbans and find their voices. *The New York Times,* p. A4.

Sen, A. (2006a). *Identity and violence: The illusion of destiny.* New York: Norton.

Sen, A. (2006b, March, 29). What clash of civilizations? Why religious identity isn't destiny. *Slate.* Retrieved from http://www.slate.com

Sequeira, N. (2009, March 2). The culture of arranged marriages in India.. *Indiamarks.* Retrieved March 5, 2009, from http://www.indiamarks.com/guide/

Sharma, K. L. (1997). *Social stratification in India: Issues and themes.* New Delhi, India: Sage.

Shastri, S. R. (1969). *Women in the Vedic age.* Bombay, India: Bharati Vidya Bhavan.

Shattuck, C. (1999). *Hinduism.* Upper Saddle River, NJ: Prentice Hall.

Shepherd, J. (2007, October 9). Education: Schools: Uniform dissent: New government guidance on religious symbols worn in school doesn't help much. *The Guardian, London,* p. 5.

Shutter, R. (1993). On third-culture building. *Communication Yearbook, 16,* 429–436.

Smith, D. (1995a, January 29). A fine mess? *Journal & Courier,* pp. A1, A12.

Smith, D. (1995b, June 17). Fight to let yard grow wild continues. *Journal & Courier,* pp. A7, A8.

Smith, D. (1995c, July 11). Petition for yard growing. *Journal & Courier,* p. A1.

Smith, D. (1995d, August 12). WL yard dispute settled. *Journal & Courier,* pp. A1, A2.

Sole, R. (1995, September 15). Lifting the veil of fear this week the French education minister, Francois Bayrou, banned girls from wearing Islamic headscarves in school. *The Guardian,* p. 15.

Spencer, R. (2006, January 12). The Economist's surrender. Front Page. Retrieved February 12, 2009, from http://frontpagemag.com/articles/Read.aspx?GUID=4E8203E2–1AB3–4486–8155–7EEC529D3AE1

Stanley, A. (2000, July 4). French bishop, disciplined over gay pride issue, still speaks out in Rome. *The New York Times,* p. 4.

Starosta, W. (1991, May). *Third culture building: Chronological development and the role of third parties.* Paper presented at the annual meeting of the International Communication Association, Chicago, IL.

Starr, M. (1990, November, 26). The writing on the wall. *Newsweek,* p. 64.

Stavans, I. (2000a). Spanglish: Tickling the tongue. *World Literature Today, 74,* 555–558.

Stavans, I. (2000b, October 13). The gravitas of Spanglish. *Chronicle of Higher Education.* Retrieved from http://chronicle.com/free/v47/i07/07b00701.htm

Stinson, J., & Hampson, R. (2006, February 14). Cartoon crisis frames Europe's conflict within: Underlying tensions across the continent, over Muslim immigration and fear of terrorism, help feed the furor over paper's publication. *USA Today,* p. 1A.

Sullivan, K. (2006, February 11). Muslim's fury rages unabated over cartoons; Demonstrators in 13 countries ignore leaders' appeals, newspapers apology. *Washington Post,* p. A12.

Sullivan, K., & Adam, K. (2006, October 21). Veil debate in Britain is also divisive for Muslims. Retrieved May 7, 2008, from http://www.washingtonpost.com

Sunday Mercury. (2008, July 6). Bishop's blast at opposition to gay clergy. *Sunday Mercury,* p. 17.

Sur, A. K. (1973). *Sex and marriage in India.* Bombay, India: Allied Publishers.

Surowiecki J. (2004). *The wisdom of crowds: Why the many are smarter than the few.* London: Little, Brown.

Sydney Morning Herald. (2004, February, 12). Paris moves closer to headscarf ban. *The Sydney Morning Herald.* Retrieved January 26, 2008, from http://www.smh.com

Tagliabue, J. (2007, November 10). Denmark's unabashed lightning rod on immigration. *The New York Times.* Retrieved May 7, 2008, from http://www.nytimes.com

Taher, A. (2006, October 29). Veil teacher was obeying a fatwa. *Sunday Times, London,* p. 4.

Tarlo, E. (2007). Hidden features of the face veil controversy. *ISIM Review, 19,* 24–25.

Taylor, M. (1990, September 20). Racist remarks spray-painted at 2 schools. *San Francisco Chronicle,* p. B7.

Teitel, R. (2004, February 16). Through the veil, darkly: Why France's ban on the wearing of religious symbols is even more pernicious than it appears. Retrieved March 3, 2008, from http://writ.news.findlaw.com

Telegraph, The. (2006 February 4). What they said. *The Telegraph.* Retrieved February, 12, 2009, from http://www.telegraph.co.uk/news/worldnews/northamerica/usa/1509638/What-they-said.html

Tharu, S., & Lalitha, K. (1993). *Women writing in India: 600 B.C. to the present.* New Delhi, India: Oxford University Press.

Thayer, L. (1987). *On communication: Essays in understanding.* Norwood, NJ: Ablex Press.

Thayer, L. (1995). *Pieces: Towards a revisioning of communication/life.* Greenwich, CT: Ablex.

The Economist. (2004, February 7). The war of the headscarves. *The Economist,* p. 24–26. (Volume # 370 Issue 8361)

The Guardian. (2003, November 14). MPs urge French ban on religious symbols. *The*

Guardian. Retrieved on February 26, 2008, from http://www.guardian.co.uk/world

Thomas, R. E. (2006). Keeping identity at a distance: Explaining France's new legal restrictions on the Islamic headscarf. *Ethnic and Racial Studies, 29,* 237–259.

Time. (2004, February 22). After the head-scarf ban. *Time*. Retrieved 3 March, 2008, from http://www. time.com

Times. (2006, February 6). Danes in despair as protesters set fire to consulate in Beirut. Retrieved May 7, 2008, from http://www. timesonline.co.uk

Tutu, D. (1999). *No future without forgiveness.* New York: Random House.

Uberoi, P. (Ed.). (1996). *Social reform, sexuality, and the state.* New Delhi, India: Sage.

United Nations Education and Scientific Organization (UNESCO). (2005). *Towards knowledge societies.* Retrieved from http://unesdoc.unesco.org/images/0014/001418/141843e.pdf

Veliz, C. (1994). *The new world and the gothic fox: Culture and economy in English and Spanish America.* Berkeley: University of California Press.

Vervort, L., & Lievens, S. (1989). Graffiti in sports centers: An exploratory study in East Flanders. *Tijdsch Rift-Voor-Sociale-Wetenschappen, 34,* 56–53.

Voice of America. (2004, September 20). On the line: The veil in France. Retrieved February 26, 2008, from www.voanews.com/uspolicy

Wagner, G. W., Pfeffer, J., & O'Reilly, C A. (1984). Organizational demography and turnover in top-management groups. *Administrative Science Quarterly, 29,* 74–92.

Walsh, M., & Taylor, J. (1982). Understanding in Japanese marriages. *Journal of Social Psychology, 118,* 67–76.

Walzer, M. (1997). *On toleration.* New Haven, CT: Yale University Press.

Warakowski, J. (1991). The humor of graffiti. In G. Bennett (Ed.), *Spoken in jest* (pp. 279–

289). Sheffield, England: Sheffield Academic Press.

Watson, W. E., Kumar, K., & Michaelson, L. K. (1993). Cultural diversity's impact on interaction process and performance: Comparing homogeneous and diverse task groups. *Academy of Management Journal, 36,* 590–602.

We. (2004, February 1). Controversial ban on religious articles of clothing passed in France's lower house. *We,* Retrieved March 5, 2009, from http://www.newser.com/archive-world-news/1G1-114983152/controversial-ban-on-religious-articles-of-clothing-passed-in-frances-lower-houseissues.html

Weil, P. (2004, March 25). A nation in diversity: France, Muslims and the headscarf. Open Democracy. Retrieved March 4, 2008, from http://www.opendemocracy.net

Weissberg, R. (1998). *Political tolerance.* Thousand Oaks, CA: Sage.

Western Resistance. (2006, October 20). UK: The Muslim veil row continues. Retrieved February 4, 2009, from http://www. westernresistance.com/blog/archives/003238.html

Why-War.com. (2004, February, 24). Transcript: Al-Qa'ida's Al-Zawahiri Attacks. *Why War News.* Retrieved January 31, 2008, from www.why-war.com/news

Widule, C. J. (1995, July 22). Let owner manage own yard. [Letter to the editor]. *Journal & Courier,* p. A 4.

Wikipedia. (n.d.). Jallands-Posten Muhammad cartoons controversy. Retrieved May 7, 2008, from http://www.wikipedia.org

Wikipedia. (n.d.). Timeline of the Jallands-Posten Muhammad cartoons controversy. Retrieved May 7, 2008, from http://www.wikipedia.org

Will, F. G. (2007, November 10). The limits of inclusion. *Newsweek,* p.74

Williamson, D. (2008, July 14). Archbishop's gay bishop comments spark new controversy. *The Western Mail,* p.1.

Windle, J. (2004). Schooling, symbolism and social power: The Hijab in republic France. *The Australian Educational Research, 31,* 95–112.

Winter, B. (2006). Secularism aboard the Titanic: Feminists and the debate over the hijab in France, *Feminist Studies, 32* (2), p 279–298.

Wright, R. (1999, November 8). We invite the hostages to return. *New Yorker,* pp. 38–47.

Wright, S. C., Brody, S. A., & Aron, A. (2005). Intergroup contact: Still our best hope for reducing prejudice. In C. S. Crandall & M. Schaller (Eds.), *The social psychology of prejudice: Historical perspectives* (pp.115–142). Seattle, WA: Lewinian Press.

Wyatt, C. (2004, February 11). French headscarf ban opens rifts. *BBC News.*

Xiaohe, X., & Whyte, M. K. (1990). Love matches and arranged marriages: A Chinese replication. *Journal of Marriage and Family, 52,* 709–722.

Yahmid, H. (2004, October 2). French school girl shaves head protesting Hijab ban *Islamic Online.* Retrieved March 4, 2008, from http://www.islamonline.net

Yelsma, P., & Athappilly, K. (1988). Marital satisfaction and communication practices: Comparisons among Indian and American couples. *Journal of Comparative Family Studies, 19,* 37–54.

Ziegler, R. R. (2007). The French "headscarves ban" intolerance or necessity. *The John Marshall Law Review,* 101–131.

Zuhur, S. (n.d.). The power of division and unity. Carlisle, PA: Strategic Studies Institute.

Zysk, K. G. (1989). *The origins and development of classical Hinduism.* Boston: Beacon Press.

Index